THE VULGARITY OF CASTE

THE VULGARITY
OF CASTE

Dalits, Sexuality, and Humanity in Modern India

SHAILAJA PAIK

STANFORD UNIVERSITY PRESS
Stanford, California

Stanford University Press
Stanford, California

Printed in the United States of America on acid-free, archival-quality paper

Library of Congress Cataloging-in-Publication Data

Names: Paik, Shailaja, author.
Title: The vulgarity of caste : Dalits, sexuality, and humanity in modern India / Shailaja Paik.
Other titles: South Asia in motion.
Description: Stanford, California : Stanford University Press, 2022. | Series: South Asia in motion | Includes bibliographical references and index.
Identifiers: LCCN 2022005752 (print) | LCCN 2022005753 (ebook) | ISBN 9781503632387 (cloth) | ISBN 9781503634084 (paperback) | ISBN 9781503634091 (ebook)
Subjects: LCSH: Dalit women—India—Maharashtra—History—20th century. | Women entertainers—India—Maharashtra—History—20th century. | Tamasha (Theater)—Social aspects—History—20th century. | Tamasha (Theater)—Political aspects—History—20th century. | Vulgarity—India—Maharashtra—History—20th century. | Caste—India—Maharashtra—History—20th century. | Patriarchy—India—Maharashtra—History—20th century.
Classification: LCC HQ1744.M33 P35 2022 (print) | LCC HQ1744.M33 (ebook) | DDC 305.48/44095479—dc23/eng/20220224
LC record available at https://lccn.loc.gov/2022005752
LC ebook record available at https://lccn.loc.gov/2022005753

Cover design: Susan Zucker
Cover art: From a photo (by the author) of Seema Pote, at a Tamasha. Background pattern, Shutterstock

To Tamasha people,
and
David Hardiman, Douglas E. Haynes,
Sharmila Rege, and Eleanor Zelliot

CONTENTS

ACKNOWLEDGMENTS

This book has been made possible by the deep commitment to transformative politics of Tamasha and Lavani women and friends, fellow-travelers, and colleagues from a range of castes, genders, and races. My thanks to their labor of love, support, and care. I have relied on their trust, warmth, generosity, friendship, and intellectual sustenance. Tamasha people shared their hopes, fears, anxieties, elations, and triumphs and contributed their time, affection, and insight with faith, trust, and bonds of samaj.

I had the privilege of engaging with scholars and friends who have been model scholars, thoughtful interlocutors, and dedicated mentors. Our intellectual exchanges and shared commitment to anticaste scholarship, Dalit studies, and feminist inquiry has enabled new forms of political solidarities. My deep gratitude to David Hardiman, Projit Mukharji, Rupa Viswanath, Joel Lee, Balmurli Natrajan, Prathama Banerjee, Thomas B. Hansen, Shefali Chandra, Durba Mitra, Douglas E. Haynes, Christian Lee Novetzke, V. Geetha, Anna Schultz, Ajit Chittambalam, Debjani Bhattacharya, and Erynn Masi Casanova for engaging with my work at critical junctures, offering generous criticism and advice, and gently but continually posing intellectual challenges. I remain deeply grateful to Douglas E. Haynes, Christian Lee Novetzke, V. Geetha, who read the entire manuscript and offered profoundly knowledgeable feedback. They, along with Joel Lee and Balmurli Natrajan, who read different parts of the manuscript, were always ready to thrash out every idea. They readily and energetically engaged with my endless queries and offered valuable counsel at important junctures. Prathama Banerjee, Anna Schultz, and Thomas Hansen read some chapters and provided incisive comments. I would like to single out V. Geetha who closely read all chapters, provided detailed and insightful comments, and helped in anonymous ways. She remains a deeply humane and inspiring intellectual. I thank David Hardiman and Lucinda Ramberg for their thoughtful feedback on early drafts of some chapters.

My deep thanks for the financial support of several granting agencies, including the American Council of Learned Societies, the National Endowment for the Humanities, the American Institute of Indian Studies, Stanford University, and the Luce Foundation during the preparation of this work. At the University of Cincinnati, my research was supported by funds and a center fellowship from the Charles Phelps Taft Research Center.

I thank colleagues and friends for inviting me to give talks and providing feedback on this project: audiences at the American Historical Association, the Annual Conference of the Association of Asian Studies, the Annual Conference on South Asia at the University of Wisconsin–Madison, the School of African and Oriental Studies, the University of Goettingen, the University of Washington–Seattle, King's College (London), the Tata Institute of Social Sciences, the Nehru Memorial Museum and Library, Jawaharlal Nehru University, New York University, the New School of Social Sciences and Research, the University of Minnesota, Stanford University, Columbia University, and the University of California at Berkeley. Some portions of chapters 3 and 4 appeared in "Ambedkar and the 'Prostitute': Caste, Sexuality, and Humanity in Modern India," *Gender and History* (August 16, 2021) and *Bombay Brokers* (Durham, NC: Duke University Press, 2021). Portions of chapter 6 appeared in "Mangalatai Bansode and the Social Life of Tamasha," *Biography* 40, no. 1 (2017). My thanks to both journals and Duke University Press and to numerous anonymous readers for their feedback.

My thanks to the archivists, librarians, and staff at the Maharashtra State Archives, the British Library, the Savitribai Phule Pune University, the National Film Archives, the Nehru Memorial Museum and Library, the Bhandarkar Oriental Research Institute, the Deccan College, the Gokhale Library, the Gokhale Institute of Economics and Political Science, Mumbai University, Mumbai Marathi Granthsangrahalay, and the families of the late Vasant Moon and Lokhande kaka. Thanks to Milind Kasbe, who readily shared some Marathi books and helped with fieldwork in Narayangao.

I am grateful to the anonymous reviewers for Stanford University Press, who helped push my arguments to greater clarity. Thanks to the patience and support of the editorial and publication teams: Marcela Maxfield, Sunna Juhn, Dylan Kyung-Lim White, Tim Roberts, and Barbara Armentrout at Stanford University Press and S. Anand and Alex George at Navayana. Thanks also to James Warren and Ajitkumar Chittambalam, my editors, who stepped in at a formative stage and carefully worked with the manuscript. They, along with Barbara Armentrout and Alex George, provided excellent editorial advice and I am grateful for their keen critical eye. Theirs is indeed a magical touch!

The book is my tribute to Sharmila Rege's and Gail Omvedt's indomitable scholarship-activism on anticaste movements, Ambedkar and the Dalit movement, and gender and labor. I miss them immensely.

My deepest love and thanks to my family for the unstinting support over long years—Aai, Rani, Maitreyee, Advait, Keisho, Harsha, and Kirti. Thank you, Amit, for reading! I dearly miss my early mentor and uncle Santosh K. Bhalerao, who passed away as the book was nearing completion. My thanks to Kali-ma and Khanderao-Shiva, who were always ready for long walks in the woods as I ruminated on my days watching Gondhal, Jagran, and Tamasha in Takali with my cousins, aunts, and Aajji Tanhaai (Tanhubai Fakira Paik). I am deeply thankful for my good fortune to be sustained by my daughter, Gargi, and my partner, Pravin. Thanks for the boundless joy, understanding, staunch support, and providing a foundation of happiness, love, and stability.

Though *The Vulgarity of Caste: Dalits, Sexuality, and Humanity in Modern India*
is written in English, I have maintained the Marathi for many terms throughout. This choice reflects my innovative vernacular methodology.

ada; adakari	gestures
adani	ignorant, uncouth
ashlil	vulgar
ashlilta	vulgarity
assli; assal	authentic, legitimate, or genuine
Ati-Shudra	literally, those below the Shudras; a term used to describe Untouchable castes
brahman	the first and the most sacred of the four varna divisions and whose members, in theory, provide society's intellectuals, priests, and scholars
brahmani; brahmanical	pertaining to sensibilities that demarcate high and low, pure and polluted; potentially found in all castes and thus not limited to brahmans
brahmanya	brahman hegemony
bibhatsa	disgust
Chambhar	Maharashtra's third largest caste of Untouchables
daulat jada	flirting with and presenting gifts of cash and kind to women dancers
dharmantar	religious conversion and apostasy from Hinduism
ijjat	respect, honor, dignity
Jalsa (pl. Jalse)	song-drama of Satyashodhaks and Ambedkarites on social and political themes; also referred to as poetics-politics.

kala	art
kalavant	artist
khandani	ancestral lineage
Lavani	a form of poetry involving different genres; the love-song and erotic are the most popular
Lavanikar	composer of Lavani
Lavanya	Lavani poems
Mahar	Maharashtra's largest caste of Untouchables
Mang	Maharashtra's second largest caste of Untouchables
manus	literally, a person or a human, frequently associated with *man* or *men*
manuski	human dignity, humanity
maratha	the dominant peasant caste of Maharashtra
marathamola	the ways and practices associated with a genuine maratha identity, especially the prohibition of women from being in the presence of strangers
Marathikaran	making Marathi identity
masti	carefreeness, passion; in the context of Tamasha and Lavani, a gamut of affects unleashing unruly masculine sexual energy
Murali	girls given in dedication to local deities by a range of dominated lower castes
nachi	women dancers
nachya	men dancers
pandharpesha	urban, urbane, white-collar, privileged, and dominant classes
Pavada	a panegyric; Marathi poetic form usually recounting heroic military campaigns and the lives of famous kings or warriors
phad	troupe
prachar	program of propagation
samaj	group, society, community
shil	decency, modesty, virtue

shilvan	decent, modest, virtuous
Shudra	fourth of the four varna divisions, whose members, in theory, provide servants and laborers to the three higher varnas
sringar	sensuality or romantic love; eros
sringarik	sensual, erotic
svabhiman	self-respect
svavalamban	self-reliance
Tamasha (pl. Tamashe)	traveling secular popular theatre
Tamasgirs	people associated with Tamasha
Tamasha women	women performers in Tamasha
vatan	fixed, rent-free land
vatandari	duties in exchange for vatan

FIGURES

THE VULGARITY OF CASTE

PERFORMING PRECARITY
Sex-Gender-Caste/Ashlil-Manuski-Assli

On the afternoon of July 14, 2016, we—Meena Javale, a Dalit ("Untouchable") Tamasha woman in her early fifties; her sister Veena; their friend Rupali Jagtap; and I—were discussing the lives of women in Tamasha in Meena's apartment in Somvar Peth-Pune (Maharashtra, a strongly nationalist state in Western India).[1] Tamasha is a popular form of public theatre practiced predominantly by Dalits and is considered a traditional Dalit cultural performance art. This secular traveling public theatre that involves music and dance is often branded *ashlil* (vulgar) by the larger society. Fighting back tears after glancing at her housemaid, who had just entered the room and become an unfortunate point of comparison, Meena expressed a sense of desperation: "This [Tamasha] life is such a despicable one. . . . Even this *kamvali* [maid] has honor. [But] we [dancers in Tamasha] are looked upon with such disdain [by respectable society] that we will not be hired even as [lowly] maids." Meena's shame is evidence that she had internalized Indian *brahmani* (brahmanical, with reference to notions of high and low, pure and impure) society's moral hierarchy of respect and decency that stigmatized Tamasha women as supposedly immoral, lowly, dishonorable, and lacking *manuski* (human dignity, humanity). Because their sensual and sexual stage performances and thus their labor were also performative iterations of Dalit womanhood, Meena's participation in an economy of sexual excess confirmed her presumed ashlil quality and her status as a surplus and thus sexually available woman within what I call the sex-gender-caste complex. Her maid, while of a lower economic class, enjoyed the esteem of a supposedly moral life: asexual, respectable, and full of hard work—cooking, washing clothes and dishes, and cleaning the house. Meena's wages, in contrast, were construed as unearned, the wages of play, of excessive sexuality, of the surplus woman. The discourse

1

of the ashlil had prevented Meena from translating her economic and cultural successes into the symbolic capital of respectability, into manuski, and into being recognized as an *assal/assli* (authentic) Marathi.

Meena and Veena are second-generation Tamasha women. They followed their parents' profession of performing with their bodies: singing (often sexually explicit lyrics), dancing, swinging, stomping, leaping, shimmying, and gesturing lewdly on stage. Historically, Tamasgirs—as those associated with Tamasha are called in Marathi, and whom I refer to as Tamasha people and Tamasha women—have disproportionately come from Dalit communities, and Meena was troubled by the centuries-old performing art that cast her, even beyond the stage, as a "dirty," denigrated, salacious "vamp," nothing less than a "prostitute."[2] She was the opposite of the stereotypical "good," "respectable" caste Hindu woman, who was construed as chaste, modest, protected, and dependent on men. Tamasha was rooted in the critical labor of the sex-gender-caste complex, which, on the one hand, reduced women to their biological functions and social roles as wives and mothers to produce and reproduce the economy of caste and, on the other, assigned to women different sexual statuses according to their position in the caste hierarchy. As a result, while dominant caste and in general caste Hindu women are deemed socially respectable, Dalit women are exploited, denied respectability, and rendered sexually available. Caste violence is central to constituting Dalit women's subjectivity. Meena had played the role of the sexually available Tamasha woman long enough and was thus considered brazen, reckless, and rebellious—a desirable and dangerous woman on the loose. Tamasha converted her and her practice of dance, song, and gestures into a sexual-desire-producing machine, and the conflation of her stage performance and her personhood offstage relegated her to the lowest rungs of hierarchies of caste, gender, and sexuality—a mere puppet in the theatre as well as in the larger social play of Tamasha.

Yet she stuck to her assigned role throughout her life. Even though, singing from the wings, she was no longer center stage in 2016, she had grown accustomed to her embodied identity as a Tamasha woman. For, as much shame as Meena felt over her complicity in her own exploitation, her performances in Tamasha—which had been recuperated by various agents within the state of Maharashtra in the second half of the twentieth century as an icon of an assli regional and global Marathi identity (see chapter 5)—and the performativity of a labor that had constituted her as a Tamasha woman had also supplied her with the means to support herself and her family. Such entangled and complex historical processes as the radical politics of manuski of anticaste activist, intellectual, and formidable leader of modern India Dr. Bhimrao Ramji Ambedkar (see chapters 3 and 4) and postcolonial *Marathikaran* (literally, becoming Marathi, but here constituting a distinctive Marathi identity; see chapter 5) produced in Tamasha women a certain ambivalence about the violence they experienced and the pleasure they provided as they performed both the legacies of caste slavery as well as their own agency as artists and women. As a result, Meena was exhausted, angry, and in pain: "What do you want to know about me, and how will it help us [Tamasha women] anyway? How will it change my life?" Meena asked me.

Meena's comparison of herself to her maid highlights Tamasha women's exploitation and subjection, as well as the regimes of power they have been both constituted by and implicated in. Their dual constitution-implication is at the heart of Tamasha performativity. Meena exposed the discrepancies between high and low, moral and immoral, decent and vulgar, which are central to the history and politics of caste, gender, sexuality, modernity, and morality in India. Even in the safe space of her home, Meena avoided the Marathi word *ashlil* to describe her immoral, peripatetic, performative, and performing life. It was difficult for Meena to express the banal equation between Tamasha and the ashlil that paradigmatically represented her life in the presence of her family—her sister, daughter, son, and ailing mother—and her friend. Rupali was, however, able to succinctly capture the "stickiness"[3] of the ashlil, the way it attaches not to the task or even the art primarily but to the body of the person that performs it and thus forecloses economic opportunities beyond Tamasha: "Even if we want to seek employment as maids, nobody will employ us." Although Ambedkar did not himself use the word *ashlil*, he did capture the essence of the ashlil sticking to the Untouchable when he referred to a "protective discolouration"[4] that cannot be peeled off and that prevents the realization of an authentic selfhood. Untouchables could not escape their ascribed status due to the caste order.

Blind to the implications of Meena and other Tamasha women's sociosexual labor, which stigmatized them as ashlil, and to their financial difficulties and consequently their inability to move out of Tamasha, Chetan Hivale—an eloquent male *sutradhar* (leading narrator in his Tamasha troupe) who belonged to the lower touchable *shimpi* (tailor) caste but replicated the *savarna* (touchable, high-caste) value system—argued vehemently against Tamasha women's dancing: "This is all vulgar. These women can easily take up [honest and honorable menial] occupations, like working as maids, washing dishes and clothes in many homes, or maybe selling vegetables. Why engage in this vulgar dance and song?"[5] Chetan was outraged by Tamasha women because of the sexualized stigma—the fetishistic image of the vulgar, disgusting, raunchy, and bawdy things they sang about and performed with their bodies on stage. He reduced Tamasha women to their bodies alone, to salacious vamps seducing men. In the process, he constructed binaries of modest, respectable, restrained non-Tamasha women and salaciously and gloriously gyrating, unhindered, untethered Tamasha women.

Although our entire conversation was in Marathi, Chetan, like many fellow Maharashtrian interlocutors, used the English word *vulgar* to describe Tamasha. Unlike Meena, who refused to name it, Chetan (like many Dalits, touchables, and agents of both the British colonial and postcolonial Indian state) easily pinned down the vulgar using the modern and universal English language. In so doing, he vocalized his anxiety and fear about the corrupting influence of Tamasha women and also underlined the views of the larger, so-called honorable Dalit-and-touchable society regarding the elimination of vulgar Tamasha women and Dalit Tamasha women's immoral performative profession.

Chetan could not hide his reworked bourgeois hypocrisy. He was the sutradhar of a Tamasha troupe led by a Dalit woman, Chandni, and he and his family depended upon Tamasha for their livelihood, yet he denigrated Tamasha and Tamasha women. He did not acknowledge—or perhaps recognize—the ambivalent tension Tamasha women enacted in consenting to their coercion through both their stage and iterative performances of Tamasha: Tamasha women were dangerous and powerful at the same time. Chetan was not troubled by the way Tamasha capitalized on the sexual and social labor of Dalit Tamasha women to provide a regular, decent wage to men like him and thus support their families, kin, and many members of the Tamasha troupe. He completely ignored the sociosexual labor of caste, the violence of Tamasha, and the skill, training, and virtuosity of Tamasha women. Chetan conveniently concluded that Tamasha women and, by implication, Dalit women were vulgar. The performativity of his aesthetic judgment functioned as a "gimmick,"[6] conflating the use value of Tamasha and the abstract labor of Tamasha and Dalit women—supposedly nonproductive and contingent workers at the margins of the market. As a result, he underlined a strict sexual morality for *all* Tamasha women. Both he and Meena were complicit in adhering to social norms; they created a hierarchy of women: honorable women sell vegetables or wash dishes and clothes, and dishonorable women sell bodily performance. Neither Meena nor Chetan thought about how caste violence, the sex-gender-caste complex, and economic relations constituted and created Dalit women's subjectivity and their vulnerability. Yet, unlike Meena, who covertly challenged the duplicity of men who both benefited from (either financially or as audience members) and stigmatized Tamasha as well as her exploitation and subjection that limited her possibilities in the context of the sexual-caste economy (that is, the sexual and economic arrangements producing the caste system), Chetan reveled in that duplicity and his denigration of Tamasha women.

The fear of ashlil performativity and performance here is overdetermined. Tamasha, through the mundane and quotidian, concretized anxieties and fears about caste transgressions, the obscene, the ashlil, sex, and sexuality in Marathi society. The repetitive, iterative performativity of women living a Tamasha life ultimately produced a "truth" about Tamasha and Tamasha women: (1) both are subject to the sex-gender-caste complex that perpetuates the sexual-caste economy ; and (2) both are characterized by an ambivalence (of pleasure and violence) about their complicity with strategies of subjection. Many dominant-caste (and Dalit) men were oblivious to the deep systemic work of the sexual-caste economy, the sex-gender-caste complex, that generated both difficulties and possibilities for Dalit women. Scholarly and popular treatments of Tamasha have rarely commented on the conditions of disempowerment, poverty, and caste violence under which women performed. Indeed, some of these have reinscribed and perpetuated its reputation for sexual innuendo and moral depravity, displacing Tamasha women from the center of their commentaries and reducing Tamasha women to objects of pleasure that serve only to corrupt men and shape touchable men's subjectivity. In these studies, Tamasha is thus a commodity through which men's emotions and masculine fantasies are created, circulated, and regulated. In *The Vulgarity of Caste*, I center the lives of Tamasha women and connect them to male leaders, poets, and state patronage and regulation, which disproportionately affected Dalit women.

This book is the first full-length monograph on the social and intellectual history and the affective life of Tamasha, and it offers an argument for the critical place of sociality, of sexuality, and of humanity in the Dalit world. I focus on three moments: pre-Ambedkar, Ambedkar, and post-Ambedkar to analyze the contested cultural politics in Maharashtra (and broadly India)—the ways in which a proper brahmani-Hindu and assli nationalist Marathi modernity were constructed—and how the Dalit woman's body became a site for affirming male heterosexual desire, male sociability, and sexual identity. In so doing, I illuminate the sexual-caste economy—that is, the caste-based social, sexual, and economic arrangements of Tamasha as both stage performance and iterative performativity. I put forward a history of Tamasha from the vantage point of the Dalit women who were most easily accused of sexual excess by the larger society. To do so, I root my examination of Tamasha in the sex-gender-caste complex and its entanglements with sociality, humanity, untouchability, and sexuality. In the process, I unpack different articulations of Dalitness and present Dalits as complete, complex, undiminished *manus* (human beings). I analyze how the ashlil stuck to Dalits, how the processes and politics of Tamasha extended and consolidated caste stigmatization and the subjection of Dalits, and how Tamasha people and Tamasha women nonetheless exercised a constrained agency. Although Tamasha exploited Tamasha women, women also exploited the ambivalent relationship between pleasure and violence in Tamasha to create opportunities for themselves. Although shameful, stigmatizing, and socially ostracizing, Tamasha, as their only means of earning a living, offered Tamasha people possibilities and was economically empowering. On top of this, the literal analysis of Tamasha is also set against a figurative or metaphorical (or metonymical) one, where the performativity of caste and gender are accentuated in Tamasha such that Tamasha operates as a metonym for the sex-gender-caste complex as a social performance in general.[7]

The Sex-Gender-Caste Complex:
Surplus Women and Caste Slavery

This book is an exploration of what I call the sex-gender-caste complex—that is, the sexual and gendered arrangements of the caste system as they operated to oppress Dalit Tamasha women and from within which those women sought to constitute themselves as strong, successful, and willful artistic agents. The control of sex and female sexuality leads to the social reproduction of caste. The dialectical processes of oppression and self-definition played out on the integrated terrain of caste politics and contested patriarchies as manifested in the entertainment, pleasure, and violence of Tamasha. The mechanisms of caste created and maintained hierarchy, untouchability, and inequality and strengthened boundaries, reinforcing the benefits of the sex-gender-caste complex for touchables and the basis for the exploitation of Dalits. Dominant castes invested in classifying and elevating themselves above Dalits and dehumanizing Dalits. Dalits, however, also adopted various strategies for contesting, navigating, and surviving the structures of caste and Tamasha, wrenching agency, humanity, and respectability for themselves.

In 1916, Ambedkar launched a critique of brahmani patriarchy and endogamy, which he called the mechanism of caste, as it functioned to regulate the sexuality, social mobility, and economic resources of women—especially *surplus* (i.e., unmarried or "unmarriageable") women—and thus safeguard brahman male power and sexual privilege by preventing those women from seeking intercaste marriages and transgressing the boundaries of the caste hierarchy. Ambedkar applied theories of economics and value to the institution of marriage and endogamy to understand the surplus woman who as an excess became a danger to brahmani patriarchy.[8] In so doing, he offered foundational critiques of the gendered and sexual power of caste domination. Whereas *surplus men* were revered, *surplus women* were seen as a menace to brahmani male power, always threatening to entice men to transgress caste. Women were, insofar as their sexuality required regulation, central to the institution of caste. Endogamy restricted conjugal mixing across castes and perpetuated inequality by fusing social and sexual reproduction. I extend Ambedkar's analysis of the irresolvable problem of the surplus woman and the construction of caste through endogamy—the sex-gender-caste complex—and apply it to the historical performativity of Tamasha and such Dalit Tamasha women as Pavalabai Tabaji Bhalerao Hivargaokarin (1870–1939; chapter 2) of Mahar caste and Mangalatai Bansode (1965–; chapter 6) of Mang caste, as well as the mobilization of the prostitute and other public women in constructions of the new Dalit woman in Ambedkar's Dalit humanist and liberation project (chapters 3 and 4), and in defining Marathi identity either in films, film advertisements, or Tamasha education in Maharashtra (chapters 5 and 6).

Although on the one hand, performers in South Asia typically hailed from a range of lower-caste and Dalit communities,[9] and on the other, all performing women were, through a generalized logic of good and bad women, viewed as tainted Dalit women performing in Tamasha and shouldered a specific burden determined by the logics of the sex-gender-caste complex. Tamasha people and Tamasha women, or "dancing girls," were always on the move, performing in cities and villages. Their constant movement without a settled location was seen as evidence of their unstable, illicit, and uncivilized character. Tamasha women did not measure up to the moral benchmarks necessary to achieve the status of woman or even manus. Although many Tamasha women were married, had monogamous relationships, and bore children (especially sons), elites viewed them as surplus women operating outside the marriage-and-family scheme, and as such, they were characterized primarily by perceived flexible sexual arrangements with many men. Consequently, they became women on the loose or "common prostitutes"—marked by both their superfluity and sexual excess and availability—and as agents of moral and sexual contamination, they had to be contained and even eliminated. I do not aim to vilify prostitutes but rather illuminate how elite British and touchables, through the sex-gender-caste complex, cunningly amalgamated a range of dancers and singers, including Tamasha women, into the category of the prostitute. For them, the cause of her violation was her (surplus) sex and (excessive) sexuality, which naturally sought to entice and expropriate. Whereas Ambedkar observed that the surplus quality of the widow was managed through a set of iterative practices of negative control, that of the Dalit Tamasha woman, linked more closely to the prostitute as sexually charged and available, was viewed as both negative and corrosive and yet necessary in order to assert the authentic caste selfhood of the savarnas and later, in the radical politics of Ambedkar and the Ambedkarite Jalsakars, of Dalits too.

Thus the "play" of Tamasha successfully occludes "work" in the sense that the always already alienated sexual labor of the Dalit woman performer produces the surplus that keeps the sexual-caste economy in place (chapter 1).[10] Tamasha and its practitioners paradigmatically represented excess, a kind of waste of the world. Tamasha was a carnivalesque and bawdy performance, a pure amusement, and the performativity of the Dalit Tamasha woman could not be put to productive use in the eyes of most elite. Caste violence remained at the root of these contestations between the colonized and colonizers, between Indians and the British, as well as among Indians themselves. Although Dalits' life-world changed over the century, the systemic caste mechanism, steeped in sexual purity, maintained differences between Dalit and higher caste women.

When I spoke to each of them in 2016, Meena Javale and Chetan Hivale rehearsed a more than century-old debate over prostitute women and their corrupt *dhanda* (business, profession). Since the end of the nineteenth century, all paternalistic, masculine actors—colonial and postcolonial state agents, elite touchables, and radical Dalit men—formed a tripartite patriarchal structure, sharing a discourse of decency through which they engaged in debates over ashlil and reinforced the social power of the sex-gender-caste complex. As symbols of the ashlil and the *bibhatsa* (disgusting), Tamasha women were at the center of this patriarchal triangle, objectified by a common desire to police public morality in order to govern (themselves) and build a moral and modern India.

Historically, the sexual excess—that is, the immoderate and overabundant sexuality—of Dalit Tamasha women at the center of this patriarchal triangle was a consequence of the cunning mechanisms of caste slavery.[11] The sex-gender-caste complex and the mechanisms of agrarian caste slavery limited Untouchables' freedom to speak, act, think, dress, and have honor, respect, virtue, education, wealth, and resources; they were coerced to follow the dictates of the dominant castes and prescribed callings not of their own choice. Even the caste mechanism of endogamy—and the accompanying regulation of women's sexuality, social mobility, and economic resources—and its observance among non-brahmans,

Ambedkar argued, is evidence of the consolidation of brahmanism, reinforcing brahman exceptionalism and brahman ideals (chapter 3). In his speech to the Bombay Presidency Mahar Conference on May 31, 1936, Ambedkar argued that "Untouchables were worse than slaves" in the Hindu religion, and untouchability was thus more cruel than slavery: "The Untouchables can claim none of the advantages of an unfree social order and are left to bear all the disadvantages of a free social order."[12] As such, there was always a violence at play with regard to Dalit culture, artistry, and creativity in the fun-filled Tamasha. Tamasha people, like radical Dalit leaders, may not have presented any overt opposition or defiance to the mechanisms of caste, but Tamasha did produce a unique Dalitness. It signified the assigned vulgarity, vitiated being, and mutilated humanity of Dalits and at the same time also opened up opportunities for radical insurgency and covert, clandestine forms of resistance.

While Tamasha provided livelihoods for Tamasha people and granted some independence to Tamasha women, it also stigmatized them as inherently ashlil—these were the double binds of subjugation and liberation. Tamasha women especially carried the burden of being inherently indecent and ashlil, which extended to the Dalit *samaj* (community). Poor Dalit Tamasha women's bodies and work (like those of maids, nannies, and nurses) associated with moral and physical taint were most stigmatized and evoked moral rhetoric. This is also an effect of the sex-gender-caste complex. The larger society considered them "dirty," involved in doing dirty work connected with sex and body, which offended brahmani society's moral conceptions. And to civilizing Dalits seeking self-respect, Tamasha women wounded the dignity of their samaj. They were objects to stroke men's egos and to help them attain and enhance their manliness; Tamasha women were to serve all men and were essential to constructing male sexuality—this was the gender imbalance. Sex plays degraded the Tamasha woman but not the man. Stripped of her personal identity, she became an image and construct of a woman desired by men. She was brutalized by caste violence, the social and sexual inequalities of caste slavery, dislocated from home, her domestic marital space, domestic propriety, and was naturally pursuing her rape and was blamed and even held responsible for it. Civilized Indians, therefore, had to abandon the ashlil and become *shilvan* (decent, modest, virtuous). Yet, the struggle for Dalits, Dalit

Tamasha people, and especially Dalit Tamasha women was to become not only shilvan but also assli in order to negotiate and survive the terrors of caste. Only by becoming shilvan and assli could Tamasha women gain legitimacy. The pursuit of legitimacy—of becoming shilvan and thus assli—by Dalits and Tamasha women is a political strategy formed both in the context of and in response to caste slavery, sexual violence, and the sex-gender-caste complex. Understanding it as such is crucial to writing Dalit history.

In 2018, after I had presented a conference paper on Ambedkarite *Jalse* (song dramas focusing on social and political themes and their poetics-politics), a renowned male brahman scholar in his early sixties who had not attended my talk had the audacity to ask me, "But why don't these [Dalit Tamasha] people own their art? Why don't they own it with pride like we see with other communities?"

I answered him, "If all Dalits were so powerful as to assert themselves and their presumably degraded arts, they would not have needed a social and political revolution. We need to pay attention to the deep problems at the root of caste violence."

This exchange reveals the historical and ongoing entanglements of the politics of caste, class, gender, respectability, vulgarity, and artistry in Tamasha. Some non-Dalit scholars and laypeople romanticize Tamasha without understanding the ongoing context of structural violence encoded in it and its ultimate social effect on Dalits. The apathetic brahman scholar, blinded by his supreme caste location, was limited in his understanding of what depictions of vulgarity meant for Dalits. He philosophized on who should be doing what and did not consider the social and sexual problems faced by Dalits, both elites and ordinary. He easily patronized and paternalized Dalit women and their arts, paying scarce attention to the numerous struggles—social, political, intellectual, psychological, and cultural—that ordinary Dalits have waged over centuries to earn their livelihoods and generate Dalit *manus* (human) and manuski. Only recently have some Dalits begun to proudly claim their supposedly polluted arts, such as drumming, as in the case of the Parai of Tamil Nadu.[13] However, the drum is different from the body, and reclaiming the stigmatized drum is much different from extracting a valorized sensual body from the sex-gender-caste complex.

Performance and Performativity

Tamasha is both a performance and performative; its practitioners not only dance and sing on stage to entertain but also, through their bodily and embodied performances, create meaning about their caste, gender, and sexual identities. I am building on and deepening Judith Butler's analysis of performativity here by theorizing performance and performativity together and analyzing the order, the systemic and systematic work, of the triple jeopardy of imperialism, caste, and sexism afflicting Tamasha women in twentieth-century Maharashtra. The stylized, iterative, and eroticized performativity of a Tamasha life creates the social reality of Dalit women's labor, caste, gender, and sexuality.[14] The performativity of Tamasha is not limited to a single act but to a whole range of stylized repetitions that, on the one hand, normalize and naturalize the sex-gender-caste complex and its violent effects on Tamasha women and, on the other, produce new Dalit and Marathi subjectivities.

Through the constrained "reiteration of a set of norms" that concealed, through normalization and naturalization, the conventions and power relations of the sex-gender-caste complex, Tamasha gained authority and became a nexus and discourse of power in Western India from the early twentieth century, riling both caste and sexual anxieties; caste distinctions operated to defend against certain socially endangering sexual transgressions. Embracing men (in the audience) from a range of castes who produced, reproduced, and preserved among themselves *masti* (intoxication, carefreeness, and a gamut of affects unleashing unruly masculine sexual energy), male homosociality, and the masculine bonding enjoyed in the libidinous space of Tamasha, Tamasha and the pleasurable effects of a Tamasha performance created an illusion of normalcy and concealed the feudal-patriarchal sexual-caste violence it was rooted in.

Dalits negotiated the caste violence, brutality, and exploitation recast as seduction and desire in Tamasha, however, struggling, on one level, to negotiate this violence-pleasure nexus for their own personal, artistic, and material gain and, on another, to transform themselves from ashlil to assli human beings (manus) in twentieth- and twenty-first-century Maharashtra. In taking the stage and, indeed, living a Tamasha life, women such as Pavalabai Tabaji Bhalerao Hivargaokarin (1870–1939; chapter 2) and Mangalatai Bansode (1965–;

chapter 6) illustrate Tamasha women's ability to capitalize on their artistry and define themselves as Dalit Tamasha women on their own terms, even as their negotiation of the ambivalent violence-pleasure nexus was always limited by the constraints of the sex-gender-caste complex. In the colonial and postcolonial periods, Dalits' status as both shilvan and assli was significant insofar as it formed the basis for their inclusion in the regional processes of Marathikaran (chapter 5) and eventually in the Indian nation, thereby becoming good citizens of modern India.

Historically, savarna elites worked hard to construct and naturalize the idiom of the ashlil and one of its tools, Tamasha, as a symbol of Dalitness—ambivalent, contradictory, unstable and at the same time dangerous, resilient, and insurgent. Tamasha in the garb of nonsense and play became performative of the paradoxical conditions of Dalitness. It represented a complicated nexus of fear, vulgarity, anxiety, and enjoyment. Poignant social and intellectual contests over vulgarity, disgust, and extracting the labor and creativity of Tamasha women illustrate that management of gender expression, sexual behaviors, domestic arrangements, conjugality, community honor, and intimate relationships were most germane to Indians of a range of castes and classes and the colonial British and postcolonial Indian government.

The social and sexual arrangements of the ashlil uniquely illuminate the claims and counterclaims of elite touchables and subaltern Dalits, revealing both the possibilities and limits of attempts to contest the boundaries of caste and sexuality over the twentieth century. In this period, sexuality and ashlil emerged as a crucial modern conjuncture to frame the political recognition of Dalit humanity and the Dalit samaj. Tamasha was a precarious product of repetitive acts of caste, work/labor, and embodied performativity to produce untouchability, surplus women, and the caste game—that is, the reproduction of the contingent social structure of caste, domination, and humiliation that obscured the conditions of playing by securing the willing participation of Tamasha women.[15]

Vulgarity and sexuality, enacted through Tamasha, remained central to the social upheaval of the modern period and resulted in the creation of new differentiations of caste and distinctions of high over low. Paradoxically, although there was power in the performative to violate and breach the walls of domination, Dalits could not simply celebrate vulgarity and Tamasha because it became an essence of and, indeed, an injurious element of Dalitness and their "social death."[16] Unlike non-Dalits, Dalits, as liminal and condemned, did not have the luxury to play with or romanticize either vulgarity or their humanity. Becoming assli Marathi meant defining themselves in opposition to what was ashlil. They could establish their new status in an independent Maharashtra by condemning the ashlil in Tamasha, learning the epithets and imitating the grammar of brahmani, cultured *natak* (drama)/*sangeet natak* (song drama), and joining in on the violence in sanitizing and regulating Tamasha and themselves to prove worthy of admission to the new nation (chapters 4 and 5). The making of modern and respectable citizens was predicated upon the policing of Dalit women's sexuality and indeed on the performance of respectability by Tamasha women.

Tamasha, Dalitness, and Ambivalence

The history of Tamasha and Tamasha women is rife with ambivalence. Dalits were implicitly involved in the mimetic enactments of identity, personhood, and entitlements. Mimicry is a production of the subject as both the same and other,[17] and colonial mimicry and hybridity can be understood in terms of an ambivalence by which colonial subjects simultaneously inhabit opposing cultural (colonial and their own) perceptions and dimensions. This ambivalence—this duality that presents a split in the identity of the colonized other—creates subjects who are of both their own cultural identity and the colonizer's. In Tamasha, the cultural location of the performance and the performers is ambivalent, marked by a tension between the cultural identity of the performers (female, Dalit, Marathi) and that imposed by the interests of others (male, touchable, high caste and hence Indian, colonial).

Tamasha itself is arguably an ambivalent performance art, inhering both repulsion (and compulsion) and attraction. On the one hand, it reproduces the violence of caste slavery and the sex-gender-caste complex by forcing sexualized bodily performances from Dalit women, and, on the other, it is a source of pleasure to both the audience, in terms of its eroticism and masti, as well as the performers, in terms of their artistry and skill. Tamasha women are also characterized by an ambivalence about their Tamasha performances and performativity. As the stories of Pavalabai (chapter 2) and Mangalatai (chapter 6) illustrate, although Tamasha exploited Tamasha women, these women also exploited the ambivalent relationship between pleasure and violence in Tamasha to create opportunities for themselves and constitute a Dalit subjectivity—abject, ravaged, pained, and resilient. This not only allowed them to profit (materially and socially) from their own exploitation, but it was also the source of great pain, as revealed by Meena Javale above.

The performativity of Tamasha—as a ritualized production of sanctioned and unsanctioned sexuality and caste transgressions under the force of prohibition—was ambivalent. The simultaneous processes of production and subjugation of Dalits in ashlil Tamasha illuminate how Tamasha both dehumanized Dalits and produced occasional spaces for them to rework the norms of caste, ashlil, and sexuality and thus reshape what it means to be Dalit. This mechanism reveals the ambivalent regimes of power at work in the ashlil, caste, and Tamasha through and in which Tamasha women were constituted and implicated. In reiterating caste, gender, sexuality, and ashlil norms, Tamasha women participated in the painful pleasures of miming norms that wield power.

Indians of various castes negotiated tradition, modernity, sexuality, and the nation by morally and materially policing the vulgar, especially Tamasha, at specific historical conjunctures. Concerns over vulgarity and Tamasha reveal a multitude of sensoriums and visceral feelings that strategically encoded caste, gender, and race. The social and sexual arrangements of vulgarity in the context of Tamasha uniquely illuminate the claims and counterclaims of dominant-caste elites and subaltern Dalits, revealing both the possibilities and limits of attempts to contest the boundaries of caste and sexuality over the twentieth century. The normativizing power of caste-based shil-ashlil-manuski-assli inscribed capacities and characteristics that made only certain people's lives valuable and worthy of rights and protection.

Ashlil, Manuski, Assli

The ashlil, manuski, and assli are Marathi concepts coded with deep vernacular contexts in the colonial and postcolonial period that provide insights into our affective understanding of the hierarchical caste order.[18] Tamasha's politics and process of struggle are embodied by these concepts, which generated and embodied more or less force at particular conjunctures. I pay close attention to the content of concepts that nurtured and strengthened sentiments according to graded social status as well as their form as they forcefully shaped and transformed Dalits. Ashlil is a paradigmatic symbol of Tamasha and denigrated Dalitness. The turn to manus and manuski was a Dalit response to the dehumanizing politics of the ashlil. Although touchables and Dalits sought assli status during the colonial period, this pursuit sharpened during struggles over regional and linguistic authenticity in the new nation-state of Maharashtra and in India during the postcolonial period as anxious touchable elites appropriated Tamasha as a sign of assli Marathi identity. Tamasha people repurposed hegemonic norms and politics of assli, newly reinforcing Tamasha as their *jativant* (caste; see chapter 5) or *khandani* (ancestral lineage; see chapter 6) capital and asserting their traditional roots in the arts form. The ashlil has stuck to Dalits *because* they are Dalits, and on this basis they have been denied manuski and assli status. Touchables are not subject to the stickiness of the ashlil; even when they appropriate ashlil aspects of culture, such as Tamasha, they remain assli and retain their humanity.

Ashlil

The English word *vulgar* generally corresponds to a single Marathi and Hindi word: *ashlil*. *Ashlil* summarizes a constellation of concepts: *anuchit* (improper, inappropriate, or flawed), *gramya* (literally rural, but meaning disorderly, inappropriate, uncouth, coarse), and *asabhya* (indecent and not acceptable to civilized, cultured people). All these words evoke the vulgar in terms of masses, "folk," commonality and evoke vulgarity in people's minds. The British predominantly used the word *obscene* in their official record; yet the bookish, elitist word intersects and is in tension with the vernacular and colloquial term *vulgar*, which was used by my interlocutors. Modern colonial governmentality and Victorian values, through detailed analytical methodology, deployed bourgeois technologies of sex and sexuality and cracked down on obscenity because it depicted sex as dirty, corrupt, and a negative force.

From the end of the nineteenth century, caste became one modality by which the ashlil was ascribed. In Maharashtra, vulgarity stuck to Dalits, who were easily blamed for society's ills and thus ideal for absorbing all that was characterized as ashlil within the Marathi, not to mention the larger Indian community. This characterization of Dalits as ashlil was also forged by both the colonial state and the independent state of Maharashtra, as well as the civil society. As such, at the turn of the twentieth century, the ashlil deployed through Tamasha accelerated the dehumanizing effects of caste for Dalits. There was a key principle at the heart of paradigmatic caste society—a deep correlation between Dalit Tamasha peoples' social-structural abjection and ashlil status that lasted into post-independence (1947) and the early 1960s, when they began to claim their assli identity. As a result, the discourse of modernity deployed the ashlil and bibhatsa as intrinsic to the humiliation and negation of Dalits, thus accentuating their pollution, their impurity, and rendering Dalitness into a permanent, generational, and genealogical identity.

Touchables used the normativizing power undergirding the ashlil, caste, and culture hierarchies in Tamasha to marginalize, exclude, and dehumanize Dalits, denying them certain rights. Being ashlil intensified the idea that Dalits were inferior and backward in a caste hierarchy ruled by dominant castes. It degraded them further; being characterized as ashlil became evidence of Dalit identity and inferiority and, concomitantly, abstinence from ashlil became proof of touchable, especially savarna caste superiority and power. Caste was thus constantly altered and updated through shilvan-ashlil-assli to fit the requirements of dominant elites. Caste mutated to keep its systemic structure and hierarchy intact and protect its beneficiaries. As I show throughout this book, it operated through the ashlil, assli, and Tamasha.

Ashlil functioned on a ladder of honor and denigration. To Ambedkar, "Castes form a graded system of sovereignties, high and low, which are jealous of their status and which know that if a general dissolution came, some of them stand to lose more of their prestige and power than others do."[19] The mechanism of caste was a peculiar system of "graded inequality," ranking human beings and assigning them value—"the higher the grade of a caste, the greater the number of these [social and religious] rights"[20] and also the greater amount of decency its members supposedly possessed. Conversely, the lower the grade of a caste, the fewer the rights and the more likely its members were to be indecent and hence contemptible.[21] The exploitation of Dalits and the dispossession of their social and cultural capital and decency worked according to a scale that marked Dalits as wild, primitive, uncouth, animallike, childlike and hence ashlil. The worst features of the caste system and untouchability were its antisocial spirit, isolation, and exclusion, which produced Dalits as inferior humans and led to a social psychology of contempt and hatred toward them. Yet each caste was oppressor and oppressed—Dalits were oppressed by touchables, and Dalits stigmatized and oppressed those of their own caste, especially Tamasha women. As a result, ashlil deployed through the caste system thrived on dissension and inequality, thus maintaining the hierarchy.

The complex and mutual constitution of the ashlil and caste necessitates rethinking the concept of labor, especially by centering a particular Dalit: the Tamasha woman. Tamasha normatively sharpened the constitution of Dalits as ashlil and derived its power through recurrent sedimentation or materiality of Dalits' labor, mutilated humanity, and abjection embedded in the caste system. By analyzing the material conditions of Tamasha as a form of labor susceptible to exploitation like other forms of labor and at the same time recognizing Tamasha women's resistance, refusal, resilience, manipulation, and negotiation, we can develop a nuanced understanding and new knowledge about Tamasha women's experiences.

The ashlil stuck to Dalit Tamasha and, at moments, to the Dalit community as a whole. While all Dalits are considered polluted, particular Dalits— Tamasha women, for instance—were seen to be more ashlil than others and hence unapproachable and unseeable. The ashlil also encoded sexism in its conceptual structure: *ashlilta* (vulgarity) sticks to Tamasha women but not to men, even men who attend Tamasha. As a result, to radical Dalits, ashlil disrupted their march to modernity and manuski. The ashlil, in every minute form, prevented Dalits from becoming fully human. Thus, for Dalits, the stickiness of vulgarity compounded caste pollution. The ashlil, characterized by its tendency to stick, accumulate over time, and not easily be altered, stuck to Dalits and compounded Dalit subalternity, stigmatizing and subjecting them even further. Ashlil legitimized Dalits' difference and untouchability. Ashlil meant different things even for Dalits, who variously inhabited, disputed, resisted, and reclaimed it.

Manuski

Dalits used vernacular concepts and categories to recuperate their manuski and connect with and even expand who was included in a universal, global humanity. The most vital of these concepts, manuski, was introduced by Ambedkar in the 1920s and represented the fundamental Dalit response to their designation as ashlil. Ambedkar wrote profoundly and prolifically about manuski, theorizing it from the position of self-in-community of Dalits who were not recognized as humans. Manuski was a praxis to achieve excellence and virtues in the context of caste inequality, violence, and untouchability, and it propelled Dalit worldmaking on their terms.

Ambedkar inaugurated an ideological revolution by deploying the moral economy of manuski to unstick Dalits from the ashlil and accelerate the reconstruction of Dalits as manus. I pay close attention to contingent forces, ideas, and complicated historical processes of Dalit humanism, respectability, and anticaste liberation, what Ambedkar and his followers, including Ambedkarite Jalsakars (makers of song-drama), called manuski, examining how it functioned under social and political constraints in the face of multilayered power relations (chapters 3 and 4). To Ambedkar and Ambedkarite Jalsakars, Dalits should conform to the moral economy of manuski-*ijjat* (respect) and focus their efforts on resisting stigmatization, annihilating caste, achieving liberty, and avoiding the empty pleasures that thwart oppositional consciousness. During the interwar period, when Ambedkar and the Jalsakars were at the forefront of an emerging radical Dalit politics of identity and collective agency, they did not approve of either alternative Dalit sociality or different ways of being Dalit. Each chapter focuses on the ways Dalits created new modes of humanness and opened up new claims in the category of manus and procedures adopted to connect to a global humanity.

Ambedkar deployed manuski to enable a far wider conception and politics of the good, self-mastery, and recognition—embracing practical reason and a broad range of emotions. To Ambedkar, "to be manus is to not be [or behave like] a slave." Most importantly, he declared, "ours is a fight to achieve manuski." Manuski brought together moral and material claims about fundamental equality and possessed a potential to connect with others across caste, class, political, and religious divisions. Despite some ambiguity and differences of opinion over what defined morality, Dalits resolutely agreed that manuski required decency for the samaj as a whole. The new political Dalit was contingently constructed as samaj, and family became a site of resistance and solidarity against caste violence in the context of specific histories of double colonization—British and brahmani. Ambedkar critically analyzed the connection between caste and the position of women and how Dalit Tamasha women suffered more deprivation, social exclusion, and harassment from touchables because of caste violence and untouchability. He and other Dalit radicals recognized how brahmani touchables depicted Dalit women as prostitutes and all Shudras (and Ati-shudras) as Chandals (bastards and sons of prostitutes, scum) because of their caste status and reminded them and Dalit men of the latter's degraded caste status and put them in line. As a result, Dalits wanted to stop the sexual exploitation of Dalit women as well as uplift them and the community to new standards of respectability. The primary focus on the struggle against caste slavery, however, complicated Dalit women's relationship with their samaj. Dalit humanity here is not the self-constituting human subject of liberalism. Indeed, the discourse of humanism and liberalism has focused on selective recognition of humanity and excluded Dalits. As a result, Dalit radicals, especially Ambedkar, made Dalits the subject of human freedom.

Dalits would have to continuously and consistently work hard to push against becoming ashlil both in their own eyes as well as in the eyes of others. Their critiques of democracy, differentiated citizenship, internal colonialism, and ordinary human rights transformed debates and the trajectory of Dalit emancipation and larger Indian politics.

Assli

In the context of mobilizations in the formation of linguistic states, and after the creation of the new state of Maharashtra in 1960, Tamasha was reconceived as assli regional Maharashtrian identity providing new grounds for the valuing of Dalit women's cultural production. Chapter 5 illuminates the contests, collusions, and contradictions between elites and Tamasha people over constituting an assli Marathi identity. For elite Marathis, Marathikaran (making Marathiness) was about creating a robust masculine Marathi iden-

tity, an assli *marathamola* (genuine maratha identity) for a new Maharashtra
state. This was quite distinct from Ambedkar's conception of manuski. For
Ambedkar, manuski was a process and politics, a path toward becoming assli
for Dalits. Yet this path was less relevant than the process of Marathikaran
or assli marathamola to Tamasha performers. Ambedkar left no space in
his idea of manuski for Tamasha women, who would have to abandon their
ashlil business in its pursuit; Marathikaran and assli marathamola, however,
did leave some space for Tamasha women. But to be recognized as manus
and assli in postcolonial Maharashtra, they had to operate according to the
terms of the elites who regulated, disciplined, and shaped a new Tamasha for
the new state. On the surface, Tamasha people conformed with these terms,
but underneath, they manipulated the art to give up things that made them
ashlil to conform to assli.

The construction of Marathi identity in the specific political conjuncture
of the formation of the state of Maharashtra was a hierarchical and tenuous
process. Dalits responded to the formation of the state of Maharashtra and
creation of assli Marathi identity by imitating the epithets and grammar of
elitist rhetoric, reinforcing state and elites' efforts to sanitize and standardize
Tamasha, and by reforming themselves and their art to become assli. Though
stigmatized as ashlil, Dalits continuously threatened the monopoly of dominant castes over decency, first by exposing the spuriousness of their exclusive
claim and second by consistently performing on stage as singers and dancers,
reinforcing their assli status. The specter of ashlil-assli haunted Dalits. Even
after these struggles, recognition of Dalits' manus, manuski, and assli status
remained elusive for Tamasha people.

All three patriarchies—the British colonial and postcolonial Maharashtra
state, the elite touchables, and the Dalits—agreed on the importance of authenticity, and yet there were differences in what legitimacy meant to them
and their goals for achieving it. The British sought legitimacy as a modern
colonial authority; the dominant castes sought legitimacy with the brahmani
order; and the Dalits struggled to be recognized as respectable and legitimate
humans. But being shilvan and possessing manuski would prove to be insufficient for Dalit inclusion in postcolonial Marathi society, though as part of the
process of annihilating caste and unsticking the stigma of ashlil from Dalits,

these would propel them toward claiming assli status in modern India. The challenge for Dalits post-1960 was to erase the disgust of the past, the darkness of history, and to carry the decent conditions of the present forward into the future where these conditions would not exist, thus reinforcing their assli status and worthiness as citizens of the new state of Maharashtra (and larger Indian nation) in the 1960s.

Tamasha Women and the Dalit Question

The vernacular concepts of ashlil, manuski, and assli are at the heart of sexual-caste politics of the performative in twentieth-century Maharashtra. While scholars of Tamasha have produced tremendous work on the art form, they have completely neglected the sexual and gendered politics of caste in the performative. I ask how and why vulgarity and disgust became a primary framework to understand Dalit sociality. How did Dalits come to be designated as ashlil, and how did some Dalits, especially Dalit Tamasha women, come to be designated more ashlil than others due to the politics of caste, gender, sex, and sexuality? How can we illuminate the state of domination and possibilities of covert resistance seized in the performative? How did the forms, relations, and institutions of caste power condition the exercise of agency and change for Dalits? How did Dalits contest the sexual-caste economy to expand the terrain of the social, sexual, and political and create possibilities, however limited? What is the ambiguous and limited legacy of universalisms—liberalism, humanism, agency, and consent—with regard to Dalits? In sum, what is the history of Dalits and the Indian nation from the vantage point of Tamasha women, who never made it to the benchmarks of full womanhood and humanity?

In pursuing answers to these questions, *The Vulgarity of Caste* provides a new interpretive framework and a wide variety of hitherto unexamined vernacular Marathi sources to examine the genealogy of Tamasha and the volatile and contentious process of negotiation between divergent social actors whose social, political, cultural, intellectual, and literary transactions shaped and governed Maharashtrians. The loud merriment and amusement of Tamasha neutralized the caste violence it contained, rendering it quotidian and unremarkable. Yet, at the same time, ironically, Tamasha offers an opportunity to analyze the Dalit human condition and especially the elasticity of Dalitness. The political discourse of the ashlil was deployed in public contestations over moral norms, in the workings of the sexual-caste economy, in shaping a new politics around erotic excess, and in legitimizing a homogeneous and authentic Indian subject—in short, in setting the terms on which the moral foundations of a new modern nation would be based.

Stigmatized Dalit women (and men) singers and dancers are central players in this history. Tamasha women may not have openly voiced defiance and opposition to the mechanisms of caste, but they were willing to risk everything to transform the conditions of their existence. They were the shame and dishonor of caste oppression. Each envisioned and imagined her or his freedom in different ways. Different Dalit performers continued to fracture and produce tensions in the order of governance. They deployed various strategies and made a range of persistent efforts to question, challenge, or embrace certain strategies and ignore certain claims at specific times, evading, resisting, and surviving. They continue to create themselves in the hostile world of Indians, making new possibilities out of dispossession, vulnerability, and subjugation. Yet the vulgarity of Tamasha as a process and politics created irresolvable predicament and tensions, and moral fault lines divided Dalits.

The sexual-caste labors involved in the Dalit question, the woman question, and the prostitute question were inextricable. Respectable Dalit women were key driving forces in the Dalit movement and the ensuing social and political transformation. My first book, *Dalit Women's Education in Modern India: Double Discrimination,* focused on respectable women who were central to the struggles of building a civilized and honorable community. Dishonorable Tamasha women posed a threat to the agenda of Dalit regeneration. What connects my two books is an interest in the shifting relations between castes, cultural expression, historical transition, identity, and political transformation that shaped modern India. At the center of my scholarship are issues of how Dalits may gain a more equal status in one of the world's biggest democracies, India. My book contributes to Dalit studies, Ambedkar studies, and histories of women, gender, and colonial and postcolonial sexuality. Although these debates took place in the colonial Bombay Presidency, my analysis suggests the contours of interrelated conflicts regarding anticaste thought, performance, gender, and freedom in the larger

Indian nation and beyond. The story is unique and yet offers insights about South Asia and beyond. Across six chapters, I analyze the ways the violence of Tamasha reconfigured dominant-caste prejudice and privilege to shape social and moral boundaries and to homogenize and even exclude certain communities of people. Caste itself was systemic sexual violence. With Dalit Tamasha women's struggles for freedom as an axis, I trace how a range of dominant social actors deployed the vulgar to facilitate the construction and consolidation of caste patriarchies and polite society across the twentieth century. Yet, they failed to entirely eliminate the vulgar or suppress Dalit artists and art forms. Dalits responded with multiple strategies to work for liberation.

To date, scholars have neglected this story. There is no systematic analysis of what I call the interlocking technologies[22]—that is, the politics and processes of sexual-caste violence, gender, class, and the ashlil; contested patriarchies of colonizers and colonized; and Dalit human revolution in Tamasha. Scholars have tended to focus either on particular castes like brahmans or Dalits or, if examining wider caste relations, have continued to maintain polar dichotomies between purity and impurity, high and low castes, or culture and counterculture.[23] Scholars have neglected the relationality between different castes—high, middle, and low. Some have also burdened only Dalits with the caste question and left others free. Instead, I focus on the *circularity* and relationality between different caste communities, traditions, and cultures to show how they contradicted, coexisted, and developed in conversation with each other. I analyze the dialectic and complementary process of how the rights, respectability, and privileges of "good" touchables became a reason for the non-respectability, denigration, disadvantage, and deprivation of "bad" Dalits. I concentrate on the *connected histories* of Dalit and non-Dalits to trace the complex and contradictory legacies, shifting linkages, similarities, and conflicts among them and to create a conversation between various apparent dichotomies: human/inhuman, high/low, polite/vulgar, wife/whore, and urban/rural.

I break significant historical, societal, intellectual, ideological, and scholarly silences and bring the ashlil Tamasha woman to the center of the discipline of history. Elite scholars writing in the English language have seldom considered Tamasha or Tamasha people worthy of systematic analysis. Scholars have continually marginalized Dalit epistemologies and histories. By contrast, scholars of Marathi literature writing in the Marathi language have mined the literary content and form of Tamasha, Lavani, low-caste art, aesthetics, and culture in the vernacular Marathi language.[24] Yet, except for one article by Sharmila Rege, there are limitations in existing scholarship, especially with regard to the sexual-caste economy.[25]

Scholars have also focused on the lives of Nautanki performers, Tawaifs in North India, and Jogatis and highly trained, higher-status Devadasis, and Tamil Special Drama in South India.[26] Like Devadasis, Tamasha women fell outside the strict and exclusive brahmani norms of conjugal monogamy enforced on their respectable sisters; they embodied dishonor, and even criminality. However, scholars have worked in a regional vacuum, paying little attention to similar practices and lives of stigmatized Murali and Tamasha women in Western India. Through an exploration and interpretation of novel archival material, I first investigate the contradictions and antagonisms in the Maharashtrian social imaginary and modern regional identity as it was shaped by Dalits, and in doing so I connect the histories of Western, North, and South India to provide broad contexts within which we can understand the messy processes of historical change over time.

Scholars have used labor, a metacategory in the social sciences, to understand exploitation. As a result, feminist scholars have replaced "prostitute" with "sex-worker." But centering the Dalit performer on stage in the context of caste slavery of Tamasha itself makes us rethink the concept of labor/work as well as the ways her presence leads to a sharpening of the excesses of caste inequality, the ashlil, and a culture of sexual voyeurism.[27] Her "birth-defined-bondage"[28] led the Tamasha woman to reproduce her lowness and remain trapped in her caste location. Her labor was made invisible, not worthy of valorization. Feminist scholars working on prostitutes, sex, and sexuality have yet to pay attention to this sexual politics of caste, wherein the sexual exploitation of Dalit women is a mechanism of social inequality. Scholars studying sex and sexuality have also tended to focus on enclaves of autonomy and resistance. They have neglected the complex set of relations and broader struggles of how gender intersected with and profoundly shaped sociality, sexuality, and manuski of Dalit women. Like them, the larger Indian society barely recognized Dalit humanity and excluded Dalit women from becoming fully human.

Ambedkar constituted a new Dalit woman through these interrelated ideas of an intrinsically caring humanity. Yet, he created binaries of respectable "asexual" women toiling away in factories and dishonorable "sexual" prostitutes. Nevertheless, his strategy of manuski infused humanism with new knowledge and understandings. This moral sensibility is absent in the savarna-dominant world that excluded Dalits from becoming fully human, fully manus. The moralities of the dominant and dominated were distinctly different. Nevertheless, they can be bridged.

Despite Ambedkar's radical anticaste agenda of recuperating manuski, not all Dalits followed him to discard the ashlil and seek manuski and liberation to become assli. Many Dalits made different choices and continued with their ashlil professions, including Tamasha people, sanitation laborers, Devadasis, and so on. Dalits did not always resist or try to eliminate the systems of hierarchical value they found themselves in, nor could they reinvent themselves freely in the cultural construction of their own choosing. Social changes occurred under variable and determinate circumstances—Dalits resisted, manipulated, shaped, accommodated, adapted, and jettisoned their cultural understandings, or alternatively, they found themselves blocked in doing so. I show both processes: attitudes of touchables revaluing the vulgarity of Dalits and also how the vulgar emanates from the lives of people.

To date, historians have focused on the singular political narrative and homogeneity of Dalit movement. Ambedkar Studies has come into fashion in the last decade, and everyone—scholars, political parties, civil society—who had neglected Ambedkar suddenly started appropriating him and his work for their own purposes. I depart from the Ambedkar-centered historiography and movement-focused approaches to analyze the ordinary and everyday in Dalit studies. My archival research positions me to investigate the internal dissensions among Dalits themselves on issues of caste, gender, and sexuality at specific historical conjunctures and reconsider the meaning of Ambedkar from the perspective of the everyday.

My emphasis on the heterogeneity of Dalit struggles allows me to contest the work of feminist scholars who hardly recognize or dismiss the relevance of caste to center the analysis of patriarchy. By analyzing primary Marathi source material that captures Dalit women's and men's voices, I delineate the complex entanglements of caste, gender, sexuality, moral reform, manuski, labor, and affect, all threads in the Dalit struggle to construct a humanity for themselves, one that feminist scholars have labeled a form of patriarchy. Dalits' focus on manuski had gendered implications, including the purging of female characters and artists in Ambedkarite Jalsa 1930 onwards, which may have even been a response to the feminization of Dalit men and the hypersexualization of Dalit women, but as political strategies they were not primarily about gender but about annihilating caste and claiming or generating a new Dalit manuski for both men and women (chapters 3 and 4).

Moreover, scholars, have also paid little attention to the intersections of popular practices of such caste-based cultural forms as Tamasha with sexual labor, gender, humanism, and Dalitness. And even when scholars have brought gender and Dalitness into the same analytic frame, their analyses tends to flatten or misinterpret certain gendered processes vis-à-vis Dalitness. Anupama Rao, for instance, argues that "the degraded status of women was seen to be closely related to the emasculation of Dalit men."[29] As such, Dalits' strategies for the "reform of gender and the defense of community honor" actually "reconstitute[ed] masculinity."[30] She simplistically argues that the reconstitution of Dalit masculinity as a whole throughout the colonial period was predicated on the regulation of degraded Dalit women's sexuality.[31] Rao does not, however, detail the specific contents and contours of "Dalit masculinity" and its historical transitions in the early twentieth century. Her sweeping analysis of Dalit masculinity in colonial India obscures the details of the conjunctive moments and awkward contingency of constellations involved in constituting Dalit identity, humanity, and masculinity.

Anticaste movements and thinkers have not engaged with the conjoined emergence of masculinity and humanity. While working toward a united community and Dalit power, Dalit men include women in a tokenistic way and pay less attention to the specific problems of Dalit women. Sometimes, men's assertions of rights and social status for Dalits strengthened certain patriarchal formations and notions of masculinity in the community. Yet, Dalits' sense of maleness differed significantly from that of the touchables. The paradoxical position of Dalit masculinity deserves more attention. Dalit masculinity was mocked and beaten down every day by dominant castes, and yet Dalit men oppressed Dalit women.

I analyze the contingent historical decisions by which manuski and masculinity were constituted and the difficulty of conceptualizing manus for Dalits. Dalits' critique of sexuality and brahmani sexual violence was an aspect of not only patriarchal power but also caste power. The caste system denied equality, freedom, and manuski to Tamasha women. They suffered most due to caste, untouchability, social exclusion, and harassment from touchables. Touchables also depicted them as prostitutes to keep them in line with their degraded caste status. Untouchability and caste norms determined the social and cultural status of Tamasha women and negatively impacted their control over resources, rights, and freedom. Caste and untouchability distinguished Dalit women as ashlil and differentiated the problems of Dalit women from those of touchable women.

Charu Gupta, focusing on dominant-caste representations of Dalit women in Uttar Pradesh, has devoted some attention to issues of Dalit masculinity, contending that through a language of manhood and dignity, Dalits argued for their moral, social, and economic progress. Gupta rehearses Rao's argument, with some difference, by delineating the specifics of Dalit masculinity and claims to respectability. To her, Dalit masculinity "was neither heterocentric nor misogynist, but developed out of a unique Dalit experience."[32] While I agree with the link between masculinity and dignity, Gupta's discussion of Dalit masculinity is problematic insofar as it, on the one hand, reduces Dalit masculinity to "mimicry"[33] of dominant norms of manhood and, on the other, reproduces a one-dimensional view of "suffering, battered, thrashed" Dalit women at the hands of Dalit men.

As such, Gupta (following Rao), by casting Dalit men as passive emulators of high-caste norms who accentuate violent patriarchy, erases Dalit agendas and agency in reconstructing their life-worlds. Moreover, in offering her "hope that Dalit men will evolve and ultimately dismantle the very ideological fetters that fasten them to a corrosive paradigm of masculinity,"[34] Gupta both absolves touchables from their responsibility in the construction and consolidation of the sex-gender-caste complex and endorses dominant-caste Hindu men as the "standard" for masculine evolution. Implicit in her linear, teleological, social Darwinistic argument is the claim that high-caste men have already evolved and Dalits should follow them toward the same endpoint. Thus, unlike

Ambedkar, Periyar, and Gandhi and like women feminists of the early twentieth century, with this regrettably patronizing language, Gupta returns the
burden of evolution to Dalit men (and women) alone.[35]

Although at times mindful of overlapping patriarchies, some feminists
have paid little attention to the way patriarchy operates through caste technologies, by entrenching divisions among caste communities and reproducing caste hierarchies. In accusing Dalit male leadership, the above feminists
have not examined the broader politics of the ideological and institutional
apparatuses shaping Dalits' lives. "Patriarchy is first a hierarchical relation
among men"[36]—British and touchable in this case. The British characterized
colonized Indian men as inherently inferior but also differentiated among
them through a hierarchy of manliness and masculinity. Patriarchies operate
in a relational manner and are subject to a wider political economy, occupying
different configurations, and to continual reformulation. Elite feminists easily elide how masculinities are produced differently at different and complex
intersections of age, class, family, gender, caste, community, religion, and nation. It was Dalits' subordinate, uncivilized masculinity that rendered them
not-male, irrelevant, threatening, and dangerous to the touchables, all at the
same time. It is these tenuous processes that made Dalit men more vulnerable to disciplining and sanitization. Feminists have yet to grapple with the
context, content, and impact of the discourse and practices of caste slavery
that burdened Dalits simultaneously in structural, material, and psychological
ways as they sought their freedom.

In the case of Dalits, these tenuous processes did not necessarily lead to a
complete mimicry of dominant norms or to the production of new patriarchy.
Elite scholars have completely neglected how masculinity and patriarchy were
equally contested internal colonial processes. Under British and brahmani
colonialism, Dalits were torn between emulating and rejecting touchables'
gender and sexuality norms. Dalits challenged brahmani patriarchy, yet at
times in this subversion, they reproduced patriarchal norms. However, for
them, their genders and sexualities constituted through caste produced severe
problems. Hence Dalits' efforts exceeded the production of a new patriarchy.
Merely focusing on gender in isolation, expanding the plight of elite touchable women and their problems to all Indian women, and concentrating on

feminism as "battle of sexes," "man as enemy," or "war on men" obscures the social roots of the caste violence and exploitation that Ambedkar and other Dalits were responding to.

Talking about gender oppression outside of the caste question is a problem—we need to examine how gender relations were mutually constituted through larger social and political processes and analyze how Dalits critiqued caste and exercised control and resistance at the same time. Dalits had to secure power continuously through extraordinary and violent struggles as well as mundane and quotidian practices. There is thus no one straightforward answer to whether Dalits were merely "mimicking" or "asserting," because they are using the hegemonic idiom to constantly negotiate the "traditional," "modern," ashlil, and assli and reconstruct their present and futures. Dalit women were fighting the triple jeopardy—imperial, brahmani, and sexist oppression—to transform their lives. Although at odds with elite feminists, family as a kinship structure was important to Dalit women. While the issue of masculinities is surely configured in the construction of any community, my stakes here are higher: building on my previous work examining Ambedkar's contradictory thinking on women, I argue that Dalits' engagement with the sex-gender-caste complex was also an effort to reconstitute a collective humanity.

Some feminist scholars argue that in writing the history of Dalit women, we must also pay attention to how women mobilized all possible means of livelihood and not just understand sex in terms of violation or exploitation. Although I concur with them on this point, I nevertheless depart from them in their romanticization of the alternative lifestyles of Jogatis, which they contend are subversive of housewifely domesticity.[37] They ignore that routine rape and sexual exploitation rooted in caste violence are an extreme form of hurt and humiliation for Dalits and fail to explain why and how Dalits and Ambedkar adopted a discourse of "progress" and "purifying" politics.

By contrast, some sociologists look upon Devadasi dedication as oppressive and uncritically celebrate Ambedkar's intervention.[38] Sharmila Rege insightfully notes that the "options [Ambedkar] presents to women at Kamathipura are actually between enduring degradation and refusing long-term humiliation enforced by the Hindu brahmani order."[39] Rege argues that Ambedkar's critique of "the disgraceful profession" is not a moral reproach but rather a clear and effective statement on how caste actually gains legitimacy through graded violence. Thus, Ambedkar's "statement is less about women being the 'honor' of the community than about cultivating self-respect as a mode of protest."[40] While I broadly agree with Rege's empathetic reading of Ambedkar, she unfortunately creates dichotomies between choice and coercion, community honor and *svabhiman* (self-respect). Anxiety, authority, and ambiguity in their engagement with the overarching questions of political rights and citizenship constrained radical Dalits in their work with prostitutes in the awkward contingencies of 1930s. Rege pays less attention to the historical motor of contradictions, intersections, and tensions in the Dalit movement. I contend here that Dalit self-governance and liberation, like many other human projects, worked within pressures and awkward historical contingencies. It succeeded and faltered and has been ambiguous. There is no finality to these sheer contingent complicated processes, and Dalit liberation had a particular fixed telos but no guaranteed triumphalist outcome.

And most significantly, none of the above scholars have examined the interconnections between the effort to recuperate the manuski of the most polluted prostitute and Ambedkar's concept of manuski created in historical flux. I offer an important caution against the romanticization of the supposedly liberatory potential of Devadasi lives, as well as the uncritical celebration of Ambedkar, to bring out the conditions of possibility for his emancipatory project.

The Tamasha Archive

In the chapters that follow, I piece together a view of Tamasha women's lives. I focus on the double movement of sexuality: sexuality as a logic of the totalitarian state to discipline Dalits, as well as how local Dalit actors interacted with, negotiated with, colluded with, and confronted them. My book combines ethnographic fieldwork with close readings of a variety of hitherto unexamined Marathi archival materials to record the multilayered, fragmented, and contested narratives about Tamasha and Tamasha women. The patchy Tamasha archive illuminates the differences in touchables' and Untouchables' readings of Tamasha's performance and performativity. For example, there were contradictions, inconsistencies, and anxieties between touchables and Untouchables in the representation of Pavalabai (chapter 2). Departing from the recovery mode of archival investigation, I consider the plurality of the forms of knowledge—written, verbal, performative—to bring out the deeper interactions, contexts, contested processes of marginalization, identity formation, norms of conjugality and sexual propriety, social inequality, regional politics, and the production of a modern vernacular morality under modernity.

Significantly, I focus on the vernacular as a method to piece together a fuller history of Tamasha. Dalit vernacular speech allows us to chart Dalit Tamasha womanhood, selfhood, and empowerment, something glaringly absent in South Asian studies. Vernacular sources help us move away from the narrow imperial and English language frameworks to concentrate on the local politics, ideas, and actions of most marginalized and stigmatized Dalit women. They offer not only a corrective by subaltern Dalits to official history but quality details that are missing or glossed over in the often quantitative, objective, and dry deliberations of the colonial registers. I deploy Marathi sources, which had a larger audience compared to English, as fundamental rather than supplementary archives. I use a wealth of hitherto unread, underread, underexamined, and neglected vernacular Marathi sources, including newspapers, magazines, biographies, songs, memoirs, films, documentaries, photographs, private collections, and other material often dismissed as trivial to write the first social and intellectual history of Tamasha in twentieth century Maharashtra.

Vernacular sources are essential to move away from strictly colonial and touchable-centric understandings of sexuality, caste, untouchability and Indian society and contribute to the global history of sexuality and humanity. These sources connect affect and ideology and illuminate historical actors in their immediacy, expressing emotions, feelings, and ideas. For example, chapter 3 focuses on Ambedkar's Marathi-language speech to a conference of stigmatized women, including prostitutes and shows his emotion and humanity by revealing his anger, frustration, and aggressive authority, which is glaringly absent in the English. Such overlooked references illuminate how Dalits radically transformed the meanings of universal concepts such as equality, democracy, and humanism in the immediate, everyday, and local contexts. I have translated all vernacular materials into English. Translation is also a political act, in terms of increasing access to the vernacular archives and voices, improving teaching materials for classrooms, and creating a robust understanding of India by complicating narrow scholarly understanding of history, politics, and the Dalit social. I have retained the ways in which Marathi-speaking communities have addressed the cities, as Pune and Mumbai. Thus, I use the colonial names Poona and Bombay only when contemporary sources have referred to the cities as such.

Popular writings on Tamashe and Lavanya have been more successful than scholarly analyses in making the Marathi past familiar and tangible. These popular writers, outside formal academic structures, who straddled history and literature, history and memory and shaped the idiom and categories of Marathi identity, are the focus of this work.

Marathi regional imaginations contingently emerged alongside and in negotiation with the national. I have also drawn upon national archives, especially for Tamasha films, and I juxtapose different source materials—written and oral—and combine theoretical frames provided by historians, anthropologists, and scholars of women, gender, and sexuality studies to offer a fresh perspective on the role of sexual-caste politics and subject formation.

Like other communities inside and outside Maharashtra, the Dalit community engaged in the vibrant print and public culture in the late nineteenth century. They contested the existing idiom, codes, and practices of caste, gender, religion, and sexuality, and so they created their own new versions to supplant them. Marathi newspapers published by dominant castes do not have even fragments of the news I refer to in my book. English newspapers and literature produced by dominant castes perpetrated social violence and were barely interested in Dalit affairs or what Dalits thought about caste, untouchability, identity, or sexuality. They also neglected the Dalit prostitute. Like them, upwardly mobile, anxious Dalits also did not want to associate themselves with, or even mention in their newspapers, any sort of ashlil and stigmatized women of ill repute, such as Tamasha women or prostitutes. As a result, the Tamasha archive is patchy and inconsistent, and I reconstruct the muted voices and suppressed subjectivities of supposedly unapproachable and unseeable Tamasha women through writings of men and, most significantly, through oral histories.

Different Tamashe: Open, Rural Fields and Enclosed, Urban Theatres

Because Dalit Tamasha peoples' lives are not officially recorded, ethnography and oral histories are necessary for illuminating how their expressive cultures have historically shaped and reflected their emotions, desires, fantasies, and pursuit of rights. Collecting such life stories provides a way of putting on record the ideas of, experiences of, and inaccuracies about Dalit women, whose ways of knowing the world have rarely been acknowledged, even by Dalits themselves. I followed Tamasha people as they performed in Pune, Mumbai, Ahmednagar, and Narayangao. It was a unique experience for me as a woman to enter the hitherto forbidden masculine space of unbridled masti in theatres such as Bal Gandharva in Pune and Damodar Hall in Parel-Mumbai. This was certainly different from my childhood experience when entire families watched Tamashe in open fields. Back then, we children and women carried our *bardan* (gunny sacks) and thin, torn *godhadi* (quilts made from old rags) and sat with our families, somewhat at a distance, separating ourselves from men who did not belong to our families. During my fieldwork, I noticed a similar approach in the village of Narayangao. Women watched Tamashe in the late nights, but they sat in the well-lit front rows and were closer to the parked police vans—perhaps they and their families felt protected by the proximity to the stationed police symbol. The police offered protection to Tamasha people and troupes in case violence and rowdiness erupted. Tamasha troupe managers had to bribe and keep the police and politicians happy (in monetary and nonmonetary ways) and secure their support.

In Tamashe performed in villages, if some men in the audience wanted to dance to the songs or dance along with the Tamasha woman on stage, they separated themselves from the larger audience and continued their masti at the back or to the side of the larger audience, away from the lit and loud stage and public and police surveillance. In this manner, the larger audience managed the rowdy men and saw to it that the latter did not interrupt or disturb the enjoyment of the former. It was in the enclosed space of modern and urban theatres and auditoriums that I witnessed a clear separation of genders and a more masculine masti. Urban theatres invariably catered to male audiences. Men bought more expensive tickets to view Tamashe and

Lavanya so that they could relax, flatter their ego, and express their masculinity, which was intertwined with entertainment of Tamasha women and their accentuated femininity. Tamasha women sold sexuality to men, and men's play among themselves as well as with the former exaggerated the inequality of gender and caste.

The theatre was alive with Tamasha and Lavani women dancing and singing. While some men were seated, most reciprocated to the dancing women in whatever way they could from their seats, shaking their heads, approving the song and dance, and making gestures to the dancer, thrusting their hands or thumbs in the air, and whistling loudly to applaud a performer. When they could not control themselves, some even got out of their seats and danced frantically in the aisles. They looked like a united, uniform group sharing their manhood, unmindful of caste, class, and gender differentiation, actively consuming the Tamasha woman's offering of the dream of sex and entertainment. It was difficult to record this display of energetic and enthusiastic masti on camera because there was no light in the libidinous theatre—it was pitch dark. By contrast, when women attended special Lavani for women only, the theatre was semi-lit. Nevertheless, even the powerful iPhone camera was powerless to compete with the hypersexual, promiscuous men. In order to capture whatever, I could from different angles, I discreetly moved among the different spaces of the theatre—the wings, the front row, the sides, and the back. I did my best to not disturb the male audience with my womanly presence, especially because I was recording them on my camera. I had to be brisk, so as not to infuriate them as they amused and entertained themselves, many practicing their covert regime of sexuality.

I mostly sat in the front row of the theatre, sometimes with two or three women from Tamasha families. I felt comfortable with them, especially when a theatre full of men narrowed their eyes to glance at me—who is this woman, and what is she doing in our dark, oversexed, manly space, they may have thought. At times, I sat at the back of the theatre so I could observe the full sensual and performative play between the artist and the audience. Men of different ages—young adults (high school and college students), middle-aged, and maybe some elderly—attended Tamasha and Lavani. The middle-aged were predominant, and their watches and cellphones flashed in the dark theatre.

They took photos and videos of the dancers to be circulated on social media. Some high-class gentlemen were selective; they walked through the back door to watch only select popular dancers they chose to view or patronize. They were a part apart—consuming the performer and performative and yet, cunningly keeping their distance from the larger hypersexual, lewd, low-class, and low-caste audience. They also watched from special seats reserved for them.

Tamasha and Lavani performances in the city were held midday or in early evenings, catering to the presumably plebian and supposedly insignificant population. By contrast, the evenings were devoted to supposedly brahman, high-cultured classical *natak* (drama) and *sangeet-natak* (song-drama), serving dominant-caste elites—that is, the salaried class who could relax and enjoy leisure after a day at the office. In this manner, theatre owners created a discrepancy between natak and Tamasha; the high and the low; the elite civilized urban and the supposedly uncivilized rural, modest, and risqué performers, arts, and audience. They thus kept the twain separate, not allowing them to intermingle. Even during the annual Bal Gandharva festival that celebrated the arts of Maharashtra, the organizers followed a similar scheme: Tamasha, Lavani, and other popular arts in the afternoon and natak, classical singing reserved for high-class, high-caste, leisurely, civilized, urbane, and polite evenings!

Plan of the Book: Dissenting Dalits

The story of Tamasha herein—of the ambivalence and performativity of Tamasha women, of their subjection to the sex-gender-caste complex, of the process of struggle embodied by the tripartite concepts of ashlil, manuski, and assli—maps the transition of Tamasha for different publics—from popular, peripatetic, and ashlil performance art to, first, a foil for a radical Dalit politics of manuski and then an assli icon of Marathi identity as mediated by the Marathi film industry and various education programs, mass culture, changing aesthetics, and different publics. Tamasha culturized Dalit identity and reproduced Dalit labor for a sexual-caste economy. Most importantly, Tamasha amplified feelings of caste, community, and class differences between touchables and Dalits and among Dalit themselves: urban, educated, upwardly mobile Dalits denigrated village-based, low-class Tamasha performers because, in their eyes, the latter continued to perform their degraded caste duties, thus stigmatizing the entire community. The three-part struc-ture of the book corresponds with three moments: pre-Ambedkar, Ambed-kar, and post-Ambedkar.

Chapter 1, "Policing Untouchables and Producing Tamasha in Maharashtra," examines the history of Tamasha embedded in the sex-gender-caste complex up to the early twentieth century. I pay particular attention to the complex ways in which caste operated to marginalize, render invisible, and appropriate Un-touchable women's bodies and labor. Within the socioeconomics of caste slavery, Untouchables were expected to provide free labor as a form of pastoral servitude. As servants, Untouchables were denied manuski and ordered to perform menial and agrarian tasks and to perform dance, music, and song for the entertainment of touchables. These forced performances were part of a broader system of caste slavery and reinforced the low and degraded status of Untouchables. From at least the late eighteenth century, the social labor of performing was combined with the free sexual labor of Untouchable women in Tamasha, which made their bodies available for the pleasure of others and normalized the violent and sexually exploitative relations. By the late nineteenth century, caste was infused with a Victorian-brahmani bourgeois alliance that characterized Tamasha and its performers as ashlil. Respectability made Untouchable Tamasha women ob-jects not only of normalized sexual violence but also, as ashlil, of campaigns to regulate, reform, and discipline their performances.

Chapter 2, "Constructing Caste, Desire, and Danger," examines the entan-gled personal and professional lives of the Tamasha couple Pavalabai Hivar-gaokarin and the *Lavanikar* (composer of Lavani) Patthe Bapurao in the first decades of the twentieth century to focus on the stickiness of the ashlil and assli. Because Bapurao was a brahman, he was always already knowledgeable, meritocratic, wise, scholarly, and therefore assli. And the Untouchable Pava-labai was already ashlil, dull-witted, dumb, and inferior because she was an Untouchable. The partnership between Pavalabai, a Mahar *Murali* (a woman dedicated and given to local deities in fulfilment of vows), and Bapurao, a brah-man, and the transgression it represented was a threat to the caste hierarchy. I explore Pavalabai's life and her emergent Dalitness vis-à-vis the sex-gender-caste complex, examining the paradox of Tamasha as simultaneously a tool of pleasure, amusement, and caste violence, as well as an expression of Dalit culture. Bapurao's ability to transgress caste and appropriate Mahar culture by living and performing as a Lavanikar, even as he was attacked by other brahmans, contrasts Pavalabai's struggles to contest the forms of patriarchy that circumscribed her life and to carve out fame and wealth for herself through her art and her own agency.

Although touchables celebrated her dancing and singing skills, they reserved the right to look down upon her with disdain as an ashlil Tamasha woman. As long as she stayed in her place and conformed to the dictates of touchables, they were fine with her. Yet, in different historical conjunctures, she consented and complied but challenged them. She also did not adhere to the respectable norms or dignified living as preached by Dalit reformers. She did not pay any attention to Ambedkar's call for Dalits to challenge caste-based exploitation, abjection, and humiliation of Tamasha women; to eradicate caste-marked cultures; and to annihilate caste. She continued to practice her Tamasha profession all over Maharashtra while transgressing the Mahar community and building fluid and mobile ties of kinship across different castes—even practicing free love and living with many touchable men, including brahman and maratha. She threatened the Dalit social that sought to homogenize or repress the plurality and multiplicity of political action in her excessive, frivolous attempts to create new relations and new realities for herself by inhabiting both the vulgar and human. Despite the modernizing and moralizing mediations and pressures of the colonial government, touchables, and elites, the story of Pavalabai demonstrates that the ashlil continued to flourish in early twentieth-century Maharashtra.

Pavalabai's improper politics were not assimilable within the radical anticaste Dalit politics and samaj that emerged under the leadership of Ambedkar from the 1920s, as I show in chapters 3 and 4. On the one hand, stigmatized Tamasha women were destined to be minor figures, deprived of voice and agency, and rendered invisible as historical subjects. But at the same time, they came to be seen as a social and moral danger, haunting the progress of Indian society as specters of perversion and deviance. As a result, Indians of various castes and classes sought to discipline Dalit women's excesses—that is, their immoderate and overabundant sexuality—through divergent methods of sexual violence and social control. This process was important to all paternalistic actors seeking to build a new social, moral, and modern order. In this complex caste-based social and sexual arrangement of vulgarity, the Dalit woman's body became not merely a passive "site" but a *situation* of control, identification, suffering, resiliency, survival, and creativity. Stigmatized Dalit women were made to bear the entire weight of the Indian citizen's moral anxieties as well as caste slavery.

Chapter 3, "Ambedkar, Manuski, and Reconstructing Dalit Life-Worlds, 1920–1956," focuses on Ambedkar's invention of new Dalit politics and contributions to the disciplining of ashlil Dalit women's sexual excesses as part of his agenda to generate the respectable manus and manuski of the Dalit samaj when contours of the Dalit social were being visibly and contingently put together in a brief moment of flux. Ambedkar's Dalit movement did not simply lay claim to certain human rights; it did so through a radical anticaste politics of suffering—and a Marathi vernacular—that understood the samaj as engaged in an existential struggle for identity, humanity, and dignity. To radical Dalits, becoming modern meant abandoning agrarian bondage and caste slavery; seeking education, employment, and manuski; and becoming assli, decent, and rights-bearing citizens of free India—this was the defiant path of coming into consciousness, reconstructing of new worldviews, and fighting for liberation. Historically, the economy of caste did not allow Dalits to build communal and kinship bonds; as a result, both individual dignity and collective community dignity were more important to them. The taint of being ashlil compounded Dalits' Untouchable caste status and threatened their social cohesion, the collective identity of the community. Ambedkar's construction of Dalit as a collectivity was a political achievement that was necessarily contingent and enabled in a specific historical context. Thus, those stigmatized as ashlil—for example, Muralis or Tamasha women—caused pain and shame to the community as a whole; they threatened to impede Dalits' path to an egalitarian modernity. He therefore put forth a new ideal Dalit woman, one free from the sticky evidence of ashlil untouchability, and a new body politics aimed at reforming Dalit practices regarding dress, food, jewelry, and certain vatandari duties and thus leveling caste distinctions. In order to generate their manuski, fight the stigma and shame of caste slavery, and belong to the Dalit samaj, Dalits worked meticulously to expunge all ashlil elements, erasing and discarding the caste markers that had over centuries concretized Dalitness.

Dalit radicals like Kisan Phaguji Bansode, Baba Valangkar, and Ambedkar recognized the power of cultural forms, including Tamasha, to communicate with an audience that was mostly nonliterate. Ambedkarite Jalsakars (makers of Jalsa), as I explore in chapter 4, "Singing Resistance and Rehumanizing Poetics-Politics, Post-1930," toured remote villages and modern cities, singing and playing music to bring about the social changes that Ambedkar preached would lead to Dalit manuski. Jalsakars such as Bhimrao Dhondiba Kardak (1904–1990) and, later, Bhimsen Barku Gaikwad (1940–2021) appropriated Tamasha in order to broadly appeal to Dalits. They sanitized the form, reducing the sensual and sexual appeal of Tamasha, which they argued thwarted the emergence of an oppositional consciousness, and redirecting its energy toward the generation of Dalit manuski. To this end, not only did Ambedkarite Jalsakars regulate and sanskritize Jalsa, but they also eliminated female actors and characters, hoping to underline propriety and shed Tamasha's potentially ashlil elements. As J. Lorand Matory argued, "Honor is a zero-sum game, with particular intense implications for the discredited, because there is so little honor to go around."[41] In this manner, caste kept Dalits divided against themselves on the issue of respectability, reconstructing their lives, and liberation.

Chapter 5, "Claiming Authenticity and Becoming Marathi, Post-1960," moves from Dalit radicals' appropriation and politicization of Tamasha to its mobilization as an icon of a regional-ethno-linguistic Marathi identity in the new postcolonial state of Maharashtra. The nationalist state of Maharashtra, touchable elites, and Tamasha people in the state adopted various strategies to both recuperate and regulate Tamasha as part of the politics of Marathikaran, putting Tamasha and its practitioners in the service of regional nation-state building. Troubled by the hegemony of North Indians and Hindi language and the market share captured by the Hindi film industry, Marathi filmmakers and *pandharpesha* (white-collared, urban, urbane, powerful, and privileged elites) sought to capitalize on the rowdy and carnivalesque energy of Tamasha—despite it being banned by the colonial government in the 1940s—to appeal to audiences, increase profits, and constitute Marathi culture and a virile, proud, masculine Marathi manus (here, "man"). Though wanting to capitalize on the energy of Tamasha, filmmakers and elites, like Ambedkarite Jalsakars, first had to sanitize Tamasha for consumption by the respectable middle classes. This sanitization is evident in filmmaking and film advertisements from the 1960s and 1970s. The state also promoted and patronized Tamasha as a regional art form through conferences and other events from the 1960s through the present day, reappropriating the social and sexual labor of Tamasha artists to serve the state of Maharashtra. In this conjunctural moment, the difference of caste and identity as Dalits for Tamasha people became a creative impulse for distinction of their art. Tamasha artists grappled with these changes and diligently worked to seek inclusion in the assli Marathi identity by preserving as well as transforming Tamasha and themselves from ashlil to assli. To do so, they engaged with pandharpesha; sanitized the rough and bawdy songs, dances, and jokes; participated in political party campaigns; entered academic spaces; asserted their traditional assli roots; and strove to keep their arts alive and new and standardized Tamasha and Lavani for wider consumption. Nevertheless, paradoxically, the regional state further subordinated and stigmatized Tamasha people and also recognized and sustained their labor by celebrating them by giving token awards to them. Except for such stars as Mangalatai Bansode, Tamasha people continue to struggle for their survival.

History, the history of Tamasha in this case, is thus an open wound, as Jamaica Kincaid writes, that started in the 1800s and has come to no end yet. Like Pavalabai, Mangalatai Bansode, who is the subject of chapter 6, "Forging *New* Futures and Measures of Humanity," grew to be a resilient and resistant, desirable and dangerous woman; yet, unlike Pavalabai, she gradually assumed a somewhat assli status, authority, and virtuosity and asserted her power in Tamasha. For Mangalatai, Tamasha was khandani, an ancestral-lineage, cultural and caste capital, an entrepreneurial endeavor, a profession that had provided and would provide for her family for five generations. She successfully exploited Tamasha as a business enterprise, transforming *hagandari* (fallow lands used for defecation) into *vatandari*, an inherited right, thus both mocking the system of inheritance in caste-based agrarian slavery[42] and capitalizing on Tamasha; she employed a troupe of two hundred belonging to different castes and religions, acted in Tamasha movies, and received state awards. Mangalatai drew upon Bollywood song and dance to produce hybrid versions that further popularized and eroticized Tamasha. She also drew upon networks with politicians, sympathetic touchables and Dalit men, and other women to counter the harmful effects of the moral fault lines that converged on Tamasha women, opening up different possibilities for herself and future generations to reclaim her humanity. Yet her success, like that of Pavalabai, was an individual success and did not extend to the Dalit samaj, and neither did it end the stigma of being a Tamasha woman, a *nachi* (inferior dancer), which haunted and humiliated her to no end. The book concludes with new generation of Dalit artists—for example, Megha Ghadge and Madhusudan (Madhu) Shinde—who experiment with the old and new Tamasha to transform the meaning and practice of Tamasha in the context of a new political and sexual-caste economy. Madhu and his associates focused on the queer performativity in contemporary Tamasha through their group called Bin Bayakancha Tamasha (Tamasha without women), which challenges the hyperpatriarchy of neoliberal India as it continues to grapple with the politics of ashlil and assli, pushing the boundaries of vulgarity, respectability, honor, and freedom to capitalize on Tamasha's ambivalence.

I grew up watching Tamasha along with other popular art forms like Jagran and Gondhal during the summers I spent in my village, Takali (Kopargao, Ahmednagar district, Maharashtra), and Tamasha films broadcast on local television by the Government of India's public service broadcaster Doordarshan (or DD) in the 1970s and 1980s. While playing with friends and family, we children also sang songs and enacted the dances of Muralis and Tamasha women. It was only after I embarked on my field research with Tamasha women, starting in 2003, that I turned my attention to the systemic sexual-caste violence of Tamasha that, despite some breaches, served to keep the structure of agrarian-caste slavery intact.

Each chapter illuminates the stickiness of caste, gender, and sexuality and a variety of ways Dalits negotiated with it in order to create and re-create a new Dalitness. Each Dalit actor you come across in this story—Pavalabai, Ambedkar, Kardak, Gaikwad, Mangalatai, and Madhu—had a different dream of what might be possible. Their life histories suggest different moralities, opinions, and options. We come across their precariousness as Dalits as they created new kinships that were as much about exclusions as affiliations. All Dalits wanted to escape the sticky impoverishment of the present and dreamt of different futures. While upwardly mobile Ambedkarite Dalits insisted on eliminating caste customs and their stigmatized past, others like Pavalabai, Madhu, and Mangalatai wanted to reclaim and repurpose those customs and pasts with performative cultures to their own ends. I show how these actors tried to re-solve moral and material tensions and reimagined the new political. These individual life narratives bring out the general in the particular and reveal the Dalit self-in-society/community. I record the larger social history by working with the ever-energetic Tamasha to analyze the stickiness of vulgarity that many Dalits continuously struggle with. In so doing, I re-create the fugitive world of young urban Dalit women (and men) who transformed the social and political landscape of twentieth-century India.

Part I

Chapter 1

POLICING UNTOUCHABLES AND PRODUCING
TAMASHA IN MAHARASHTRA

Tamasha and Lavani are important popular arts in Maharashtra and have played a vital social and cultural role for many centuries. Touchables deployed mechanisms of the sexual-caste system to demand Untouchables' production of Tamasha culture as essential to the former's politics and processes of differentiation, exclusion, domination, and legitimizing discrimination, stigmatization, and exploitation. This chapter situates Tamasha and Lavani within the specific context of the sex-gender-caste complex and the tripartite framework of ashlil-manuski-assli in Maharashtra from the twelfth up until the early twentieth century.

While scholars, activists, and intellectuals writing in Marathi have devoted tremendous energy to studying Tamasha, those writing in English have paid less attention to these carnivalesque art forms of the subordinated, the non-elites—Dalits and low-caste touchables. None of them, however, have analyzed these in terms of social performativity, especially as it relates to caste: the sexual economy of excess, amusement, and enjoyment, on the one hand, and of the culture and oppression of Dalits, on the other. There is no systematic analysis to date of the role of supposed folk Tamasha and Lavani performance, its context, and its connections with broader social, ideological, and political changes and the Dalit movement in Maharashtra or how popular Tamasha performances were experiments in political pedagogy and a crucial conduit for the transmission of new ideas. In a powerful article, Sharmila Rege argues that dominant castes appropriated Tamasha and Lavani and represented female sexuality and the performer herself as unbounded and wanton, which led to the "drain of [women's] sexuality."[1] Yet she obscures the complex power operations of caste that marginalize, make invisible, and appropriate women's bodies and labor and simultaneously enable women to also exploit small cracks in the hegemonic order.

Tamasha, Work, and Play

Tamasha is a form of secular theatre in Maharashtra that brings together skit, song, dance, mime, poetry, and farce. Historically, Tamasha is rooted in *khel ani gammat* (play and humor). Colloquially, the word *Tamasha* has come to mean "fun," "nonsense," "tantrum," or even "disorder and commotion." Tamasha artists, like their Bengali jatra and Gujarati bhavai counterparts, toured cities and villages, performed in public squares and open spaces, and drew a mixed audience of high- and low-caste women and men. Etymologically, the word *Tamasha* has roots in Persian and literally means "a show, spectacle, or a sort of theatrical entertainment." Tamasha as a form of entertainment that elicits pleasure and *masti* (a gamut of affects unleashing unruly masculine sexual energy) is evidence of the interconnections between Marathi, Persian, and Arab cultures, languages, and societies since the medieval period.

Tamasha embodied the dangers of the Tamasha woman's body and audiences' desires to simultaneously see and experience the prohibited. Through the word *Tamasha* and its fraught associations, ruling elites expressed their fear of and prejudice toward the genre's performers, and the *ashlil* (vulgar) started to stick to rural Dalits more broadly. Tamasha was a paradox—women performed in Tamasha due to the demands of the market and the male viewer, but touchable men who patronized Tamasha neither afforded Tamasha women dignity nor acknowledged their own complicity in creating meaning about Tamasha via their participation in it.

More than mere entertainment, Tamasha was a social, political, and ideological sexual-caste game born precisely from the interplay of relationships of power, and as such it produced and reproduced the social relations of caste—that is, caste sociality, as well as performers' consent to the exploitative and humiliating relations between mainly low-caste and Dalit female performers and the touchable male audience. Historically, Tamasha women were coerced to provide sexual service to all men, especially touchable, dominant-caste men. This coercion rendered them both objects of predatory desire and objects of vilification as the embodiment of vulgarity. Constituting the work of Tamasha

as game and play between Tamasha women, managers, and the audience countered the ennui and arduousness because it became a tool of pleasure and
survival, enabling Tamasha women to endure the work.

Tamasha conveniently naturalized and normalized a nexus of play and
work. Many Tamasha people agreed that Tamasha was both *kala* (art) and
Lakshmi (goddess of wealth, here referring to a means of livelihood), with
some underlining the hard work of training and rehearsing for such play. In
Tamasha, however, Tamasha women were expected to play rather than work,
and understanding Tamasha as only kala and play rendered the work and the
relations of power, caste, and economics in Tamasha invisible. Tamasha women
worked on a reiterative body politics of erotic excess, emphasizing bold bodily
gestures—for instance, winking the left eye or accentuating the breasts and
hips—and openly expressing sensuality and sexual mores, lovemaking, and
sexual enjoyment for their predominantly touchable male audience.

Work was productive, and play was its antithesis, unproductive. Labor is
the force, action, and process that accomplishes work. Different touchables
and Untouchables harnessed Tamasha as work, putting the unproductive to
productive use. Tamasha women did much of the important work that was
rendered play, presumably because the unruly energy and aimless, simple en-
joyments that resulted from play—in the sense of drama or even play between
the artist and audience—lacked utility. The play and playfulness of Tamasha
has mass appeal, and touchables and Untouchables deployed it for different
purposes. By sanitizing Tamasha in the twentieth century, for instance, touchable elites put the rebellious energy of Tamasha to work in carving out an *assli*
(authentic) Marathi identity.

Tamasha not only reflected but also constructed and reproduced social relations of caste, gender, and sexuality. Tamasha and Tamasha women solidified
a relationality and a certain normative construction of Marathi masculinity
and femininity—that is, a marathamola man and woman. Writers of Lavanya
described men as brave, virile fighters, as tall and muscular, with broad shoul-
ders and thick moustaches, and they depicted women as fair, delicate, doe-
eyed, and draped in tight *cholis* (traditional blouses) and nine-yard saris that
accentuated their figures. While men were depicted as patronizing patriarchs,
Tamasha women were rendered as manipulative and cunning home wreckers.

Tamasha women's supposedly unbridled sexuality was readily associated with the ashlil, which stuck to Dalit women, thus further cementing their Dalitness. Women were socially Untouchable, but sexually touchable.

Tamasha emerged from local Maharashtrian forms of entertainment such as Dashavatar, Gondhal, Lalita, Shahiri (a song genre) comprising Lavani and Pavada (a panegyric recounting the achievements of a warrior). Unlike saints, who were relegated to spiritual affairs, the *shahir* (singer of Shahiri) engaged with the sensual.[2] Lavani is the song with *adakari* (gestures) in the broader Tamasha art form. The roots of both words relate to and even originate in rural culture. There are at least five types of Lavanya, including the puranic, devotional, and *sringarik* (sensual, erotic). Not all Lavanya are erotic songs; yet, a titillating, at times explicit *sringar* (eros) of lovers has become essential to this form of entertainment, especially to cater to the predominantly touchable male audience. Lavanya were written about sensual and sexual relationships between women and men, and sung by women and men, for the entertainment of men. As a result, Dalit Tamasha and Lavani woman became an image of woman desired by men.

Tamasha and the Performativity of Caste Slavery, ca. 1200–1818

Since the thirteenth century, Tamasha was recognized as khel-Tamasha, which used song, dance, and mimicry to entertain people. *Balutedars* (village artisanal castes and hereditary functionaries) were remunerated in cash and kind for khel-Tamashe, thus strengthening the caste system that sustained agrarian slavery. The stock characters of Tamasha included the *sardar* (main interlocutor), the *songadya* (buffoon/comedian), the *nachya* and *nachi* (men and women dancers), the *dholkya* (drum player), and the *surte/ jhilkari* (chorus singers and musicians playing the *tuntune*, a one-stringed musical instrument, and *tal*, cymbals). The main components of Tamasha are *gan* (Tamasha starts with worship of Ganesh/Ganapati, the Hindu deity of wisdom and the arts and the remover of obstacles), *mujra* (salutation to audience), *gaulan* (sensual play between Krishna, his maidens, and *maushi*, a man cross-dressed as woman, who was often portrayed as a silly old aunt), *batavani* (comedy, parodic verbal exchange), *savaljavab* (question-answer competition), and *vagnatya* (skit). It is possible that the short song at the beginning of Tamasha hailing Ganapati for the success of the long play became a required component during the peshva regime (the brahman prime ministers who usurped power to emerge as leaders of the Maratha Empire from 1707 to 1818) because the peshve were followers of Ganapati.

As popular arts, Lavani and Tamasha also embraced people of a range of castes and religions and have thus been regarded as one of the more important *lokakala* (popular arts), cultural touchstones, of the majority of people of Maharashtra. Traditionally, traveling Tamasha artists largely belonged to stray or "nomadic" castes (Kolhati, Asvalvale, Bahurupi, Vasudeo) or to low castes such as Dhobi (washerman), Kumbhar (potter), Sutar (carpenter), Teli (oil presser), and Untouchable (Mahar, Mang, Chambhar), and *bara* (twelve) balutedars who performed different services for the village community in return for specific payments in kind, sometimes supplemented by cash. Mangs and Mahars are among the many Dalit castes that largely supply South Asia's labor force. In the twenty-first century, Mahars are about 58 percent of the Dalit (Scheduled Caste) population in Maharashtra, followed by Mangs, who are about 20 percent,[3] and following the logic of caste games, Mahars see themselves as superior to Mangs.

Tamasha was related to Dashavatar and influenced by Bharud, a form created by Mahars.[4] "The first people to [perform Tamasha as a] form of entertainment were Mahars and Mangs, two outcast[e] communities," notes Balwant Gargi.[5] As mentioned in both the *Kavyanushana* (twelfth century) and the *Dnyaneshvari* (thirteenth century), Lavanya were sung by Untouchable women belonging to the Dom and Mang castes.[6]

Historically, Mahars functioned as landless agricultural or field servants, menials, and messengers and attended to the odd and sundry throughout the year, and they continued to be the most rebellious of all Untouchable castes. They were laboring servants, who suffered bondage by birth, and their subordination was principally maintained by their landlessness. Untouchable artisanal castes, such as Mangs, made ropes and brooms, wove baskets, and functioned as executioners. In contrast to Mahars, these artisanal castes (sweepers, leatherworkers, weavers) could be easily dispensed with if the landlord and peasants so desired. As a result, Mangs and Chambhars were tightly tied to their occupations in the villages. The specific duty of Untouchables was to carry society's burdens: Mahars were menial village servants who were to do everything they were ordered to by any authority—the headman, the village corporation, or the colonial government. Many a time, they were obligated to provide free labor and reproduce Untouchable labor for a caste economy. Tamasha was a performative of the hierarchies of labor and social life, reproducing sociopolitical power and stigmatizing Untouchables even further. We need to attend to this context of caste slavery, violence, and sexually exploitative relations to analyze Tamasha women's lives.

Caste institutionalized social hierarchy and labor inequality not only between touchable dominant (exploiters) and Untouchables (exploited) but also among the exploited groups themselves. The caste system sowed dissension among Dalits, and rivalries and jealousies thrived along with some commonality. As a result, many activists and leaders, including Ambedkar, made efforts to unite Dalits. All Dalits were subject to a double colonization—external British and internal brahman—and hence a united front of Dalits could pose a formidable challenge to both sets of colonizers.

Some brahman men, like Ram Joshi and Patthe Bapurao also performed in Tamasha, which opened up avenues to make kin and construct close affective communities of different castes. Yet, due to the mechanisms of the caste system, each group was bound by occupations of their kinship groups by birth—for example, a potter was held to pottery work and married only other potters. Tamasha possessed the potential to undermine or resist the institution of caste and untouchability and challenge social reproduction. Nevertheless, the caste mechanism naturalized the constitution of particular caste communities. As such, they reduced Untouchables to singing, playing music, and dancing until the current day. Madhu Shinde, a transgender person, or TG as transgender people described themselves, belonging to the troupe Bin Bayakancha Tamasha (Tamasha without women; this troupe showcased straight and gay male dancers), asserted that their group had "70 percent of *our* [Dalit] people."[7] Whether Tamasha is performed by men or women, the underlying caste structure remains intact in twenty-first century India. Even though we met for the first time and very briefly, our Dalit backgrounds helped Madhu create a common bond between us belonging to the same Dalit community—they a Chambhar (leatherworker caste) and me a Mahar!

Along with engaging in a certain kind of labor, upholding the institution of caste also meant performing a touchable-dominant or Untouchable-subservient role. As part of their *baluta* (responsibilities as defined by the village servant system),[8] trapped in their caste location Mahars sang and drummed not only to carry out one of their fifty-two duties to spread the message of the state to the larger masses but to entertain. More significant, however, is that their stage performances were also a form of political protest, performative of Dalit resistance, during the twentieth century. The village looked after those balutedars—such as Chambhar and Dhor leatherworkers, smiths, and carpenters—whose productive labors were essential and whose absences would cause difficulty. But those—such as Mahars—whose labor though significant was seen as unproductive, excessive, as play, were ostracized. The Mahars were much more alienated from the village system than other caste functionaries.

Further, intercaste relationships also resulted in individuals and communities modifying and inventing new customs to their own advantage. There is a saying in Marathi that crystallizes the practices of certain castes: "Brahmana ghari lihina, kunbya ghari dana, ann Mahara ghari gana" (The top-most caste, brahmans, are to read and write, Shudra maratha peasants to produce grains, and Ati-Shudra, Untouchable, Mahars to sing and dance). Agrarian caste slavery set the parameters for the roles brahmans, marathas, and Mahars were to perform. Caste is not merely a division of labor, but of laborers, as Ambedkar argued. Caste difference led to discrimination through a crippling distortion of human values and relationships—higher castes subjected Mahars to large amounts of labor, including entertainment, which itself was a form of servitude in the pastoral economy. Mahars were to subserviently perform unproductive and excess labor through, song, music, and dance, while marathas would work the fields, tending to crops. Brahmans, of course, engaged in cultivating his intellect, produced knowledge and literature, and looked down upon manual labor of Shudras and Atishudras. Brahmans enjoyed caste supremacy and they graded knowledge systems, placing intellect higher and practical arts and crafts lower. Bitter contests for political power and social status thrived in the idyllic village, and they continue to embolden ethnic boundaries in the present day.

The caste system reduced Untouchables to singing and dancing, and the ensuing fun and frolic degraded their innate talents and intelligence they might have had. Poverty, economic dependence, and social weakness subjugated Untouchables in both the economic and ritual domains and prevented self-assertion and upward mobility. The ancestors of marathas and brahmans captured for themselves the top and the middle of the caste hierarchy—that is, a human hierarchy—and over centuries reinforced their position, growing accustomed to deference from Mahars. They saw Untouchables not as humans but as means of securing social, political, and economic superiority; Untouchables were only objects over whom touchables could exert total control.

Caste hierarchy functioning through exclusion and imitation is insidious; at all levels of difference, the brahmans look down on marathas, who are lower than them on the caste ladder. Marathas do the same with Untouchables. They are below brahmans but above the Untouchables. While being anxious to pull down brahmans, marathas brooked no challenge from the Untouchables. Instead of allying with them, marathas committed atrocities and policed the Untouchables. Due to graded inequality, as Ambedkar noted, "Each caste takes its pride and its consolation in the fact that in the scale of castes it is above some other caste." Dominant castes lived in the glory of their innate superiority, entrenching the presumed inherent inferiority of Untouchables, reducing Untouchables to servility and, in the process, solidifying the caste system. Untouchables were rendered and required to be dumb, childlike creatures, not mature men, not women, uncivilized, animalistic, and vulgar.

Dominant castes also demonstrated their caste-pride and domination by enacting their power and privilege within and outside the performing arts, which in turn became performative of caste hierarchy. For centuries, the ruling castes forced Untouchables to perform at command—the degradation of Untouchables was entertainment to the former. Cruel caste slavery orchestrated coerced performances by Mahars for the enjoyment of dominant-caste brahmans and marathas, who had rights to lands and controlled state administration and expanded their exploitation.[9] Agrarian caste slavery systematically alienated Mahars from notions of honor; they were to be entertainers while also toiling away in the fields. Even the Mahar headmen were not spared by the ruling classes; their servitude was maintained and their obedience compelled under the threat of violence. The Mahar headman from the Sasvad village (near Pune), for instance, was forced to play music during festivals.[10] Clearly, the doctrine of perfect submission reconciled the headman to violence and subjection, making him fall in line and stay in his lowly place and setting an example for the rest of the Mahars. If dominant castes could control and terrorize the headman and conjure up the threat of punishment, certainly the rest of the Mahars would easily comply. Dominant castes thus policed the social-sexual reproduction of caste, forcing Mahars to witness beating, torture, and humiliation, reminding them of the total proprietorship over their being. Such demonstrations of power were essential to producing, reproducing, and reinforcing domination.

The constitution of Maharness (and of Untouchableness in general) as an abject and degraded condition was closely connected with performance, and touchables' enjoyment and entertainment at the expense of Mahar subjection was part of the performativity of caste domination. These supposedly innocent pastoral amusements and festivities conveniently camouflaged the cruel violence of caste and the relationships of mastery and servitude, dominating and dominated, exploiter and exploited. To achieve peace, Untouchables would accommodate such torture and brutalities, allowing some injustices to survive, even as some would later turn their compelled performances and the talent they built from them to their advantage and dominate Tamasha, Jalsa, Lavani, and other art forms in Indian culture.

Caste also institutionalized forced labor, which bound Untouchables as slaves (or semi-slaves[11]) to landlords or peasant cultivators in the form of *veth begar* or bonded servitude. Under caste slavery, Mahars were not permitted rights to land, yet their duties included a primary role in settling boundary disputes. As Antyaja (the last people or castes), they were "*Maha-ari*,"[12] or big or great enemies of the (Aryan) invaders and sons of the soil, thus staunchly resisting Aryans and establishing their ancient connection to the land. Tamasha was also a performative of forced labor. In 2016–17, when I met the octogenarian Dalit shahir Bhimsen Gaikwad, he reaffirmed Mahars' connection to both agricultural labor and creativity in Tamasha: "*Our* people were farmers who sang, played music, and earned some income based on their art during the summer season [when they were not working the fields]. My uncles, cousins, father played [musical instruments like] *halgi, dhol, tutari*, and also sang in Tamasha. Some traveled and others did not. At times, they devoted themselves entirely to Tamasha. This is how I was *born* into the culture of Tamasha and developed my song and music [skills]."[13] Gaikwad underlined his inherited artistry and ancestry in Tamasha to establish his assli status as a performer. Gaikwad also referred to me with the collective "our people," thus underlining our common bond as Mahars, as belonging to the same community. This was also reinforced when his nephew introduced me to Gaikwad, saying, "This is *our* madam." As a Dalit woman, I could establish these bonds and reconnect with my community.

Untouchables developed music and singing while working in fields or attending to other duties. Yet the performance and music were not for the sake of having a good time or "merely entertaining,"[14] as I discussed above. Songs, dances, and jokes normalized caste violence and made it socially endurable and a vehicle of excessive enjoyment of Mahar performances by others. And yet sometimes the material performed possessed glimmerings of Dalit insurgency and rebellion. Historically, Mahars' crucial role in agricultural production also led to their growing consciousness, unlike Mangs and Chambhars, who complied with the hierarchical order and were used by touchables against Mahars.

Along with social labor, Tamasha engendered the performativity of the coerced sexual labor and objectification of Untouchable women. Historically, Tamasha women were coerced to provide sexual service to all men, especially the dominant and privileged high-caste men. This coercion rendered them both objects of predatory desire and objects of vilification as the embodiment of vulgarity. Although caste created social and sexual boundaries, these were continuously violated by dominant-caste men who routinely asserted their virility by sexually violating and raping Untouchable women, as if it were their birthright. Tamasha normalized and disavowed touchable men's violence toward and injury of Untouchable women, appropriated their bodies, and made them available for the pleasure and amusement of others. The institution of caste yoked sexuality to the subordination of Tamasha women and elided their sexual violation by constituting the structural presumption that they lacked virtue and thus did not merit status as manus (human) and therefore as a woman.

Dalit Tamasha women's labor completely encapsulated in the caste system takes us beyond conventional notions of labor. While regular forms of labor permitted the possibility of protest and resistance, Tamasha women's labor, like that of scavengers, was implicated in the very regimes of power that generated it—their ownership of their labor, their "consent" to it, was itself a state of subjugation of the most extreme order. This was the cruel paradox—their labor reproduced their lowness and birth-based bondage.

In general, there is a strong connection between Tamasha, Lavani, Pavada, and military culture. Khel-Tamashe were used in the seventeenth and eighteenth century to amuse the Mughal army.[15] From the middle of the eighteenth century, they were patronized by the peshva as a stylized form of court entertainment. The peshva referred to them as Lavanya Tamashe. During this time, shahirs focused on *sringar* (sensuality, eros) and their Lavanya described the lives of the queen, the nobility, and the courtiers, as well as the spiritual and divine.

The peshva amply rewarded high-caste male Lavanikars (Lavani composers). There is only one reference to a woman Lavanikar, and women's performance of the sringarik Lavani was predominant between 1796 and 1818, the late peshva period. Although the peshva patronized brahman Lavanikars like Ram Joshi and Anant Phandi, as well as Honaji Bala, who belonged to the Gavali (cowherder) caste, and Prabhakar, who belonged to the Shimpi (tailor) caste and may have also resided at the peshva residence of Shanivarvada-Pune, they did not patronize Untouchables—with one exception: Dhondya Mahar, who was the teacher of Ram Joshi.[16] Yet, when scholars sing the praises of the brahman Ram Joshi and Patthe Bapurao, their caste status blinds them so deeply that they forget Dhondya Mahar and his exceptional contributions in shaping Ram Joshi's skills at Lavanya.

The peshva and touchables enjoyed Mahar-Mang Tamashe Lavanya, and at the same time exploited them and further entrenched caste distinctions and caste-based feudal patriarchy. The eleven-year old Mang student Muktabai Salve from Pune noted the atrocities of the peshva: "The peshva drove us Mang Mahar away from our lands to build their own mansions. They buried them in the foundations of their mansions. Under Bajirao's rule, if any Mang Mahar happened to [transgress caste-based spatial boundaries and] pass in front of the gymnasium, they cut off his head and used it to play 'bat ball,' with their swords as bats and his head as a ball, on the grounds." The peshva bolstered caste slavery in Pune by reinforcing the brahmani ideology of purity-pollution and inflicted severe punishment and death on transgressors, including touchables.[17]

The intense degradation, humiliation, and vitiation of Untouchables took extreme forms: Untouchables were forced to tie brooms (resembling a tail as if they were two-legged animals) to their waists so that the broom would sweep away the dust they trod on lest a Hindu be polluted by walking on the same dust. They were forced to carry an earthen pot around their neck wherever they went "lest their spit should fall on the earth and pollute a Hindu who might unknowingly tread on it."[18] They were forbidden to enter the town premises in late afternoons as their long shadows might pollute the ground and thereby others who trod on it. They were made to carry sticks with bells to announce their presence so that others could take care and not be polluted. And each Untouchable was "to have a black thread either on his wrist or around his neck, as a sign or a mark to prevent the Hindus from getting themselves polluted by his touch by mistake."[19] In this manner, the peshve consigned entire groups of Untouchables to animal status and reduced them to "walking carrion."[20] As a result, the Untouchable body and being became deeply repulsive and socially dangerous. Brahman hegemony dehumanized Untouchables and robbed them of their sociality, self-respect, and manuski (humanity, and human dignity).

During the late peshva period, the peshve enslaved many errant Shudra-Ati-Shudra (non-brahman-Untouchable) caste women, and they were called *bateek* (whores). These women may have performed in Lavanya Tamashe patronized by peshva. The last peshva, Baji Rao II, also procured many bateeks to work for high-caste savarnas in dance halls, homes, stables, granaries, cattle houses, and construction projects.[21] Though little work has been done on shahirs' patronage records, it seems that many women from the Shudra-Ati-Shudra castes were bought for domestic or sexual labor by the Maratha state and then presented to shahirs as slaves in lieu of payment. In characterizing lower-caste women as bateeks, the state objectified and commodified their bodies—an important site for articulating the state's power. Hiroshi Fukazawa notes that the caste of slaves played an important role in the kind of services forced upon them, and in this way the peshva maintained the hierarchies of caste slavery.[22]

Social distinctions were also mirrored in the songs of Lavanikars, who created dichotomies of the "*saubhagyavati* (wife) and the *bateek* (whore)."[23] While the wife expressed her pain of separation from her lover and took pride in his virility and excessive desire, the low-caste bateek pleaded with men to exercise their right over her, to give her pleasure, and invited rape.

After the British defeated the peshva regime at the Battle of Koregaon on January 1, 1818, to end the Third Anglo-Marathi War, they built a memorial to commemorate their victory, The memorial listed twenty Mahars who fought with bravery and strength, virtues that were denied to them by the horrors of the caste system. Following Ambedkar's call for celebrating Mahar heroes who routed the tyrannical brahman rule, the Koregaon monument has become a pilgrimage site for Mahars even in the present day.[24] The false dichotomy between colonialism and nationalism constructed by elite reformers of modern India as well as scholars easily elided the internal colonialism of brahmans and touchables over the Untouchables.

After the fall of the peshva in 1818, it was mainly traders, landlords, local princes, and, most significantly, ordinary people who patronized and maintained Tamasha performers and put on their shows. As a result, practitioners of Tamashe and Lavanya flourished in private *baithaks* (seated performances) and salons, as well as public *maidan* (open spaces). Into the nineteenth century, although Tamasha and Lavani were considered lower forms of art for the exchange of sex and wealth, they were not stigmatized as ashlil, even if *nachya-pore* (boy dancers) cross-dressed, danced, and performed as women. This stigma emerged and stuck to Dalits in the late nineteenth and twentieth centuries.

Victorian-Brahmani Morality Making Modern India in the Late Nineteenth and Early Twentieth Century

After the rebellion of 1857, the British Crown consolidated its power over India. While the Proclamation of 1858 stated that the British would not interfere in the social and religious realms, in practice, although they were divided on the political costs of intervening, British officials did precisely that. They intervened to police the mechanisms of caste, the woman question, and the lives of prostitutes and Tamasha women. From the last decades of the nineteenth century and especially in the early twentieth century, British intrusion in the Indian economy and society also resulted in changes in Tamasha. Performances moved into closed auditoriums. Industrialization and commercialization gave rise to new middle-class patrons and consumers of Tamashe Lavanya. A contract/manager system of middlemen, who employed Tamasha artists and troupes on salaries or against advance payments, further commercialized Tamasha. Modernity led to the emergence of *talim-masters* (teachers) focusing on training, rehearsals, and regimented, structured presentation of Tamasha (like that in high-caste-dominated theatre). Most importantly, women replaced nachya-pore in Tamashe in cities like Mumbai and Pune. Women also led *sangeet-bari* (sequences of song-dance by different groups) theatres. From 1900 to the 1920s, Pavalabai Bhalerao Hivargaokarin (see chapter 2) was the first Mahar woman to perform in Tamasha in the modern theatres of Mumbai and Pune. Namdeo Vhatkar provides evidence of rare advertisements of Tukaram Mhar (Mahar), Satya Mhar, and Raghya Mhar performing at the New Elphinstone Theatre, Grant Road, Mumbai on June 28, 1898, and May 7, 1899 (figs. 1.1 and 1.2).

The professionalization, feminization, commercialization, and broader middle-class patronization of Tamasha in the late nineteenth and early twentieth centuries spooked British colonial officials, elite Indian liberals, popular writers, and Dalit gentlemen, who feared and were anxious about ashlil Tamasha. Yet these same men secretly enjoyed Tamasha through a covert regime of sexuality. Their furtive enjoyment of Tamasha and Tamasha women and the resulting anxiety led British colonial officials, elite brahmans, and other savarna Hindus to seek to discipline Tamasha women and the larger realm of the ashlil, unleashing a modern sexual economy and politics of caste in colonial Western India.

The fusion of a Victorian-brahmani bourgeois alliance critically shaped the deployment of the sexual-caste economy, stigmatizing Tamasha and its practitioners as ashlil and transforming Tamasha into a modern vice. Colonial governmentality, the discourse of decency and respectability, marriage and family, Victorian sexual puritanism, Indian religious revivalism, and liberal reformism all converged to regulate the ashlil sexual deviance. The elevation of dominant-caste women and proper demeanor eroded the agency of Dalit

FIGURE 1.1. A contest between Krishnya Mhar (Mahar) and Raghya Mhar (Mahar) at New Elphinstone Theatre, Grant Road, Mumbai, May 7, 1899. Source: M. R. Lamkhade, *Tamasha and Lavani* (Pune: Navin Indalkar, 2014), 35–36.

Tamasha women, assigning to them a perversion and erotic excess requiring disciplining. Along with prostitutes, hijras, and criminal tribes, stigmatized *Muralis* (lower-caste girls given in dedication to local deities) and Tamasha women were depicted by enlightened liberal British officials as a moral contagion that had to be controlled or eliminated through legal and social reform. Since the beginning of the twentieth century, a range of dominant paternalistic actors, including the British colonial government and elite Indians deployed the ashlil and its multiple valences to facilitate the construction and consolidation of

FIGURE 1.2. A contest between Indurkar Kalgivala (Tukaram
Mhar and Raghya Mhar) and Dhayarikar Turevala (Satya
Mhar and Saghya Mhar) at New Elphinstone Theatre, Grant
Road, Mumbai, June 28, 1898. Source: M. R. Lamkhade,
Tamasha and Lavani (Pune: Navin Indalkar, 2014), 35–36.

racism, inherited caste inequalities, caste patriarchies, and repressive polite
society by disciplining the production of a decent, modern public sphere and,
later, "Marathi" identity.

I am not necessarily endorsing a narrative of decline with the ascendance
of the colonial order in India. I have already analyzed the false dichotomy of
colonialism and anti-colonial nationalism elsewhere.[25] British rule unleashed
modern forces that opened up new employment opportunities for Dalits. The
British enabled Untouchables' access to law, education, and the political realm,

yet such access was frustrated by ambiguities, uncertainties, and contradictions. For instance, the British also upheld religious restrictions, favored the dominant castes, and reinforced caste ideology.

The bourgeois Victorian-brahmani order of respectability and decency ensured the proliferation of specific pleasures, fixed on certain polite tastes and practices, thereby producing perpetual circuits of power, the ashlil, violence, and pleasure. This covert regime of sexuality and its Victorian ideals distinguished civilized from uncivilized Indians. Some dominant-caste Indians appropriated Tamasha in content and form, simultaneously negotiating their relationship to, emulating, and distinguishing themselves from both European Victorians and Untouchables. To maintain their hegemony and retain their sense of self as possessors and producers of the finest arts and culture and more human value, elite British and touchables colluded to institutionalize the supposedly high arts of *natak* (drama) and *sangeet-natak* (song-drama) while diminishing the value of Lavani-Tamasha as vulgar. To generate Dalit manuski and establish their status as assli, ostracized and exploited Dalits accepted some terms of the dominant ideology and, in the process, abandoning and manipulating the ashlil. The ashlil was foisted on Dalits for the purposes of subjugation.

Colonial British Sexual-Caste Governmentality
From the middle of the nineteenth century, the British embarked on a modernizing mission in India and critically engaged with the sex-gender-caste complex to police, cleanse, and regulate ashlil elements of society. They mobilized the nexus of "power-knowledge-pleasure"[26] that sustained the ambivalent discourse of sexuality in Tamasha. In establishing India's incapacity for self-government, the colonial state entrenched discourses regarding the inhumanity of natives; benevolently supported suppressive legislation to save women from sati, child marriage, and temple prostitution; and managed Indian bodies and dispositions. To normalize its power, the colonial government strictly surveilled the social, sexual, moral, and political behavior of Indians. Discourses about masculinity became entangled in contagion, hygiene, and obscenity. As a result, the colonial state actively monitored "obscene" and "seditious" publications and presentations—books, dramas, speeches—as well as other cultural practices such as Tamasha, plays, and

nationalist activities. The government subjected the above productions to a "test of obscenity" and surveilled those that might incite violence, disturbances, and immorality. The state framed rules for Theatre and Performance licenses and controlled song, dance, music, smoking, and liquor consumption. For example, colonial bureaucrats in 1903 debated if certain plays were "objectionable," framed "rules regarding playing of music in streets and public places," and in 1911 agreed on the "suppression of obscene publications."

Dalit Muralis and Tamasha women who performed mainly on the street could not afford to apply for licenses like the elite theatre companies did. Hence, official documents rarely mention Tamasha performances. British officials spent long hours watching "dancing girls," Tawaifs (courtesans), even recording classical music. But they did not record any observations about popular arts, perhaps because they were too marginal to be of concern or because officials were prejudiced against Tamasha and Murali performers. Although colonial officials desired dancing girls, they were also anxious about their own moral reputation. As a result, they engaged in a covert regime of sexuality and the discursive management of obscenity. Configured as dishonorable and ashlil, a range of Dalit women—Muralis, Jogtinis, and Tamasha women—came to be seen as a threat to the civilizing impulses of modern, colonial Indian society. These Dalit women were triply stigmatized: for their caste, gender, and sexuality. Some of them were married but most were not, and they often entered into sexual relationships with male patrons of various castes. Falling outside the conjugal norms of the monogamous family unit, they were classified as non-wives, a category defined only in the negative.

The ambivalent position of Tamasha women, indeed of Dalits as a whole, emerges from this negative position of birth-based bondage. The sexual availability of Tamasha women made them integral, indispensable to the entertainment of and release of masti for elite men, but Tamasha women were also dangerous, threatening the conjugal norms outside of which they operated. In human terms, these surplus women were of little significance to elites, yet they threatened the modern order. Here, I am expanding on Ambedkar's thinking about the "surplus [brahman] woman" to include Dalit women. As surplus women, Dalit Tamasha women were seen as always available sexually, and they were deprived of the right to family and kin. They were scorned and yet desirable, and as such acquired a liminal status. Gender, labor, and sexuality were accentuated differently for Dalit women performers.

Tamasha itself and Tamasha women in particular were surplus, untamed, unruly, and signified enjoyment and excess in increasingly complex ways into the twentieth century. Although many touchable men enjoyed Tamasha and Tamasha women, they also devalued their work and rendered them and their labor unproductive, both excess and surplus. On the one hand, there was a management of surplus through a set of iterative practices of negative control. On the other, this surplus was marked as negative and corrosive; in the same turn, it was deemed necessary to assert the assli caste selfhood of the touchables. The play of Tamasha successfully occludes work and in so doing, the always already alienated sexual labor of the Dalit woman performer produces the surplus that keeps the sexual economy in place.[27] Independent, Untouchable Murali and Tamasha women did not fit Victorian modernity. Colonial liberal reforms ended up devaluing and denying Muralis' and concomitantly Tamasha women's precolonial customary rights to property inheritance. The shift from precolonial customary rights to colonial ones further weakened women's claims to a share in the family wealth. Colonial liberalism was successful in silencing Muralis and erasing Tamasha women from the official record, and this became the foundation for postcolonial problems.

Savarna Elites' Brahmanizing of India

Elite savarna reformers focused on brahmanizing Marathi society (and by extension Indian society) and joined the British in manufacturing a moral crisis and sexual panic in modern India. Ruling elites adopted many racist Victorian ideas and suffused them with their brahmani values to reform and remake India and prove their cultured status and fitness for self-rule. While dominant-caste theatre such as *natak* (drama) and *sangeet-natak* (song-drama) were construed as high, moral culture, Tamasha and Lavani were rendered licentious and immoral. Elites strictly surveilled emergent and existing practices of supposedly illicit sexuality among all sections of society, especially the lower castes.[28] They cultivated higher tastes and cultures of music and song, favoring those brahmans and non-brahmans who fit brahmani ideals and disciplining those who did not. Under the guise of reformists, they emerged as architects of caste segregation, social-sexual reproduction, and social selection. Reformers thus constituted an elaborate enforcement of a new Marathi social imaginary by creating new differentiations of "high" and "low" communities, policing pollution and purity, and implanting an oppressive hierarchy in everybody's imagination, including Dalits'.

In the late nineteenth and early twentieth centuries, elite brahman liberal reformers sought to build a sexual and social order, debating the scope of *samajik* and *dharmik sudharana* (social, religious, legal, and moral reform and improvement) necessary to attain a certain *naitik adhunikta* (modern morality) in the private and domestic spheres. Marathi elites aimed to cultivate sudharana through a certain *shastric* (cultured, cultivated and hence modern, scientific) thinking and *shista* (discipline, both individual and social). The resulting social order relied on the distinction between ashlil and *shil* (decent) to reinforce inequalities between high and low castes, communities, and cultures. The construction of high and low caste and polite and impolite cultures, in part, entailed policing the production of modern Marathi public culture. This included attacks on supposedly vulgar festivals, behaviors, and lower-caste dance forms and music, which further cemented caste distinctions. In the process, elite reformers described lower-caste art forms like jatra and Tamasha as vulgar, crude, rural, and unrefined. They also promoted brahman superiority in the field of Marathi culture, introducing shastric dramatic performances, singing, and amusements and appropriating and reinforcing emblematic traditional arts, like natak and sangeet natak.

From the mid-nineteenth to the mid-twentieth centuries, elite brahmans strengthened the Marathi natak tradition. For example, the well-to-do brahman Balwant Pandurang (alias Anna) Kirloskar (1843–85) started a sangeet natak group called Bharatshastrotejak Belgaokar Mandali (Cultivating cultured, regimented, and scientific Indian by a group from Belgao). He moved to Pune in 1878 and established himself as a theatre personality and founded the Kirloskar Natak Mandali (1880–1935), whose many stars gained a legendary status.[29] Most of the teachers and performers of the Pune Gayan Samaj established in 1874 were brahmans and they aimed to "revive a taste of *our* musical science amongst our brethren of the upper class, and to raise it up in their estimation."[30] Two brahman men, V. D. Paluskar and V. N. Bhatkhande, made enormous efforts to give a distinctive shape, form, and identity to Indian classical music and turn it into a high art in the late nineteenth century. Historically, brahman elites preserved the supposedly inherent respectability of Marathi natak as distinct from disrespectable Tamasha. Between 1856 and 1862, Parshurampant, Tatya Godbole, Krushnashastri Rajvade, and Ganeshshastri Lele presented natak dramas based on Sanskrit literature. Later, Janardan Kirtane and others produced many dramas based on historical, mythical, and Shakespearean stories that were translated into Marathi.

Between 1880 and 1920, the famous five men—Kirloskar, Deval, Kolhatkar, Khadilkar, and Gadkari—took Marathi theatre to its pinnacle, creating a wave of enthusiasm with their different art forms. They rarely mentioned arts like Tamasha and showed no inclination to systematically preserve them. Although ignored and denigrated by elites, Tamasha thrived in the public realm, which is most clearly evident in the rise of Tamasha films in the 1940s. The popularity of Tamasha films and the ashlil elements they promoted threatened elites and their construction of an assli Marathi identity. Marathi elites disapproved of Tamasha and the way it controlled the Marathi cinema industry as well as a majority of the population.

Modern bourgeois reformers strategically constructed an axis for the "inclusion/exclusion"[31] of a range of communities: the lower classes, prostitutes, hijras (persons born male who describe themselves as emasculates), dancing girls, Tamasha women, Muslims, and Untouchables. They emerged as the "others" of Hindu India. Brahman elites cleverly fused the regional and national to shape Hindu ascendancy, a Hindu public sphere, drawing selectively from such regional culture as Marathi theatre as a modern form of entertainment and avoiding contamination by the West as well as the seemingly coarse, uncouth, rural, and ashlil Tamasha Lavani and its low-caste practitioners. Drawing on regional culture enabled elites to prove their difference from the British colonizers as well as Untouchables and Muslims to create systematic and indigenous music and a moral and modern India in the early days of cultural nationalism. In the process, Marathi elites created caste and cultural differences.[32]

Elites were mindful that playful and carnivalesque Tamasha was intensely popular among Marathis of different castes and genders and as such posed a threat to savarna elite art forms. In this new social order, Tamasha, by now a paradigmatic symbol of excess—in terms of uncontrolled expenditure and lack of utility and productivity—was symbolic of Dalitness. It was—alongside Tamasha and Lavani forms and actors—a backward religious custom, licentious, with *"bomb"* (loud) merriment in *kilasvana* (disgusting, nauseating) festivals such as *shimga* (Holi)[33] and immoral practices such as prostitution. It became more frequently attacked as "kilasvana and ashlil."[34] Women especially demarcated inclusion and exclusion within this social order. Elite reformers clearly differentiated between "our *kulin* [high descent] family women" and "nautch women" (dancing girls) or Tamasha women, a necessary distinction made to save brown men from brown "fallen" women, and ultimately, to save Hindu religion from European ridicule. At the same time, there was a parallel engagement in a covert regime of sexuality—explicitly diminishing cultural forms and their practitioners, which they deemed ashlil while covertly attending dancing-girl performances in salons or other gatherings. In line with traditional Victorian-brahmani patriarchal norms, dances, dancing girls, and Tamasha women who performed in public before predominantly all-male audiences, especially to provide pleasure through their bodily art form, were seen as dishonoring women and womanhood. Although they enjoyed it in private, elite men argued that there was a critical conflict between women dancing in public for the entertainment of men and the norms of bourgeois Indian respectability. There was thus a significant tension between the dishonorable body art of Tamasha women, their low-caste status, and the powerful patriarchy constructed in a colonial setting. Women dancing in public conflicted with patriarchal patterns and were seen as sexually available and even erotic.

Conclusion

Caste privilege enabled touchables to accuse Dalits of being ashlil. As a result, dominant castes reconstituted their privilege, accumulated caste capital, and further consolidated their high-casteness. Even if savarnas practiced the ashlil, they could reform and become decent and venerable. The ashlil did not stick to them in the way it does to Dalits. As a result, touchables writing and singing sringarik Lavanya were not stigmatized in the way Dalits were.

And while touchables in different regimes—peshva, British, or postcolonial Indian—constructed and sang explicitly sringarik Lavanya, it was accepted as art, but the same entertainments became ashlil when performed by Dalits; vulgarity stuck to Dalits, further solidifying their Dalitness, in a vicious circle. Reformers used tropes of the ashlil and *bibhatsa* (disgust) to shape normative ideas about propriety and restructure India's social geography, gender norms, and sexual mores. They believed that social and sexual evils emanated from the very nature of certain Untouchable people rather than from the structural and material conditions of caste, class, capitalism, poverty, and unemployment. The ashlil extended caste stigmatization of Dalits, producing social differentiation and reproducing structures of caste inequality. This is the exceptionalism of caste. The ashlil could be used—or in the case of Tamasha and Lavani, could be appropriated—by touchables, but it defined the essence, and the difference, of Dalitness. Vulgarity works through social and sexual differentiation—marking food, language, music, and dance—to generate inequality and amplify the subalternity of Dalits and their ongoing struggle against sexual-caste. It legitimized their social and sexual difference and solidified caste hierarchy.

Colonial officials colluded with genteel *pandharpesha* (white-collar, privileged, powerful, urbane elites) in depicting language, behavior, attitudes, and, most importantly, *"bhadak"* (ostentatious, loud, boisterous, lewd) Tamasha and sexual gestures expressed unhindered in the public domain as ashlil. Consequently, the colonial state eventually banned Tamasha in the 1940s. Extending this regulation, although for the purpose of creating a robust masculine regional-nationalist identity when the new State of Maharashtra was created on May 1, 1960, it further clamped down on all that was deemed ashlil—Tamasha, cinema posters, *chumban* (kissing) on screen, prostitution, alcohol consumption—in the name of protecting the morality, sentiments, and culture of Marathi people.

Nevertheless, there was the predictable transgression that is provoked by any prohibition, as we see with marketing strategies and state and court bans, which accentuate the desirability of vulgar products, making them even more controversial. In this manner, dominant castes used the ashlil as a discursive trope to produce, reproduce, and consolidate their domination and hegemony, deploying it to regulate and condemn those lower in the caste hierarchy. In the modern liberal discourse, privileged touchables also become casteless and mark Dalits as caste subjects, especially due to the latter's position in the social structure of caste that is simultaneously a division of morality, decency, and vulgarity. The ashlil was indeed a strategy, a bourgeois polysemic political process that colonial officials and touchables of various castes and classes deployed to negotiate tradition, modernity, sexuality, and nationalism. In certain circumstances, the ashlil also had the potential to organize consensus and achieve agreement by creating a set of norms and obligations. Thus, although the ashlil created distinctions, it also paradoxically created a commonality between people of different castes and classes.

Chapter 2

CONSTRUCTING CASTE, DESIRE, AND DANGER

An encounter between Dr. Bhimrao Ramji Ambedkar, the brahman *Lavanikar* (maker of Lavanya) Patthe Bapurao, and the Mahar artist Pavalabai, Bapurao's former partner, in the context of the Mahad Satyagraha of 1927 is legendary among some of my Dalit interlocutors. Realizing that his campaign for Dalit *manuski* (humanity, human dignity) and liberation would require financial support, Ambedkar requested donations from both Dalits and sympathetic touchables. Several *sangeet natak mandalis* (song-drama troupes) offered to donate funds to support Ambedkar's ongoing attempts to open the Mahad water tank to Untouchables. Patthe Bapurao also sought to donate and met with Ambedkar on September 10, 1927. By this time, Pavalabai was in her late fifties and estranged, both professionally and romantically, from Bapurao, who arrived for the meeting magnificently attired and escorting two Mahar women, one on either side. When Bapurao offered to donate the proceeds from eight of his shows, Ambedkar angrily refused, much to Bapurao's surprise. It was well known that the main attraction of Bapurao's shows—and therefore the chief source of his earnings—had been the seductive singing and dancing of Pavalabai.[1] Ambedkar argued that it was extremely insulting and degrading for him to accept money that Bapurao earned through the *sringarik* (erotic) spectacle of Pavalabai's dance. The accumulation of Bapurao's wealth was predicated on the alienation and invisibilizing of Pavalabai's labor. Although Ambedkar enjoyed watching Tamasha, he was deeply concerned by the generalized depiction of Untouchables as *ashlil* (vulgar) and by the systematic stigmatization and exploitation of Untouchable women in Tamasha. As a result, following his anticaste liberatory agenda, he wanted to break the historical association between Untouchable female promiscuity and Tamasha. The story of this encounter reveals the tangled politics of caste slavery, gender,

71

and sexuality—the sex-gender-caste complex—and colonial modernity running through Tamasha life. Departing from conventional Tamasha scholarship and feminist readings of the binaries of pleasure and violence, I excavate the story of Pavalabai to illuminate how the nexus of coercion, brutality, pleasure, and violence imbricated in Tamasha contributed to sexual-caste games and contested notions of Dalitness.

Pavalabai's Tamasha life illuminates the ways in which vulgarity, sexuality, and sexual exploitation were integral to the functioning and reproduction of caste. For Ambedkar, female subordination and sexual exploitation through endogamy were mechanisms that perpetuated the system of caste, safeguarding the privilege and power of both the brahman caste and men. In this chapter, I re-create the life history of Pavalabai and the emergence of her Dalitness in the context of sexual-caste politics and the economy of excess and enjoyment, understanding Tamasha as an ambivalent tool of pleasure, amusement, and enjoyment—as well as an expression of Dalit culture—on the one hand, and of caste games and violence, coercing and enforcing social compliance, on the other. I deploy Pavalabai's history to argue that the pleasure of performing in Tamasha was inseparable from subjection and exploitation; it normalized caste violence and cemented patriarchal control of Tamasha women, transforming them, as the case of Pavalabai demonstrates, into objects, paradoxically desirable as well as dangerous. Like many Tamasha women, Pavalabai transformed, through the elements of her art form—her dance, gestures, songs, and jokes—and her own agency, her wretched condition into contentment and pleasure for her male audiences and fame and wealth for herself.

Central to the social history of Tamasha in Maharashtra is the historic love story of the most *sringarik jodi* (sensual couple): the famous singer and dancer Pavalabai Bhalerao Hivargaokarin (1870–1939)[2] and the *suprasiddha shigrha kavi* (famous poet who quickly composed poems) Patthe Bapurao, born Shreedhar Krishna Kulkarni (1866–1945). Both not only worked together in Tamashe in Mumbai, Pune, and beyond in the early decades of the twentieth century but were its biggest stars from 1900 to the 1920s.[3] Pavalabai was the first important woman actress. She was dedicated as a Murali and entered Tamasha, associated and worked with men from different castes, especially touchable men, and traveled throughout Maharashtra's cities and villages to perform. She was a brilliant performer, one smart enough to play in Tamashe that delighted and aroused audiences of mixed-caste and mixed-class men. She contested Dalit and brahman patriarchal structures, was the head of her household, and was the main breadwinner for her family. Despite the constraints of her social status, she fought for her right to live on her own terms, however limited these were. She did not desire power like Bapurao, but instead she desired to be protected and cared for and to lead a life free from caste resentment and patriarchy. In short, in the context of caste slavery, she desired to govern herself. Yet in the eyes of socially mobile Dalits and privileged touchables, she was an ashlil, surplus woman; her dedication as an Untouchable Murali and status as unmarried marked her as an excess woman, both surplus to and yet significant within the economy of caste. This excess was doubled through her art form, Tamasha, which its critics viewed as an ashlil indulgence within an economy of excess that valued individual gain and pleasure. As such, her performances in Tamasha were seen as performative of her Dalitness, and in this way demonstrate just how the ashlil stuck to Tamasgirs *because* they were Untouchables. While to many socially mobile Dalits, she was an object of condemnation, to many ordinary Tamasha-loving Dalits and touchables, she was source of both male pleasure and caste consternation.

Through Pavalabai's and Bapurao's life histories, I unpack the social, economic, sexual, and emotional histories of Dalit women. Pavalabai's life-world offers a unique and unexplored perspective from which to examine the larger societal, political, cultural, and statist transformations of which she was a part. While, at times, Bapurao contested caste and the injunctions of *brahmanya* (brahman hegemony), I must underscore that he simultaneously participated in the discourse of caste inequality and enjoyed his exceptional brahman status and brahmani male privilege. It was his brahman power and popularity, as well as elite efforts to erase his vulgarity and canonize him in the 1940s, that led to the documentation of his Lavanya. Despite performing Tamasha and Lavani together, the ashlil stuck to only Pavalabai and not Bapurao. This was a function—and for Bapurao, a privilege—of caste, which was brahman for Bapurao. Bapurao was always already knowledgeable, meritocratic, intelligent, scholarly, assli, and so on *because* he was a brahman. And Untouchables were always already dull-witted, dumb, inferior, and ashlil because they were Untouchables.

Unlike Bapurao, the lives and artistry of many Dalit artists who are alive in popular memory, including Pavalabai, were not documented and have been lost to history. I illuminate the contingent, undulating terrain of power, inherited and acquired privilege, and powerlessness to demonstrate how brahmans constructed, colluded with, and at times—though rarely—challenged brahmanya, thus simultaneously reproducing, reinforcing, fracturing, and destabilizing it. At the same time, however, only privileged brahman men such as Bapurao could possess such power of construction, destruction, and reconstruction. Untouchables, especially doubly burdened Untouchable women such as Pavalabai, who were at the lowest end of the caste structure and seen as excess women, continually contested caste patriarchies, exercising their constrained agency and pursuing their freedom in various ways.

In the process, I closely connect the "big history" of Dalit oppositional political, social, and intellectual agitations to the supposedly smaller cultural contestations that were rooted in caste, gender, desire, and sensual personhoods. While Ambedkar operated overtly in the political public sphere, Pavalabai—as well as Bhimrao Dhondiba Kardak and Bhimsen Barku Gaikwad (in chapter 4)—connected Tamasha and Jalsa performance cultures with radical social and political activism, enacting new and radical Dalit pedagogical performativities. Indeed, they exceeded mere performance to present performative spectacles of Dalitness.

Contested Archive: Dalitness and the Memory of Pavalabai

The images in figure 2.1 are certainly what both Pavalabai and Bapurao would have wanted: she seated under a tree, beautifully adorned with flowers and jewelry, and he seated in a chair at a table full of books, writing Lavanya to be bound in many volumes; she a Mahar, a sensual beauty enticing her audience, and he a writer and singer and a meritocratic brahman man. She is exposed, outside, vulnerable; he is housed, encased, safe. He is the master of a home; she is without a home. They perfectly embodied the caste hierarchy. We do not know if Pavalabai and Bapurao sat for these portraits, or if they were even drawn at their request. The discrepancy in their labors, however, is evident: she performing her physical (social and sexual) labor, enticing her audience, and he engaged in his intellectual labor, writing Lavanya. Both

के. सुप्रसिद्ध श्रीप्र कवि श्रीधर कृष्ण उर्फ पट्ठे बापुराव कुलकर्णी

के. सुप्रसिद्ध गायिका सौ. नामचंद पवळाबाई हिवरगांवकर

—: जन्म :—   —: छायाचा प्रकाशन :—   —: मृत्यु :—
११-११-१८६६   वी. एम्. जिंतीकर   २२-१२-१९४५

—: जन्म :—   —: छायाचा प्रकाशन :—   —: मृत्यु :—
१८८१, हिवरगांव.   वी. एम्. जिंतीकर   १९२०, मुंबई.

FIGURE 2.1. Patthe Bapurao and Pavalabai. Source: B. M. Jintikar, *Patthe Bapurao's Lavanya Part 1* (Pune: Published by Jintikar).

touchables and Untouchables reviled Pavalabai, holding her in contempt for the very qualities that provoked their desire. All men—including touchables such as Bapurao and two of his life chroniclers, Bapurao Mahadev Jintikar and Govind Purushottam Dange, and Dalits such as Pavalabai's nephew Lahuji Namdeorao Bhalerao and his son Changdeo Namdeorao Bhalerao—adored and desired Pavalabai's beauty as both clean and white, which, following a color logic, privileged fair-skinned over dark-skinned people.[4]

Connected to ideas about cleanliness, discourses about skin color have throughout South Asian history mediated stereotypes about both labor (those with dark skin perform manual labor; those with light skin, intellectual labor) and the social capital of caste (Untouchables are dark and dirty; touchables are white and clean) to enforce caste divides. As a result of this colorism, people of various castes have engaged in lightening their skin tone. This includes Dalits, many of whom also discriminate according to skin color and harbor disdain for everything black. Scholars have yet to appreciate the connections

FIGURE 2.2. Detail of Pavalabai's portrait (Figure 2.1) in Changdeo Bhalerao's home.
Source: Photo courtesy of author.

FIGURE 2.3. Author at the far left with Changdeo Lahuji Bhalerao, Pavalabai's grand-nephew, in the center, and his wife and two sons. The photo of Buddha and Ambed-kar on the wall suggests Bhalerao's Ambedkarite leaning. Source: Photo courtesy of author.

between colorism and caste and the impact of colorism, or skin-color privilege and stigma, on caste identity. Pavalabai's fair skin, as compared to "darker" Untouchable women, was a privilege, and it marks the dangers of Untouchable female sexuality for touchables and brahmanya. Her fair skin tone helped her to be assimilated—she could have passed—as a touchable Arya(n)-Hindu woman. Yet, she was stigmatized as an ashlil Mahar, a stigma that stuck to her as a Untouchable because she was rendered a lascivious, wayward, and rebellious Tamasha woman. A pink-hued reproduction of her portrait in figure 2.2 adorned a wall in her grandnephew Changdeo Bhalerao's home in the city of Nagar in Ahmednagar district when I visited him in June 2016. His pinkish reproduction of the original black and white portrait artificially whitened her appearance further, accentuating her fairness and, by extension, her beauty, thus perpetuating its legendary status.

As a Tamasha woman, Pavalabai was gawked at by audiences of a wide range of castes and classes. Her performing and performative body was for the pleasure and amusement of others. And though her direct gaze in the portrait insists on her agency, to many elites, she was just another Untouchable, with no art form as such, because they considered Tamasha to be ashlil—loud, ostentatious, sensual, and carnivalesque, lacking art and hence inferior. The perceived inferiority of her art form reinscribed her Untouchable status; through it she performed an abject and vulgar form of humanity, an ashlil nature that would not come unstuck, and as such she was, in their eyes, a dangerous woman on the loose, moving from place to place and from man to man, dancing, singing, and entrancing. Her mobility and illicit sexuality threatened the gender and caste superiority of touchables like Jintikar and Dange, on the one hand, as well as the reformed image of the Dalit promoted by Ambedkar, his associates, and followers, on the other. And although everyone praised her white and boundless beauty, she knew it was not a luxury but a requirement for living inside and outside of Tamasha.

Excavating Pavalabai from the written sources, as well as from the portrait in figure 2.2 and Changdeo Bhalerao's pinkish reproduction, requires some imagination and attention to the politics of the archive as well as of sex-gender-caste complex. There is no solid record of Pavalabai's voice or life. Barring the few minibiographies and memoirs that constitute this chapter's main archive, which are neither easily dismissed nor sources to celebrate, we have little firsthand knowledge of Pavalabai and Bapurao, and we must navigate the imprint of caste, gender, and sexuality on those sources as they construct Pavalabai and her Dalitness. Pavalabai's life is available to the historian only through contrasting and competing representative fragments: on the one hand, insider accounts of her from within the Dalit community—the memories of her nephew Lahuji Bhalerao, who spent time with Pavalabai both as a member of her family and her troupe, and short essays by Kanta Achalkhamb and Tamasha scholars Rustum Achalkhamb and Milind Kasbe—and, on the other, the selective anecdotes of touchables, those outside the Dalit community—Bapurao's associates and biographers Jintikar and Dange, and Chandrakumar Nalge.[5] Moreover, all these authors, except for Kanta Achalkhamb, reproduce the same stories about Bapurao and Pavalabai from a male point of view. Kanta Achalkhamb, the only female source on Pavalabai, stands out in her emphasis on the agency and artistry of Pavalabai—a woman author praising a woman artist. Chandrakumar Nalge's writings are especially problematic; published by the state of Maharashtra, Nalge's study of Bapurao gives state legitimacy to Jintikar's hagiography of Bapurao and denigration of Pavalabai. Taken together, these accounts present difficulties, contradictions, inconsistencies, and misunderstandings as each engages in hagiography of either Pavalabai or Bapurao. And although scholars might be skeptical of these sources on this basis, I need to reiterate that scattered references, fragments, eulogies, and minibiographies are significant sources of historical study of ordinary Dalit women's lives. The official archives as well as elitist writings of Tamasha either erase, exclude, or objectify Tamasha artists. Hence, I have tried to re-create Pavalabai from the available, though inconsistent and problematic, fragments.

Jintikar and Dange focus on the recklessness of Pavalabai and easily forget that of Bapurao, vilifying Pavalabai in order to clean up his image. In the process, they deny her respect, recognition, individual autonomy, and agency. To them, her accomplishments and her artistry did not have the same weight as Bapurao's. Bapurao's claim to fame is that he was a shighra kavi who composed 240,000 Lavanya.[6] By contrast, they already marked Pavalabai with vulgarity, humiliation, and negation. Despite some differences between them, she and Mangalatai (chapter 6) have come to symbolize the vulgarity, tumult, upheaval, and open rebellion attributed to Tamasha women. Every line of Jintikar's and Dange's texts aims to violently disfigure the humanity and destroy the legacy of Pavalabai. They consistently represent her, and Dalits generally, in terms of excess and the ashlil in order to naturalize innate brahman supremacy, diminish Dalit artistry and cultural forms, legitimize Bapurao's appropriation of those forms, and secure his legacy by developing a lasting sense of the ashlil, anxiety, and animality about Pavalabai.

By contrast, the Dalits Bhalerao, Kanta Achalkhamb, Rustum Achalkhamb, and Kasbe portray a different sense of Dalitness in Pavalabai: subjected and exploited but confident, brave, rebellious, and full of artistry and agency too. The most important source for reconstructing Pavalabai's life is the short memoir narrated by her *nachya* (dancer) nephew Lahuji Bhalerao. Moreover, in contrast to the brahmani Jintikar and Dange, Lahuji Bhalerao's memoir and Kanta Achalkhamb's and Milind Kasbe's short essays in Marathi seek to understand the pressures on and the fears, limitations, and potential of Pavalabai. Achalkhamb provides some details from Pavalabai's perspective as a performer and constructs her complex subjectivity as an artist, family member, and generous woman. To her, while Pavalabai forgave the mistakes of her co-workers, Bapurao conspired against and sought revenge on Pavalabai. Pavalabai's and Bapurao's contributions together actually provided opportunities for the two artists to make history in Tamasha in modern Maharashtra.

The sense of Pavalabai's Dalitness and the violence that emerges from the two sets of texts is exemplified by the sexual-caste politics of naming. First, none of my interlocutors, save her nephew and grandnephew, knew her full name, Pavalabai Tabaji Bhalerao Hivargaokarin—such a detail about a Tamasha woman was trivial. Some knew she hailed from the village of Hivargao in Sangamner, Ahmednagar district, but only because Tamasha women and their troupes took village names as their last names. Second, Jintikar and Dange refer to Pavalabai by the shortened "Pavali," which could certainly be construed as a moniker of endearment but, given their denigration of her and her agency in her artistry, it was more likely intended to be derogative and patronizing.[7] Third, and by way of contrast to Jintikar and Dange, Kanta Achalkhamb and Kasbe address Pavalabai as Namchand (renowned or famous one). The contrast between how Pavalabai is named by insider Dalits and outsider touchables— renowned on the one hand and patronized on the other—is exemplified in the acts of appropriation (by Bapurao and Jintikar and Dange) and erasure (of Pavalabai and other Mahar-Mang singers) that Bapurao's signature on each of his works—an act of patriarchal caste pride, power, and privilege—enacts, as I will discuss below. And lastly, elites, both outsiders and insiders—touchables and Dalit writers—evidence brahmani domination in their writing, participating in brahmani norms, sanitizing and sanskritizing names: for example, while Jintikar, Dange, and Kasbe mention Kavthekar, the less educated Lahuji Bhalerao writes "Kauthekar." I retain Bhalerao's version. And both Achalkhamb and Kasbe are mistaken on Maruti Kauthekar's name—instead of Maruti, they call him Madhavrao.

To touchables in general, Bapurao was a "good" brahman man engaged in the vulgar business of the "bad" and "ignorant": Mang-Mahar Tamasha. Maharashtrians, both elite and non-elite, place him on a pedestal, obscuring the contributions of Pavalabai to the history of Tamasha. Jintikar and Dange both sanctify Bapurao as the good brahman and vulgarize Pavalabai as the bad Maharin who enticed and hindered Bapurao, tapping into the trope of ashlil Untouchable women corrupting brahman men. Moreover, both strive to show that Pavalabai was dependent on and derived her success from Bapurao rather than her own artistry and agency. Dange even regards her as a prize won by Bapurao: "During one competition, marshalling the force of his poetry, Patthe Bapurao won an *amol kalagooni ratna* [valuable jewel full of art]—'Pavali.'"[8] Their narratives situate Bapurao as the supreme, benevolent, masculine patriarch who tried to rescue the disrespectable, but beautiful Mahar Pavalabai from her degraded caste and oppressed sexuality, which elevated her status and reputation through her association with him. Although they praised her art when alongside Bapurao, they also objectified Pavalabai as a prize, a jewel. Moreover, they obscured the fact that Pavalabai was successful and famous in her own right prior to performing with Bapurao. Refuting Jintikar and Dange's claims, Lahuji Bhalerao elaborated on Pavalabai's artistry:

> She has a wonderful voice and intonation. Her singing, dancing, and acting were exceptional. She was a fantastic dancer. Using her ankle bells, she used her flexible body successfully. Her facial expressions and gestures pierced audience [men's] hearts. As a result, they showered her with *daulatjada* [flirtatious expressions of audience appreciation through gifts in cash and kind)].[9]

Pavalabai's clean, white beauty and her artistry provided the essential architecture of her existence and her agency as a Tamasha performer. She was a proud dancer who, for instance, did not accept daulatjada that she felt were insufficient: "In comparison to other Tamasha women in the bari [competition], Bapu's Pavala never took even a *chavali* [silver coin equivalent to two anas, or three-eighteenths of a rupee] from anybody. She however, accepted a *banda rupaya* [full rupee]. Other women and [men] dancers however, accepted the chavalis [as daulatjada gifts]."[10] Pavalabai, a Mahar Tamasha woman, thus fixed certain high standards and status to wrench honor for herself in the stigmatized Tamasha.

Lahuji Bhalerao's memoir lauds Pavalabai and recognizes her skill and artistry. He records the subjectivity and agency of Pavalabai, portraying her as a strong and brave woman, the head of her household. His memory, though riddled with gaps and slips, still presents psychological truths to represent the symbolic and political world of Pavalabai. In contrast, Jintikar and Dange use selective moments from the lives of Pavalabai and Bapurao to paint a prejudiced portrait of her wayward life, objectifying and denigrating her as a prized item, characterizing her as desperate, reckless, and hopeless in describing her romantic and/or sexual relationships. Their celebratory recuperations of Bapurao, though biased, are significant for the fragments of Pavalabai's life they do provide, however. In this chapter, I critically navigate and balance these patchy, inconsistent, and fragmented sources to reconstruct the life of Pavalabai. Because she did not leave any sources of her own, my reconstruction of her Dalitness is an act of moral imagination.

Pavalabai: Artistry and Agency

Pavalabai Tabaji Bhalerao Hivargaokarin was born on August 12, 1870, in the small village of Hivargao Pavsa, about five kilometers from Sangamner in Ahmednagar district.[11] Her parents, Tabaji and Reubai Bhalerao, earned their living performing feudal Mahar caste duties (see chapter 1) in the village. Hivargao Pavsa is home to the most popular deity—Khanderao of Jejuri—and houses the biggest Khanderao *yatra* (pilgrimage to worship) in Ahmednagar district. Although Khanderao is the most popular deity for Hindus in Maharashtra, women of Untouchable castes are dedicated, or ritually married, to him in disproportionate numbers. Though they disagree on the details, both Jintikar and Lahuji Bhalerao provide accounts of Pavalabai's dedication to Khanderao as a Murali. According to Jintikar, when Reubai was pregnant with Pavalabai (Reubai's fourth pregnancy), she was very sick. In order to save the child and mother, Tabaji and Reubai made offerings and vows to many deities, as was common practice. However, Reubai's health worsened, and Mahars in the village advised Tabaji to make a vow to Khanderao that, when born, the child would be offered to the god. To support his family and ailing wife, Tabaji found work in Mumbai as a *hamal* (head loader) at Boribunder Station. When Reubai again fell ill, Tabaji worried that Khanderao was furious with him for failing to fulfil his vow. However, according to Lahuji, an astrologist advised the ailing Reubai that she should give her daughter Pava-labai to Khanderao to be free of all illness. As a result, both Tabaji and Reubai got scared and immediately "took Pavalabai to Khandoba temple, sprinkled turmeric powder as a sign of wedding, and gave Pavalabai to Khanderao as his wife, a Murali."[12] Thus, Pavalabai was dedicated before birth to Khanderao. As a consequence, she became his wedded wife, a Murali.

As girls and women wedded, or "given," to a god, Muralis existed outside the marriage plot; they were surplus women, deviant women of untethered sexuality consorting with men of a range of castes, stigmatized as prostitutes. Muralis did what was necessary to survive, sometimes entering Tamasha to support themselves financially, often through long-term relationships with patrons who paradoxically exploited them but also provided some care, com-fort, and resources. Most Tamasgirs do not understand their performing lives to be a choice; they were pushed to perform because of poverty—they per-formed to survive. And although feminist critics have challenged Orientalist representations of Western women as full of agency and Asian women as powerless victims, the dichotomy between choice and coercion is a false one; women did what was necessary within certain structural limits to survive. For Tamasha women, Tamasha was an ambivalent endeavor—opening up possibilities within the constraining structures of gender, caste, and poverty, but any possibility that a woman pursued by using her body was stigmatized by moralistic men as embodying a dangerous sexuality—that is, prostitution. I do not want to romanticize the lives Tamasha women led or the possibilities they were able to pursue. Tamasha women were implicated in the very regimes of power that constituted them.

Information about Pavalabai's childhood and her early artistic life prior to collaborating with Bapurao starting around 1900, compared to what we know of her after 1900, is especially lean. But what little we can glean from Jintikar and Lahuji Bhalerao, speaks to the construction of her Dalitness as it was contained in her artistry and agency. In his short memoir about his aunt, Lahuji Bhalerao reported that after her dedication as a Murali, Pavalabai lived with her fellow Muralis and Vaghyas (males dedicated to Khanderao) and followed the traditional practice of begging alms. The *devacha niyam* (divine rule) was that both Murali and Vaghya had to beg for alms from at least five homes every day.[13] As they begged for alms, Murali and Vaghya also sang and danced. Pavalabai, with a *ghati* (a metal bell used by Muralis when they sing and dance) sang:

> Malhari [Khanderao] is my husband
> Khanderaya [Khanderao] on his horse is riding everywhere
> there is a loud rising, my husband is Malhari.[14]

Bhalerao's account emphasizes the allure of her voice even at this time; many people, including Tamasha artists, were attracted to Pavalabai's singing. Sometime before the end of the nineteenth century—certainly prior to her collaborating with Bapurao from around 1900—even the famous Tamasha troupe leader and comedy artist Namdeo (Nama) Dholvadkar[15] had learned about the beautiful singer. In accepting his invitation to perform in his troupe and thus seizing the opportunity to use her body as a sensual and sexual tool and consort with different men, she performatively transformed her Dalitness and artistry into possibility. She was both exploited by and exploiting the art. Lahuji Bhalerao reasons that Pavalabai's family felt sad to part with their daughter; however, they were also poor and helpless at that time.

Jintikar's account, in contrast to Lahuji Bhalerao's, does not characterize the young Pavalabai's talent and artistry as self-evident but as something that others identified and developed for her. Jintikar contended that Pavalabai's family sent her to the nearby village of Vaghapur, where her older sister lived, to learn dance and music from Ranuji Roham and the famous shahir Haribaba Gholap.[16] To Jintikar and Dange, Pavalabai's use of her body through dance as a sensual and sexual tool and her relationships with different men, such as Roham and Gholap, were indicative only of her ashlil Dalit character. Nevertheless, leaving her family and Gholap to once again create a life from nothing, Pavalabai then proceeded to work with Nama Dholvadkar's troupe.

From the first decade of the 1900s through the 1920s, Pavalabai emerged as a popular artist, and her fame spread everywhere. But her performances on the theatre stages of Mumbai cannot be taken for granted, for Dholvadkar, for the first time, introduced a Mahar woman, Pavalabai, to perform as a *nachi* (supposedly inferior dancer) in Tamasha theatres in Mumbai. A Mahar woman performing Tamasha on the stage of a closed theatre in Mumbai was significant in terms of gender, caste, sexuality, urbanization, and performance history. As people increasingly moved to urban areas, especially at the end of the nineteenth century, they took their culture and art, including Tamasha, with them. As Tamasha grew increasingly professionalized in urban centers such as Pune and Mumbai, performances moved from open fields to closed theatres. In these urban theatres, however, because patriarchal modesty norms did not allow "respectable" women to perform in public, men performed women's roles. Even in Mumbai in the early 1900s, all famous Mahar, Mang, and maratha Tamasha troupes—for example, those of Bhau Phakkad, Kadu Subana, Shiv-Sambha Kaulapurkar, Dagdu Tambe Shirolikar, and Bhau-Bapu Narayangaokar[17]—featured nachya men in the garb of women. Some, including the brahman Narayanrao Kulkarni (under the alias Bal Gandharva), even transgressed gender boundaries by cross-dressing and performing *as* women. Bal Gandharva became the epitome of feminine beauty and appropriate womanhood, a status he, as a brahman man, was able to enjoy because his gender transgressions were palatable, whereas, as we will see, Pavalabai's caste transgressions were not.

Remembering her initial days in Mumbai, Lahuji Bhalerao reported that "the beautiful Pavalabai enamored the audience with her Lavanya, sung in her cuckoo-like voice."[18] She regularly performed at the pilahouse (playhouse) Elphinstone and other theatres in Mumbai and Pune. Gradually, Pavalabai's fame spread, and many men wanted to include her in their Tamasha troupes. Deploying her body as a sensual and pleasure-producing machine, Pavalabai, on the one hand, performed her Untouchable marginality and exploitation and, on the other hand, deployed myriad and infinite ways of exercising her artistry and agency. Her Dalitness reinscribed her liminal status, as she performed a different articulation of Dalitness—covert and manipulative. In the process, she engaged in an "improper" politics—performatively complying with and yet exploiting the mechanisms of caste.

During the 1890s, she seems to have fallen in love with the famous wrestler Maruti Kauthekar, who was also a lender and *savkar* (trader or merchant) from Kauthe.[19] In general, wrestlers were doubly helpful to performers: they not only performed but also protected women artists from the abuse of male co-artists as well as men in the audience.[20] She also may have been in a relationship with Dholvadkar, who kept her close to him and allowed her to perform only in closed theatres. Men thronged to theatres in the thousands to see the beautiful Pavalabai, the only woman performer, who performed to full houses and made the "Nama Dholvadkar saha [with] Pavala Bhalerao Hivargaokar Tamasha Phad" all the rage in Maharashtra.[21] According to Lahuji Bhalerao, the shows in front of full houses were almost like Divali (festival of lights) celebrations, and he described Pavalabai as so beautiful that when she chewed betel, her throat turned red;[22] in suggesting that her delicate skin was white to the point of being almost translucent, thus revealing the color of the red betel, Lahuji peddled the legend (and the colorism that informs it) of Pavalabai's beauty. Perhaps Lahuji Bhalerao was drawing on other examples, such as the legendary Mughal-era artist Anarkali, to describe Pavalabai's physical beauty. Pavalabai was a not only good-looking; she was also a fantastic singer and dancer. Men watched and gawked at her at Mumbai's playhouse, or pilahouse, as millworkers referred to it. Her white beauty and gracefulness were requirements for her to earn living, allowing her to navigate her liminal status between willful agent and will-less, abject object as well as the ambivalence between the pleasure and violence of Tamasha as mixed-caste male audiences consumed her beauty and arts, even from a distance.

Bapurao: From Flour-Mill Songs to Lavani

Patthe Bapurao was born Shreedhar Krishna Kulkarni in Harnaksha Rethare, Valave taluka, in Satara district in 1866. Though as a young man, he followed his caste occupation and worked as an accountant in Baroda (likely in the early 1880s), his boyhood love of poetry, which was influenced by the songs flour-mill women sang while on the *jata* (grinding stone) and supported by the Aundh and Baroda states, persisted. He increasingly devoted himself to writing Lavanya, even penning one on an accounting worksheet. Bapurao's Lavanya and his transgressions in immersing himself in Tamasha in the Mahar neighborhoods where they were produced—as both a young man and a seasoned professional—were acts of appropriation, a fact that is laid bare in his sanskritization of Lavani, a product of his caste background. The social, sexual, geographical, cultural transgressions that his Lavanya were predicated upon were actualized and permitted by the very caste privilege that some in the brahman community felt he threatened to undermine and destroy, and they served to confirm the ashlil that stuck to Untouchables. Moreover, these acts of appropriation—and the construction of Untouchables as ashlil that they upheld—were further entrenched by the writings of the touchables Jintikar, a Gurav (castes serving as priests, maintainers, and managers in temples devoted to Shiva), and Dange, a brahman. In recuperating Bapurao from being outcaste by the brahman community—and making the case to include Lavani in the Marathi canon of popular art forms—they and other elites such as D. D. Parchure argue,[23] despite no evidence that his Lavanya were any different in imagery and language than those written by Untouchable Lavanikars, that Bapurao had sanitized Lavani and made it palatable to respectable audiences. Parchure argued, "Bapurao's poetry does not seem only a tool of Tamasha, but *superior* literature."[24]

After the death of his father sometime in the early to mid-1880s, Bapurao left Baroda and returned to Harnaksha Rethare. There, he was attracted to the sounds of *tuntune* (stringed instruments), *dhoki* (drums), *paijan* (the ankle bells worn by Tamasha women), and Lavanya emanating from the Maharvada (Mahar neighborhood) across from his house; he would sneak out of the brahmanvada (brahman neighborhood) to attend Tamasha performances. Although Jintikar and Dange both likely exaggerate the spatial proximity of the Mahar and brahman neighborhoods—placing them across the street from one another though they likely would have been more segregated—the influence on and allure of Mahar cultural forms for Bapurao is clear.[25] As a brahman man, he had the power and privilege to visit Mahar homes and comfortably move across caste hierarchies and cultural forms, whereas Untouchables could not. The caste privilege that allowed Bapurao to move between neighborhoods defined by caste was crucial to his appropriation of Tamasha as an art form. The account of Bapurao given by the Dalit shahir Bhimsen Barku Gaikwad, who was a boyhood neighbor of Bapurao's in Pune in the late 1930s and early 1940s when he lived with his father near the famous Aryabhushan theatre, illuminates how the younger Bapurao might have negotiated his caste position in pursuit of his love, Mahar Lavanya, and how he profited from it:

When I was 6–7 years old, I picked up songs and tunes from my father and other artists. I used to listen to gramophones as I played in the neighborhood and sang. Bapurao made me sing the tunes and used these to set his songs to them. He paid intense attention to all the pronunciations, grammar, writing them down and then constructing his own songs, using the stories of deities like Radha and Krishna. He wrote and then made me sing, checked tunes, and perfected everything. This is how he became the Guru, the Master. Gradually, the Tamasha troupes at Arya bhushan used his songs and gave him two anas, and some even four anas in compensation. Sangeet bari artists earned more money, and they gave him four anas. That was his everyday honorarium.[26]

In this manner, Bapurao appropriated and sanskritized Mahar Lavanya with his authoritative brahman voice and his signature, all of which underpinned his popularity into the 1940s. But all of this was predicated on his power, pride, and privilege as a brahman man.

Bapurao's Lavani learning emerged as a historical conjuncture of caste contestations. Bapurao's mingling with Mahars and appropriating their Lavani culture did not go over well with the orthodox brahmans in the village. By worlding with Mahars, by frequenting their "dangerous" urban environs, whether in Harnaksha Rethare or later in Mumbai and Pune, as a brahman man, Bapurao had the power to threaten the brahman caste-pride and power as a whole—he was polluting it by potentially transgressing caste boundaries. As a result, the orthodoxy was outraged at the disruption of the so-called natural order of brahman dominance. In this manner, brahmans created caste distinctions and consolidated their caste privilege. By his actions, both in Harnaksha Rethare in the 1880s and later through his association with Pavalabai in particular and Tamasha generally, Bapurao threatened *brahmanya* (brahman order and hegemony) and emerged as a "bad" brahman in the eyes of the brahman orthodoxy and caste and cultural vigilantes. His recuperation by Jintikar, Dange, and other Marathi elites in the 1950s, which I return to below, was not only part of the attempt to regulate and sanitize Tamasha and Lavani for inclusion in the Marathi regional canon of popular art forms but also a response to his outcasting by the brahman orthodoxy. Since the 1900s, Marathi elites seeking to standardize modern Marathi cultural norms felt threatened by the popularity of Tamashe Lavanya among non-elites, and this continued into the post-independence period. As I show in chapter 5, elites set the terms of how sanitized Tamasha Lavani could become regional popular theatre. By this time, professional *natak mandalis* (drama troupes) were already on the decline and almost died out in early 1950s.[27] Elites were gatekeepers who included or excluded Dalits and their arts as it suited them.

In Harnaksha Rethare in the mid-1880s, Bapurao's uncle, Haripant Kulkarni, had faced the ire of orthodox brahmans, who said to him, "Your Bapu was talking to a Maharin [Mahar woman] today; he went to Maharvada and was performing in a Mahar Tamasha at the fair."[28] The conservative Kulkarni could not tolerate Bapurao's ashlil Tamasha and Lavani habit any longer, and he decided to confine Bapurao to the orderly and pious world of marriage and household, arranging for Bapurao to wed Sarasvati Badve. However, Bapurao was not interested in the secure domestic and familial arrangements of the marriage plot. Consequently, he left his wife and home to pursue Lavani.

Bapurao declared, "I will shame Kuber [the god of wealth] and earn enormous wealth and fame through Tamasha,"[29] laying bare the objectives of the cultural plunder his brahman privilege made available to him. At the same time, he also crushed orthodox brahman's caste-pride. Throughout the late 1880s, the 1890s, and indeed until his death in 1945, Bapurao continued to mingle with Mahar-Mangs, traveling with them and performing in their Tamasha. Soon, with Bapurao working diligently, Harnaksha Rethare Tamasha grew very popular. According to Jintikar, people thronged to see his Tamasha, because the brahman Bapurao started entering the lower-caste sensual culture of ashlil Lavani. People in villages and kingly courts enthusiastically repeated "*shabash* [well done, skillful young] Patthe Bapurao."[30]

When the "brahman boy [Bapurao] started doing Tamasha," people went hysterical and crowded to see him perform. Dange, once again, underscored the magical quality of Bapurao's poetry: "Bapurao retained the sensual, erotic sringar in Lavani and structured it in a specific manner to further sharpen its [robust and rebellious] marathamola form."[31] For example, "when he sang his '*pikachi lavani*' [harvest Lavani], farmers who had toiled away in the fields would feel the evening breeze and enjoy it." They could take some time off to engage in romance when they heard words of Bapurao's Lavani, "Your shapely body is very ripe. Your beauty is exquisite, you young one. You are well-shaped like a snake."[32] In this manner, to Dange, Bapurao sang about the sensual young women and "presented the overtly erotic in simple, beautiful, live language to connect with both the intelligent and ignorant."[33]

The casteist editorializing of Jintikar and Dange suggests that Bapurao's Lavanya were sanitized improvements on the form: "Because Bapurao did not find other [Mahar] poets' Lavanya *good enough*, he started constructing *shastra shuddha* [pure, cultured, regimented] Lavanya."[34] Dange seconded this idea that Bapurao's Lavanya were both original and surpassed those of Mahar poets: "Bapurao felt that Mahars' Lavanya were made hastily and forcibly"[35] and hence, they did not have a structured form of poetry. Most importantly, Dange could not hide his elitist, patronizing, casteist notions regarding *"ajaan"* (ignorant) Mahars:

> Bapurao made Mahars understand and improvised the Tamasha performance for Mahars. Mahars could not separate the good from bad and were naïve and ignorant. In this manner, Bapurao worked on the jewels [of songs] that fell out of [Mahars'] broken *gadgya madkyatoon,* pots, polished, and uplifted them, thereby providing them a golden supreme status.[36]

Thus, both Dange and Jintikar differentiated the Lavanya of Bapurao from those of Mahars according to caste—brahman versus Mahar—a distinction characterized as between high and low, pure and polluted, assli and ashlil. Similarly, Chandrakumar Nalge noted that Mahar Lavanya were *obaddhobad* (uneven, uncultured):[37] "Mahar, Mang, were ignorant, illiterate and this reflected in their Lavanya. But Bapurao had studied English books and even knew Sanskrit. He thought Mahar Lavanya need to be culturized. Bapurao provided an intellectual speculation, more attractive form to these Lavanya."[38] There is no evidence, however, to suggest that there was any difference between the Lavanya written by Bapurao and those written by Untouchables—except the caste locations of their authors. When a brahman man wrote sringarik Lavanya, they were seen as better, and their betterness was described as magical; when an Untouchable did the same, it was ashlil—ashlil stuck to Untouchables, and therefore Lavanya were ashlil when written by Untouchables precisely *because* they were written by Untouchables. Moreover, Bapurao's knowledge of supposedly higher languages such as English and Sanskrit further reinforced his privilege, pride, and power as a brahman man.

In arguing over the quality and respectability of Lavanya along caste lines, touchables like Jintikar and Dange created disparities of the human species, consigned Mahars to an inferior status, and consolidated caste divisions. This process of constructing caste divisions inside the colony and colonizing Untouchables was similar to the larger racial imperial colonizing project. Touchables denigrated Mahars, the creators of Lavanya, and moreover argued that Mahars had limited, if any, intellectual capacity to create "good" Lavanya. In this manner, touchables created false knowledge and misunderstandings about Untouchables. These were based essentially on a massive labor of imagination rooted in rumors and erroneous and unverifiable suppositions and stereotypes. In the process, touchables constructed caste difference and defined Mahars as biologically, intellectually, and culturally inferior and dumb. These traits stuck to Mahars on the basis of caste. Touchables created graded knowledge systems and thrived on false knowledge and fantasies, thereby enclosing themselves and excluding and socially isolating the Untouchables. They marked Bapurao, the brahman man, as possessing the innate excellence to do so. To them, Bapurao the brahman was naturally gifted with skills; he did not have to work hard to gain them. This merit itself was a product of brahman caste status and stuck to him on that basis alone. Touchables thus engaged in the tactics of meritocratic claim-making. They eulogized Bapurao's magical abilities to rescue Lavani from its degraded Mahar manufacturing location of flour mills or fields and situate it in a pure, shastric, sanitized, brahmani home. To them, Bapurao, a brahman man, had the so-called innate intelligence and innate striving to excel. Moreover, to Jintikar, simply because Bapurao was brahman by birth, he did not have to strive for excellence and had no obligation to be excellent. He was already the best and could thus immediately work upon the stray words (which were like uneven pebbles) that fell from ashlil Mahari mouths, skillfully transforming them into precious, sanskritized, brahmani gems. Meritocracy, intelligence, and skill all stuck to Bapurao *because* he was brahman.

His brahman caste was an inherited merit that enabled him to consolidate brahmanya further. In fact, Bapurao muffled Untouchable voices and silenced them as soon as they produced Lavanya. He appropriated their Lavanya and even imprinted his signature on his Lavanya. Even though he sang Lavanya, he did not become ashlil, like Untouchables; as a brahman, he was not subject to the stickiness of the ashlil—it stuck to Untouchables and left touchables free. The politics of naming becomes especially clear in Jintikar's argument that Bapurao's fame derived from his signature: "Because Bapurao added his name 'Bapurao Kulkarni' at the end of every Lavani couplet, large crowds of people gathered to see his Tamasha." Whereas Bapurao's brahman signature appeared on each of his works, Mahar-Mang singers such as Pavalabai enjoyed no such recognition; Untouchables sang, danced, and played music without identifying themselves or authorizing their skills.

Significantly, unlike the Lavanya by the privileged Bapurao, those by Untouchables did not find a dedicated disciple or patron like Jintikar and, as a result, have left no trace in the historical record. Even some the works of the Dalit activist-dancer-poet Bhau Phakkad Bhandare, an active member of Ambedkar's Bahiskrut Hitakarini Sabha (Society for the Benefit of the Boycotted Indians), have been lost to history. The writer Bandhumadhav notes, "There was a serious fifteen-day [Lavani] competition between Bhau Phakkad and Bapurao in Mumbai. In this performance, Bapurao lost the battle. Shahu Maharaj of Kolhapur celebrated Phakkad's victory by honoring him with a title, scarf, and other gifts. After this Bhau Phakkad started constructing poems for [socially motivated] Satyashodhaki (non-brahman truth seekers) Jalsa and reached a peak during 1920–30."[39] Both memory and history do not serve Dalits. And except for such fragmentary accounts of loss as the one above, we encounter only the triumphs and eulogies of Bapurao in the historical record.

Nonetheless, in the late nineteenth and early twentieth centuries, Bapurao's brahman and non-brahman contemporaries—Keshavrao Jedhe, Popatlal Shah, Datto Vaman Potdar, Siddheshvar Shastri Chitale, Kakasaheb Gadgil, Nanasaheb Gokhale, Annasaheb Sahasrabuddhe, and Govindswami Aphale—watched his Tamasha and praised his Lavanya. Jintikar noted that many brahmans in their laced *pagadis* (turbans), conservative Hindu *sanatanis*, and educated liberals watched Tamasha in secret.[40] This points to the duplicity of mixed-caste audiences. Moreover, the ashlil did not stick to the male audience members; they did not become ashlil like the Tamasha women performing for them. Tamasha and Lavani emerged as spaces of exception where hypocritical elite men could comfortably enjoy and denigrate Mahar-Mang arts. They engaged in a covert regime of sexuality—they understood the potential difficulty that could come from watching sringarik Tamasha and Lavani, yet they could not resist indulging in their insatiable desire for sexual masti—masculine performances of intoxicated unruly energy transforming the theatre into a libidinous space. They could not entirely follow the restrictions of the modern age on cultured individuals and repress their inner human nature of sensual and sexual energies. To negotiate the systemic societal forces and avoid being exposed, they continued covertly watching Tamasha, hypocritically reinforced their discourse of ashlil Mahar Lavanya, and created caste, culture, and taste hierarchies.

These tensions were especially apparent in Pune, where Bapurao would have performed many times over the years and where he settled in the late 1930s, toward the end of his life. Many Tamasha theatres flourished in Pune and shaped the city as a Tamasha *pandhari* (capital). The highest Chitpavan brahman peshva had made Pune their social, political, and cultural capital since the eighteenth century, and over the years, under the hegemonic brahman peshva regime, Pune emerged as the capital of orthodox brahmanhood, with Sadashiv Peth and Narayan Peth as the polis. The peshva hegemony converted Pune into a cultural capital in Maharashtra not just for brahmans but also Untouchables, who also found the city receptive to their cultural forms. The peshva also patronized Lavanya of high castes but marginalized its Untouchable producers. A Tamasha contractor, Hasanbhai Pativadekar, argued that unlike Mumbai, Pune retained its rural ties and hence Tamasgirs, many of whom were Muralis like Pavalabai, have flocked to Pune city and its outskirts up to the present day.[41]

The location of Tamasha theatres in or near the red-light districts in Pune and Mumbai exacerbated the sense of Tamasha as a dangerous indulgence for brahman men. Reminiscing about the vibrant Tamasha of 1940s Mumbai and pilahouse, the octogenarian Madhukarsheth Nerale of Hanuman Theatre (Parel, Mumbai) invokes its unrespectable, unapproachable, and low-caste setting, near Batatyachi Chal (chawl) in central Mumbai, then a lower and lower-middle-class hub where artists found audiences and patrons from among the upper-caste merchants of Girgaon, the millworkers in Girangaon, and the red-light district of Kamathipura, all nearby:

> Pilahouse is the lower-caste-class playhouse. During that time traders and travelers passed through or came to Mumbai in their bullock carts. This Dadar-Parel area was forest then. Men gathered here, tied the animals close by, and made a big circle lowering all carts. At times they got gunny sacks and built tents. In the middle of the lit circle Tamasha was performed. The ticket was a mere 1 rupee. Artists often took loans from a Pathan, Ahmad-sheth Bangdivala and performed to earn their living. Artists stayed close to pilahouse in the Batatyachi Chal.[42]

And Jintikar's description of the Tamasha theatre in Satranjivala chowk in Ravivar Peth, the red-light district of Pune, evokes its bustling and dangerous setting:

> The doors of the theatre were decorated with banana stems [signifying auspiciousness]. The bright gas-lights spread everywhere. The theatre was protected [from the public street] by iron rods and well-lit by gas lamps, which illuminated the displayed prizes for winners of the competition: embroidered turban, golden *salkadi, toda* [jewelry], and so on. Tamasha people moved briskly about their business. The beautiful dancers who may have shamed *apsaras* [celestial consorts] sat outside the theatre on a para-pet [to entice men].[43]

Clearly, touchable men could not control their sexual appetites, as evidenced by the iron rods and gas lamps that were installed to protect Tamasha theatres and Tamasha.

Bapurao and Pavalabai lived in the tenements of Batatyachi Chal in Mumbai and performed at Satranjivala chowk in Pune from 1911 to 1915 along with Shiv-Sambha Kaulapurkar, Arjun Vagholikar, Dagdu Sali, and so on. It was in these settings that men from different castes—high, middle, and low—enjoyed the ashlil, stigmatized Tamasha and Tamasha flourished. It was also, in part, Bapurao's movement through these dangerous social and spatial geographies that had unnerved the brahman community and his uncle in Harnaksha Rethare in the 1880s and would inform later charges that Pavalabai had polluted Bapurao.

Bapurao was known as a fine dresser, which maintained his image as a "winning" artist and also emphasized his status as a privileged, mobile brahman man. Whenever Bapurao visited Pune, for instance, the capital of Tamasha art, he dressed up a *jaripatka* (embroidered turban), competed with other artists, and most often gained first position. In Pune, as Gaikwad notes above, Bapurao, as a brahman man, moved freely through the Maharvada and was embraced by Untouchables. He lived with Untouchables in their neighborhoods—Yerawada, Ganesh Peth, and Ravivar Peth—that is, on the margins of the Pune polis. Gaikwad recalled Bapurao's time in Pune, when he transgressed caste, living with Dalits and Muslims and eating nonvegetarian food: "He used to eat whatever my mother cooked—mutton, fish, *puranpoli* [sweet stuffed bread], *bombil* [dry fish that is depicted as Mahar food]. He loved bombil. Moreover, *our* people were proud when he, a brahman, came to *us*, ate with *us*, lived with *us*, engaged in *our* arts."[44] Untouchables and Bapurao befriended each other. In so doing, while Untouchables enjoyed brahman Bapurao's presence, in turn Bapurao, though his appropriation of Lavani, his talent, and his status as a brahman man, created some cracks in brahmanya. Gaikwad reported that Bapurao was a loud, arrogant, and aggressive master: "Nobody challenged him because they were scared that he may not give them his songs. Tamasha artists took care of him—gave him food, money, *ganja* [marijuana], home. He did not have to pay rent. He was arrogant and not scared even of police."[45] Yet, this is not entirely true because, as I illuminate below, the brilliant and beautiful Pavalabai would pose a challenge to Bapurao.

Pavalabai and Bapurao: Entangled Lives and Caste Games

Though each was famous in their own right before the beginning of the twentieth century, Pavalabai and Bapurao's professional, erotic, and romantic union between 1900 and 1920 aroused audiences to new peaks of desire, secured their status as Tamasha legends, and threatened the stability of caste boundaries, brahman hegemony, and attempts to define Untouchable-ness in terms of either the ashlil, by brahman commentators, or manuski, by such Dalit radicals as Ambedkar. By the 1890s, Pavalabai's fame had spread so far and wide that, as Lahuji Bhalerao speculates, Bapurao must have visited Mumbai to see her perform;[46] Kasbe reports that upon meeting her and see-

ing her perform in Mumbai, he was so struck by her beauty and skill in singing, dancing, and winning over the audience that he sang her a song:[47]

> Don't just touch, but kiss me from afar
> I will buy Mumbai for you
> Above the Bhaykhala bridge
> The Parsi feudal seth [*saramjamseth*] Batlivala, has provided for
>   your sleep.

He was so inspired by her beauty, in fact, that he composed "*sringarik va shas-
trashuddha*" [erotic and cultured, sanitized] Lavanya for her troupe to perform,
which only enhanced their success. The death of Pavalabai's troupe leader,
Dholvadkar, around the turn of the century created the opportunity for Bapurao and Pavalabai to perform together. Although the sources disagree on the
details of their union—Jintikar insists that Bapurao invited Pavalabai to join
him, and Lahuji Bhalerao recounts that Pavalabai invited Bapurao to join her
own new troupe[48]—the Pavala Hivargaokar with Patthe Bapurao Retharekar
troupe made big waves in Maharashtra.

The synergy between the *Lavani samradni* (empress), Pavalabai, and the
Lavani samrat (emperor), Bapurao, drove each to new artistic heights. Mes-
merized by, in Lahuji Bhalerao's words, "Pavala's fair complexion, her watery
eyes like that of a doe, the electric agility of her body, her singing like that of a
cuckoo, and her attractive gestures,"[49] Bapurao was quick to produce Lavanya
full of pleasure and eroticism:[50]

> Out of a hundred thousand women, the one [Pavalabai] is the most
>   beautiful
> We have never seen anyone like you
> You are the one with a well-shaped voluptuous figure and with fem-
>   inine airs, blandishments, flirting, swaggering
> It seems as if an example from the heavens [Indra's consorts] has
>   appeared
> You are the most beautiful, arousing sexual passion [*madanma-
>   jiri*] . . .
> [I] have never seen such a beautiful face in the entire continent.

Lahuji Bhalerao summarized Pavalabai's effect on Bapurao as follows: "Just like a tree blossoms in spring, Bapurao's poetic interest and enthusiasm also fully blossomed due to Pavalabai's youth, beauty, voluptuous figure, and boldness."[51] Pavalabai sang and also gave shape, motion, and affect to Bapurao's Lavanya, enacting them through her beautiful gestures and dance, which matched the sensuality and eroticism of the song. Their artistry and the chemistry between them onstage, in turn, fueled their romance offstage, and their professional success became entangled with their personal lives. With the beautiful Pavalabai standing in front of him on the stage, Bapurao sang Lavanya praising her, and she responded favorably to his every sensual song, and thus they gradually fell in love.

The love between them flourished in the tenements at Batatyachi Chal, along what is now Patthe Bapurao Street. The two took comfort in one another. For instance, Pavalabai kept Bapurao's beloved, fine, and unique turban secure in her own trunk, which prior to one performance she had locked. Unable to find his turban and perhaps feeling insecure about not performing in it, he sought succor in her clothing, draping Pavalabai's green sari decoratively upon his head before taking the stage.[52] And at times acting like his devoted wife, Pavalabai was also very cautious about finances and always alerted Bapurao: "You always want to spend money. If you continue this *dhooldhan* [wasteful expense], all gold, and everything including the home, will be ruined."[53] Although, Pavalabai was at times strict with Bapurao, she also immensely cared for his welfare and wanted him to flourish. Audiences were thrilled by the love life of this couple, appreciating them as the god Indra and his consorts Apsara and Rambha. Men in the audience responded to Pavalabai and Bapurao's experiments on stage and thoroughly enjoyed the sensual and sexual play between the couple, fueling their fame (and their earnings) and drawing audiences from throughout Mumbai and beyond.

Their success, however, was predicated not just on their love and sensual play, but on the dream of sex and the promise of the sexual availability of Pavalabai to all men, especially touchables, as an excess woman, both a Murali and a Mahar Tamasha woman. Her alluring stage performance was both performative and ambivalent, both meeting and challenging expectations of her as an Untouchable woman. Her sexual availability—rooted in the political economy of caste slavery and entanglements of power, violence, and pleasure—was both the basis for her sense of possibility as an Untouchable woman—affording her mobility and agency—and also a sort of enclosure perpetuating her subjection to brahmani patriarchy. And both the entrenchment of brahmani patriarchy as well as the agency Pavalabai carved out for herself—and the danger she posed to brahmani patriarchy—through Tamasha were reinforced by the relationships Pavalabai had with touchable men of different castes. While Pavalabai expanded the sense of what might be possible, she also created new enclosures for herself.

As her fame grew and men flocked to such theatres as pilahouse in Mumbai only to catch a glimpse of her, Bapurao suggested to Abu Sheth, the theatre owner, that they capitalize on her raw sexual availability by dropping the pretense of Tamasha: "People can pay for a ticket to see Pavalabai (and me). We will sit in chairs in the middle of the theatre." He could not hide his love for Pavalabai and continued: "Because it will not be good to have Pavalabai sit alone, I will also sit with her."[54] Bapurao's idea was instantly successful. People rushed to the theatre to merely see Pavalabai, who was styled in "*motha thata*"[55] (grand, pompous) attire that hinted at a magnificent lifestyle: "a traditional nine-yard Paithani sari embroidered with gold and silver, silver anklets like of royal Shinde lineage, golden necklace, golden armlets, earrings, golden bangles, golden rings on fingers, nose ring, and gold decorated hair plait."[56] In these shows, Pavalabai exaggerated her womanliness and became an image of a woman desired by men of varied castes. She was stripped of her identity as she indulged men in the expression of their desires constructing their manliness and masculinity. Pavalabai's sexualized body eroticized the space of the theatre, as the audience observed and examined her. The power of her artistry provoked the audience to accede to the world of desire and enjoy the hitherto condemned. The ashlil that stuck to her because she was Mahar made her sexually exciting to the male audience. She was, as Lahuji Bhalerao argued, a "queen," and "people were happy to see this beautiful woman in the prime of her youth."[57] The audience caressed her with their eyes as they engaged in an interplay of intense sensations, their power anchored in pleasure, as they enjoyed nonconjugal and nonmonogamous sexuality and transformed the theatre into a libidinous erotic space. The owner collected Rs. 100–125 for this show and about Rs. 500–600 for Pavalabai's actual performance in the Tamasha.

In this manner, Bapurao and Pavalabai's professional and personal popularity reached every nook and corner of Maharashtra. Bapurao underscored his success in his Lavanya: "The horse of poet Patthe Bapurao is riding wild; the Turevala [his opposition party] followers dare try to control it."[58] Dange seconded the idea that Bapurao thus conquered every troupe in Maharashtra from atop his Tamasha horse.

Many artists in postcolonial Pune and Mumbai argued that "artists do not have a caste" ;[59] however, even the famous couple Pavalabai and Bapurao were not untouched by the caste-ridden colonial brahmani society they were rooted in. Once again, some orthodox touchables who felt their high-caste dominance was threatened objected to Pavalabai and Bapurao's successful partnership *only* because "Bapurao brahman had *sambandh* [conjugal personal connection outside marriage] with Maharin Pavali."[60] While some argued that a *"Maharnine brahman batavala"* [Mahar woman polluted a brahman man], others disagreed, arguing that theirs was merely a professional relationship.[61] The question of caste and the propriety of the relationship between Mahar woman Pavalabai and brahman man Bapurao was a serious one, resulting in not only verbal but actual physical battles within their troupe as well as among brahmans.[62] Ultimately, the charge that Pavalabai had polluted Bapurao reached the local court of law in Thana-Mumbai,[63] and Pavalabai was summoned by the court on October 11, 1905.

Given the celebrity of the couple and the significance of the caste-related charge, people packed the court and its premises. Danseuse Pavalabai and shahir Bapurao arrived at the court in a horse-drawn carriage. The police had to help them enter the court because of the large crowd that had gathered to see these stars. Once the proceedings were under way, the judge questioned Pavalabai: "What do you have to say regarding the accusation that *tumhi batavile* [you polluted the] brahman."[64] Jintikar, Dange, and others have suggested that Bapurao immediately sang a Lavani in response. However, Lahuji Bhalerao argues that, at this juncture, Pavalabai was direct and unhesitant in answering the judge: "I request that the Court ask the accused brahman who is said to be polluted for clarification."[65] Only following her direct address to the judge did

Bapurao stand up, greet the judge with *Namaskar* (respectful bow and greetings), and humbly say, "I will answer this question with evidence, in front of
everybody during our performance in the theatre. The Court can decide the
day."[66] The judge decided on a specific date, and on that day the theatre was
over capacity, all the tickets having been sold and some resold on the black
market.

Both Pavalabai and Bapurao entered the stage and the latter sang a stanza
from his famous Lavani: "Don't touch, kiss me from a distance, I will buy Mumbai for you."[67] As he sang, Bapurao walked toward Pavalabai and fed her a *pedha*
(a traditional Maharashtrian sweet)[68] to express his love for her and explained:

> Although, I am a *sreshtha varna* [highest brahman],
> I have stayed away from *sovale* [the ideologies of purity pollution].
> I am wielding the *mashal* [lamp] of [low-caste-class culture of
>   ashlil] Tamasha
> and I have thus, given up shame and honor of my caste....
> I have followed my ambition of writing Lavanya despite other prob-
>   lems.
> I have enjoyed life immensely. I married, but my family life col-
>   lapsed.
> I knew all this and yet I leaped [into Tamasha]....
> There were many obstacles and because I did not engage with them,
>   many associates are angry.
> I gained a Maharin [Pavalabai] and I am earning my living.
> I have been singing all over for fifty years now....
> I also brought to light the *moti* [pearl, referring to Pavalabai] which
>   was hidden in darkness....
> I have worked very hard; however, you men have given me only half
>   the credit.[69]

Though on the surface a defense of Pavalabai and a claim to his agency in their
relationship, Bapurao's testimony reveals the tension both in his position as a
brahman Lavanikar—who both contested caste injunctions and participated
in the hierarchical discourse of caste—and between his position and that
of Pavalabai's as a Mahar woman. In the mid-1910s, through his testimony,

Bapurao took pride in his high caste and confirmed that his brahman caste was the highest, and he took credit for bringing Pavalabai into the limelight of the theatre, forgetting that she had not been in darkness earlier. In so doing, he assumed an iconic status for himself and become a larger-than-life figure. However, in pursuing his love for Lavanya, he challenged caste injunctions by entering Tamasha, writing Lavanya, giving up married life, and loving a Maharin. Bapurao's understanding of his relationship and position vis-à-vis Pavalabai was complicated. On the one hand, he recognized that he earned his living through her physical and sexual labor; on the other hand, he objectified Pavalabai as a pearl he worked hard to bring to light and for which he deserved more credit.

The judge ruled that Pavalabai never polluted Bapurao and that, in fact, Bapurao was the one who fell in love with her and persuaded her to perform with him. She never forced him to lose his caste, as Jintikar argued. On this point, Kanta Achalkhamb challenged Jintikar: "Bapurao's assertion of his highest brahmanhood is very selfish. It was he who pursued Pavalabai."[70] Nevertheless, after this event, the shringarik couple gained even more fame and fortune. Remembering them, Gaikwad pithily notes, "Master (Bapurao) loved and lived with Pavalabai, it is a matter of heart. The heart may die but not desire, the body may die and hope too, but not desire—says the poet Kabir."

Bapurao affirmed Pavalabai's partnership in love as well as in the Tamasha business because it was also due to her central role that his troupe was doing well. He continually affirmed to the people, "Hence I became Mahar for Pavali [here, indicating love] for the art of Tamasha and for Pavali. I left a tulsi leaf at the door of my house and disavowed kith and kin to become a Mahar!"[71] Bapurao left the auspicious tulsi leaf at the door of his house to signify his relinquishing the auspicious marriage plot and household and stepping into the inauspicious Mahar Tamasha. Now that he had given up his brahman home, he rhetorically asked, "Can I now regain my caste as a brahman?"[72] To further underscore his decision to renounce his brahman status, he ate the food offered to him by Pavala Maharin on the Tamasha stage and Mahars off the stage. As a result, Dange reports, "the majority of Bahujans were raving for him."[73] Bapurao's claim to Maharhood through his actions on stage was akin to Gandhi proclaiming himself as Harijan, a name he gave to Untouchables, which many of the latter found nauseating and patronizing.

In 1946, Gandhi tokenistically visited Harijan neighborhoods, such as Balmiki Colony in Delhi, which he noted as dirty, to show his deep empathy for the wretched condition of Harijans. Once during such a visit, he was offered milk by a Harijan. Gandhi cleverly refused to drink the milk, saying, "I carry my own goat milk. If you are keen I should take food prepared by you, you can come here and cook for me."[74] Again, when an Untouchable gave him nuts, Gandhi fed them to his goat, saying he would eat them later in the goat's milk. In so doing, he demonstrated his lack of enthusiasm for intercaste communal meals, thus consolidating caste divisions. Gandhi's double standard did not sit well with Untouchables, and hence, they did not trust him. Unlike Gandhi, however, Bapurao did make a public show of feeding and eating food at the hands of a Maharin. The Tamasha of a brahman man eating from the hands of an Untouchable woman was not mere spectacle; he was expressing his love for Pavalabai and also puncturing caste boundaries. However, by inviting pollution on himself in such a performance, he also put himself on a pedestal.

The public and ambivalent (inhering both repulsion and attraction) performance space of the Tamasha theatre allowed for Bapurao's caste-violating performativity; it was a liminal space between the realities of caste and pure fantasy, a space where the normally impossible was made possible. What emerges in the theatre is a world of pleasure and provocation that invites the audience to suspend their disbelief and accede to the world of desire, and this liminal world of Tamasha authorized Bapurao's violation of caste.[75]

Bapurao's transgression, however, still existed within a broader social logic of caste and brahman pride, power, and privilege; as he declared, "A brahman can become a Mahar, but a Mahar cannot become a brahman."[76] In other words, according to the logic of caste, a brahman has the freedom to descend to the status of Untouchable if he so desires; however, it is impossible for an Untouchable to attain brahmanhood. Brahman men could do whatever they pleased.

Most significantly, brahmanya, though hegemonic, at that same time emerged as an unstable and flexible identity for a brahman man—it could be constructed, challenged, transgressed, and even recovered by penance. The tulsi leaf and the waters of the river Ganga, through the power of penance and purity, could salvage the polluted brahman Bapurao. After the Thana court incident, Bapurao and Pavalabai performed in Pune for three years. Later, as their love deepened, Bapurao took Pavalabai to his village, Rethare. However, villagers were upset with his caste and cultural transgressions and discussed his polluted status, which breached brahmanya, with him. And though they first readily outcaste him, later they collected funds (Rs. 3,000) and suggested to him that he "go to Kashi and purify himself," thereby regaining his brahmanya.[77] Brahmanya could be temporarily lost and regained, thus suggesting some flexibility and constant updating by brahmans; yet this was available to only brahman men. With his expenses on the rise and his income declining, Pavalabai perhaps even encouraged Bapurao to consent to his caste-fellows' suggestion, accept the money, and travel to Kashi to purify himself of Pavalabai's blot. And though he did accept the money—giving it to Pavalabai—he refused to pay heed to caste constrictions, perform penance, and regain his purity, telling his brahman brethren, "Once I have become a Mahar, I am a Mahar, why do I need to convert now?"[78] In declining the demands of the orthodox brahmans of Rethare, Bapurao was steadfast in his decision to renounce his brahman status, doing so, however, by virtue of the assumed innate superiority of that status, which afforded him the privilege to become anything: brahman, Mahar, Chandal, and so on. Like Gandhi, who conveniently chose to become a Bhangi (sweeper, the lowest Untouchable) in the 1930s, Bapurao could transform himself into a Mahar in the 1910s. Both the Bania (Gandhi's caste, a grocer) and the brahman did not understand the plight of Untouchables, who had no such playful choices. They were ascribed to be Untouchables.

Pavalabai Contests Powerful Patriarchy

Despite the love and inspiration that Pavalabai and Bapurao drew from one another, their relationship always operated within the sexual-caste economy and was subject to the regulatory norms and mundane displays of brahmani patriarchy. The coupling of Pavalabai and Bapurao and her later reunion with Kauthekar illuminate the intimacy and violent domination of brahmani patriarchy and its regulatory norms. She was desperate not to be a servant or drudge, insistent that she be independent and own her Tamasha troupe instead of partnering with Bapurao or even with Kauthekar. Her life demonstrates the nexus of desire, consent, coercion, pleasure, and violence that both constrained the possibilities for a stigmatized Tamasha woman and shaped her opportunities to disrupt the sex-gender-caste complex. In it, we can appreciate both the potential as well as the restricted scope for Dalit manuski, as well as the limitations of Pavalabai's agency. While the elite men who wrote about her referred to her reckless freedom, Pavalabai's life illuminates the negation of virtue and status as manus (human) for Untouchable women and the presumption of sexual promiscuity and availability that stuck to her as an Untouchable woman. Pavalabai was strong, brave, assertive, and successful on her own terms and performed her agency as a Tamasha woman in her dealings with audiences as well as with her professional and romantic partners Dholvadkar, Bapurao, and later Kauthekar. But the demands of caste patriarchy, as enacted by Bapurao and Kauthekar and reasserted by Jintikar and Dange in their recuperations of Bapurao, constantly—even after her death—sought to negate that agency, constrain her performativity of Untouchable womanhood, and subject it to control. I examine these forms of domination that usually go undetected.

Pavalabai's skill as a Tamasha woman resulted in celebrity and financial success. This allowed her to buy, among other things, farmland for her family in Hivargao, which she would visit during the monsoons, arriving in an embroidered buggy that she had bought for herself. Pavalabai traveled to the fields in Hivargao in style, like an empress, the buggy driven by a pair of robust bullocks and decked out with special velvety curtains in the front and rear.[79] Her popularity also allowed her and Bapurao to tour different parts of Maharashtra: Sangli, Satara, Kolhapur, Karad, and so on. Bapurao's most popular *vag* (poetic skit) was "Mitharani," which was again inspired by Pavalabai, who portrayed Queen Mitha. The popularity of this vag and Pavalabai's performance in it brought it and her to the attention of a local prince and social reformer, Shahu Maharaj of Kolhapur. Shahu Maharaj encouraged shahiri performances of the Bahujans. On his special request, in 1908 or 1909 Pavalabai performed the vag at the *divankhana* (special chamber) of the Kolhapur court. Both Shahu Maharaj and his queen were immensely impressed with Pavalabai's *adakari* (skill at gestures) and presented her with an expensive nine-yard sari and silver anklets and Bapurao with a *jari patka* (turban decorated with gold or other expensive threads).[80]

Pavalabai was not entirely dependent on, nor was her success derived from

Bapurao, as Jintikar and Dange would like us to believe. She was a strong and brave woman, head of her Tamasha troupe, a breadwinner who took care of the Tamasgirs who depended on her. Unlike Jintikar and Dange, Lahuji Bhalerao spent a long time with her and provides an insider's insights. He asserts, "She was authoritative and powerful. When she cast her critical eye on a Tamasgir, they trembled with fear. She was dictatorial."[81] For instance, on one occasion when Pavalabai and her co-artists were at Satranjivala Chowk in Pune, somebody stole all her gold jewelry and nobody could locate it. Frustrated, Pavalabai lodged a police complaint, which resulted in an investigation that revealed a member of the troupe had committed the theft. Both Lahuji Bhalerao and Kanta Achalkhamb argue that "if Pavalabai had decided, she could have punished and sent this co-worker to jail. However, she did not do so."[82] Whether her decision was out of compassion or out of fear that news of the transgression would negatively affect the morale of her troupe, the incident illustrates the agency she was able to exercise in such situations. After consulting with government officials, she withdrew her complaint, putting an end to the criminal matter, and donated all the recovered jewelry to an orphanage, retaining not a single piece. Although Kanta Achalkhamb mobilizes this story as "evidence of a *mahan* [great, venerable] and *mayalu* [sympathetic and loving] Pavalabai,"[83] it also suggests her subjectivity and agency as the head of a successful Tamasha troupe.

Incidents like the one above, however—as well as other conflicts over finances, such as the sort of exploitation present in the pilahouse theatre story recounted above; incidents of violence toward Pavalabai that are suggested by but not always spelled out in the sources; and Bapurao's resentment toward Pavalabai when she refused to follow his direction or imposed her will on the troupe—strained her personal and professional relationship with Bapurao past the breaking point. The enactment of caste patriarchy by Bapurao—and also Kauthekar, whom Pavalabai reunited with in the 1920s—and his use and appropriation of Pavalabai's image, success, and labor for his own personal, artistic, and financial gain did not sit well with a strong, successful agent like Pavalabai, and she left him. Moreover, Jintikar's and Dange's recuperative texts perform that recuperation by dehumanizing Pavalabai (as animal, as slave), thus doubling the effect of caste patriarchy on her. Those texts sought to accomplish in writing what Bapurao had failed to do in reality: to control

Pavalabai, or at least the memory of her. And in them, for instance, in their treatments of the separation between the two, Bapurao emerges as the brahman savior to Pavalabai's animalistic, tyrannical, degraded Mahar woman who, tragically, would not submit.

Though he discussed fights between Bapurao and Pavalabai, Dange shrouded any direct violence or exploitation by deflecting blame for their professional and romantic separation onto Pavalabai. He completely dismissed any legitimate reasons that Pavalabai might have had for separating from Bapurao; to Dange, she embodied a vulgarity and excess sexuality characterized by ignorance, unruliness, coercion, desire, animality, and submission. Caste, for Dange, was nothing more than a benign institution, and Bapurao, a paternal brahman who could regulate Pavalabai's Mahar excess through bonds of affection, protection, and patriarchy. Caste along with patriarchy worked to negate the manuski of Untouchables and perpetuate the presumption Tamasgirs' sexual promiscuity and availability, but Pavalabai's refusal to submit illuminates the limited dominion of both brahman and non-brahman owners-lovers.

Pavalabai's decision to split from Bapurao did not go over well with his supporters. Even in recognizing that as a Tamasha woman—a desire-producing machine—she had been crucial to Bapurao's success, they degraded her, reducing her to a tool used to excite audiences and elevating Bapurao as the paternalistic brahman savior. Dange, in his moralistic, patronizing, brahmani tone, exalts Bapurao and vilifies Pavalabai for leaving him: "Pavala was getting away from Bapurao. Wonder whether her *kotya man* [cunning heart] was at all affected by his venerable heart's teachings and actions? *She remained a* [thorny] *babhal* [acacia] *even in the shadow of the fragrant chandan* [sandalwood] *tree*.[84] To him, Pavalabai was an ashlil, dumb Mahar woman with limited or no intellectual capacities who could never grasp the essence of Bapurao's higher actions and motives. Bapurao's reward for "discovering" and revealing her talents was that her thorny cunning in leaving Bapurao—for another man rather than for other personal or professional reasons, Dange argues—destroyed his brahmanya and his life:

> Maybe, she felt uncomfortable. The Pavala who had been transformed
> into gold through her association with the *paris* [magical stone that turns
> into gold; here, Bapurao is that magic] was once again attracted to rusting

iron, [that is her earlier lover/owner Maruti Kauthekar]. [As a result], she disavowed the great *kumbha of amrut* [heavenly vessel containing elixir, or Bapurao] and embraced the *phutaka ranjan* [broken water pot/jar, or Kauthekar]. She carved out her success due to Bapurao and yet she left a *kalank* [blot] on him, and left him. The one who for the sake of art destroyed his brahmanya, kith-kin, home, and everything, she with her deeds clearly in turn, broke him and destroyed him.[85]

Dange was attempting to construct a benign romantic fantasy between the two actors by precariously balancing Bapurao's civilized brahman behavior with her animalistic Mahar barbarism, his fragrant sandalwood essence with that of her thorny acacia. And by mythologizing Bapurao as the magical *paris* (stone) who had transformed Pavala into a golden girl, Jintikar, Dange, and others elevated Bapurao as the good, large-hearted, magical brahman who made every effort to uplift the opportunistic and degraded Pavalabai. In place of specific reasons for why Pavalabai might have chosen to split with Bapurao personally and professionally, Dange relies on the explanatory power of Pavalabai's status as a Tamasha woman, and unfortunately no other sources discuss their fights, the reasons for their separation, or the whereabouts of Pavalabai.

The characterization of Pavalabai as reckless and unstable stuck so well that in 1984, she was still described as "inherently of a *chanchal* [unstable] nature. She never valued the boundless sacrifices Patthe made for her. On the pretext of a trivial misunderstanding, she left Patthe and ran away with Maruti Patil Kauthekar."[86] To touchables, Pavalabai thus became both property and a person—in other words, in this dual invocation was the idea of her being a slave. She was owned by touchable men—Dholvadkar, Bapurao, and Kauthekar—who became her lovers and owners, and the elites made her absolutely subject to the will of Bapurao. She had no agency and was not human in their eyes. They also tried to intimately connect Pavalabai and Bapurao's intimate relations with his domination, as well as with the legitimacy of brutality, violence, subordination, exploitation and the necessity of his protecting her. To them, she was an animal to be herded or tethered to them alone, even if she was not Bapurao's wedded wife. She was disposable and replaceable. Functioning in the agrarian caste slavery, Tamasha inscribed subjection into the daily life of Pavalabai. Tamasha normalized this caste, sexual, and gendered violence and dehumanized Pavalabai. In these contestations, Pavalabai, to touchables, emerged a hypersexualized will-less object, an animal randomly, recklessly, and will-lessly shifting from one man to the other. They completely ignored that Pavalabai may have made strategic decisions based on the contingent historical circumstances. To them, the focus on the supposed wrongdoings and the utter negation of Pavalabai's will was necessary to demonstrate her submission to her "master" Bapurao.

The nexus of desire, consent, coercion, pleasure, and violence at work in Tamasha and the threat that Pavalabai's success and agency posed to the regulatory norms of caste patriarchy are also evident in her personal and professional relationship with Kauthekar. After leaving Bapurao, she sought to work independently and to assert her agency, to the degree that both were possible, once even declaring publicly during a performance at Karad: "I am leading my independent bari. I have no relationship with Bapurao. I am not going to sing his Lavanya."[87] In this manner, Pavalabai tried to distance herself from Bapurao and carve out her own identity. She formed a new troupe with Shahu Sakharam that enjoyed some success.[88] Soon, however, she encountered her former lover Maruti Kauthekar, who was by then a rich maratha (peasant cultivator) Patil, a village headman. Performing for Patils and negotiating the nexus of caste, desire, and danger in those performances was especially perilous for Tamasha women, according to Lahuji Bhalerao:

> In those days, Patils were very fond of Tamasha. Even if a Tamasha show was organized in faraway villages, they bullock-carted all the way to enjoy and immerse in daulat jada. After watching the performances, they invited Tamasha women they liked to their villages. If anybody declined the invitation, then given the circumstances, the Patil either forcibly brought them or even engaged in killing them. Hence, Tamasgirs have feared such devotees.[89]

Though Patils ritually occupied a relatively low position in the agrarian caste hierarchy, they were still dominant as owners and cultivators of land and above Untouchables. They were thus able to oppress Untouchable men and women generally and sexually coerce and act upon the perceived sexual availability of Tamasha women. After seeing Pavalabai on stage, Kauthekar fell for her and persuaded her to join him. Like Bapurao, however, Kauthekar was also subject to scorn and abuse from among his caste in his village for consorting with an Untouchable woman. And thus, regardless of whether or not she was in a position to refuse his advances, Pavalabai was able to use, first, the community scorn to make him understand that there was no use simply keeping her at home and, second, their relationship to persuade him to fund a new Tamasha troupe. Their hard work was realized in Pavalabai's renewed fame in the mid to late 1920s. By contrast, Bapurao's troupe had completely collapsed, and Achalkhamb went so far as to argue that it was during this period with Kauthekar, and not with Bapurao, that she was at the height of her fame. This claim, however, seems an exaggeration given the stories about Pavalabai and Bapurao, not about Pavalabai and Kauthekar, and about their performances and even the 1905 "pollution" court case that were still circulating in Maharashtra in 2016, clearly affirming the fame and persistence of the legend of the sringarik couple.

Pavalabai was, however, once again entangled by the combination of caste and patriarchal control in her new personal and professional relationship with Kauthekar. Kauthekar bought all the equipment needed to start the Tamasha troupe in Pavalabai's name and he became her agent, organizing the shows. This sense of financial obligation and control manifested in jealousy and eventually legal proceedings. Once during a performance, one man in the audience announced a daulatjada of Rs. 5 for Pavalabai. While she was accepting it, the man caught her hand and refused to let it go. Pavalabai, however, through the artistic skills, false flirtations, and pretense that she was adept in as a Tamasha woman, freed herself. Yet her lover, agent, and former bodyguard, Kauthekar, who observed the scene from afar, was very angry with her about this physical and financial exchange, and he started a fight. As a Tamasha woman, such performances of ownership over her body and being were not new to Pavalabai. She immediately retorted: "You are not my *lagnacha navra* [wedded husband]. I meet many people like you who are crazy about me. That does not mean that I go about distributing my love for them. If you keep troubling me unnecessarily as you have done, our relationship will soon turn sour."[90] In asserting her agency by challenging Kauthekar's jealousy and control, Pavalabai challenged caste patriarchy. Her angry rebuttal only stoked Kauthekar's ferocity, however, and he started calling her names. Pavalabai threw at him the jewelry he had given her and asked him to leave the troupe. Unwilling to let the matter rest and wanting to enforce his financial and social control over her, Kauthekar filed a complaint that the jewelry actually belonged to him and that he should receive compensation in the amount of Rs. 30,000 for his loss in Tamasha. But Lahuji Bhalerao reminds us that Pavalabai was not a *lechipechi* (fickle) woman.[91] She mentioned in the court of law that she owned the jewelry and also produced receipts. Although she won the case, her Tamasha troupe did not do well because Kauthekar was successful in breaking it and her in the process. Worn out after this, Pavalabai returned to Hivargao.

Although we do not have direct evidence for her side of the story, even this fragmentary evidence attests that Pavalabai was a brave, proud, and dignified woman who spoke her mind and made decisions in her best interest. Gradually, as she aged, her beauty waned, and artists left her for better opportunities. Maharin Pavalabai was a strong woman who consistently contested the supposedly formidable walls of powerful patriarchy. Kauthekar and Bapurao loved her, Kauthekar did not heed to the village Patils, and Bapurao challenged brahmanya for her, but both of them—and later, through their writing, Jintikar and Dange too—also sought to control and conquer her through their spectacular caste patriarchal power. Touchables and scholars have easily obfuscated the quotidian routine of violence that assured and sustained terror in Tamasha.

The poles of brahman patriarchy, intimacy and violence, and the nexus of caste, danger, and desire in Tamasha are further evident in Bapurao's attempts to reenter Pavalabai's life over the years. During one incident, while on tour with Kauthekar and her troupe, she discovered that Bapurao was aboard the same train, though travelling to a different destination. When the train stopped and Pavalabai attempted to alight, Bapurao and Kauthekar both imposed and enacted their claims to ownership over her, with Kauthekar pulling her off the train and Bapurao pulling her back on. It is unlikely that either was unfamiliar with manifesting caste patriarchy through physical violence and desire for perfect submission from Pavalabai. At another time, Bapurao "requested" that Pavalabai accompany him to Rethare to seek the blessings of his guru Jangali Maharaj, and "after that she was *free* to go anywhere."[92] Dange's language—his use of *request* and the idea that she would be "free"—once again suggests a benign interaction between Bapurao and Pavalabai, which serves to hide the implicit violence of caste patriarchy in Bapurao's assertions of his uncontested authority over her. Pavalabai's agency and Untouchableness were always contingent, her resistance and freedom staged and performed vis-à-vis terror and caste slavery. When she refused and instead toured with Kauthekar and the troupe, Bapurao was furious because, in the words of Dange, "Pavalabai had now become dauntless, and [hence] argued that her relationship with Bapurao had ended."[93] On another occasion, Pavalabai again refused Bapurao's invitation to accompany him to his village, saying, "Whatever happens, I will not join you."[94]

To Dange, Pavalabai's decision to separate from Bapurao was just *"popat-panchi"* (repeating like a parrot)[95] because to him the so-called intellectually inferior Pavalabai could not take such a major decision in her life. To him, "she was taught by Kauthekar"[96] and merely reproduced his speech. In this manner, Dange reduced Pavalabai to a nonhuman, a tiny bird dependent on and derived from Kauthekar. Thus, once again, Dange blames the "dull-witted" Maharin Pavalabai for not having the intelligence to understand Bapurao's love for her and in fact, casting away her brahman lover.

By the beginning of 1930s, a physically and psychologically diminished Bapurao, burning with hate and unable to come to terms with Pavalabai's agency, made one final attempt to avenge the insult of Pavalabai leaving him. At the theatre in Karad, as his last gift to her, Bapurao offered Pavalabai four expensive saris and requested she wear one. Though she recognized this as an attempt to lure her back to him, she acquiesced and draped the sari. Bapurao then went to the police and lodged a complaint: "I had brought four jari saris from Mumbai and somebody stole them. Here's my receipt." The police found one sari on Pavalabai's body and three in her trunk. Pavalabai was thus helpless and she was found guilty of theft. In this manner, Bapurao deployed legal means to avenge and police Pavalabai. Dange once again contrasted them, celebrating Bapurao as *thor* (venerable, great) because he did not actually call Pavala a *"chor"* (thief).[97] In Dange's opinion, Bapurao was blinded by love and hence all his actions, even to insult and punish Pavalabai, should be seen as episodes in their grand love story. By contrast, to Kanta Achalkhamb, this incident, when compared to the jewelry event in Pune, clearly revealed Bapurao's vengeful mindset.[98] To her, Pavalabai had forgiven her co-artists, whereas Bapurao sought vengeance on her.

Most significantly, Dange continues to sing praise of Bapurao's gloriousness. He observes that Pavala could not gather the courage to look into Bapurao's eyes because her pride was replaced by *paschhatap* (repentance) and she immediately fell at Bapurao's feet crying, "Bapurao is mine."[99] As a result, to Dange, "Love won in the end!" Bapurao and Pavalabai came together again and spent time in Mumbai. However, they could not recuperate and relive their past fame and economic prosperity. After some time, Pavalabai retired from Tamasha.

Canonizing Bapurao and Sanitizing the Ashlil

As I have suggested at various points throughout this chapter, caste and patriarchy structure not only Pavalabai's relationships with Bapurao and Kauthekar but also the memory of both Bapurao and Pavalabai in the writings of Jintikar and Dange. The legacy of Bapurao, secured through Jintikar's three-volume collection of his Lavanya, is revealing of the ways in which privileged brahman male performers such as Bapurao, as well as other touchable public intellectuals and artists, both appropriated Tamasha and Lavani for personal, political, and social gains and slighted Tamasha and Lavani as well as their performers as ashlil and backward. Janaki Bakhle has gone so far as to argue that these intellectuals and artists abandoned Lavani and concentrated on sanskritized "Marathi theatre and classicized music drama well into the first four decades of the twentieth century."[100] This focus, Bakhle argues, affected Tamasha and Lavani to the extent that, "with very few exceptions, there were no more Lavanya or gondhals on the stage, associated as they had become with bawdy and lewd entertainment, and even when some of the music of these forms permeated newer compositions, it was not acknowledged as such."[101] Bakhle, however, focused on only brahman men, thus erasing Untouchable Lavanya from the Marathi music tradition. Tamasha and Lavani performances in the rural and urban spaces of Maharashtra continued to flourish into the 1940s (and indeed, continue to do so up to the present day), precisely the time when Jintikar was securing Bapurao's legacy and Marathi elites were seeking to regulate and sanitize Tamasha and Lavani for inclusion in the regional Marathi canon of popular art forms.

Canonization was also a performative gesture that led to credibility and authority for and produced the received truth about Bapurao, thus creating a lasting sense of anxiety, perversity, and uncertainty about the patchy and inconsistent information about Pavalabai. Capitalizing on the popularity of and productive spaces for Lavanya in the new Marathi cinema (chapter 5), as well as to continue Bapurao's legendary success of shighra kavi, Jintikar published three volumes of Bapurao's Lavanya in the 1940s and 1950s. Jintikar—a postman by profession, who had played drum at Satrangiwala chowk Tamasha theatre in the 1910s—met Bapurao in 1939, when the latter was seventy-three years old and no longer accustomed to writing in the comfort he enjoyed in the portrait in figure 2.1. According to Jintikar, Bapurao was then writing Lavanya at Jintikar's small dronpatravali shop near Phadke houd, near the red-light district in Ravivar Peth, Pune. Between 1939 and 1945, Jintikar financially and emotionally supported the old man.[102] As a man of some local prominence, Jintikar also worked as the editor of the periodical *Shaiva Samachar* in 1941 and participated in debates about caste, most notably one on whether Guravs were brahmans or Shudras. Clearly, he wanted to legitimize his low-status Gurav caste to a higher placement in the hierarchy. Continuing this exaltation of himself and his community, he also sought to recuperate his brahman friend Bapurao as a classical hero for Tamasha and Lavani. Jintikar was well aware of the broader stereotype of the "polluted" Tamasha. Consequently, he argued, his book on Bapurao was pedagogical and instructive, especially because Tamasha *"mhatala tar tyat phajilpana asavayachach"* (Tamasha has to be useless and therefore vulgar).[103] Therefore, in order to discipline and make this phajilpana (vulgarity) more palatable to readers, Jintikar and his associate Dange invited some significant Marathi elites to comment on Bapurao's contributions to Tamasha and Lavani. In their short write-ups, each author, with painstaking effort, contributed to the construction of Bapurao's prominent patriarchal and, moreover, mythic brahman, masculine status.

Jintikar, along with such leading Pune intellectuals and leaders as N. C. Kelkar, Master of Music G. N. Muzumdar (aka Abasaheb Muzumdar), Keshavrao Jedhe, Datto Vaman Potdar, and Kakasaheb Gadgil, contributed prefaces to Jintikar's three volumes of Bupurao's Lavanya. Several of them also attended a series of events in 1942–43 to contextualize and secure the legacy of Bapurao, of which Jintikar wrote, "Bapurao would certainly be happy with this celebration!" Continuing the celebratory note, in his preface Gadgil noted, "Bapurao did not care about caste differentiations and tried to disseminate his poetry deploying the weapons of *dholki, jhanj, tuntune* [musical instruments]. He sought to educate Bajujan samaj (majoritarian community) through sensual, attractive, and even harsh words."[104] Jedhe agreed: "Bapurao was an icon of Maharashtra."[105]

In his preface, the renowned reformer and litterateur N. C. Kelkar argued, "It was well known why [urbane] educated elites *nak muradtat* [twist their noses and express disgust] at Lavani and Tamashe." However, despite his claims that he was providing an objective assessment, scientific and free of bias toward Lavani, he could not hide his prejudice: "I have tried to keep away the *dushit* [polluted] bias and focus on the poetry of Lavanya." Lavanya thus were always already vulgar and hence, to Kelkar, "Lavani books should not be given to people of all classes" because, to him, people might be waylaid or misuse them. Yet, Kelkar would appropriate Lavanya by sanitizing them, because, as he reasoned, "When we see *ker* [rubbish] in a glass of milk, do we not remove it and still drink the milk? In the same manner, [one should] pick good Lavanya, absolutely delete or improve some [ashlil] words in there, and use it in books for adult education." Kelkar could be a paradigmatic representative for Pune brahman elites who reinforced caste-pride, emphasized a "purified" and "high" moral tone, and hence looked down upon ashlil Lavanya because of the latter's always already corrupting nature.

In the process, Kelkar strategically created distinct differences in class, caste, knowledge, and literature. Nevertheless, continuing his praise for Bapurao, Kelkar proudly noted that Bapurao continued the legacy of shahirs in the peshvai and, most importantly, was not affected or influenced by poetic traditions and insights that emerged in the colonial English period. Thus, to touchables protecting their inner spiritual core, it had been important to create a new wave of cultural nationalism since the end of the nineteenth century. Both the European and lower-caste influences threatened their supposedly glorious and pure past and scientific order. To prove their exceptionalism and superiority in the cultural realm, the former had to be kept lower and at a distinct distance.

In contrast with Kelkar, Jedhe argued, "If Bapurao's poetry was in the hands of ordinary people and in libraries, they would help reform and improve the morals of Bahujans."[106] D. D. Parchure compared brahman Lavanikars Ram Joshi and Bapurao: "Joshi and Bapurao have a vast vocabulary. But Bapurao does not cross limits, like Joshi. Those trying to find ashlil in Lavani-Tamashe will be disappointed when they read Bapurao's poetry."[107] Thus, in contrast to Kelkar, to Parchure, Bapurao's Lavanya were absolutely clean, devoid of the ashlil.

The poet Lahiri Haidar also praised Bapurao and argued that "his books show that Bapurao intensively fought orthodox casteists and was a reformer. His actions are evidence of this."[108] Thus Tamasha scholars and biographers of Bapurao construct him as oceanic—boundless and vast, not a person at all. They transform him into a god, the protector, provider, and liberator of Pavalabai. Bapurao's biography follows a pattern like those of some famous musicians, which are mostly the collections of moral lessons that transform the actors into exemplary men and women. The authors depict Bapurao's life as a series of minor epic battles over evil and malice and turn him into a godlike figure. The authors except for Nalge are rarely concerned with narrative of history writing. However, they pay great attention to history through a simple chronology. Most significantly, they praise the brilliance of Bapurao, and though he was at times irrational, they mark such tendencies as signs of his naivete. The authors staunchly supported family tradition and acceptable boundaries of conjugal behavior and were deeply spiritual and sometimes even devout.

Although Jintikar and the contributors to his volumes drew sharp distinctions between the artistry and Lavanya of Bapurao and that of Untouchable artists, denigrating Mahar and Mang arts on the basis of caste, Bapurao refused to participate in this. Toward the end of his career, during a felicitation organized by Jintikar on January 2, 1942, in John Small Memorial Hall, Pune, Bapurao told the audience: "I have been in the dhanda of Tamasha for 52 years and pursued it living among Mahar-Mangs. I have a different outlook on these people. They are like pearls and diamonds in a broken pot. This society should not look at their exteriority, but interiority. You will find a flowing brook there."[109] Although

Bapurao recognized the innate intelligence of Untouchables, which had been broken and denied by caste slavery and the stickiness of the ashlil, he also objectified them.

By performing in Tamasha, which was traditionally dominated by Mang-Mahars, disregarding conservative brahmani traditional notions of *sovale* (purity and pollution), and, most significantly, by partnering professionally and romantically with Maharin Pavalabai, Bapurao radically challenged his brahmanya. Yet there were limitations to this good brahman man. Certainly, Bapurao's actions and efforts became controversial and his public performances of Lavanya were full of intrigue. Even spatially, even if Bapurao lived in Pune for some time, he always resided on the margins, in low-caste localities such as Yeravada, Somvar, Ganesh, or Ravivar Peth and was never close to the orthodox chitpavan brahman polis of Sadashiv Peth.[110] Thus Bapurao is many a time out of step with his brahmanya, but yet, it enables him to enter with confidence a world that his brahman caste despises, derides, and requires only to affirm their always already superordinate status.[111] Although Bapurao concurred with the supreme status of brahmanhood, at the same time, he was critiquing and contesting brahmanya and confirming his outcaste status because he had such brahman power. Such brahmani critiques are also themselves acts of brahmanism because the power to critique oneself in this way reinforces the exceptional, and Bapurao's control of discourse also is a display of power.[112]Although some brahmans watched his Tamasha, many brahmans outcaste him. But Mang-Mahars embraced him, because he was in *their* Tamasha.

The sanitizing and sanskritizing that Jintikar and Dange argued were crucial to the success of Bapurao's Lavanya are not only key features of their recuperation of Bapurao but even, by the end of their narratives, of Pavalabai too. Patriarchal touchable men continued to play many caste games while narrating Pavalabai's life. Dange reports that toward the end of her life, Pavala found herself "*nirarthak*" (meaningless) and transformed herself into a "*yogini*" (recluse). "She prayed like [Hindu mythological figures] Sita or Radha, 'Krishna assimilate me into yourself. Grant the remaining of my life to Sridhar [Bapurao]. The world needs him more than me.' This was the setting point of the light of sensuality."[113] Dange draws upon Sita, for whom the earth created fissure to "take her in" and accept her prayer of ending her life to save her husband Ram. Similarly, to Dange because Pavalabai had lost interest in living, she turned to Krishna and asked him to deliver her from her life. And most significantly, he accepted her prayer. Unlike Sita however, Pavalabai was not wedded to Bapurao. She was like his unmarried second wife though. They had flexible arrangement, they were free lovebirds, freely and flexibly loving different men and women. Yet, Dange and Jintikar slander Pavalabai for her flexible relationships with men and never provide much detail about the many women in Bapurao's life.

Most significantly, Dange deploys sanskritic, shastric, and puranic texts and seeks to cleanse and civilize artists and Tamasha itself. According to Dange, Pavalabai transformed into a true lover only when she was near death, pining for Bapurao's long life. In a similar vein, the biography and movie on Ram Joshi also highlights the ways that a brahman man, Ram Joshi, gradually awakens to the real meaning and motive of music and poetry. The movie ends with Joshi turning into a recluse to purify his association with the ashlil Lavani and Tamasha performance. He thus abandons Lavani singing and grabs *kirtankar* (devotional singer's) musical instruments, chipalis, thus sanitizing and sanskritizing himself by transforming himself into a kirtankar. He would henceforward use his poetic skills to sing kirtans and bhajans providing moral guidance, departing from the merriment and extraneous, unproductive pleasure of Lavanya. Mahar women, however, could not become dignified kirtankars, so they repented like tapasvinis or yoginis and sought forgiveness. Touchables appropriated Pavalabai for many purposes—in her youth, they used her energetic, enticing, sexual beauty, and in her death, they used her as a repenting renouncer praying for Bapurao's life.

By contrast, Kanta Achalkhamb suggests that both Pavalabai and Bapurao turned into alcoholics and constantly fought with one another. Once again, the evidence is thin. Denying her claims, Pavalabai's grandnephew Changdeo Bhalerao argues that "she chewed tobacco and ate betel, but she was not an alcoholic."[114] Clearly, Changdeo Bhalerao was trying to portray a decent image of Pavalabai because he recognized how moralistic elites rendered tobacco, betel, and alcohol as stereotypical of Tamasha people and the ashlil. He added, "She was getting older and also suffered from asthma. People who made her famous forgot her, and her luxury was a temporary wave in her life. Hence, her last days were full of sorrow." She traveled to Duncan Road (Maulana Azad Road), Mumbai to stay with her niece, Chandrika Gholap, to seek treatment for asthma. However, the doctor could not detect the ailment, which grew by leaps. According to Lahuji Bhalerao, it seems she developed diphtheria.[115] She soon died "helpless, poor, and neglected," at the age of sixty-nine, on December 6, 1939.[116]

After Pavalabai's death, Bapurao tried to renew his Tamasha with the help of other women: Tai Parinchekar and the dancer Chandrabai; however, it seems Pavalabai took Bapurao's wealth and fame with her. His weakening will power and declining health led to his demise. He was not successful anymore and his life and popularity waned. Bapurao passed away in Pune on December 22, 1945.[117] Jintikar is more reliable here because he was with Bapurao at this time. In 1961, shahir Shankarrao Nikam and others agreed to repay the debt to Bapurao. He argues, "Tamasgirs earn their living by singing Bapurao's Lavanya. They haven't repaid their debt to Bapurao."[118] He wanted people to celebrate Bapurao and requested the leading Mang Tamasgir, Bhau Narayangaokar (the grandfather of Mangalatai Bansode; see chapter 6) to make efforts to build a memorial for Bapurao in his village of Sangli.

To commemorate Bapurao, brahmans like Raja Nene also directed and acted as Patthe Bapurao in his movie titled the same in 1950 (see fig. 2.4). Anant Mane co-produced the movie. Anant Mane also produced his sixty-first film, *Lavanyavati* (The graceful, beautiful), on the life of Pavalabai in 1992 (see fig. 2.5). Reproducing the sex-gender-caste complex in practice, Varsha Sangamnerkar, a Lavani woman from Kolhati caste and Girish Oak, a brahman man played the roles of Pavalabai and Bapurao respectively.[119]

Conservative caste strictures haunted Bapurao in his life and death. He was a privileged brahman, who was held in low esteem by elite Pune brahmans. To them, he had transgressed brahmanya by entering Tamasha, performing Lavani, inhabiting with lower castes and Untouchables, and loving Maharin Pavalabai. He resided in Untouchable neighborhoods of Pune. He was befriended by Shudra caste Gurav like Jintikar and Untouchables, away from brahmans. As a result, Bapurao asked Jintikar to perform the last death rites for him. To keep his word to Bapurao, as well as to not invite the fury of Puneri conservative brahmans, Jintikar did not cremate Bapurao's body at

FIGURE 2.4. For shahiri, Patthe Bapurao left government employment and became the favorite shahir of Maharashtra. Source: "Patthe Bapurao," *Chhaya*, May 22, 1960. National Film Archive of India.

Omkareshvar in the brahman neighborhood but at non-brahman and Dalit Lakdipool crematory.[120] However, because Ambedkarite Jalsa (see chapter 4) was so powerful in purging ashlil elements and even Tamasha itself from the Dalit samaj that, as activist Appasaheb Ranpise reported, no Dalit shahir attended Bapurao's cremation.

Pavalabai's and Bapurao's lived experiences highlight the ambivalence of these actors as well as the simultaneous everyday construction, flexible and rigid structures of caste, gender, sexuality, and patriarchy. The famous couple immensely enjoyed their popularity and fame. They dissented against societal structures and strictures. Yet, unlike Maharin Pavalabai, Bapurao was a privileged brahman man who could easily break boundaries. Bapurao tried to intervene in the social movement of the Mahad Satyagraha of 1927; yet, because he earned money deploying the social and sexual labor of Pavalabai, Ambedkar refused to accept Bapurao's financial support. Ambedkar frontally attacked the brahmani circular logic of tightly tying caste, gender, and the doubly stigmatized sexuality of Muralis, Tamasha women, and prostitutes especially from the 1930s, as I discuss in the next chapter. Given the pressures of manuski,

FIGURE 2.5. Varsha Sangamnerkar as Pavalabai and Girish Oak as Bapurao in Patthe Bapurao. Source: *Rasrang*, 1993. National Film Archive of India.

samaj, and dharmantar, he sought to cleanse, civilize, and reconstruct their life-worlds. Yet, by also affirming the agency of women, he departed from the orthodox Hindu agenda of seeking spiritual purity and penance. Ambedkar was furious with ways the sexual-caste slavery reinforced their status as property, possession, perversion, profit center, and item—nonhuman. He would fight for their manuski and freedom.

Conclusion

Pavalabai's life illuminates the ambiguous and entangled interconnections between choice and compulsion and the absolute inability to escape the binding ropes of willfulness and will-lessness, the constant caste games of ashlil and assli that constitute Dalit subjectivity. This double bind of freedom—the generativity and constraints—were the entanglements of bondage and liberty. Pavalabai's determined will enabled her to rise to fame and carve out a name in Maharashtra. She was a Mahar, Untouchable artist who paved the way for Tamasha artists and also propelled upward social mobility for her family. Yet she was also constrained. Her inferior, Untouchable caste and gender status, compounded by Tamasha, further solidified her ashlil status, while Bapurao was always already assli due to the privilege of his superior brahman caste status. He was always meritorious, intelligent, knowledgeable, and higher than human, even when he appropriated Untouchables' arts to become a star. While Pavalabai's outcaste status denigrated her, Bapurao kept accumulating his caste capital and consolidating and updating his brahmanya.

The very nature of the space of the Tamasha performative was outcast and liminal. Liminality was simultaneously constraining and liberating. Tamasha enabled Pavalabai to navigate her liminal status between willful agent and will-less, abject object as well as the ambivalence between the pleasure and violence as touchable men consumed, enjoyed, and exploited her beauty and arts, even from a distance. While Bapurao did not renounce his brahmanya, he was also not always tied to it. Brahmanya's liminal moments, historical as they were, were constantly undercut by the difference that the individual brahman man came to mark, establish, and enjoy in all instances.

Both Untouchables and touchables normalized caste violence in the supposedly fun and frolicking Tamasha, an ambivalent cultural form through which Pavalabai performatively enacted and negotiated her Untouchableness. Untouchableness was diverse, unstable, and constantly produced and reproduced through multiple processes of caste subjection, exploitation, brutality, rivalry, jealousy, ambivalence, ambiguity, and complicity. Pavalabai's strategy, skill, and modern existence were crimes to Ambedkar and his followers (see chapters 3 and 4) because they perpetuated the stickiness of the ashlil to and confirmed the backwardness of Dalits, especially in the context of caste slavery. As such, she remains a minor figure in even her own Tamasha history, despite her artistic skill. Her peripatetic, wayward life and inability to marry like her Murali and Tamasha sisters rendered love and all desire illegitimate.

Untouchables were a mutilated humanity, abject and deprived of manuski, but they possessed the power of resilience necessary to radically remake themselves. Ambedkar mobilized Tamasha as evidence of Dalit abjection and the basis for constructing Dalit manuski. Tamasha women, as objects of male desire and caste exploitation, were denied status as manus, or even women—theirs was a body of extraction, exploitation, and perennial excess, and they ultimately could not wield their own sexuality as a robust emancipatory weapon. Even as they used their sexuality and their artistry to make money, travel, and, as the story of Pavalabai demonstrates, contest brahmani patriarchy, they appeared complicit in their exploitation, and their untethered sexuality as Tamasha women made them available to touchable men and converted them into profit centers.

To commemorate her artistry, Pavalabai's grandnephew, Changdeo Bhalerao and his sons Nitinchandra and Abhijit sought support from the Ministry of Culture, Maharashtra, to start the organization Kala Samaradni Pavala Kalamanch (Art Empress Pavala's Art Association) on January 28, 1993, to celebrate popular art and artists and to encourage students to train in the arts. They have also worked with the Ministry of Education to provide opportunities for students to gain extra credit in the realm of art as they would in sports.[121] They wanted students to reap the rewards of their artistry, talents, and skills.

The history and memory of Pavalabai are fraught: the fragmented archive illuminates the caste and gender war between Dalit and touchable actors and authors. While Pavalabai's family and some scholars from Dalit backgrounds have celebrated her agency, artistic skills, and achievements, elite touchable men attended to Pavalabai's desperation, recklessness, and hopelessness characterized by choosing her lovers or moving unhindered between them. While Lahuji paints the subjectivity and agency of Pavalabai as a strong and brave head of household, Jintikar and Dange objectify her and denigrate her as a prize item. Jintikar and Dange credited Pavalabai with nothing. They condemned her in advance for wrongdoing. These are touchables' narrow judgments of Dalit women. I showed how these contradictory and contested narratives and views bear on each other to reconstruct Pavalabai's life-world.

Part II

Chapter 3

AMBEDKAR, MANUSKI, AND RECONSTRUCTING
DALIT LIFE-WORLDS, 1920–1956

Ours is a fight for *manuski* [human dignity].
–Dr. Bhimrao Ramji Ambedkar (1891–1956)[1]

After two decades of continuous struggle for the political, social, and cultural liberation of the Untouchables, Ambedkar launched a historic debate in Indian society on October 13, 1935. Speaking to an audience of more than ten thousand people at the Depressed Classes Conference in Yeola (Maharashtra), the formidable intellectual, anticaste activist, and leader of modern India thundered: "I am born a Hindu, but I will not die a Hindu, for this is in my power."[2] For Ambedkar, the only rational strategy to escape from the historical hurt and humiliation of caste slavery was *dharmantar*, religious conversion and apostasy from Hinduism, and he exhorted his followers to do the same. Ambedkar forcefully declared: "[Hindu] *dharma* [religion] that does not treat humans with *manuski* [human dignity], how [can we] call it dharma?"[3] Liberation for Untouchables could be found only through a new project: rejecting brahmani Hinduism and annihilating caste in an effort to create a new Dalit political *samaj* (community), to establish an equal, just, and inclusive society, and to build manuski among Dalits and new futures for them.

Manuski as praxis was most essential to Dalit women, especially those women stigmatized as immoral—Tamasha women, Muralis, and prostitutes— who were doubly excluded from the statuses of woman and *manus* (human). Although Ambedkar watched Tamasha, he was also deeply troubled by its exploitation and sexual violence, which institutionalized caste slavery and reproduced the sex-gender-caste complex and lowness of Untouchables. Ambedkar recognized that brahmans viewed Shudras and Ati-Shudras only as dispensable and inferior workers, and the term itself indicated lowness and powerlessness and invited opprobrium[4] and referring to all Shudras and Untouchables as Chandals (bastards and sons of prostitutes). Ambedkar worried that Tamasha and Murali women such as Pavalabai (chapter 2) were defined in terms of their sexual servitude, succumbing and performatively confirming the *ashlil* (vulgar) that stuck to them through their *sringarik* (erotic) stage performances. As a Dalit man, he understood how the larger society of dominant touchables exploited them socially and sexually and associated Tamasha women with sex and sex work, prostitution; thus, Ambedkar's thinking about the prostitute in articulating a radical Dalit politics also applied to other women stigmatized as immoral—including Tamasha women. Tamasha women suffered from caste slavery, social exclusion, discrimination, and the stickiness of the ashlil differently than respectable Dalit women. Not only were they denied manuski, the dignity of being manus, by brahmani society, but even the Dalit samaj regarded them as contemptible, unseeable, and unapproachable. The status of Tamasha women, Muralis, and prostitutes as ashlil threatened to undermine Ambedkar's collective radical politics of manuski for Dalits, and he put forward a vision of a new Dalit woman who was an agent of social transformation capable of, and burdened with, generating manuski for the Dalit samaj and reconstructing Dalit life-worlds.

This chapter focuses on the inextricable connections between the larger Dalit question and the Dalit woman question, especially as it was articulated through the figure of the prostitute, who stood in for, among others, Tamasha women. Along with other disputes between Dalits and touchables over the right to public spaces such as schools, temples, and water tanks, the Dalit woman's body became a site of violent assertion of touchable men's sexual privilege. In this manner, social and sexual reproduction coincided, and Tamasha women, like Devadasis, Jogatis, and Jogtinis, became the most vulnerable. Dalit women's different life experiences require us to deal with differences in the caste question, the woman question, and feminisms.

Seven months after his comments at the Depressed Classes Conference, Ambedkar affirmed his decision to follow the path of dharmantar (conversion) at the Mumbai Mahar Parishad (conference), May 30–June 1, 1936. Two weeks later, a collective of Murali, Vaghe, Potraj, and Jogtini women and men of the "red-light" district of Kamathipura, Mumbai, organized a meeting at Damodar Hall, Parel-Mumbai, on June 16, 1936, to engage with the larger politics of Ambedkar's new direction, and they invited Ambedkar as their chief guest. This collective was largely made up of women who, much like Pavalabai and other Tamasha women—were "dedicated," or ritually given to deities in fulfillment of vows, and thus obligated to provide sexual services to men of all castes.[5] Ambedkar was troubled by ritual commitment of the sort, like playful Tamasha women such as Pavalabai, whose art and bodies were appropriated for the pleasures of touchable men, where Muralis and other dedicated women served the predatory sexual desires of privileged touchables and further entrenched caste patriarchy intrinsic to Hinduism. Poor Dalit women who worked in public were already marked for their unruly behavior and supposed sexual excess; dedicated women were thus doubly stigmatized on account of both their (Untouchable) caste and their non-conjugal sexuality. The Dalit newspaper *Janata* referred to them as *batalelya baya*, which literally translates to "stigmatized women" but was used to mean "common prostitutes,"[6] women of no significance to respectable society. In presiding over the meeting, Ambedkar emphasized the significance of the women's meeting:

> Today's meeting is more significant than the just concluded Mahar Parishad. Your part of the samaj is considered the most inferior or *takavu* [trashy]. Under the protection of religion, you women are earning your lives in immoral ways. Your *svabhiman* [self-respect] has died away because you are selling your bodies to earn your living. That such a class is curious to know what is happening in the larger world and shows readiness to improve your character is certainly to be applauded. I am more impressed by your actions. Your assembly of 400–500 here is more important to me than the Mahar Parishad of 25,000 people. Hence, I thank you.[7]

Why would Ambedkar invest this smaller gathering of prostitutes with such seemingly disproportionate significance? An answer lies in Ambedkar's articulation of the relationship between manuski, dharmantar, and samaj—three interdependent political strategies that had come to form the core of Ambedkar's multilayered anticaste liberation agenda. From the 1920s, Ambedkar deployed the concept of manuski to frame the Dalit movement as not simply demanding political, economic, and social rights but also as an almost existential struggle for the recognition of Dalit personhood and humanity. Manuski was important conceptually to mobilizing Dalits to move away from the ashlil, to become manus, and to gain assli status as good *pandharpesha* (white-collar, powerful elites) citizens. As Ambedkar's thinking evolved, he came to believe that manuski could be obtained only through dharmantar—constituting for him a kind of epistemically revolutionary moment when he acknowledged the impossibility of any reform of Hinduism. But for Ambedkar, dharmantar was not a matter of individual morality but of mass, collective politics—a widespread mobilization to form a new Dalit samaj. Dharmantar could create a "collective effervescence"[8] stimulated by Dalits and would promote community life. It was essential to end Dalits' social isolation and energize their sense of belonging to samaj. This agenda would allow Dalits to step out of the darkness of prehistory into the light of civilization and history. Within this framework, stigmatized women—the Mahar prostitute as well as other Dalit women associated with sexual availability, including Tamasha women and Muralis—represented for Ambedkar a contradiction and an embarrassment. By focusing on the trajectory of his thinking on and strategic positioning of "the prostitute,"—and, by extension, Tamasha women—and revealing the contradictions therein, this chapter explores how Ambedkar sought to construct collective Dalit agency. He situated the conceptual capaciousness of manuski within the awkward contingencies and complex conjuncture of heterogeneous socioeconomic, sexual, and material forces of the period.[9] These included debates about Hari Singh Gour's Age of Consent bill in the mid-1920s, the publication of and debates about *Mother India* in the late 1920s, the Sarda Act of 1929, the Kalaram Temple satyagraha in March 1930, the Temple Entry bill of 1933, the League of Nations inquiry into the condition of prostitutes in the 1930s, and Gandhi's Harijan Sevak Sangh of the 1930s.

Feminists studying prostitutes' lives have yet to recognize how the social organization of sexuality in South Asia informed Devadasi devotion, which then led to prostitution as well as Ambedkar's Dalit politics. Also, the contemporary reformist discourse to end the Devadasi practice by Muthulakshmi Reddy addressed only elite class Devadasis who traditionally enjoyed royal and feudal landlord patronage. Unlike conventional feminist readings of the prostitute,[10] Ambedkar centered sexual inequality and endogamy as the mechanism of caste—the *sex-gender-caste complex*, as I call it. To him, the issue of touchable men's erotic, sensual, and sexual claims to Dalit women's bodies constituted a systematic rape. These entitlements and acts based on them did not threaten, as did intercaste marriage, the caste status of touchables but, rather, reproduced caste hierarchies.

To date, scholars have paid little attention to this sexual-caste economy or the complex matrix of tenuous historical contexts, political pressures, decisions, and emotional human interiority that inhered in the conjuncture of debates about Dalits and women in the early twentieth century. Ambedkar excavated this economy and deployed it in elaborating a Dalit politics aimed at the recuperation of manuski for stigmatized women, who symbolically and materially embodied the most egregious violence Dalits suffered under agrarian caste servitude. Dalits were fighting to carve out their svabhiman and assert their common humanity and in doing so placed the onus of community honor on women through acts of social and sexual self-discipline. There were no clear-cut answers to the predicaments that emerged in this complex matrix (nor a clear resolution to the tension in Ambedkar's thinking about the prostitute); as Dalits resisted and rebelled, they also consented, appropriated, negotiated, and made difficult choices under constrained circumstances.

In this chapter, I recognize the very real, deleterious, and limiting effects of the discourse about supposedly ashlil Dalit women as well as both the possibilities Dalit women crafted for themselves in their performances of Dalitness and how that discourse was mobilized by Ambedkar and Ambedkarite Jalsakars (chapter 4) as a political strategy in pursuit of manus and manuski for Dalits and the Dalit samaj in the interwar period. Ambedkar's construction of Dalits as a collective community was a political achievement born of the national and international focus on the woman question and national caste politics.

Historically, such stigmatized women as Tamasha women, Muralis, and prostitutes were corporeally violated by the sexual-caste economy, which denied them claims to personhood, protection, privacy, property, and prosperity. Equally, for Ambedkar, they were worthy of blame and in need of cleansing. In tension with much of his thinking on gender, Ambedkar invested the prostitute (and other stigmatized women) with a heavy burden, simultaneously holding her morally responsible for both the liberation of all Dalit women as well as for the social status of the emergent Dalit samaj. She signified the hurt and humiliation of the Untouchables' past, Ambedkar argued, because caste was in and of itself a form of systematic sexual violence through the mechanism of endogamy. *"The problem of Caste,"* Ambedkar wrote, *"ultimately resolves itself into one of repairing the disparity between the marriageable units of the two sexes within it."*[11] As such, the prostitute, like the widow, was a *surplus woman*; she was a consequence, a symptom, of caste who, because of her very excess, was significant to its operation. It was this paradoxical position of prostitutes within the Dalit samaj that constituted a doubled "inclusive exclusion"[12]: she occupied a fraught position within the samaj, which was in turn subsumed within Hinduism and the Indian nation.

Although Ambedkar was deeply radical in provoking and seeking the transformation of the Untouchables into moral and fearless citizens of modern India, his thinking about women stigmatized as immoral—Muralis, Tamasha women, and prostitutes—was at times far from radical; to him, they represented an impediment in the march toward an egalitarian modernity, a predicament for his liberatory praxis and its concept of Dalit manuski. The articulation of gender developed by Ambedkar over his corpus of writings and speeches—that is, his critique of caste patriarchy—intended to make possible the liberation of Untouchables from caste oppression; yet this very articulation, I argue, was a kind of conceptual trap that prevented him from imagining those women as having any place within this liberation without their complete moral transfiguration. This conceptual trap is precisely what makes Ambedkar's relationship to the question of feminism so difficult to parse. The concerns of achieving manuski for the samaj in the 1930s curbed the radicality of some of his early insights into the intersections of caste, gender, and sexuality. Yet, I argue that it is difficult to dismiss him as a Dalit patriarch, simply mirroring touchable attitudes and moralities. Instead, we need to understand Ambedkar's stance toward women stigmatized as immoral through his own vision of manuski and dharmantar and the national and international interwar forces that provide the context for the reconstitution of Dalit politics and feminism.

In the context of overlapping and contested patriarchies, social movements and new ideologies constructed new ideals of womanhood. In the process, actors drew new boundaries, which gave rise to tensions. By engaging Ambedkar's ideas of dharmantar, manuski, and samaj and his mobilization of the figure of the prostitute as an example of women stigmatized as immoral, I elaborate the possibilities for a Dalit feminist politics in colonial times. My focus is on both Ambedkar's critical analysis of intercaste differentiation as well as his understanding of how caste instituted and intensified Mahar intracaste divisions between virtuous and vulgar Dalit women.

Unlike touchables' new ideal of female domesticity in the form of *grihalakshmi* (goddess of the home), Ambedkar's ideal was the *kashtakari-mahila* (working woman)[13] with a work ethic, engaging in hard, menial labor. Mainstream touchable reformers, including Gandhi, were little concerned with Dalit women's lives and also did not engage with prostitutes. They focused on rights and respectability for high castes and saw prostitutes as overtly sexual figures who contrasted with ideal Hindu nationalist womanhood.[14] By contrast, Ambedkar's position on the prostitute is located in his critique of caste hierarchy, untouchability, and social exclusion. Fighting sexual inequality and sexuality of religion were essential in annihilating caste slavery and for the larger project of social equality, social responsibility, and liberation of the community.

Unfortunately, the voices of the women stigmatized as immoral are not recorded in official archives. Their silence suggests difficult and painful moments, embarrassment, and shame. Certainly, indecency was to be omitted in the larger collective narrative of the nationalist movement, the Dalit movement, and concerns of history. Hence, prostitutes, Tamasha women, and the like rarely represent themselves in the official record. In tracing the trajectory of Ambedkar's thought on the figure of the prostitute, however, one can faintly discern the constrained subjectivities of these women that emerge through his hitherto under-examined speech of June 16, 1936. This chapter offers the first analysis of Ambedkar's speech to examine the interrelated social, political, cultural, economic, emotional, and moral battles of constituting Dalit humanity in a doubly colonial (British and brahmani) context.

In the first section of this chapter, I focus on Ambedkar's radical insights on what I call the sex-gender-caste complex in 1916. In the second section, I analyze Ambedkar's forging of a new, ideal, and respectable Dalit womanhood in articulating the goal of manuski for the Dalit samaj in the late 1920s. In the final section, I examine how Ambedkar's thinking about the political signifi- cance of prostitutes and other women stigmatized as immoral transformed after 1929, paying attention to the suturing together of his concepts of samaj, manuski, and dharmantar. This chronological development in Ambedkar's thought must *not* be simply considered as evolutionary. Rather, I focus on how manuski and dharmantar were mediated by the contingency and spe- cific context of the late 1920 and 1930s and tensions in Ambedkar's writing and practice. Indeed, the awkward contingencies of political mobilization and solidarities and the different imperatives and exigencies of the political moment both offered new possibilities and closed off others for both Dalit women and the larger Dalit samaj.

Sex-Gender-Caste Trouble

On May 9, 1916, in his paper "Castes in India: Their Mechanism, Genesis and Development," a twenty-five-year-old Ambedkar stated to a Columbia University audience that "when I say *Origin of Caste*, I mean *the Origin of the Mechanism for Endogamy*."[5] A "closed-door system" of marriage, rooted in numerical equality between the sexes, he argued, was the fundamental characteristic, or "essence," of caste: "Endogamy [is the] key to the mystery of the caste system. . . . It is only through the maintenance of . . . inequality between the sexes that the necessary endogamy of the group can be kept in- tact."[6] How do we understand Ambedkar's analysis of the economy of caste, with endogamy as its mechanism, in terms of his project to release Dalits and Dalit women from the oppression of caste through the construction of a new social formation (the Dalit samaj) and new terms of sexual exchange (for Dalit women)? To Ambedkar, Dalit women suffered a special burden due to the complex interaction of caste, gender, and sexuality that assigned women different sexual statuses according to their position in the caste hierarchy. The control of Indian women and their sexuality through endogamy was, for him, the very mechanism that produced rules of marriage and mating, and reproduced caste, and Dalit women, especially Muralis, Tamasha women, and prostitutes, who were seen as sexually available to all classes due to their status as surplus women, were especially crucial figures in the battle to define Dalits and the Dalit samaj in terms of either the ashlil or the manus.

In this 1916 paper, Ambedkar articulated a gendered and sexual analysis of the construction of caste through endogamy in India—what I call the sex-gender-caste complex—and analyzed the role of sexuality in safeguarding the power, pride, and privilege of the brahman man and the caste as a whole. The sex-gender-caste complex deployed women's biological sex and their social roles as wives and mothers to produce and reproduce the economy of caste. Gender affected the operations of the sexual-caste system and Dalit women suffered most due to caste violence, untouchability, and social exclusion. Women's social mobility, economic resources and sexual freedoms were seriously limited. Endogamy, Ambedkar argued, was deployed by brahmans, and as it—and the accompanying regulation of women's sexuality, social mobility, and economic resources—became more widely observed among non-brahmans. As such, the sex-gender-caste complex consolidated brahmanism by reinforcing brahman exceptionalism and brahman ideals, hierarchizing caste practices, and creating discrepancies in social and sexual labor, which became a cause of disadvantage, discrimination, and deprivation for Dalit women.

In Ambedkar's analysis, the (violent) control of and traffic in women, especially surplus women, through endogamy, was central to the foundation and maintenance of the caste system. The endogamous nature of caste enabled the regulation and control of women's sexuality, thereby preventing caste miscegenation and maintaining purity of blood. As such, women's sexual subordination was institutionalized by ancient male lawgivers and, increasingly in the late nineteenth and early twentieth centuries, the state. Brahmani patriarchy and gender codes highly valued and closely guarded the sexuality of brahman surplus women: "*Sati, enforced widowhood,* and *girl marriage* are customs that were primarily intended to solve the problem of the *surplus man* and *woman* in a caste and to maintain endogamy"[17] by preventing them from transgressing the boundaries of caste. Marriage thus emerged as a regulatory tool for entrenching social and sexual orders and maintaining the caste hierarchy.

Both the surplus woman and surplus man constituted a menace to the sexual-caste hierarchy by potentially marrying outside their caste circle and thus breaking boundaries. Brahmani patriarchy, however, distinguished between the dominant *surplus man* and the disposable *surplus woman*. The surplus man created all religious, social, and economic injunctions and, despite being a danger to the morals of the group, cunningly constituted himself as a "sturdy soul" and an asset to the caste mechanism of endogamy. While brahmani patriarchy promoted surplus men, allowing them to remarry, keeping them as *grahasta* (one who raised a family), it sought to conveniently eliminate—even through killing—the surplus woman.[18] Without a sanctioned sexual partner inside her prescribed caste, the surplus (widowed or unmarried) woman constituted a menace to the entire edifice of brahmani male power.

While caste sociality regulated the sexuality of all women, the real sexual violence of caste slavery lay in the differentiation of sexuality and ritual exploitation of Untouchable women. I am extending Ambedkar's analysis of brahman surplus women to the Mahar prostitute and other women stigmatized as immoral, including Tamasha women. I recognize that these women do not figure in Ambedkar's 1916 theoretical analysis; if, however, we extend Ambedkar's theorization, we can appreciate the specific nature of their exploitation: their physical labor was always open to appropriation *and* they were surplus women without a legal partner. The very mode of evaluation that subjected the brahman woman to an assessment of her as "surplus" was additionally weaponized against the Mahar prostitute, as well as those women—Tamasha women, Muralis—seen to be sexually available and thus associated with her. In her case, sexual labor was not restricted to marriage or caste; it was obscured and universalized. By ensuring that all people had access to her laboring body and that all men could claim her sexual body, she was rendered, through the sex-gender-caste complex, both surplus and constantly available. As such, she raised concerns and doubts about her own status inside and outside the samaj. She transgressed what was normal and deemed proper. The double work of caste games thus (1) sexually differentiated Untouchable and touchable women while making invisible the extraction of labor and (2) engendered caste violence as sexual exploitation. The Mahar prostitute's outcaste and "nonwife" status determined that she was unprotected both inside and outside the samaj. Both Untouchable caste and sexed female, the doubly stigmatized Mahar prostitute endured centuries of caste slavery, produced her lowness, and embodied the double negation of manuski.

From the middle of the nineteenth century, the conditions of work in modern colonial cities—transformed by the growth of modern technology (factories, railways, print media) and education (schools)—changed, attracting many Mahars. As such, many Muralis and Devadasis dedicated to rural gods and goddesses also migrated in search of new opportunities. While many worked as unorganized labor, some turned to prostitution for their daily survival and were exploited anew in these modern cities. A disproportionate number of prostitutes in Mumbai were Mahars; census statistics of 1921 show 2,330 "Hindu prostitutes," of which 716 were Mahars, 208 Kalavantin, and 85 Kolhati.[19] The conditions of enslavement in which most Dalits lived and worked were harsh and exploitative and exacerbated the cruelty against all Dalit prostitutes.

It was in that context that Ambedkar argued for the complete dismantling of caste itself: "It is our responsibility to attack the tradition of [caste] slavery. And towards this end, we should first abandon filthy customs."[20] He continued, "There is more damage in giving girls as Muralis. The tradition of dedicating young girls to Hindu deities has continued in our people in certain regions for centuries. . . . It is true that servants of the goddess are *vishvachi yoshita* [the world's whores]."[21] Here, Ambedkar lays bare the sexual politics of caste patriarchy and their effects on Muralis: deemed unmarriageable, they are categorized, through the sex-gender-caste complex, as surplus and thus in need of control so as not to upset the strictures of caste. According to Ambedkar's reasoning, as unmarriageable within her caste community, a Murali's potential for sexual transgressions of caste boundaries posed a threat to the system of caste and the hegemony of brahman patriarchy. Thus, her dedication as a Murali subordinated her sexuality to the needs of all men through sexual service and labor in order to consolidate both caste and brahmani patriarchy. Oppressive brahmani Hindu customs of dedication transformed Untouchable women into public women sexually available to touchable men. This was a sex-caste atrocity and the magnification of the mode of predatory caste violence and touchable hegemony.

Caste was not, as some touchables and scholars have argued, just about the stigma of impurity or pollution. The specific sexual economy of caste slavery was political and organized into systems of power: it rewarded and encouraged touchables, while punishing and suppressing Dalits.[22] Patriarchal caste games enabled touchables to enjoy the right to consider Dalit women as property that could be violated—a form of sexual access that provides ongoing testimony to touchable mastery and sexual morality. The lack of legal apparatus of rape entrenched this violence. Touchables naturalized the subordination of Dalits by associating them with excessive sexuality, and customary dedication practices allowed touchable men to use Dalits to prove their virility (and, in doing so, to denote Dalit men's inferiority). As such, caste led to the most intimate forms of social and sexual violence.

Along with touchables, Ambedkar also challenged Untouchables for perpetuating prostitution through dedication. Addressing the Mumbai district Conference of the Boycotted on April 11, 1925, he blamed Untouchable parents for blindly following customs and endangering the lives of their daughters:

> She is to sell her body to ensure the survival of her kith and kin! This tradition is so deeply rooted that people who adhere to it are no longer afraid of legal consequences. These people are not only the enemies of the girl's welfare, but also of the larger society. How many such cases will there be if parents decide to seek education and become aware of their real responsibility? [Instead, they] take loans to get their sons married or abandon their daughters as Muralis and do unforgivable things, like surviving on their income.[23]

Ambedkar thus attacked both the patriarchal property rules embedded in the sex-gender-caste complex that enslaved Untouchables and those Untouchables who reproduced the game and reaped its benefits by forcing girls into prostitution. To him, custom was not be be viewed lightly because the compelling force of an organized people is far greater than the compelling force of the state.

What resources did Ambedkar, a Dalit man, have to re-create manuski for prostitutes, as well as Tamasha women, and the larger Dalit samaj they would inhabit? Ambedkar tried to approach this question with logic and reason, but his previous theoretical analysis confronted messy contingencies on the ground. One resource was the figure of the prostitute herself, whom Ambedkar reconstituted through a campaign for social and sexual propriety for all Dalit women and men. He also reframed such customs and duties as dedication and vatandari as oppressive structures from which Dalits needed to liberate themselves. His robust moral, civilizational, and intimate agenda of regenerating Dalit women and men formed the core of his philosophy, based on the three principles of freedom, equality, and fraternity for the entire Dalit samaj. Constituting a sexual propriety or modern morality for all Dalits, then, was vital—in particular to build the Dalit woman's manuski and protect her inside the samaj as well as from the disdain of outsiders. Thus, the project of annihilating caste would require, for Ambedkar, nothing less than the construction of a new, ideal, respectable Dalit woman.

New Dalit Women Making Manuski and Samaj

By the 1920s, Ambedkar viewed Dalit women as makers of manuski, as agents of social transformation for the entire Dalit samaj. Time and again throughout the 1920s and 1930s, Ambedkar returned to the core ideas of manus and manuski in his multilayered liberation agenda for Dalits. When addressing the community at the famous Mahad conference of December 27, 1927, Ambedkar posed a stark choice: "Do you want *sukh* [comfort, happiness] or manuski?"[24] Similarly, in his speech to the Conference on the Protection of Self-Respect on May 26, 1929, in Chittegao-Nashik, Ambedkar radically asserted, "We need to fight intensively to reclaim our manuski," and "Unless we revolt, we will not get the rights to real manuski."[25] To the six thousand in attendance, Ambedkar continued:

> It is necessary to reenergize the movement to protect and awaken svabhiman. This will illuminate the distinctions between touchables and Untouchables and establish an opportunity to create equality. It is only because Untouchables are born to a low caste that, even if they possess innate superior qualities compared to touchables, they are helpless. The circumstances created by touchables are antithetical to our efforts to recuperate svabhiman and manuski. Untouchables are not allowed to enter temples, use water tanks, wells, and they are subjugated.

Ambedkar reminded Untouchables of their discrimination, stigmatization, and exploitation and argued, "In order to liberate themselves from such oppression, Untouchables should awaken their svabhiman and launch *halla* [an aggressive attack] for manuski rights." He was certain that education on its own would not provide manuski; as a result, direct action and attack was required to fight the blot of inferiority.

In March 1936, echoing these terms, Ambedkar asked Untouchable women and men in Mumbai, "Do you want to remain *gulam* [slaves] or live as *svantantra manus* [free universal human beings]?"[26] Associated with honor, decency, and improvement, manuski was central to his project of cultivating a new Dalit samaj, asserting civility and securing legitimacy for Untouchables at the level of both the individual and the samaj.[27]

To a vast number of Untouchables, the denial of manuski was a function of the brutalizing history of caste violence, changing modes of sociality, the oppression of women, and the sexual politics of caste, and it could be realized only through a larger ethical, emancipatory struggle that was both anticaste and assertive against Hinduism. In order to create a new Dalit sense of self-in-community, Ambedkar deployed a multipronged regenerative agenda— political, social, educational, legal, and cultural—aimed at both the external and internal transformation of Dalits. At the core of this agenda for Dalit reconstruction was the modern politics of manuski, that is, for Dalits to be regarded as dignified humans on their own terms within their own samaj and by the larger society as a whole. Even the smallest characterizations of Dalits as ashlil, animalistic, or nonhuman disrupted their march to manuski and modernity. Ambedkar and his followers and associates, aiming to destroy the characterization of Dalits as ashlil, thus sought to counter caste aspersions of Dalit male effeminacy, abolish the exploitative social labor under the practice of vatandari, cultivate a new Dalit body politics, and, as I will discuss in the last part of the chapter, eliminate any ashlil elements, including prostitution. Possessing self-respect, dignity, and decency were important to the new Dalit pride and power and necessary to Ambedkar's call to Dalits to challenge touchables and fight for equal human rights.

On April 5, 1946, on behalf of the All India Dalit Federation (AIDF), Ambedkar would present to the British the Dalit *khalita* (petition) in figure 3.1, which focused on the all-round development of Dalits. V. N. Shivraj was the president; P. N. Rajbhoj, a Chambhar from Ghorpade Peth, Pune, was the general secretary of the AIDF; Dadasaheb Gaikwad represented Mumbai province; and Shantabai Dani represented women. On the eve of independence, on April 4, 1946, at

FIGURE 3.1. Dalitancha Khalita (petition by Dalits).
Source: Ambedkar Collection, University of Mumbai.

a meeting of the AIDF in Delhi, Ambedkar advised AIDF members to remain united and organize on deeper levels especially through villages. He argued, "In this emergent situation, Untouchables should remain alert regarding their future and work on the success of AIDF. AIDF at provincial and district levels should spread the message and work in a disciplined manner." Members of AIDF entrusted full rights with Ambedkar to negotiate with the British as well as future politics for Dalits in independent India.

Manuski as Praxis

In English, the Marathi term *manus* translates literally as "person" or "human"—woman or man. *Manuski*, which I translate as "human dignity," summarizes a constellation of vernacular Marathi concepts—*nitimatta/*

naitikta (morals/ethics), *svabhiman, svavalamban* (self-reliance), *shila* (good character or disposition), *ijjat* (honor, dignity, respect), *mansikta* (abilities of the mind), *susanskrut vyakti* (cultured personhood), *sudharana* (improvement), and *abru* (honor)—that were important to build a dignified humanity for Dalits. These concepts were central to how Ambedkar reimagined both the new Dalit samaj as well as its individual members, especially the new Dalit woman, as beacons of a caring humanity.[28] Through the epistemic eruptions of these vernacular concepts, Ambedkar transformed the normative category of human from within a subordinated, anticaste, and assertive Dalit politics. Scholars have yet to appreciate this transformative potential of Dalit political thought that gave them a manus status in the world—which they had never enjoyed before. Thus, although he borrowed from liberal humanism, he did not—indeed, could not—merely extend the rationality of liberal humanism to Dalits; rather, he offered an alternative, radical vision of humanism, one that defined humanity from a subaltern position of suffering and in vernacular terms. Although Dalits used these vernacular concepts to connect with a universal, global humanity, Dalit humanism and anticaste writing, as Subramanian Shankar has argued, express a fundamentally different "temper," one that evokes a sense of struggle and combativeness that is absent in liberal cosmopolitan humanism.

Ambedkar elaborated that Untouchables lacked social liberty and freedom of mind to become fully manus. To him, a free manus was "with consciousness awake, realizing his rights, responsibilities, and duties; he who is not a slave of circumstances, and is always bent upon changing them in his [and her] favor."[29] This free manus deployed reason and was not "a slave of usage, customs, and traditions, or of the teachings because they are brought down from the ancestors."[30] Subject to a dominant touchable worldview that denied Dalits' humanity because their status as "untouchable" was constituted as a state of injury and punishment, Dalits had no choice but to struggle to win the status of manus; they could not wait to receive it. Dalit humanism, lacking the luxury of cosmopolitan humanism to assert "we are all human" and speaking from an anxiety about Dalits' *own* humanness, asserts "I too am human—just the way I am."[31] "A world of difference," Shankar writes, "exists between *we all* and *I too*";[32] it is the difference between a liberal humanism of tolerance and a radical humanism of assertion, between a generous humanism that speaks comfortably within the universal and a humanism that resists exclusion and must struggle to make a place for itself within an estranging universal. Dalit humanism worked to create more than mere civility and decency; Ambedkar encouraged Dalits to resist, to struggle, and to radically assert. Instead of depending on touchables' gradual reformism, especially Gandhi's, to change touchable hearts, Ambedkar wanted Dalits to be self-reliant, fight sexual-caste violence, and work toward their own liberation. As a result, he thundered, "We ourselves have to fight our Untouchable status."[33] He was aware of touchable prejudice and presumptions, arguing, "Even if you fight for simple manuski, touchables oppose you aggressively. Do away with your vulnerability and weaknesses."[34] In this manner, although Ambedkar drew upon the liberal tradition of humanism, he also departed from it to create a unique Dalit humanism, born from a subaltern position of suffering and infused with new, vernacular conceptualizations of humanity beyond Western and masculine dictates. Ambedkar's manuski and the critical project of Dalit studies is a reconstructive one that provides an alternative theory of manus and the sex-caste-gender complex that shapes it.

Given their special oppression, manuski was most important for stigmatized Dalit women to carve out a space in broader, modern colonial and then independent India. It would eventually end their otherness and grant them access to citizenship in modern India.[35] Dalit women deployed a robust body politics and morality of svabhiman, svavalamban, and manuski to repossess their bodies, become independent, and critically reconstruct their emotional and corporeal selves.[36] Ambedkar reinforced Dalit women's agency to fight their stigma and assert themselves through different strategies. In their struggle to achieve revolutionary modernity and to simultaneously fight against the violence of caste discrimination and untouchability, radical Dalits were (and are) also at times ambiguous about the role of women in generating manus and manuski.

Manuski, Manhood, and Masculinity
The ambiguous role of women in the radical Dalit quest for manuski resulted from the highly masculine terms of the language of politics and caste, which have unfortunately been reproduced in the historiography about Dalits. This historiog-

raphy largely fails to recognize how certain gendered political strategies, such as constructing warrior genealogies and military pasts, entering the army, and founding the Samata Sainik Dal in 1927 (Volunteers of the Army of Equality; SSD), along with attempts to eradicate supposedly ashlil women from the Dalit samaj were attempts not, first and foremost, to conform to, reproduce, or challenge colonial or brahmani gender norms but to generate a unique Dalit manus and manuski in the context of sex-gender-caste discourses about docile, dirty, delinquent, childlike, deficient, effeminate Dalit men and hypersexualized, ashlil Dalit women.

Ambedkar often intentionally invoked Dalit masculinity as a facet of manuski to challenge Dalit men *and women* to defend their rights and liberties and sustain their autonomy and independence. Building manuski was a technology of the self-in-the-community, as Dalits sought to govern themselves.[37] Upper-caste men forged their identities in response to the caste identity and classification of Dalit men. Yet more importantly, the manliness enacted by Dalits themselves reveals the creative performances of masculine identity by marginalized men that were not exclusively a reaction to dominant ideals of manhood that touchable men promoted. Establishing a distinctive masculinity in response to charges of Dalit male effeminacy was one aspect of Dalits' broader efforts to generate manuski and attain freedom from caste slavery, especially after the mid-1920s and the founding of the SSD, a youth volunteer corps for the protection of Dalits from physical intimidation and attack.

Touchables depicted Untouchables as effeminate and incapable of protecting their women, thus refocusing broader British colonial tropes about South Asian male effeminacy on Untouchable men. Both the British and touchables constructed and managed race and caste differences by reinforcing phallic masculinity. Like the British who created graded masculinity along racial lines, touchables hierarchized masculinities mirroring the caste order. Touchables debased the manhood of Untouchables while enhancing and promoting their own manliness. As a result, Untouchable men knew they had to fashion a competing vision of manhood to counter the vision of masculinity espoused by touchables. Sensing the conflation of sex, Untouchable masculinity, and political rights in the discourse of Dalit male effeminacy as a means to maintain political and social inequality, Ambedkar founded the SSD as an assertion of Dalit virility, certainly, as it offered an opportunity for Dalit men to tap into warrior genealogies and military pasts and to march in parades, carry weapons, and protect their community, especially women. In this way, there is a sense in which Dalit men participated in hegemonic masculine norms to re-dress their status—not just as men, however, but as manus. Their participation in hegemonic masculine norms was part of a strategy for generating Dalit manus in the face of the dehumanizing effects of the discourse of effeminacy; they deployed the generative power of gender to challenge the dominant brahmani social order.

Touchable men joined British men to constitute their notions of virility by emphasizing the emasculation of Untouchable men—and the hypersexu-ality of Untouchable women, which then led Dalit Jalsakars to erase the pro-miscuous sexuality of Tamasha from Jalsa. It should be no surprise, therefore, that the Dalit response entailed masculinity. However, Ambedkar invoked manhood, reason, and responsibility as aspects of svabhiman and of manus. Since Untouchables had been denied manuski, they were seen by touchables as unmanly, or *namard*, and this was the difference between them and touch-ables. The cultivation of manuski was important to protect basic civic and human rights and cultivate Untouchables' worthiness to gain citizenship, freedom, and equality. Ambedkar was aware that the sex-gender-caste com-plex treated Untouchables as less than human, disqualifying Untouchable men as effeminate, just as it asserted the sexual availability of Untouchable women and disqualified them on that basis. The problem Ambedkar faced was not of responding to characterizations of Dalit men as effeminate and Dalit women as ashlil, but of the tenuous process of generating and maintain-ing manuski, carving out a positive manus, rising in the eyes of upper castes, becoming "civilized" and "cultured," and adopting certain respectable moral standards in order to be accepted by the larger Indian society. And even as some responses, such as the founding of the SSD, entailed the performance of hegemonic masculine norms, the sex-gender-caste complex unequally burdened Dalit women with accusations of "immorality" and "vulgarity," and thus burdened the new Dalit woman with the pressures and consequences of the reform of the Dalit samaj. Caste assumptions that led to hierarchies of purity and pollution, superiority and inferiority, supremacy, deference and degradation, decency and lasciviousness, pride and disgust, highness and lowness, intellect and manual labor, full dress and tattered rags, all too human and not human, and order and danger created devastation on both sides of the caste divide and produced a less generous society and excluded Untouchables from the commonweal.

Under sexual-caste slavery, Untouchables bore the weight of what was ejected; depicted as waste, trash, and refuse and made to eat leftover grain or food, clean up the defecation and mess of others, remove dead animals, and care for the dead, Untouchables were seen as "rag-humans"[38]—degraded, damaged, ruined. As the wretched of the earth, they were constantly injured and defined by indignity and vulnerability and a mutilated humanity. Like slaves, Untouchables suffered invalidation, abrogation, and annulment of being in an ontological sense. Deprived of any authenticity, Untouchables were at once outside and within human and at the mercy of touchables. Deploying caste, touchables—that is, internal colonizers—insisted on treating Untouchables as animals, denying them recognition as co-humans, thereby transforming them into animals. There is an ambiguity for Untouchable humanity, similar to that for Black humanity—an animal possibility within man.[39] Touchables used terror, violence, and cruelty as means of control and condemned Untouchables to insignificance. This is how Untouchables were produced—ashlil, abject, exploitable, and lacking agency and manus. Ambedkar wanted to rupture and rearrange Untouchables' interiority and exteriority through the modern notions of rights, svabhiman, and manuski and assert their eruption into manus. He wanted all Dalits, women and men, to discover their existence and sense of creation in a responsible way.

Ambedkar argued that if Untouchables had to have the feelings of manus, they ought to be aware of the difficult battle they faced in overcoming touchable depictions of them as inherently effeminate and ashlil. Competing models of manhood—colonial British, touchable, higher and lower, Untouchable— and competing languages of masculinity were central to how Dalit men interpreted colonization and caste. Untouchables recognized that their manhood was measured in part against the standard default of other non-Dalit men. As a result, Ambedkar invoked the language of manhood and citizenship in his appeals and protests—manuski was at the core of *nagarikatva* (citizenship) in modern India. Dalits would have to fight a multipronged battle—social, economic, religious, political, cultural, and ideological—to gain freedom and rights. Considering these diverse responses exposes the interactions of the sex-gender-caste complex and demonstrates how Dalits were constrained by and yet subverted normative gendered discourses.

Dalits were not simply responding to dominant-caste conceptions of caste, race, and gender; rather, they were cultivating a new anticaste Dalit selfhood on their own terms, an "I too" claim in Shankar's language, insofar as it was rooted in and asserted, struggling to have recognized, certain vernacular concepts associated with manuski. They were challenging, though an anticaste politics and Dalit humanism, the caste mechanism and dominant-caste discourse of decency and creating their own interpretation of the meanings of manhood and womanhood within strategies for nationalism, citizenship rights, freedom, and communal and individual survival. Manuski was significant to carving out a new morality, respectability, civilized self-in-community, cleanliness, rationality, and a certain scientificity. Developing manuski would stimulate the psychological foundations of virtue and contribute to creating family, self-in-community, good moral character, and meaningful work for Dalit power.

Realizing individual manuski was also linked to collective samaj identity. From the 1920s, Ambedkar deployed a multipronged strategy on different fronts—social, political, ideological, educational—and scales—internal and external—to build a Dalit samaj and Dalit power on a national scale. Dalits embodied their samaj with a common essence and affinities of culture, religion, history, and tradition in order to gain a higher status within Indian society. They drew upon historical experiences of exploitation as they forged a new language of rights. Dalits also practiced what I call *samaj governmentality*,[40] a form of radical organizing bent on abandoning old forms of hierarchy and creating new bonds of attachment, commitment, and kinship hitherto denied to them by the caste mechanism. They worked on multiple fronts: the entire gamut of Dalit habits, aspirations, beliefs, ideas and subjectivities were all worked on and worked over in constructing the Dalit social and determining its boundaries. If someone became ashlil, they caused pain and shame to the community and, as a result, could be alienated and cut off from Dalit society. There were material contradictions and ideological challenges and these processes were unstable and tenuous.

What were the procedures Ambedkar adopted to cultivate a liberatory anticaste politics, inculcate Dalit humanity, and constitute the new Dalit modern manus away from the ashlil and the stereotypical depictions of British and touchables about Dalits as dirty, wild, feeble, and backward? To create manuski, Ambedkar focused on attacking caste markers, such as clothing, customs, hereditary vatandari, that stigmatized, hurt, and humiliated Dalits and building inner resources, such as svabhiman, shila, and svavalamban to create fearless Dalit citizens of modern India. Along with outer legislation, inner legislation that they would impose upon themselves would be important for Dalits. Yet, there were tensions, and Ambedkar faced serious challenges from different quarters—Untouchable and touchable. While touchables ridiculed, banned, and punished Untouchables seeking manuski and transgressing caste boundaries, not all Untouchables followed Ambedkar's agenda of breaking traditions and seeking liberation. As a result, many Untouchables, including Mahar vatandars, Tamasha women, and sanitation labor castes would make different decisions for their own purposes.

Abolishing Mahar Vatandari

Mahars' inherited *balutedari* (village servant duties) provided them with a fixed amount of rent-free land and hereditary claims to local services called *vatan*. Along with land, Mahar *vatandari* (duties of vatan) also required them to perform many duties of *Taralki* or *Yeskarki* (dragging carcasses, wearing rags, performing duties of watchmen, assisting headmen), for which they were remunerated with scraps of food or clothing. They were also required to sing and dance for touchables' entertainment. Tamasha, rooted in feudal field practices, bound precarious Tamasha women to the entertainment whims of their audience, situating them as sexual commodities available to touchable males. Although vatandari provided an important source of livelihood, it was also a source of caste stigma and reproduced Untouchables as a servile class across generations.

As hereditary property, Mahar vatans emerged as a contentious economic problem in the Dalit reform movement. Although the Dalit samaj supported Ambedkar's desire to break the connections between caste and occupation, caste and the dedication of Untouchable women, and caste and the rape of women, not many Mahars were ready to abandon an economic gift that they looked upon as *hakka* (a right), even if it stigmatized them as inferior

Untouchable servants of the government and other touchable castes such as marathas. Mahars also managed to keep the customary right of vatandari inside the family by not marrying off one daughter into another household. Yet, Mahar vatan underwent a number of changes after 1857, and there were increasing conflicts over land between Mahars and other agriculturalists.

Building on earlier efforts by D. D. Gholap, the first nominated Depressed Class member to the Legislative Council, Ambedkar was adamant about the need to abolish the exploitative social labor performed by Mahars. He argued that Mahar vatandari was stigmatized slavery that required Mahars to perform degraded labor and, in the process, victimized them. He explained:

> As vatandar workers, Mahars are servants of the government; however, the government does not compensate them with payment for their services. Their payment is in the form of *balute* [share in kind] and this is given by the touchables! The work is to be performed for the government; however, the touchables decide whether Mahars are to be remunerated or not. They exploit Mahars and do not pay remunerations unless they think that Mahars are falling in line and behaving appropriately. Thus, Mahars caught between the government and these people have become slaves of the touchables. If Mahars want to free themselves from this slavery they have to gain economic emancipation and hence they should improvise Mahar vatan.[41]

Ambedkar pointed out the discrepancy between the policy and practice of vatandari. These gaps benefited touchable intermediaries working between the colonial government and Mahars. As a result, touchables exploited Mahar vatandars by demanding the latter's services and not offering compensation in return, imprisoning them in the institution of caste.

As result, Ambedkar encouraged Mahars to fight their economic slavery and work toward social and economic liberation from caste by abandoning their vatans and the vatandari associated with them. The first step was "to completely do away with vatani *nokri* [service] and become economically independent from touchables. [However], if they cannot do so, they should at least ask for regular salary payment from the government instead of taking balute [and feeding on begged leftovers]."[42] Ambedkar asked Mahars to directly connect with the state, ask for a regular salary, and become government servants. He would work from within the state to secure protection for Untouchables. He wanted Untouchables to be viewed as working people, as laborers, not as people born servile. If vatan was made taxable, Mahars would be able to hold their property with dignity and work on it or sell it. Most importantly, "this was a historical transition as Ambedkar likened ending of vatan to emancipation of slaves in the US—[Untouchables and Slaves] were to be free, even if freedom meant uncertainty."[43]

With his agenda of abolishing vatan and vatandari, Ambedkar anticipated questions about economic difficulties from the samaj. Similar to his exhortation to the prostitutes in 1936, as I deal with later, he addressed the samaj as follows:

> When I tell Mahars to leave vatans and become free, they in turn question that what is the alternative livelihood if we leave vatans? In reality, they should not ask this question. A person does not bring the occupation of earning livelihood with him from his birth. [Only] after he is born he takes up some business/occupation according to his capacity and earns his living. Then why cannot Mahars earn their own living?[44]

To Ambedkar, many Mahar vatandars and, concomitantly, Tamasha women were complicit in their own exclusion, exploitation, and enslavement.[45] Hence, he argued with Mahars about building their independence, confidence, virtue, and svabhiman. Moreover, he wanted them to dissociate from vatandari and practices of dedication and forced prostitution, think about alternative livelihoods, and enter new occupations.

Ambedkar further compared Untouchables with pandharpesha, analyzing the precarious social and moral circumstances of Untouchables performing vatan duties:

> Your situation is *kangal* [penniless poor]. You do not have enough to eat or wear. You cannot even change your loin cloth. Opposite to this is the pandharpesha varg [class]. . . . They have tiles on their house roofs, and your house does not even have enough bamboos for support or covers. They have brass utensils and you have clay pots, this is your wretched situation. You are ruined by poverty and become dependent on others.

In this manner, Ambedkar drew attention to caste games that always already granted power, property, and privilege to touchables, and poverty, wretchedness, and vulnerability to Untouchables due to which the former considered the latter animalistic and rejected their manuski. Untouchables' wretched condition fed into their ashlil status and deprived them further of the status of manus, manuski, and required circumstances to live well and flourish.

Ambedkar analyzed the ways the caste system subjected Untouchables to inhuman treatment and servitude thus making it difficult to differentiate between them and animality. His conceptualization of manus was also relational—while touchables had the right to be fully human, Untouchables were deselected from manus. Ruling castes arrange the world according to their logic, transforming Untouchables into servile ashlil bodies. Touchables subjugated Untouchables and thrived on accumulating more and more of the human. Manuski was a liminal category that aimed to generate conscious change by exposing injustices inherent in the structure of caste. "Liminality can provide a view from which to understand the structure and ordering of the dominant worldview through which the subordinated being and the dominant referent are constituted."[46] Ambedkar's manuski give humanness and humaneness a different future by opening up new claims in the category of the human and gender and moreover points to the need to study women and gender from a broad framework of human experience. He provides an alternative genealogy of human rights and Untouchables to propel themselves to a higher level and the full height of human and create the new Dalit.

Consequently, Ambedkar once again reminded Mahars of manuski, self-determination, and anticaste liberation: "You cannot do anything with a free spirit. Even if you fight for simple manuski, touchables oppose you aggressively. [Hence] do away with your vulnerability and weak will."[47] He forcefully argued for his aim: "I want liberation in this life, and that is manuski."[48] He reminded Untouchables that "touchables and the Hindu religion have killed your spirit. You now think that you are inferior, dumb. Hindu religion treats you outcaste. If you were walking along a touchable, you give way easily. The reason is your mind is dead. Your self-respect is asleep. You don't think you are manus. And hence you are not touched by the thought that you need to rebel. Let me warn you that until you are in this structure, chained, enslaved by this religion, you

will remain inferior, poor, helpless, and vulnerable."[49] The only path to reclaiming manuski was dharmantar and exit from Hindu religion.

The exploitative and degrading caste labor of vatan that led to degradation,
stigmatization, and subjection haunted Ambedkar. Untouchables continuing
their vatandari ensured the reproduction of this Untouchable labor for a caste
economy and hindered anticaste liberation. As a result, he vehemently argued,
"Mahar means *sarkari bhikari* [beggar of the government]. Every village has
such government beggars because of the prevalence of vatans. Hence Mahars
should not insist on vatans and fight furiously."[50] Most significantly, Ambedkar as with the prostitute question connected the vatan form of stigmatized
property to the building of a human personhood as well as political ordering
of Mahars and reminded them that "ours is a fight for manuski. You have no
idea that you have become so dependent on vatan."[51] Time and again, he argued
with Mahars: "Leave your hereditary customary labor and start seeking education."[52] This was important to lay the path for a social revolution and liberation
of Untouchables from touchables. He explained to them the significance of
building manuski: "Quit ideas that are silly and deprive you of yourself."[53] Instead of spending time in scrambling over degrading "rights" to fallow lands
and related duties or in working on developing spirituality with the idol in the
temple, he wanted Untouchables to concentrate on building their manuski.

In this manner, Ambedkar centered the degraded and stigmatized Dalit
vatandar and prostitute in the fight for manuski, equality, fraternity, and freedom. He tried to carve out a respectable and moral personhood for Mahars.
He wanted them to abandon their ancestral villages and pride for these sites
where people shamed them and insulted and abused them. He also suggested
that Mahars leave the village and create their own separate neighborhoods
and that children should be raised in Mahar-dominated neighborhoods, so
that "children do not think themselves as impure and inferior from the day
they are born, and not afraid of touchability-untouchability. This would enable children to not think they are inferior to anybody."[54] Ambedkar wanted
Dalits to think about their future generations. He continued, "Just as touchables
educate their children, it is extremely important to educate our children and
enter government employment. Only if we do this, we will be able to liberate
ourselves" from the social and economic arrangements of caste slavery.[55] With

separate housing, Mahars could live freely and escape violence perpetrated by touchable goons. They could also freely take up occupations of their choice. Mahar could become Patils (headmen), grocers, tailors—occupations that they are not able to take up in villages today. Change in comportment, the construction and presentation of the body in the public sphere, was another immediate battle.

Cultivating Robust Body Politics

Cleanliness of body and clothing was important for building Dalit pride, identity, and manuski. Abandoning socially stigmatized ragged clothing and cultivating a Dalit body politics of *purna ani svaccha poshakh* (full and clean dress) was significant to the struggle for manuski. Ambedkar himself personified this most intimate war and made it a matter of routine to wear a three-piece suit. By doing this, he was expressing his community's most intimate desire of possessing the body, caring for it, and cultivating it in order to access a privilege hitherto denied to them and, indeed, to become dignified like the pandharpesha or even a European official. This was important to inculcate confidence and manuski.

Ambedkar forged an intimate body politics to remake Dalit women's emotional and corporeal selves. New respectable Dalit women repossessed their bodies and created new voices for themselves. A significant task for Ambedkar was the radical rejection of some detestable identity markers of untouchability: clothing, jewelry, naming, and housing, which were strictly policed by touchables. He underscored, "Learn to be clean and be away from all bad qualities."[56] This was a significant battle to uplift a degraded community and improve its manuski. To Ambedkar, in order to modernize, Dalits must annihilate minor caste cultural distinctions. The institution of caste commanded Dalits to appear different in order to be identified and further stigmatized. The caste mechanism, endogamy, and the need to police both unwanted sexual transgressions by Untouchable men and the sexual availability (and perceived hypersexuality) of Dalit women, especially surplus women, demanded that Dalits appear different in order to be identified and further stigmatized.

As a result, physical experiences of intentionally donning clean clothing and jewelry emerged as powerful practices of presenting Dalit women's transformed personhood, manuski, and social and moral status. By giving up caste-specific, stigmatized dressing styles and heavy jewelry, Dalit women resisted both brahmani (caste and gender codes) as well as intracaste patri-archies. By featuring themselves as paragons of *modern womanly virtue*, Dalit women politically reiterated and performed the modest, traditional, brahman normative full-sari (covering their entire legs down to their ankles) draping. Brahman sari style was central to claiming an Indian subjectivity, because despite some robust resistance, the larger society in general blithely homog-enized and fixed brahman practices as Indian culture.

On the surface, Ambedkar's encouragement of and Dalit women's sarto-rial performativity of modern womanly virtue through brahmani style might seem both like an iteration of the hegemony of brahmani culture and anti-thetical to a radical Dalit humanism that insists on Dalit humanity "as I am." However, this is not the case, because, on the one hand, it resists brahman expectations about Dalit dress and, on the other, as an assertion of "I too," it comes not out of a cosmopolitan impulse to inclusivity but a vernacular and oppositional demand for inclusion. Dalits performed higher status, individual and collective manuski and dispositions through their robust *body politics*, a form of embodied struggle that constituted a rebellion against the hierarchy of dress and comportment that produced distinctions between women of various castes. By appropriating high-caste sari draping, Dalit women were not merely sanskritizing or reinforcing touchable norms of proper femininity or sartorial morality. Rather, Dalit women were challenging the idea that touchables were the holders of values. Moreover, they were "disidentifying"; touchable-style sari draping was a political act through which they not only resisted dominant ideology but also embodied a "disempowered politics or positionality that has been rendered unthinkable by the dominant culture."[57] It was a strategy of creating self-in-community by dismantling caste ideologies and, moreover, a collective disidentification to reinforce that their bodies mattered.

Ambedkar's strategy echoed that of anti-race activist W. E. B. Du Bois for protecting Black mothers, daughters, and wives from the insults of White Americans. The protection of "our women" was important to Dalits. Virtues of a certain heterosexual sociality would be important for social reconstruction. Although this argument naturalizes the benevolent patriarchal organization of gender relations, the absence of "protection" of Untouchable women simultaneously permits privileged touchable sexual aggression alongside the caste violence and humiliation imposed upon Untouchable men. Within such a matrix, Dalit surplus women were most vulnerable because of their lack of protection in the very performance of their labor.

What could Ambedkar do? He provided an answer in his address to Dalit women at the Mahad Conference of December 25–27, 1927:

> You must realize that you possess much virtue, character, and purity like that of a brahman woman. Moreover, you have the *manodharya* [tenacity of mind], *kararipana* [resoluteness], and have the *dhamak* [power and daring], something that the brahman woman lacks. . . . So you should now pledge that you will not live in a degraded stigmatized condition henceforth.[58]

Ambedkar attacked the caste mechanism to recontextualize virtue—between the supposedly "virtuous" brahman woman and the "fallen" Untouchable woman—within the political economy of caste slavery and provoked Dalit women to recognize and combat the enormity of their degradation and violation.

In the 1920s, Ambedkar creatively forged a *new* ideal, respectable Dalit woman in colonial Western India.[59] He emphasized women's rights to live as human beings. He depicted Dalit women as agents who could challenge their humiliation, abuse, and sexual control in marriage and victimization inside the family. Ambedkar and Dalit women's political strategies then centered on the creation of Dalit womanhood, the radical remaking of the self, and the construction of subjectivity; it was not a merely a "recovery" of women, as feminist historians have argued in the context of imperial and elite women. Ambedkar put the responsibility of dismantling caste and improving the samaj on new respectable and *dhadasi* (daring) women.

Ambedkar's project of respectability was not of merely moralizing women; it was indeed a sociopolitical process of annihilating caste to secure honor. Unlike touchable women, Untouchable women were always already denied honor due to their caste status. As a result, Ambedkar constructed a "masculine Dalit womanhood."[60] In a sharp contrast with brahmani patriarchy's prescription of femininity and genteel behavior and construction of the woman as dependent and fickle, Ambedkar and other Dalit radicals emphasized Dalit women's strengths; they upheld women's equality with men and emphasized their supposedly "masculine" qualities of *nischay* (resoluteness), *dhadaadi*, and *dhamak* (daring and will power). Ambedkar wanted women and men to become more "masculine"—that is, more self-conscious and self-confident—in order to create manuski in a daring and determined manner. Much like Dalit reformers' efforts to establish new modes of male masculinity to generate manuski, Ambedkar's emphasis on a female masculinity was also aimed at generating manuski and shedding caste-assigned gender performativity. Rather than affirming a binary view of gender rooted in essentialist notions of biological sex and the sex-gender-caste complex, radical Dalit gender politics emphasized iterative gender performativities—be it of martial prowess or of dress—that promoted Dalit nitimatta/naitikta, svabhiman, svavalamban, shila, ijjat, mansikta, susanskrut vyakti, sudharana, and abru as modes of self-living, of new ways of being manus, so to speak. And in this manner of being manus, the radical Dalit politics of manuski disrupts both the sociopolitics of the sex-gender-caste complex and the mapping of gender onto biological sex. It is possible to read this as a proto-queer politics insofar as it sought to disrupt the habitual ways of being sexed male and female that were constituted by caste, even as they constituted it.

Yet, this radical Dalit politics also identified, targeted, and thus further stigmatized particular women within the community, including prostitutes, Tamasha women, and Muralis. In 1929, in tension with his earlier theoretical positions as well the practice of forging a new Dalit womanhood, Ambedkar compared Dalit women to one another, creating a moral hierarchy that threatened to withhold membership in the samaj from some Dalit women and foreshadowing his mobilization of the figure of the prostitute in the 1930s:

> Is there ever a similarity between a prostitute who lives in luxury and pomp, and a married woman who earns her living with svabhiman and hard work? Has anybody reflected on the *ghanerda prakar* [filthiness] involved in [such] luxury living? To be very direct, to live without self-respect is to be *namardpanache* [unmanly]. [Hence] keep your self-respect alive for your [own] life. Even if you face economic hardships, you should be

aware of your responsibility. You will not find sukh easily. Unless you bear laceration, you cannot attain manuski.[61]

Ambedkar characterized the luxury enjoyed by the prostitute (and by extension other women stigmatized as immoral) as resulting from a dirty and immoral gender performativity; the financial gains of prostitution were unmanly because they evidenced a lack of svabhiman and virtue. He forcefully declared that Dalits should continue to fight against the slavery of the sex-gender-caste complex and reminded all Dalits that even though caste had dehumanized Dalits and denied them manuski, "in today's new age, nobody is a slave."[62] However, in conceptualizing Dalit manus and disrupting the sociopolitics of the sex-gender-caste complex, Ambedkar constructed distinct dichotomies of moral/immoral, householder/public, working woman/idle woman, and wife/prostitute, which would inform his politics of manuski, dharmantar, and samaj—and have repercussions for views on prostitutes and Tamasha women—into the 1930s.

Dharmantar as Manuski and the Figure of the Prostitute
Throughout the 1920s, Untouchables demanded entry to such public spaces as water tanks, streets, and schools. Ambedkar experimented with direct action and other strategies and cooperated with Gandhi and other touchable reformers on such issues as temple entry, adorning the sacred thread, and intercaste dining to improve the situation of Dalits within Hindu society. By the 1930s, however, Ambedkar was increasingly doubtful that this was possible, and he grew frustrated—angry, even—with touchable reformers (especially Gandhi but also Congress nationalists), and his earlier conciliatory stance gave way to a "*chadhaiche dhoran*"[63] (aggressive policy) to create a new Dalit identity, samaj, and power.

There were several reasons for this transformation. During the Round Table Conferences of the 1930s, Gandhi declined the proposal for Untouchables to constitute a separate electorate on the pretext that they were an indivisible part of the larger monolithic Hindu community. The animosity between him and Ambedkar grew after this incident. Gandhi refused to acknowledge Ambedkar as the representative of Untouchables or mandate any rights to Untouchables because he wanted them to cooperate mutely with their touchable trustees.

Touchable reformers also were deeply uncomfortable with the very idea that Untouchables, especially Mahars, were seeking rights to enter the political public and sacred religious spaces that had hitherto been solely their domain.

In *Annihilation of Caste*, Ambedkar called for breaking—literally annihilating, reducing to nothing—past traditions and Hindu customs that enslaved Untouchables in the first place. Ambedkar's call for the annihilation of caste promised to render untouchability nonexistent. Continuing his attack on caste, Ambedkar declared in his famous speech "What Path to Freedom," delivered at the Mumbai Mahar Parishad on May 31, 1936, "Your whole future depends on dharmantar." He continued to elaborate on dharmantar as manuski and social change, saying, "The difference between an animal and a man is that the man can make progress, while the animal cannot. No progress can be made without change."[64] Caste slavery played upon the human-animal divide. As such, the Untouchable was not a man.[65] Touchables did not recognize Untouchables as human, as manus, and treated them worse than animals. Conversion was thus essential for the liberation of Untouchables from their social death.

Hindu religion precluded Untouchables from fulfilling their human capacities by refusing them equality, compassion, and freedom (both physical and spiritual). Dharmantar was necessary for Untouchables to become free. Hindu religion and its customs of vatan and dedication were a hindrance in the path of progressive Dalits. Ambedkar argued, "If there is anything that dooms the fate of Mahars it is Mahar vatan alone. And the day you will be freed of these chains of Maharki [Maharness] your path of liberation will be open to you." In order to fight the tyranny of Hindus, Untouchables would have to build wo/man power, financial and mental strength.

Disillusioned with Hinduism, with touchable reformers, and with the lack of recognition for Untouchables manus and manuski achieved by a politics of conciliation, Ambedkar encouraged Untouchables to be wary of the sociality of caste and recognize their own capacity to be agents of change. For instance, on October 9, 1932, at Belasis Road Improvement Trust chawl maidan Ambedkar declared: "Due to simple, guileless ideas, [your] already difficult life has become even more difficult and full of hurdles."[66] He continued to question touchables and Hindu religion and urged Untouchables to be watchful:

Because you wear necklace of sacred tulsi leaves on your neck, the Marvadi [money-lender] does not help you. Because you recite Ram's name your landlord does not give you discount in rent, nor does the grocer lessen prices for you. Because you are a regular Pandhari pilgrim your employer does not increase your salary. A big portion of society has been structured by such ideas, and some selfish people cunningly use their power. As a result, you should be utterly careful. If you do not use whatever political power you have gained to change your situation, there will be no end to your suffering.[67]

Ambedkar exhorted not only the larger community, but also his wife, Ramabai, to not follow Hindu religious strictures and to challenge touchable injunctions of caste discrimination against them. He tasked Dalits with recognizing their agency in achieving social transformation, to not "rely on fate, but on their own will power. Untouchables needed to be treated equally and this meant the destruction of the caste order."[68] He wanted Untouchables to "recognize the foul play of [touchables and tools of caste in suppressing them]. Abandon the thought that god has put in in a specific caste. This is god's will. Don't think about god now. Rather you need to think how others have selfishly exploited you, not because of your karma. Mahars don't have lands because others snatched them away. Untouchables don't have employment because others grabbed them. You can remedy the good and bad that happens to you."[69]

Ambedkar argued that "the nation's progress has stalled because the majority samaj was marginalized from politics." As a result, Untouchables would have to strategically plan their program of reclaiming and protecting their manuski and political power from the clutches of touchables. He was certainly not against intercaste communal meals and entry to temples, but to him, "such efforts would not grant political rights" or manuski to Untouchables.

In addition to promoting Untouchables agency in pursuit of manuski, Ambedkar promoted the collective power of the Untouchable samaj. Speaking at Balpakhadi, Gujarat, on November 19, 1932, Ambedkar argued, "We will gain political rights on the basic force of *sanghshakti* [community power]. Keep your unity, don't allow it to disperse. Do not increase caste, class, regional distinctions. Don't be waylaid by others' [touchables'] lies. United power will end our slavery."[70] Collective power and dharmantar were crucial to the idea of Dalit self-governance and self-determination, which were significant for citizenship and civil and political rights in the context of caste slavery and internal brahmani colonialism. Ambedkar urged Dalits to decolonize brahmani colonialism, create themselves as manus, and thus free themselves through their own efforts.[71]

However, some Untouchables opposed Ambedkar on manuski, dharmantar, and samaj governmentality. Ramchandra Hari Bandasode, for instance, an Untouchable and a staunch supporter of Congress, in his booklet *Ashprushyanchi Dishabhool* (Deception of the Untouchables)[72] severely criticized Ambedkar for concentrating on the *bahirmukhi* (external) aspects of the Dalit movement, instead of working on the *antarmukhi* (internal reform) of Untouchable community. Due to Ambedkar's aggressive attacks on touchables, he wrote,

> Untouchables witnessed a break in their movement, there was a corruption of principles, and it led to their weak mentality or will. Due to this bahirmukhi movement there was no development of moral enthusiasm and ethical energy in Untouchables, and hence in the first phase of the movement itself, immature and weak-willed Untouchables went cold. Some became stupid, and others started a childish, immature movement.[73]

Bandasode argued that Ambedkar's political strategies and his arrogance weakened the Dalit movement,[74] and he proposed that Untouchables "1) make their movement antarmukhi, 2) abandon the crazy thought of dharmantar, 3) and join Congress!"[75] Echoing touchable, conservative Hindus and Gandhi, he also suggested that Untouchables should wholeheartedly embrace and live within the fold of Hindu Arya(n) dharma, concluding his essay on a serious Arya(n) Hindu note:

> Once Untouchables follow [my advice], our Arya(n) dharma that illuminates the entire world with its lesson of spirituality will then become the religion of the world. Let Arya(n) dharma become the world religion! God! Let the Hindu religion expand in the whole world! May it come true! Om let it happen![76]

Despite these objections, Ambedkar's ideas gained traction among the Mahar community and formed the basis for calls to abandon the celebration of Hindu festivals. Caste associations like the Mahar Parishad of Mumbai, to whom

Ambedkar had affirmed his decision to follow the path of dharmantar in 1936, empowered the Mahar Jat-Panchayat (caste council) as well as the larger Mahar community to unite in constructing new caste cultures and the Dalit samaj by ceasing to celebrate Hindu festivals such as Ganeshotsav or Ganapati Gauri. In September 1936, the activist Subedar Vishram Gangaram Savadkar argued,

> Like in previous years, even this year we will not celebrate Gauri Ganpati festival. If anybody goes against the unanimous decision of not celebrating the festival as decided by our entire jati, then the entire Mahar community will have to think about them. Mahar panch, pudhari, and mhetre in villages and every chawl should discourage those who want to celebrate such festivals. If anybody challenges such a stance of the Mahar Parishad, they will be tried by the Jat-Panchayat and those who break rules will have to suffer strict consequences.[77]

Although there were tensions between older Mahar folks and the radical Ambedkar, on many occasions, Mahar Jat-Panchayat also endorsed Ambedkar's ideas about manuski. Eventually, the *Janata* editor declared, "If [Dalits] are to recuperate their manuski, they have to liberate themselves from [the caste] slavery [of Hinduism]."[78] Like him, Ambedkar argued, "Untouchables should separate from Hindus"[79] because "Untouchables will be considered animals as long as they live inside Hinduism [because] Hinduism is a curse to Untouchables [and] the biggest sin in the world."[80]

Ambedkar's support among Mahars is significant in the context of this study: many Mahar women—as Muralis, Tamasha women, and prostitutes— were stigmatized as immoral, and in the 1930s, the prostitute problem was closely connected with Ambedkar's broader battles to radically recuperate Dalit manuski. These included abolishing caste-specific practices such as Mahar vatandari and *khoti* (landlordism) (1930s), accessing temples (from 1927 to 1935), founding the Independent Labor Party (1938), declaring dharmantar (1935), and, as a culmination, self-publishing his undelivered revolutionary speech "Annihilation of Caste" (May 15, 1936) on the abolition of caste slavery and the destruction of the sanctity of shastras just one month before he spoke with the prostitutes at the Mahar Conference in Mumbai.

Globally, sexuality and the struggle for morality and respectability become politicized at certain historical conjunctures. To civilizing Indian reformers, the interwar period of the 1920s and 1930s was one of moral panic about prostitution, and their focus on its legal abolition emerged during a moment of historical flux for Untouchables, wherein the boundaries of public and private spheres and moral and immoral, respectable and disrespectable behaviors were radically redefined. Ambedkar's call to dharmantar was situated among a number of contingent factors: From the mid-1920s, debates over Hari Singh Gour's Age of Consent bill, Katherine Mayo's *Mother India*, and the 1929 Sarda Act foregrounded issues of sexuality and the law. The condition of prostitutes in India, as well the nature of trafficking and their rehabilitation, was also under the microscope in the 1930s as a League of Nations–commissioned survey team was active in Mumbai just prior to Ambedkar's June 1936 speech to men and women from the red-light district of Kamathipura. Further, the failure of the Kalaram Temple Satyagraha in Nashik in March 1930, as well as the conservatism of Congress's 1933 Temple Entry bill, confirmed for Ambedkar the limits of both Dalit civil disobedience and caste Hindus' sincerity about temple-entry reform. Ambedkar refused to endorse the bill on the grounds that it was not radical enough, saying that to do so would be "temporizing with evil." Finally, the success of Gandhi's Harijan Sevak Sangh (HSS), a nonprofit organization founded to eradicate Untouchability, distressed Ambedkar as he viewed it as compromising the manuski he had striven to establish for Dalits. In this context, Ambedkar's call to dharmantar exhibits an existential and political urgency, which is perhaps why he sounded so admonitory when speaking to the Murali, Vaghe, Potraj, and Jogtini who attended his speech at Kamathipura in 1936, aggressively coercing them to abandon a livelihood and the reproduction of lowness that, he contended, was rooted in caste violence and caste slavery and thus precluded manuski for the most stigmatized women. It is in this context that the June 16, 1936, conference of Mahar prostitutes must be understood.

Ambedkar's analysis of what I call the sex-gender-caste complex confronted the messy contingencies of political praxis on the ground. The timing is striking because the political conjuncture of the 1930s enveloped Ambedkar in a larger struggle of reconstructing and incorporating prostitutes—and, by extension, Tamasha women—into the new samaj, inculcating manuski and political representation, and building Dalit power. He wanted Dalits, as members of a free nation, to insist on the opportunity to work on their interiority, remake their dispositions and tastes, construct their world, and bond with global humanity to create a new future of equality, justice, and manuski. Situating Ambedkar's manuski-dharmantar-samaj triad in the context of the politics of the sex-gender-caste highlights how his thinking about manus was not simply derivative of liberal Western humanism. For him, manus was the praxis of humanness—it is not merely the biological (as suggested in colloquial Marathi), but the sociological and the performative enactment of codes of the human.[81]

Responding to Ambedkar's and Mahar Parishad's call for dharmantar, on June 16, 1936, Mumbai's dedicated women and men invited Ambedkar to preside over a meeting. *Janata* reported:

> Because these women were incapable of earning their living by moral means, they had fallen into immoral business. After the Mahad Conference [of 1927] these women started thinking about their condition and on their own initiative called for a conversation. They wanted to listen to Dr. Babasaheb's thoughts on their freedom.[82]

While the newspaper failed to record the actual voices of these women, *Janata*'s editor portrayed them as conscious of their oppressed state and eager for liberation. The editor also transformed Ambedkar into a messiah, the liberator of stigmatized women, reporting that Ambedkar motivated many women to civilize and transform themselves. Compared to men, vulgarity stuck to women who were dedicated in disproportionate numbers. The 1936 event became an occasion for action and change. As a result, some dedicated people requested that their brothers and sisters abandon dishonorable occupations. Some affirmed that they had already done so, were indeed *ghamacha paisa* (working hard deploying respectable methods to earn their livelihoods). The *Janata* happily recounted that as a result, their lives had become full of manuski, manus, and given to communitarian impulses.

Because by this time Ambedkar saw dharmantar as the only path to manuski, his response was more complex and nuanced. He thundered, "Sisters, liberate yourselves from the business-profession that blots the community."[83]

Like touchables, he considered women to be symbols of the Untouchable community, carriers of caste and culture, and a sign of civilization. Yet, he was also aware that touchables saw Dalit women as symbols of Dalitness and harassed, abused, and violated Dalit women. Unlike touchables, however, Ambedkar saw women as rights-bearing subjects and a central force in the Dalit struggle, and he provoked women to fight for equal human rights. Importantly, unlike touchable reformers and feminists who pitied, objectified, or excluded them, he addressed prostitutes as "sisters" with agency. Through these emotional claims, shaped by historical and cultural circumstances, he made the case for prostitutes' attachments and common bonds with the samaj and called on their commitment to the samaj.

Ambedkar was excited that immoral women had decided to exercise their agency and work toward constructing a moral character through dharmantar:

> Your lifestyle in your Kamathipura is *kalima* [a blot] on the community and women. Hence, you should abandon your dirty life and work towards your own uplift as well as your caste status and glory.[84]

Here, Ambedkar embraced these women as belonging to the same samaj or family, while also exercising his patriarchal authority to protect and punish them as needed. He did not fail to emphasize the dual role of the samaj: both a bounded belonging and a disciplinary institution.

Most significantly, Ambedkar warned the women to 'keep fully in mind the meaning of *our* dharmantar" (emphasis mine). For Ambedkar, dharmantar and creating a new samaj was the Dalit insurgent's goal of annihilating caste and making manuski. Dharmantar was a determined, deliberative, and rational opportunity to escape the stigmatized past and the humiliating political present. He called upon women to emerge into the light of history, remake their lives into something new and modern, and build a Dalit future.

Ambedkar challenged the inequality and exclusionary tactics of brahmani Hinduism, yet at the same time, he also drew lines between "our respectable" samaj and doubly outcaste "dishonorable" women. So, despite his hopefulness at the outset of the gathering, Ambedkar tempered optimism with a caution:

> In Mumbai today, [the] Mahar community has to walk through your Kamathipura with heads hung in shame. Every Mahar feels frustrated when

he sees the picture of how his sisters allow the rest of the samaj to ridicule and shame them. You have shown your readiness to dharmantar along
with the rest of the Mahar samaj. However, I am neither happy that your
decision will increase the number of my followers, nor am I contented that
my dharmantar decision will be supported more because of you.[85]

The institution of caste had already stigmatized Untouchables, and with the
prostitute it appeared that women were a stigma or a blot on the community.
Moving away from his earlier sex-gender-caste analysis, Ambedkar sharpened
his moral stance on noble and virtuous women. He blamed the women and
held them responsible for their *dhanda* (profession/business). The prostitute
as a surplus woman was disrupting the Mahar samaj. As a result, she was significant and yet of no significance to dharmantar or the decent samaj that he
tried to build. Generating moral manuski for the samaj would require her to
first abandon her dhanda, like vatan for Mahar vatandars.

Prostitutes thus emerged within Ambedkar's schema as interior frontiers
and dangerous classes of women against which the respectable Dalit samaj
must be defended. He continued,

> *We* are converting to get out of these *durgandhiche* [literally, bad smell-
> ing; here, offensive] circumstances. *We* are ready to convert because *we* all
> think and want to work towards the ideals of equality, fraternity, and self-
> respect, and incorporate them in *our* lives, for a better lifestyle. If *you* want
> to join *us*, that is, join with *your* caste-community, then you must abandon
> your dirty attitude, durgandhit lifestyle. Only if *you* are ready to follow this
> you can come with *us*. Or else *you* need not join *us*. *Just stay where you are.*
> You can convert to Islam or Christianity. *We* have no problem with that;
> however, if *you* want to join *us*, *you* must *shuddha* [purify] your body, lan-
> guage, and mind and only after *you* have cleansed yourself *you* can come
> along with *us*.[86]

While Ambedkar insisted on equality, fraternity, and svabhiman, he also created internal differentiations between moral and immoral, respectful and
disrespectful, and us and them within the Mahar community. Dedication was
sanctioned by the Hindu religion, so to liberate themselves, women would
have to first abandon it and thus end their exploitation, stigmatization, and

discrimination. Ambedkar supported women's conversion to Islam and Christianity and argued for renouncing Hinduism. Unlike other Dalits or touchables, including Gandhi, Ambedkar was not concerned about Dalits' conversion to non-Hindu religions and increasing the latter's numbers.

Ambedkar's also deployed the metaphor of dirt and pollution, conforming to the discourse that touchables employed to depict Dalits as a whole. Yet, Ambedkar employed and appropriated this discourse for different outcomes; in his strategy, the notion of "shuddha" was not directed at anxieties over miscegenation but was a basis of resistance to combat the centuries of caste violence and graded sexuality. For Ambedkar, a moral mind and body and powerful will were fundamental to achieving Dalit power and freedom.

Troublingly, however, Ambedkar asserted that, if needed, he would use force and violence to eliminate prostitutes and protect the samaj. He issued a strict warning to prostitutes: "If you continue your living like this, . . . being a *batta* on the Mahar community, I am warning you that I will prepare thousands of young volunteers and *uthav karin* [uproot] you from Kamathipura."[87] In order to liberate the prostitutes from caste slavery, he would not hesitate to use righteous force to compel them to not merely reform (as in the case of touchables) but reconstruct themselves entirely. This was a necessity; this was a liberatory violence to disrupt the sexual-caste order of things and open up new possibilities for women to reinvent themselves and develop a new interiority—self-directed and self-produced—to replace the one imposed upon them. And while it is important to recognize Ambedkar's liberatory intent, it is equally important to also recognize that he reserved violence as a means to realize liberation for prostitutes alone.

By the mid-1930s Ambedkar grew angry and aggressive and was desperate to stop the extreme abjection of prostitutes, and he deployed rhetoric as a positive force for valuable outcomes of protecting the life and liberty of prostitutes. He chose between different priorities and underlined self-determination, respectability, political identity, and rights of Dalits and the tragedy of Dalit female body. Such a critical and agonistic relation to social order would energize Dalits' "sense of kinship, which was based on shared principles and moral measures made for a feeling of 'sympathetic resentment'—a compound of tender emotion and anger."[88]

Ambedkar also anticipated the question of economic exigencies, as in the case of vatan. Although he advocated for svavalamban for Dalit women, in the case of the prostitutes, he also aligned her self-reliance with vice; independence and self-preservation rooted in stigmatized living under conditions of slavery was neither empowering nor did it grant moral value. Ambedkar clarified:

> You may raise a question: this dhanda is our means of livelihood. Not only this, but due to this dhanda, we are not dependent on anything; our life is happy. We also have the luxury of maintaining servants. What can we do after giving up such luxuries and pomp? When I tell you that you should leave this shameful life, at the same time, I underscore that I am not responsible for providing you alternative means of living.[89]

Although financial constraints along with caste slavery forced the women into prostitution, Ambedkar would not pay attention to their everyday survival because he focused on long-term benefits. His strategy was in line with his efforts since the 1920s for the abolition of stigmatized property and labor of Mahar vatan. Discussing the declaration of dharmantar at the Mumbai Mahar Conference on May 31, 1936, he clarified doubts among Mahars over vatan and political rights. He first assured them that vatan would not be endangered due to dharmantar. Second, dharmantar would also not harm political rights, but he cautioned, "No one should think only of the present. To forget what is eternally beneficial, and to be lured by temporary gains, is bound to lead to suffering. Under these circumstances, one must think what is permanently beneficial. Nobody should hesitate, even if political rights are required to be sacrificed for this purpose."[90] Thus, to Ambedkar, economic imperatives should not interfere with dharmantar, and most importantly, dharmantar was a means to strengthen political safeguards, as well as manuski.

Ambedkar was remaking his samaj from one that was produced by the hierarchical and unjust caste system to a community that was *not derived from caste*—that is, an ethnicized community.[91] In this samaj, all cultural traits had to be first cut off from caste—Dalits could not adhere to caste-specific symbols and practices. Ambedkar urged Untouchables to stop consuming carrion and alcohol and to give up caste-specific dress and duties. Consequently, women who were engaged in stigmatized work needed to be separated from their work and livelihood. Ambedkar asserted, "Mahars should not insist on vatans and [instead] fight furiously."[92] Paradoxically, vatan duties like dhanda of prostitution, though an important source of livelihood, wealth, and value, were also a source of stigma and hence Ambedkar sought to abolish them. This created contentious economic problems because not all Mahars were willing to abandon stigmatized labor and property. These were tenuous processes, and contestations emerged. Nevertheless, the Mahar vatan was finally eliminated in 1959. Although vatandars could abandon or keep vatans at their own will, such a recourse was not available to the prostitute.

The making of Dalit manuski historically required the complete annihilation of all that had to do with caste; it was not possible to speak of morality otherwise. The legal restraint was not adequate for his purpose. This morality, however, was constitutively gendered. In the interests of Dalits' impending manuski, the new self-in-community Ambedkar wished to forge, an ontological revolution was necessary and dharmantar was the first step. Self-in-community-making conceived of in this sense—expansive, foundational, and historically unprecedented—was a significant achievement. Dalit politics offers a new moral language of redemption through a restraint on excess and through respectable social existence.

In 1936, the respectable housewife once again emerged for Ambedkar as the anchor of the Dalit family. He continued to advise prostitutes:

> You need to understand that the woman caste is the jewel of the community. Every samaj values the character of women. Every man makes efforts that the woman who will be his wife is from *uttam kul* [the best race/family]. He does so because he knows that the prosperity of his children and family depend on her morality. Such is the venerability of women.[93]

Ambedkar's authoritative tone ascribed women, like touchables, as decorative; good and pure women were also deemed to be the center of the family cell and burdened with duties and responsibilities. In contrast with savarnas, his critique depicted family as a site of resistance and solidarity. Unlike savarnas, however, Ambedkar deployed the discourse of human rights, the politics of belonging, and notions of Mahar pride to challenge prostitutes to think both individually and collectively. Yet, such affinity making and Mahar samaj-building strategies alienated other Dalit communities, such as Mangs and Chambhars.

Ambedkar deployed a productive alliance of marriage, sexuality, samaj, and family to make the manuski and mansikta of Dalits. This went beyond the question of dedication and patronage relations to define the "proper" form of the family and its foundational relationship with the "good" society he envisioned. Reform of the Murali was only one part of a broader program of sexual propriety, including monogamy, property rights for women, and so on. Ambedkar critically intervened in the Murali question, tying it to the crisis of "family." In shaping his particular vision for the family, he intimately linked it to the project of saving Dalit personhood and building a healthy community. He explained that by dedicating girls, parents

> are attacking the basic foundation of a society, which is the family institution. One wife and one husband are the most appropriate family structure. The society has constructed family as a significant institution to protect its people and for rearing [children]. The more *shuddha, satvik va abhimani dampatya* [pure, honest, proud couples] who run this institution, they will bear children who are shuddha, satvik, and abhimani. It is disrespectful for one woman to make many husbands or one man to make many wives.[94]

Thus, at times Ambedkar aligned with the modern, middle-class morality of the nineteenth- and twentieth-century Victorian-brahmani, European and touchable patriarchs who underscored heterosexual monogamous marriage as the fittest foundation for conjugality and the family structure. In this vein, the order of the family also extended to the order of the nation. Women and men who had sexual relations outside monogamous marriage and family were essentially "dangerous threats" to the samaj and larger nation. Most importantly, only "good," "pure," and "proud" couples could make honorable children in their own image. Ambedkar sometimes conformed to the dominant ideology in terms of shuddha or satvik, yet for different purposes. Due to caste slavery, Untouchables never enjoyed the warmth of family and kinship. Feminists have yet to engage with Dalits' concerns regarding family, marriage, and sexuality. Unlike touchable women for whom the home, the private domestic sphere entrenched gender inequality and domestic violence, for Dalit women, the household and family protected them from public vulnerability and touchable patriarchal violence. Family and home were sites of resistance and solidarity for Dalit women. The family and home were the significant site to context their caste-based exploitation and at the same time they could face domestic violence inside the household.

Ambedkar was also furious that Muslim men (a marginalized community) enjoyed easy access to and expressed pride in keeping Mahar women. At a conference in Kamathipura, he recounted an incident that had occurred a few years prior that had left him furious: "One Muslim present among a few said: 'Why does the Mahar think about [the] Muslim as [an] enemy? We keep two or four Maharni.'"[95] Ambedkar was shocked at the audacity of this man, irrespective of his religion. The protection of Mahar women naturalized a benevolent patriarchal organization of gender relations inside the samaj and the predatory character of men. Ambedkar exhorted his audience on the significance of their commitment to samaj:

> I did not respond to this piercing statement [of the Muslim man]. But I really felt very bad; you cannot even think about this. The only thing that really makes me furious and my anger travels from my toes to my head is about your lifestyle and living in Kamathipura. Hence, once again, I am warning you that if you want to call yourselves Mahar, then you must abandon this dirty business. I will not allow you to join us if you remain in this business. If you do not follow my advice, I will not rest until I remove you from here. I think that you have organized today's conference due to your self-initiative and enthusiasm. You are eager to improve yourselves. I hope this is soon successful.[96]

Once again, Ambedkar attributed agency to the prostitute to question her humiliation, decide her own future, and work for individual and community improvement, however limited. This was both an epistemological and political act that was denied to Untouchables by touchables.

Both the colonial government and privileged touchable women and men had always already delegitimized the bodies of Untouchable women and depicted them as invested with excess sexuality. By contrast, Ambedkar underscored women's agency to protect their own rights and reconstruct their life-worlds. To him, women's unruly sexuality was a potentially transgressive threat that could pierce and destabilize the Dalits' collective community identity because continued touchable sexual access to Untouchable women reinforced the existing logic and power of caste. Hence, he constructed an ideal Dalit working woman who was chaste, pure, and reproductive and upon whom the Dalit future depended.

Toiling, Respectful, Ideal Dalit Woman

Time and again during the mid-1930s, Ambedkar returned to the theme of toiling *ijjatdar* womanhood. He emphasized his double ideal of woman as noble worker and agent of social transformation. While speaking to prostitutes in 1936, he once again deployed the trope of the *kashtakari mahila* (the hard-working woman) of Mumbai mills and compared the "vices" and "luxuries" of prostitutes with the "virtue" and *kashta* (rigorous manual labor) of poor Dalit women:

> Today, thousands of women marry poor men, and lead their lives in utter poverty. They toil away in textile mills to earn their living. They suffer in their family life, are starving, and they also must feed their children. But they do not enter your dhanda to seek happiness. Why do they behave in such a manner? Why do they suffer? Have you thought about this? . . . Why are you scared to work hard? Why is it so difficult for you to toil away at earning your living or doing some job, like your [other respectable] sister? Why cannot you leave this lifestyle that ruins you and blots the caste?[97]

Ambedkar emphasized the hardships of the poor but proud woman mill-worker who with svabhiman labored her entire life in the factories of Mumbai and practiced legitimate sexuality within familial domains. Her hard work, sweat, starvation, suffering, and respectable poverty imbued her with the qualities of the ideal Dalit working woman: legitimacy, culture, chastity, and steadfast morality.

By contrast, the prostitute's individual success, self-advancement, and creating value for herself and her family paradoxically denigrated the status of the samaj. Her right over her body and sexuality is not merely an individual right but has to be thought through caste, as Ambedkar argued. As such, to Ambedkar, she became a labor deserter and as such her income was unearned. Unlike a woman mill-worker, she detracted from real work. Her economy of excess focused on material advancement instead of good moral character and disrupted the cultivation of self-esteem and confidence required for the samaj. He declared at a sabha in Manmad, Nashik, on January 16, 1949, "Protect your poor hut in a strong manner. It is certainly foolish to break up one's [simple] home in order to enter a palace."[98] Thus, Ambedkar attacked excess and wanted women, men, and the community as a whole to defend their family, home, and inner values. It was no good to adopt "immoral" means to live a life of luxuries because to him "our people's morality is pure/bright."[99]

Like touchable reformers, Ambedkar burdened women with normative ideas of monogamous fidelity and chastity, yet he deployed them for his own purposes of fighting everyday caste patriarchy, social exclusion, and humiliation. He departed from the touchable, middle-class construction of the beautiful, genteel, and gentle women. Nevertheless, once again, Ambedkar constructed distinct binaries between honorable and disrespectful, pure and polluted, moral and immoral, good and bad, virtue and vice, wife and prostitute, and factory worker and idle woman. There was no middle ground in these binaries.

In the context of the rising urbanization in the 1930s, Ambedkar sought to recuperate traditional tropes of virtue and hard work to create the new Dalit model of a married woman toiling away in a factory. This new woman staunchly protected her svabhiman by engaging in hard work. Unlike the immoral prostitute, she did not exchange sex for subsistence or indulge in a life of luxury. Care and respect of the body was gained through manual labor and self-protection, not by prostitution. Hence, to become this new ideal Dalit woman, prostitutes had to recuperate their svabhiman and personhood, fighting through financial hurdles and moral sanctions in the process.

In seeking to follow Ambedkar's vision, many prostitutes conceded: "We are willing to take up married life. Ambedkar then arranged the marriages of several prostitutes. Many women also converted to Buddhism and gained freedom from this cruel custom."[100] They rejected traditional practices and stayed away from prostitution despite economic hardship. They sought refuge in dharmantar, samaj, family, and marriage to gain manuski. They entered conventional, monogamous marriages to cleanse and improve themselves, gain access to a certain respectability, and become a part of a new samaj and civil society. They were not merely mimicking hegemonic normativity; instead, they were accessing, accommodating, negotiating, manipulating, challenging, and continually affirming their right to life through marriage, maternity, and family.[101] They were appropriating certain traditions, twisting them, and generating possibilities and power for themselves.

Women innovatively redeployed marriage, chastity, and motherhood to forge new meanings as wives. They were concurring with Ambedkar's dictum that character is more important than capital. Significantly, they also transformed traditional marriage into a radically political act, carving out their own morality. Certainly, marriage need not set terms for kinship and family, because kinship can be formed outside marriage bonds and women can be subordinated in marriage structures; systems of power are multiple, and women are caught up in overlapping struggles. But Ambedkar constructed a particular vision of family formation and linked it to the project of recovering manuski and building a samaj precisely because the long history of caste slavery operated by breaking up the Dalit family, community, and social networks. Ambedkar's strategy was intended to enable unprotected women to break with their stigmatized past, protest feudal caste-patriarchy-property rules, challenge caste games, and agree to conventional monogamy and marriage. Dalit women's problems were different from those of touchable women. Women deployed the generative power of sexual norms to reimagine their becoming and social belonging, to create some stability and make their lives livable. Manuski and dharmantar would allow surplus women to be included in the fold and protection of the family and samaj. It would enable them to become venerable rights-bearing citizens and grant them the security and honor always already denied to them.

Elite feminists fail to recognize Dalits' intentions of protecting Dalit women from sexual humiliation and the derision of other castes. What is filthy and enslaving to Ambedkar is a divine miracle to them. In their opinion, even the revolutionary Ambedkar focused on reinserting women into families and traditional structures of marriage and the "protective" patriarchy, thereby cementing male domination. I agree with them that within constraints, Jogatis pushed the boundaries of Hindu tradition and sexual respectability to uplift themselves. Nevertheless, theirs was not a robust sexuality. Their strategies did not offer them much in terms of an empowered self or collective community identity, the very things that Ambedkar was trying to create through the combined framework of dharmantar, manuski, and a Dalit samaj.

Many women made different and difficult choices under constraints. Many consented to and dissented with the possibilities and conditions not of their own choosing. Many did not abandon their dhanda to remake themselves. Women faced hard realities: they struggled with poverty; they negotiated and renegotiated with the dominant power of Dalit, touchable, and statist patriarchies; they slyly subverted norms; and they attempted to piece together whatever was available to them to sustain themselves and their families.[102] While many married, many others refused to be contained by the marriage plot, husbands, and children. A full acknowledgement and accounting of their struggles and predicaments requires us to move to a third position beyond the dichotomies of constraint (by force) and consent (to reason), between mechanical coercion and voluntary, free, submission.

These differences within Dalit politics illuminate the commitment, concerns, strategies, contradictions, ambiguities, and contingent outcomes in this historical conjuncture. Ambedkar continued to work on these, as well as the complicated and different positioning of women and manuski within Dalit modernity. Speaking a few years before dharmantar at the Diamond Jubilee celebrations of Chembur, Mumbai's Ashprushya Sanghatana Mandal (Untouchable Organization) on May 29, 1953, Ambedkar was happy about changes in the dress of the youth because, their *"poshakh* [dress] could be simple but proper." It seems they were ready for dharmantar—physically and psychologically. Yet there were challenges from some older women who did find relief in their old customary ways and looked upon dressing up finely as imitating touchables, especially brahmans. Yet Ambedkar continued to coax them: "Learn to live fearlessly, do not cover your faces with your *padar* [end of the sari that veils the chest and head]."[103]

Continually working on the complex negotiations of manuski, even as late as October 1956, when he converted to Buddhism, Ambedkar continued to underscore virtue and ijjat for women:

> To tell you the truth, every human being loves ijjat, not profit. Every virtuous and well-mannered woman knows the profits of adultery or loose behavior. In our Mumbai, there is a neighborhood of *vyabhichari* [adulterous] women. These women wake up at 8:00 a.m. and order breakfast at a nearby hotel: "Suleiman, get me a plate of *kheema-paoroti* [minced meat and European bread]." Suleiman brings the food along with tea, bread, and cake. However, my Untouchable sisters do not get even simple chutney-*bhakri* [traditional Maharashtrian bread]; yet they live with ijjat. They lead their lives only with good conduct. We are fighting for ijjat.[104]

Ambedkar began and ended his speech with the significance of ijjat. In his powerful agenda, the ordinary Untouchable women may be poor and starving, yet they possess the precious power and jewel of ijjat, especially important in this historic and political conjuncture.

Ijjat allowed Dalit women to face the world in a brave manner and, most importantly, with pride––an individual pride that would extend to the whole community. Nevertheless, once again, Ambedkar constructed a dichotomy between the "rich" "prostitute" and the "respectable" working woman. He drew attention to consumerism and the variety of delicacies at a restaurant—the kheema, soft European pao, and cake that prostitutes indulged in versus the dry, slightly harder than pao, homemade crusty bhakri (bread) of working women. Moreover, the very fact that the prostitute could consume meat and cake and order food from a restaurant was a sign of her privilege over the working woman, who had no such "luxury." Dalits could eat only at Muslim eateries, because they were discriminated against by Hindu restaurant owners. Like savarnas in the interwar period, Ambedkar was anxious about the prostitute's consumerism and advocated for simplicity and austerity. Yet, Ambedkar's strategy constructed in historical flux and under contingency was important to improve Dalits' image in the eyes of others; but paradoxically, such a change would not guarantee Dalits equal rights and justice. Ambedkar also added that if one was to live with ijjat, it was also important to have a "healthy body and cultured mind."[105] A healthy and cultured mind and body full of manuski would lay the foundation for a powerful Dalit personhood and power.

Conclusion

The figure of the Dalit prostitute opens an epistemic space for archaeological work on reconstructing Dalit history and humanity and the difference of caste and Dalit feminism. The Dalit prostitute was the intermediary between Dalits' civilized and uncivilized statuses and as such emerged as a predicament to Ambedkar's liberatory anticaste political praxis of samaj, dharmantar, and manuski. Sexuality is not free floating, and historical limits hedged the practice of humanity for Dalits because masculinity and humanity constituted each other. I analyzed the historical flux and decisions through which humanity and masculinity constituted each other and the difficulty of conceptualizing humanness in the context of caste violence and caste patriarchy for Dalits.

Ambedkar inaugurated a historic change by deploying sexual reconfiguration as a motor for social transformation, yet there were contradictions that constrained his agenda. Although Ambedkar exposed the tight ties between sexuality and sociality, attacked the caste mechanism, and argued for women's humanity, he also created new distinctions and boundaries thus revealing the difficulties of conceptualizing humanness under destitute conditions. He attacked the impoverished conditions of Untouchables as well as the economy of excess. He did not want Untouchables to depend on touchables. He would make do with no political rights because as it is they would cease to exist at some time, but he wanted manuski and freedom of Untouchables. In these political processes, different Dalit women gained on many fronts, as well as lost on others as they shaped the dynamics of caste, sexuality, and equality. I illuminated the sheer contingencies of the particular politics of forces and ideas involved in reconstituting Dalit power and social imaginary had often paradoxical and ambiguous implications. His speech to the prostitutes was also a public address, and therefore it has rhetorical and performative aspects just as the speech made at the conversion ceremony.

An exploration of Ambedkar's thought allows us to bring the multidimensional prostitute to the center of Indian history and, even more importantly, to

Indian nation-building. She was pivotal to reorganizing modern Indian society. Prostitution through the ritual practice of dedication was, in its very essence, an enforcement of the caste game. For Ambedkar, annihilating caste was fundamental to recuperating individual and community respect and humanity from dehumanizing social practices. He deployed gender and sexuality as intentional generative forces while expanding their terrain to reconstruct Dalit life-worlds. My focus on the precarious position of the most stigmatized Dalit woman provides new strategies for a more productive and inclusive politics for Dalit samaj. Yet, there are tensions. In post-Ambedkar times, women would have to continuously struggle with the samaj and social responsibility to carve out their self-in-community. They would under historic contingencies consistently create new samaj, fight and create new boundaries, seek individuality, and seek political intervention.

Dalit women's sentiments, attachments, and commitment emphasize that projects of Dalit feminism and articulation of gender and sexuality, as well as the Dalit revolution are never predetermined. They are to be negotiated according to historical moments, as well as caste, race, and class positions. Dalit histories underscore the mobile, contextual, and transformative potential of gender, feminism, and its intensified significance in the modern politics of manuski. Dalit politics considers how to produce a new matrix of power within the category of the human itself and deepens connections between gender and the human.

Chapter 4

SINGING RESISTANCE AND REHUMANIZING
POETICS-POLITICS, POST-1930

Our Bhim's [short for Ambedkar's first name, Bhimrao] pious deeds give us
manuski.
He showed us a new path, the whole world now wants Buddha!

My father, Deoram Fakira Paik, constantly sang and hummed these lines
celebrating the mantra of *manuski* (humanity, human dignity) bestowed by
Ambedkar on the Dalit community. When I was growing up Dalit in the city
of Pune during the 1970s and 1980s, my father sang songs that he heard during
gayan (song, music) parties. He would often take me and my sisters to these
gatherings in the evening in the open-air circular parapet in the center of Bund
Garden, near Yerawada-Pune. These contrasted with the energetic and loud
song-dance congregations of the Rajneeshees at the Osho Ashram, on the opposite side of Bund Garden, in the elite Koregaon park neighborhood, about
a quarter mile away from where I grew in Yerawada. During these evenings,
Dalits (and Bahujans) gathered together to have a good time as a *samaj* (community) and engage in a collective reflection on their conditions of possibility.
Through song and musical performances, Dalits asserted their manuski, and
the singer and listener together performatively engendered and nourished
liberatory and utopian structures of feeling.[1]

Ambedkar enjoyed *Jalsa* (song drama, poetics-politics), and on the occasion of a Jalsa by the renowned *Jalsakar* (maker of Jalsa) Bhimrao Dhondiba
Kardak (1904–1990), he declared, "The social impact of my ten conferences
and meetings is equal to one Jalsa performance by Kardak's troupe."[2] But
why would Ambedkar invest the new medium of Jalsa with such seemingly

disproportionate significance? An answer lies in the attempts by city-based Jalsakars and Ambedkar, by shahirs and the politician, to spread manuski, and forge a respectable Dalit samaj through Jalsa's *prachar karya* (promotional work) for social reconstruction. The performativity of Jalsa was significant to the iterative production of the truth of manuski for the Dalit samaj as a whole. Through the poetics-politics of Jalsa, Jalsakars performatively enacted manuski in challenging the social stigmas against and the economic exploitation of Dalits.

A significant part of the Jalsakars' task was to bridge the divide between literate and nonliterate and urban and rural Dalits in building manuski, Dalit samaj, and Dalit power. Kardak characterized the rehumanizing and samaj-building aims of this vernacular poetics-politics as a form of service:

> Hence, we decided to deploy the weapon of Jalsa. Through this we sought to disseminate the message of Dr. Ambedkar to the *adani* [ignorant, uncouth, even vulgar] mandala in their everyday *gramin* [rural] language. We have been doing this service [through Jalsa] for the last 15–20 years.[3]

Dalit youth deployed Jalsa, addressing contemporary political and social questions and moments—such as the 1930 Kalaram Temple Satyagraha in Nashik or the 1932 Thana Boarding House closure and Poona Pact clash between Ambedkar and Gandhi—in popular culture to express an all-around fight against exploitation, including peasant and working-class struggles, and reject traditional caste duties. Jalsa was an easy, available, and effective medium to connect with nonliterate Dalits and performatively recuperate everyone's manuski—that of both actor-activists and audiences.

There were tensions between Tamasha and Jalsa, and like touchables, urban, educated Dalits were anxious and ambivalent about Tamasha, which they believed confirmed the caste-prescribed ashlil nature of Dalits. Like touchables, Untouchables sought to sanitize and purify Tamasha; however, their aims and the outcomes differed. For Jalsakars the main aim of Jalsa was to undo the ashlil qualities of Tamasha and uniquely focus, like their leader Ambedkar, on resisting stigmatization and exploitation and forging their liberatory anticaste agenda of manuski and radical insurgency. Furthermore, because Kardak and his associates recognized that nonliterate rural and urban Untouchables were invested in the tradition of Tamasha, they needed to convince this audience of the merits of Ambedkarite Jalsa and reconstruction of Dalit life-worlds. The caste system deployed Tamasha to essentialize and produce the "culture and tradition" of Dalits as ashlil, thereby differentiating, dominating and legitimizing itself.[4] As a result, Jalsakar's most important challenge was to replicate certain elements of the Tamasha art form, drawing upon its rebellious and carnivalesque energy to attract nonliterate Untouchables and propel them toward a social revolution, without having the ashlil stick to the samaj.

Jalsakars experimented with, adapted, appropriated, and improvised Tamasha to create Jalsa. They negated the sensual and sexual appeal of Tamasha. Like Ambedkar (see chapter 3), they constructed a dichotomy between claiming manuski and being ashlil and believed there was no place for the latter in a civilized Dalit samaj. To them, it was necessary to break the historical association between Dalit female promiscuity and the Mahar-Mang Tamasha as well as the giving of girls to local gods and goddesses and the emerging vulnerable Dalitness. As a result, Dalit radicals, from the early decades of the twentieth century, driven by a desire to modernize the Dalit samaj, decried performance forms that they now considered "backward," and they created Ambedkarite Jalsa to accomplish the prachar karya of Dalit social regeneration. Just as touchable elites asserted their hegemony in a standardized theatrical style, Dalit Jalsakars asserted and negotiated Dalitness through a theatre of wit, satire, humor, threat, or even sedition. Moreover, they also sought to restrict the performance of Jalse to men alone. The supposedly wayward Tamasha women consistently imperiled norms of monogamy, fidelity, and moralism and trampled on manuski, and hence, even to radicals, they were to be restrained.

As a result, Jalsakars' anticaste radicalism was subject to contingency, ambiguity, and contradiction and the ungovernability and excess of Tamasha and Tamasha women. Because they focused on the poetics and political utility of Jalsa, Jalsakars rejected Tamasha as an expression of the idea of pleasure without purpose and thus a symbol of excess. Nevertheless, Ambedkarite Jalse did not actually replace Tamasha or Sangeet-bari; the three forms thrived alongside each other. As I show below, there were differences between a variety of Dalit artists, and different popular arts flourished at the same time in the middle decades of the twentieth century.

In this chapter, I examine Ambedkarite Jalsa and *shahiri* (poetry as performed by shahirs,) to illuminate their content and the tensions within the Dalit artist-activist community since the 1930s. I focus on the ideas, actions, and life histories of two renowned Ambedkarite shahirs from Mumbai—Bhimrao Dhondiba Kardak and Bhimsen Barku Gaikwad (1940s–2021)—to reconstruct the history of Jalsa as shahirs creatively and performatively practiced Dalit manuski. In some ways, Kardak and Gaikwad are representative of Ambedkarite Jalsakars and shahirs. Kardak was, indeed, talked about as the paradigmatic Ambedkarite Jalsakar. He was a founder of the most significant and effective Jalsa for the prachar karya of social regeneration: Nashik Jilha Yuvak Sangh Sangeet Jalsa (Nashik district youth musical Jalsa; NJYSSJ). See artists and founders of NJYSSJ in figures 4.1 and 4.2).

Kardak and Gaikwad represent different eras and phases of the Dalit movement as well as the poetics-politics of Dalit assertion and power. While Kardak was an Ambedkarite Jalsakar of the late colonial period, Gaikwad was a post-Ambedkar shahir. I attend to both the similarities and differences between their performances and poetics-politics, analyzing how radical Dalit shahirs produced Jalsa and were in turn shaped by its unique politics in the cosmopolitan city of Mumbai.

These strands of social transformation and revolutionary Dalit shahirs-Tamasgirs have remained invisible to mainstream historians writing in the English language. Scholars have studied popular art forms such as abhang and kirtan, reform of Devadasis in some depth, yet they have neglected Jalsa and reform among Dalit artists. Dalit shahirs appear only in thin booklets and pamphlets that have rarely made it to the official printed record or serious scholarly attention: to elite touchables Dalit shahirs were never serious poets and singers worthy of note. And few Marathi literature scholars writing

FIGURE 4.1. Artists and members of Nashik District Youth Organization Sangeet Jalsa Mandal (1930–50). Source: Kardak, *Ambedkari Jalse: Svarup va Karya* (Abhinav, 1972).

in Marathi have engaged with Jalsa performances,[5] offering little historical, social, and cultural analysis of the particular anticaste, gendered, and sexual politics of Jalsa.

The role of song, dance, drama, and poetry in the political and social life of Ambedkarites has, however, received increasing attention in such films as Anand Patwardhan's 1985 documentary *Bombay: Our City*, and more recently Chaitanya Tamhane's award-winning 2014 drama *Court*. Yet for all their subtlety and power, such tidy framings of the relationship between Dalit poets and Dalit politics left me puzzled as well, sitting uneasily alongside what my research has found to be much more tenuous, complex, contingent, and contentious articulations. I examine the shifting and uneasy alliances between poets, poetics, and politics, both inside and outside the Dalit samaj. I also examine the gendered processes through which Jalsakars and shahirs united with respectable touchables, Dalits, colonial gentlemen, and the state to discard traditional ashlil elements

FIGURE 4.2. The founders of Nashik District Youth Sangeet Jalsa. Bhimrao Kardak in the center. Source: Kardak, *Ambedkari Jalse: Svarup va Karya* (Abhinav, 1972).

of Tamasha, an art form that had acquired the taint of promiscuity and illegality. Broadly, for urban, socially mobile Dalits, there would be no latitude for misstep; they could not slip up, and hence sanitized and cultured language, food habits, dress, demeanor, and so forth were important to the generation of manuski. Ashlil stuck to Dalits, and these urban and mobile

Dalits could not afford to dismiss the politics of respectability in ways that brahmans such as Bapurao could (see chapter 2).

Jalsa and Manuski

Kardak emphasized that "Jalsa was a live history of Untouchables' fight for full humanness and human rights."[6] As an art form, Jalsa was thus performative of the radical Dalit project to invent a new sovereignty, interiority, and manuski. To regenerate and reaffirm their fully *manus* (human) identity and carve out a future of hope and self-determination during the interwar years, Ambedkar and Jalsakars shared one important aspiration: Dalit social reconstruction. Following their leader, Jalsakars combined entertainment with social regeneration, especially for rural, nonliterate Untouchables. Kardak argues, "Through the medium of Jalsa we aimed to reach the most *adani ani ashikshit* [nonliterate] and use the medium of *karamnuk* (entertainment) to make them aware of the changes in the community, real events, in a simple *gramin* [rural] language that they would understand."[7] Entertainment thus emerged as an especially palatable path for socially regenerating Dalit samaj.

From the early decades of the twentieth century, both Tamasha and Jalsa were central to the formation of a vibrant Dalit public sphere, with traveling poets and activists using poetry and music to communicate with an audience that was largely nonliterate. The performance of Ambedkarite shahiri acquired a particular political salience beginning in the 1930s, when artists began touring villages and cities to sing about social change. The newspaper *Janata* identified the sense of service and duty that informed this poetics-politics of Jalsa, emphasizing that "*Lokshikshan* [social awakening and pedagogy] was the aim, and Jalsa troupes performed their social service with a great sense of duty."[8] Like the term *Tamasha, Jalsa* also derives from the Persian language and connotes a gathering for entertainment and music. But the linking of pedagogy to entertainment through Jalsa speaks to the performative of Dalit political consciousness; the non-brahman and Dalit movements mobilized vernacular performance traditions as critical social and political pedagogy and not merely propaganda.[9] Jalsa's prachar karya was both in the service of Dalit manuski and a new performative iteration of that manuski in the public context, enacting

Dalit thought, rationality, communication, and agency, which is evident, for instance, in Kardak's farces discussed below.[10]

The tumult and upheaval of Dalit's open rebellion for rights and freedom in the political arena was coupled with radical creative acts of art and performance that gave hope and meaning to their daily struggles. Under the influence of *Bhimvara* (the winds of change inspired by Ambedkar's ideas and actions) and *Bhimvede*[11] (the passionate, even maddening pursuit of Ambedkar's agenda of revolution and freedom), rebellious young Dalit Ambedkarite shahirs and Jalsakars deployed music as a form of political and social propagation, to fight fear and humiliation and to build manuski to bring about *Dalitoddhar* (individual and collective social awakening and improvement among Dalits).[12]

Ambedkarite shahiri and Jalsa culture, inspired by Ambedkar and his philosophy, was a creative power resource[13] employing modes of humor, irony, sarcasm, satire, and parody to mock and tear down caste slavery and challenge caste violence. Jalsa deployed humor as a subversive poetics-politics to defy the norms of the social order of caste, especially for the non-elite, lowly *adani*[14] Dalits. Due to their specific focus, Jalsakars and shahirs provided simplistic and straightforward explanations of complex and complicated problems, as I illustrate through the Satyagraha and Thana Boarding farces of Kardak and the NJYSSJ below, thus making Ambedkar's critical texts and speeches—indeed, his social and political revolution—accessible and intelligible to the most ordinary Untouchable. Through Jalsa, Untouchables would come to gain, as Kardak argued, "*manuskichi janiv*" (consciousness of their humanness) and "*manuskicha hakka*" (right to be human).[15]

Ambedkarite Jalsa, and Dalit music in general, would also become "informational capital,"[16] propelling action and transformation to bring about the social and political revolution that would potentially create a society based on equality, liberty, and fraternity. As a result, both shahirs and Ambedkar underscored the significance of Jalsa vis-à-vis Tamasha, promoting, embodying, and performing the manuski of Dalits rather than confirming their status as ashlil. Ambedkar's exhortations to discard the ashlil in all forms (see chapter 3) informed his recommendations of Kardak's Jalse to others. However, because Tamasha was the most popular form of entertainment among Dalits, supplanting it with non-ashlil Jalsa was a challenge for Jalsakars.

Like Ambedkar, Dalit radicals like Kardak also asserted that mere formal education was not enough. Other forms of social regeneration, activism, and informal education were needed to fight untouchability and exploitation. Dalit youth challenged touchables as especially savarnas who advised Untouchables to "improve in the field of education [because they believed that education alone] would automatically end *shivashiv* [pollution from touch or commingling], and higher-lower [caste] issues."[17] To these touchable reformers, formal education and cleanliness were the solution to Untouchables' social problems, and by following upper-caste Hindus' advice, Untouchables could grow smarter, change traditional ways of knowing and being, and rise in the eyes of the larger Hindu community. Yet in practice, on many occasions, even Ambedkar, the most educated Dalit, was never embraced by dominant-caste Hindus. "They did not allow his shadow to fall on them,"[18] Kardak wrote, and they humiliated him, subjecting him to continuous social discrimination throughout his life: as a student, teacher, officer in the State of Baroda, lawyer in Mumbai, and so on. Even though Ambedkar, having earned several degrees, was very well educated, in the eyes of the upper castes, he belonged to an Untouchable, "*neech*" (inferior), Mahar caste and was rendered "polluted."[19]

Kardak explicated the importance of NJYSSJ Jalsa in light of Untouchables' social position as caste slaves:

> Jalsa is the story of Untouchables' struggle for manuski rights. . . . Ambedkar led Untouchables in the 1927 Mahad satyagraha, [Nashik satyagraha], the 1956 dhammadiksha, [and so on]. We founded a social Jalsa based on Ambedkar's *sandesh ni aadesh* [message and order]. . . . It was not easy to bring about a *manuskichi janiv* [consciousness of humanness] among the Untouchables, because the samaj was downtrodden due to poverty and illiteracy, bound by the shackles of tradition, economically disabled, lacking svabhiman [self-respect], and enslaved by savarna Hindus.[20]

Like Ambedkar, Kardak elaborated on the sufferings of Untouchables without manuski. Praising Ambedkar's efforts to combat caste slavery, Kardak wrote:

> Dr. Ambedkar awakened such a samaj with his "*sanjivani*" [elixir of life] mantra. With his education and knowledge, he attacked Untouchables' ignorance, gave them the lesson of svabhiman and encouraged them to

break the shackles of slavery. He gave them the injection of introspection, recognizing *aapan kon aahot* [who we are], their new selfhood/personhood, and provoked them to fight social injustice.[21]

Kardak and his Dalit associates recognized and underlined the possibilities of Jalsa for reaching a popular audience and promoting a collective samaj and collective movement in the fight for manuski.

Kardak also pointed out that along with Ambedkar, the work of his associates and Dalit youth was very significant. In order to explain the actual meaning of certain concepts and the historical moments in which they were located, Kardak and his associates deployed the weapon of Jalsa:

> When Dr. Babasaheb started his fight against untouchability, the community of many women-men attended sabhas. They listened to his speeches and sought to actuate them in practice. However, they did not understand the real meaning at times. What exactly is satyagraha? How is it performed? Similarly, what is dharmantar? And so on. . . . Further, they only heard Dr. Babasaheb's speech with great attention. They did not pay attention to other speakers. Why would they engage with speeches of Dalit youth like us?[22]

As a result, a new figure, the Ambedkarite shahir and Jalsakar, emerged on the scene in the 1930s as a "media-intellectual" to exert considerable influence over Dalit political and cultural life.

Dalit activist-writer Appasaheb Ranpise, writing on Jalsa, refers to the renowned brahman litterateur P. K. Atre, discerning the differences between poet, Lavanikar, and shahir: "While poets and Lavani performers entertain, a shahir is to *prerna* [inspire]. When people listen to a shahir, they feel like cobras or roaring tigers. . . . Kavi and Lavanikar are the associates of leisure, while a shahir is a pedagogue of the struggles in everyday life."[23] Jalsakars, like their leader Ambedkar, spoke and sang tirelessly to awaken the Dalit community from the inside in the hope of rearranging the social order and generating manuski, which was at the core of fighting caste slavery and creating the *new* Dalit political and the new Dalit samaj.

Dalit shahirs performed Jalsas at auspicious events, including weddings, naming ceremonies, and other important social and political gatherings

organized by and for the Dalit samaj. The culture of Jalsa became so significant that, as newspapers reported, every *sabha* (public meeting) and *parishad* (council) started with the performance of Jalsas. Sometimes Jalsakars
entertained throughout the night. Jalsas thrived in Bombay Development
Department chawls in Dalit-dominated neighborhoods of Shivdi, Ghatkopar,
Bhaykhala, Matunga, Sion, Varli, Naigaon, Parel, and Bombay Central, which
were major sites of Ambedkarite and Communist activism and important to
Dalit mobilization. However, the full weight of caste slavery fell on women,
and the tension between Dalit politics and performance forms was negotiated
through their marginalization.

From Sexual Tamasha to Social and Political Jalsa

Reminiscing about his 1930s and 1940s childhood, shahir Bhimsen Gaikwad
emphasized the significance of Tamasha for Dalits: "There was no main
entertainment except Tamasha. So, people enjoyed it. They did not look
down upon Tamasha. But the educated [respectable] elites have a different
standpoint."[24] To Gaikwad, there was a chasm between urban, educated, and
respectable touchables and Dalits, on the one hand, and the largely village-
based, nonliterate or literate, Untouchable masses, on the other. How can we
understand the emerging tensions and struggles between the latter's Tamasha and former's Jalsa?

   Since the middle of the nineteenth century, although brahman elites drew
upon semi-religious themes from century-old popular arts of Dashavatar,
Gondhal, Tamasha, and Lavani, the educated among them also focused on
creating supposedly high cultures of sanskritized sangeet-natak, high-class
music and singing. The intelligentsia-led theatre flourished in cities, towns,
schools, colleges, and annual social gatherings.[25] The late nineteenth century
also witnessed a larger interest in Hindustani classical music, focusing on
the prosperous city of Mumbai. The mainstream reform discourse, focusing
on touchables, was also monopolized by brahmans. As a result, to create a
rupture, they reinforced their strong prejudice against supposedly lowbrow
fare flourishing in ashlil Tamasha as well as European theatre. Yet, at the same
time, some were influenced by and engaged in reading and borrowing from
European theatre and drama. For example, leaders like Jagannath Shankarshet

(a Daivadnya sonar, goldsmith by caste) and Bhau Daji Lad encouraged Marathi theatre toward public recreation along European lines. In general, however, they expressed distaste for Tamasha and its actors, like Bapurao (chapter 2), whose loose lifestyle was certainly beyond the limits of acceptable standards of morality.[26] Yet, at the same time, touchables were engaging in a covert regime of sexuality (chapter 1 and 2).

In contrast with touchable elites, to the subordinated either based in the villages or recent migrants to cities like Mumbai and Pune, the main form of entertainment remained Tamasha. And urban Dalit youth activists, like their elite touchable counterparts, clearly understood the vast and deep outreach of theatre as a medium for spreading social and political revolution. Tamasha (as well as Sangeet bari) was popular due to its loud, sensual, and sexual entertainment. Sanskritized elite theatre seemed alien and was not so popular among the subordinated. By contrast, large audiences of Bahujan masses, as well as some savarnas, loved Tamasha's risqué lyrics and the opportunities to openly flirt with attractive women (and cross-dressed men). The jokes, satire, and humor of Tamasha were their lifeline, and they fed on the anomalous beauty and sensuality of Tamasha women like Pavalabai (chapter 2). For example, the radical Dalit Communist R. B. More (1903–1972), who was fond of dancing and singing, attended Tamasha performances and visited the socially disreputable performers in Batatyachi chawl in Mumbai. Although a fan of Tamasha, More tried to raise funds through plays and street theatre to organize the 1927 Mahad satyagraha conference. As a part of his collection drive, he visited Ambedkar's house in Parel-Mumbai chawls. Although he supported More's efforts, Ambedkar's elder brother, Balaram, told More, "Our people do not watch plays; they like to see Tamasha. So, I cannot do anything for you in this regard."[27]

Like More, Dadasaheb Namdeo Pagare, president of the NJYSSJ, was angry about the problems Dalit organizers faced in mobilizing a community steeped in popular Tamasha culture toward social transformation in the 1930s: "People gather for Tamasha in the thousands, but not for prachar sabha."[28] Similarly, at a sabha held at Teen nalachi chawl-Mumbai, one enthusiastic Dalit shahir-activist, Keshavrao Gangurde from Kurla-Mumbai, argued, "If [the Mahars] had known that there was a *ji-ji-cha* [a specific singing] Tamasha [traditional, sensual, sexual] to be performed here, they would have brought their mats and sheets to reserve a place to sit [and see the Tamasha]. Such are the people at Teen nal!"²⁹ Thus, surmounting the social and cultural context of Tamasha emerged as a challenging task for young Dalit activists focused on spreading Ambedkar's political and social message.

Kardak reasoned that transforming ashlil Tamasha into the *samajik kary-acha* (social work) of Jalsa was necessary because, "even if the language of Tamasha was ashlil, there was no restriction on women not hearing [or engaging with] it. There was no prohibition of ashlilta." To him, the deep roots of Tamasha would lead to women, the weaker and vulnerable sex, becoming wayward and ashlil. Kardak further revealed the problems and tensions as follows:

> The only means of entertainment for the poor Untouchables was Tamasha. Tamasha had comedy, advice. But the comedy in Tamasha was *ashlil ni panchat* [vulgar and vapid]. Tamasha included some instructions related to morality and everyday course of action. [Yet] Tamasha was disconnected from *sudharana* [the improvement and advancement] of Untouchables and their circumstances, or even their manuski. Because the larger community looked upon Tamasha as the only means of entertainment, many young and old women-men sang Lavanya.³⁰

To bring about sudharana, it was important to attack Tamasha as ashlil. To Ambedkar, the caste order itself was beset by a wholesale state of promiscuity. As a result, Dalit youth sought to cleanse Tamasha for the purposes of individual and collective advancement. Kardak also expressed his fear and gendered anxiety that women, the bearers of community morality, were listening to and even singing ashlil Lavanya, potentially leading to female sexual promiscuity and immorality, both in the present and the future. The emphasis on the futurity of the carnal crime of ashlil Tamasha is significant.

Dalits' problems in attracting the masses to Jalsa culminated in their appropriating the Tamasha form, sanitizing it, and refashioning it for broader social transformation. The Dalit samaj was bound by mutual cooperation and solidarity but also contained antagonisms, as members expressed competing interests and values through popular arts like Tamasha and Jalsa. Responding to the sort of sentiment expressed by Keshavrao Gangurde above, modernizing Dalit shahirs seriously adopted the mode of Tamasha, refashioning it as

Jalsa to engage the "*nadlubdha janata*" (people devoted to Tamasha entertainment).[31] Certainly, Dalit youth critiqued Tamasha to create a rupture between the latter and their socially and politically inspired Jalsa to create a confident Dalit identity.

To Jalsakars, traditional Tamasha aimed merely at *ranjan* (entertainment); however, both the form and artists of touchable but lower-caste non-brahman Satyashodhaks (Seekers of Truth) of the early 1900s and its successor, the Ambedkarite Jalsa, were shaped by creative ideas and actions of "samaj sudhar" (social improvement).[32] For example, Satyashodhak Jalsakars severely critiqued the hypocrisy of the touchable-led shuddhi (Arya Samaj purificatory) movement. Like their Satyashodhak counterparts, Dalits borrowed song and music from Tamasha and Sangeet-bari Jalsa, deprived it of its businesslike, inferior, entertaining character, and imbued it with samaj sudhar, which constituted "*lokjagruti* [awakening], *lokshikshan* [education], *lokprabodhan* [exhortation for advancement], and *lokkalyan* [benefit of the masses]."[33]

As Bhagvan Thakur reports, "Satyashodhak Jalsa was divorced from the "traditional elements of Tamasha: free dialogues, vulgarity, *bhadakpana* [ostentatiousness], frivolousness."[34] Like Satyashodhak Jalsakars, Ambedkarite Jalsakars could not completely break with the popular Tamasha form; yet they were afraid that Tamasha would plant the seeds of future promiscuity. As a result, they bent Tamasha to their needs by abandoning the aim of sheer entertainment and infusing it with the radical political message of *vatan taka* (shedding caste-marked duties); giving up Maharki (Mahar caste labor), drinking, and gambling; and building manuski through *shikshan* (education), *svabhiman* (self-respect), and *svavalamban* (self-reliance) to build Dalit pride and power.[35]

According to Marathi literature scholar Krishna Kiravale, "Following Phule, who decried Krishna and his teasing of maidens, calling 16,000 women his wives, engaging in a *ras-krida* [dance and sensual play] with maidens, Satyashodhaks . . . abandoned gaulan,"[36] the skit that focused on the sensual dialogue and (fore)play between Krishna and his maidens, which was central to Tamasha. Similarly, Ambedkarite Jalsakars also "abandoned gaulan"[37] in creating their political Jalse, eliminating love, desire, open and at times lewd expressions of sexuality, and foreplay between Krishna and the maidens who he robbed of milk and curd and also played sexually and sensually with them.

They also eliminated characters like Krishna, Radha, and so on, emphasizing Ambedkar's strategy of subverting traditions and his gendered analysis of the "Riddle of Rama and Krishna."

To Ambedkar, Rama's marriage was far from ideal, and moreover, he was not a virtuous, monogamous man. In fact, he behaved irresponsibly toward Sita. Unlike the popular myth that Rama demanded she prove her innocence, in Ambedkar's interpretation, Sita chose to die instead of living happily with her cruel husband. In Ambedkar's opinion, Krishna actually made women tools of his pleasure. "His Krishna," writes Sharmila Rege, "is almost pathologically promiscuous, having eight principal wives won in war or carried away from swayamvara weddings and 16,108 consorts inherited from the harem of a defeated king."[38] Sharad Patil and Kancha Illaiah have defended Ambedkar's critique of Krishna and his brahmani ideology. Uma Chakravarti has also argued that the Sita myth as quintessential of wifely devotion is a relatively later invention. To her, Ram and Sita actually constitute the foundation of the patriarchal, monogamous marriage in Hinduism. Jalsakars' strategies were thus in line with their leader's thoughts and actions.

Thus, both Satyashodhaks and Ambedkarites challenged sensuality and sexuality in Hindu religion and its sensual gods like Krishna. While Satyashodhaks also did away with the silly female character of Maushi (the maternal aunt) and the songadya (the cross-dressed buffoon) and their cheap jokes, Ambedkarites retained Maushi. She emerged as a witty aunt provoking the adani audience to think. Like Tamasha, the Ambedkarite Jalsa featured the Maushi; unlike Tamasha, she was deployed as a caring aunt who fought exploitation, superstition, and vulnerability of Dalits. The Dalit artist Bhau Phakkad, for example, danced and sang in Tamasha until 1925, when he embraced Ambedkar's movement to help pave the way for a radical change through Jalsa, singing Ambedkar-inspired versions of songs and skits—gan, gaulan, batavani, vag—that were central elements of Tamasha.[39] Consequently, many Dalit artists, mainly following Bhau Phakkad, gave up Patthe Bapurao's gan, commemorating Bapurao's contributions to Tamasha, and replaced it with Ambedkar's gan, singing praises to Ambedkar and his movement.[40] The impact of Ambedkar and Ambedkarite Jalse was so deep that as Appasaheb Ranpise reports, "While non-brahman artists started the program with Patthe Bapurao's gan, Dalit shahirs departed from this tradition to sing Kavi Bhau Phakkad's gan. When Patthe Bapurao died in 1948, no Dalit artist attended his cremation."[41]

To establish new traditions, Ambedkarite Jalsa also regulated, standard-ized, and sanskritized Tamasha. Jalsakars focused on shastric (cultured) sing-ing, rehearsals, intonation, and pitch and surveilled the content of skits and songs. For example, while old Tamasha started with Ganapati worship, in the form of *stavan* or *mangalacharan*, the new Ambedkarite Jalsa started with mangalacharan deifying Ambedkar.

In so doing, Jalsakars transformed their leader Ambedkar into a *daivat* (god) and praised him and his work. For example, Kardak sang the following mangalacharan:

> Hey, Bhimrao namito paya
> dyavi mati amha tav goon gaya
> Jari amha nahi vali, tuch aamchi krupa savali
> Asprushyanchi khari mauli[42]

> (Respectfully calling Bhimrao Ambedkar and paying respect to you
>   by bowing, touching feet, or prostrating to you
> Grant us intelligence to sing your praise
> Though we do not have a patron, you are our sympathetic protector
> You are Untouchable's true respectful mother)

Jalsakars also depicted Ambedkar, a man, as a caring mother of the community, capturing Dalits' transformation of Ambedkar into both mother and father, thus queering him and blurring the boundaries of femininity and masculinity. In general, they called him Baba or Babasaheb (adding the honorific *Sir*). As in devotional kirtan, NJYSSJ started with the practice of naman and also depicted Ambedkar as "mauli" as well as god. This sublimated form of femininity in mascu-line identity is perhaps more acceptable in Indian society, wherein devotees often address their male gods as mothers, caretakers, and protectors. One of the NJYSSJ advertisements (figure 4.3) also read: "Bhimraya Prasanna [with the blessings of King Bhim]." NJYSSJ added the honorific *raya* (king) and sought the blessings of Ambedkar, thus transforming him into a godlike king who would break the shackles of slavery and establish new realities and bring about liberation.

FIGURE 4.3: Advertisement for Kardak's Nashik District Youth Musical Jalsa. Source: Bhagvan Thakur, *Ambedkari Jalse* (Pune: Sugava Publications, 2005).

The focus on the "truth" of Ambedkar here is also important; Ambedkar and Gandhi sparred both verbally and in writing about who was the true representative of Untouchables in the 1930s. Dalits started celebrating Ambedkar's Jayanti, his birthday, April 14, in the 1930s. Ambedkar expressed his discomfort with such festivities and stayed away from them until his fiftieth birthday, in 1941.

Like Ambedkar, Jalsakars attacked brahmani patriarchy and its treatment of women. One of the famous Jalsas of Bhimrao Mahamuni drew upon the radical Dalit Kisan Phaguji Bansode's poetry and produced a farce about the tonsure of a young brahman widow who tries to argue with her father:

I am your loved one, father, your loved one,
Why do you make me a tonsured widow?
Leave your adamant behavior, arrange for my second marriage,
  [like the way] it is allowed among lower castes.[43]

The attack on patriarchy was similar to that of non-brahman Satyashodhak

Jalsakars. Satyashodhaks drew upon the critiques of the revolutionary Jotirao Phule to argue that brahman men oppressed brahman women's sexuality and, indeed, considered them to be Shudras.[44] The 1933 report of the diamond jubilee celebrations of the Satyashodhak Samaj also concludes that "Satyashodhak Samaj recognizes that the brahman women and Bahujans are the victims of brahman [men's] arrogance and atrocities and will never ridicule women."[45] Yet, brahmans thought such Jalsa songs actually maligned brahman women, and hence they always counterattacked Satyashodhaks. Although both Satyashodhaks and Dalits critiqued brahman men's repression of brahman women, paradoxically they were torn by caste patriarchies. They resisted as well as appropriated gendered norms in their families and communities. These processes were complicated and tenuous.

These critiques were deeply connected with Ambedkar's analysis of the sex-gender-caste complex in 1916 (see chapter 3). It was Satyashodhaks and Dalits, exploited by sexual-caste slavery, who produced early intersectionality critiques, yet scholars have continuously obscured their contributions and denied them space to critique caste, untouchability, and the nation. Caste triumphed in creating dissension and keeping the subordinated divided. In general, Satyashodhaks, however, did not consider Dalits to be equals, thus dividing their communities and their struggles against a common enemy: brahmans and brahmanism. Yet, drawing inspiration from their precursor, the Satyashodhak Jalsa, young Dalit activists diligently deployed the mode of entertainment to disseminate their leader's social and political message among nonliterate Dalits.

These processes led to moral and gendered conflicts inside the Dalit community. In the process of social improvement, Jalsakars agreed with the dominant depiction of respectable touchables regarding Tamasha women, and the *nachi* (woman dancer) emerged as immoral and promiscuous. She posed a threat to Jalsa and its anticaste radicalism. She was a ghost that could not completely be banished. To create Jalsa in opposition to Tamasha, Jalsakars sought to eradicate women as actors and characters. Theoretically, in the context of caste slavery and heteronormative marriage market, the nachi of Tamasha became a surplus young woman, paradoxically of significance because she threatened the caste order but simultaneously was of no significance and could be easily discarded (chapter 3). Yet, Jalsakars were challenged by difficulties on the ground. Because she could not be easily discarded by them, they must expunge her through a process of sanitization.

Continuing their cleansing efforts in crossing over from Tamasha to Jalsa, the NJYSSJ also specifically concentrated on male artists, excluding women from public performances, and thus gendered Dalit sudhar. Men like Dhondi-ram Annaji Pawar, Kachar Revji Dani, Mahadev Savla Bhalerao, and Krishnaji Hari Bhalerao performed female characters, for example, in the form of the famous and supposedly conservative and silly Maushi character.[46] As Kirwale argues, Jalsakars also brought about a significant transformation in the role of the songadya (a comic pretender who assumes various disguises or personates various characters).[47] The songadya now acquired a central role in making po-litical and social parodies and jokes mocking touchables and systemic oppres-sion. Dalit gentlemen thus completely excluded women and their creativity. Dalit men drew upon songs such as palna, ovi, and other songs sung by women while they were doing housework and infused them will social activism. How-ever, they excluded women as actors and reduced the role of characters such as the Rani and Maushi (queen and aunt) drawing upon but refashioning them to a new poetics-politics. Also, the recovery and recoding of the Maushi character illuminates another figuration of gender that is juxtaposed with the erasure of the sexualized figure of Tamasha woman. The Maushi is a male person ventriloquizing a female voice. Despite making women either tokens or present only implicitly in Jalsa, Ambedkarite Jalsakars, according Bhagvan Thakur, understood women implicitly, "organizing women for the social cause, fighting for women's rights, and calling them *vir mahila* [brave women]."[48] He cites Kardak's ovya for Mahila Mandal (women's organizations)—"I wake up in the morning, I pray to Bhim[rao Ambedkar], 'Grant a long life to my husband'"[49]—and mentions one Aher master who sang "palna [songs sung at birth ceremonies], streegetey [women's songs], Pavada, Lavani"[50] for women as evidence that in appropriating women's cultural productions, Jalsakars demonstrated their *"streemanas"* (concern for women). Thus, despite men-tioning women on only two pages of a 464-page book and failing to consider the voices of women in his study, Thakur argues that Jalsakars understood women's interiority.

The purging of female artists and characters from Ambedkarite Jalsa is not simply evidence of the reproduction of upper-caste patriarchy, as argued by Rege, or reconstitution of Dalit masculinity, as argued by Rao; rather, this political strategy was part of a contingent, complicated, and tenuous processes to generate Dalit manuski (see chapter 3). Appasaheb Ranpise argued that in developing Dalit manuski through Jalsa, "Dalit shahirs' poetry is *virarasapradhan*" (dominated by the emotion, sentiment of manly valor).[51] He further linked the manly valor of Jalsa to the generation of Dalit manuski in his claim that "chhati ubharun yenara kavya" (their poetry makes our chest swell with pride). Moreover, citing non-brahman leader Prabodhankar Thackeray, Ranpise noted the relationship of masculinity to assertive, oppositional calls for social change: "The alive *mard* [heroic manliness] should do *kranti* [revolution], the dead corpse should do *shanti* [peace], revolution is of the man, shanti of the cremation ground."[52]

Ambedkar and Ambedkarite Jalsakars sought political strategies, first and foremost, to civilize, uplift, and humanize Dalits, not refashion Dalit masculinity. These strategies—for instance, the founding of the SSD or the purging of women from Jalsa—were contingent, contradictory, and ambiguous responses to the moral crisis and sexual panic manufactured by the colonial state and touchable reformers in discussing Untouchables. Ambedkar and Jalsakars attacked touchables' grading of masculinities focused on caste lines. They recognized how touchables deprived Dalits of masculine virility and rendered Dalits effeminate and timid. Jalsa culture, like its political counterpart the Samata Sainik Dal (Army of Soldiers for Equality; SSD) modeled an Ambedkarite paradigm for a certain manhood and manuski. And though the SSD fashioned Dalit men as lathi-charging, disciplined volunteers on the front lines of caste conflict, they also had a women's wing of more than five hundred women who marched like disciplined soldiers at the start of the Nashik Satyagraha. Respectable samaj governmentality, as I demonstrated in the last chapter, constrained women and at the same time provided possibilities and opened to them new arenas to practice a masculine Dalit womanhood, their manus and manuski, even in more traditionally "manly" ways.[53]

As I have analyzed in my previous work, Ambedkar opened opportunities for Dalit women to access the public realm. He and Dalits also fused masculinity with femininity by using words like *confident, brave, daring, bold*, and *resolute*, which had stereotypically been reserved for men, to provoke Dalit women to think and act. His focus on manuski certainly had gendered implications—including the purging of female characters and artists in Ambedkarite Jalsa—and the formation of the SSD in 1927, and the gender politics of Jalsa may have even been a response to the effeminization of Dalit men and the hypersexualization of Dalit women, but as political strategies they were not primarily concerned with gender per se but with annihilating caste and claiming and generating a new Dalit manuski for both men and women. Jalsakars in particular and Dalits in general thus deployed the generative power of gender to challenge the dominant brahmani caste order. Radical Dalit shahirs, in the tenuous process of both challenging and, at times, conforming to, even as they were parodying dominant-caste technologies and elite reformers, including Gandhi, also marginalized women characters and excluded women as both actors and characters in the narrative.

Jalsakars saw the marginalization of women in Jalsa as a performative political strategy necessary to the making of Dalit manuski, a new dignified humanity, a certain morality for the emerging good Dalit, a modern citizen of twentieth-century Maharashtra. In making a new Dalit manuski, shahirs attacked the sex-gender-caste complex and its particular oppression of Untouchable women. They were intensely troubled by the stigmatization, discrimination, and exploitation of women like Pavalabai in the theatre of Tamasha and sought to recuperate a certain svabhiman and manuski for all Dalits, and remaking the ijjat of the most degraded women became critical to Dalit self-fashioning in mid-twentieth-century India.

Like touchable elites, Dalits were influenced by colonial modernity. Unlike them however, they were not merely reproducing and sanskritizing popular forms. Brahmani theatre and Satyashodhak Jalsa excluded Dalit worlds, and Dalits had no choice but to use hegemonic idioms and values to raise their status. As a result, Dalits selectively appropriated dominant norms of honor and respectability, yet they continuously resisted and pursued alternatives for their own purposes. Resistance and compliance is an ongoing struggle, and especially with respect to women and gender, tensions emerged in Dalit politics between the pragmatic and liberatory aspects of the struggle. In underlining these tendencies as patriarchal and masculinist, scholars have completely obscured the political contingencies, elasticity of Dalitness, and the complex human condition of Dalits, which I analyze through the discourses of Kardak, Ambedkar, and Gaikwad.

Dalit radicals seeking change were not merely reforming but practicing anticaste resistance and generating Dalit samaj from the ground up. There were contradictions as Dalits were appropriating and resisting touchables. To upwardly mobile Dalits and Dalit shahirs, Tamasha and women dancers therein, were (and are) an embarrassing sign of their caste's feudal past, and hence they disparaged Tamasha. In their battle for higher social status, Dalit reformers sought to counter practices that they now considered immoral and sought to control the sexuality of doubly stigmatized women artists. They also supported the criminalization of their lifestyle brought about by the British officials. Dalit shahirs sought to break the association between the ashlil fun and frolic of Tamasha and Lavani and the sexual promiscuity of its female Dalit performers.

This was the double bind that Ambedkar and many Dalits experienced: the pleasure that Tamasha provided to men of all castes was contingent on the surplus labor of the (surplus) Dalit woman. She was exploited in the eyes of Dalit radicals, but at the same time, she also exposed the tensions of caste struggle, both bearing the wounds of touchable exploitation and finding new mobility through performance. As Jalsa culture gained influence and popularity, Dalits critiqued members of their own community who they thought consented to their subordination through practices like Tamasha. Nevertheless, Ambedkarite Jalsa could not displace Tamasha. Both cultural forms, Tamasha and Jalsa, thrived alongside each other. They borrowed from each other, bending certain rules without actually breaking the traditional form.

Kardak and NJYSSJ: Educate, Organize, Agitate!

The immensely popular Bhimrao Dhondiba Kardak, who performed from the beginning of the 1930s until the mass Dalit conversion to Buddhism and death of Ambedkar in 1956, was a founder of the NJYSSJ. From its founding on January 14, 1931, the NJYSSJ served the Dalit community and was at the forefront of prachar karya for Dalits' social regeneration through Jalsa in the Bombay Presidency until the troupe disbanded in 1956. During this period, Kardak and the NJYSSJ propagated Ambedkar's thoughts through 378 programs.[54] Unlike other Jalsakars who have been lost to history, Kardak documented the aims and efforts of the NJYSSJ in his 1978 Marathi-language book

Ambedkari Jalse: Svaroop va Karya (Ambedkarite Jalsas: Form and Work). Kardak's impact has been so lasting that, even in 2017, the female shahir Kadutai Kharat sang the praises of Kardak.

To illustrate how poetics-politics of Kardak's Jalsa performed prachar karya for Dalit social regeneration by transforming sringarik Tamasha into Ambedkarite Jalsa (and minimizing the voice and performances of potentially promiscuous women), I provide two examples of his farce that deployed humor as a tool of subversion. To Kardak, the main aim of NJYSSJ was certainly not mere entertainment, in contrast to traditional Tamasha and Tamasgirs. Dalit youth, including Kardak, authored socially relevant songs, and his troupe sang Lavanya and Chhakkad songs and performed Satyagraha (in terms of nonviolent demonstrations, sit-outs) farce, Maharki farce, dialogues between orthodox (sanatani) brahman and Untouchable satyagrahis, farce by the volunteers of the Samata Sainik Dal (Army for Equality), *daru ani sattebajicha* (alcohol and gambling) farce, *dharmantaracha* (religious conversion) farce, and Thana Boarding farce. The farce form, a type of comedy, became important to the poetics-politics of Jalsa, as Jalsakars mocked touchables, social conventions, and caste games. To center Kardak's politics, I quote two farces at length: the first on Satyagraha and the second on Gandhi's Harijan Sevak Sangh in the Thana Boarding farce.

Satyagraha Farce

The Satyagraha farce is set during the Kalaram Temple Satyagraha at Nashik on March 4, 1930, which Ambedkar launched in an attempt to secure Untouchables' entry into the temple. Kardak's Jalsa used this political moment of Hindu *"dharmasangram"* (religious contest)[55] that lay at the conjunction of historical, social, and cultural conflicts between Untouchables and touchables to highlight the different perspectives of Ambedkar and Gandhi in 1930 and accentuate the performative nature of manuski. Ambedkarite Jalsa and Jalsakars played a critical role in mobilizing Dalits for the Nashik satyagraha. Although they had ideological differences with the gradual reformist Gandhi, radical Dalit activists were inspired by his strategies of nonviolence and popular resistance. But by 1930, Dalits had broken with Congress nationalists and exposed the limitations of attempts to reform temple entry, which Congress nationalists framed as a "religious problem" that could lead to equality. Dalits, however, viewed it as an issue related to their right to public space.[56]

Touchable reformers were deeply uncomfortable with the very idea that Untouchables, especially Mahars, were seeking rights to enter their public sacred, religious spaces. To Untouchables, entry to the public space, including tanks, streets, schools, and temples, was a matter of winning equal rights and making manuski. Yet, Ambedkar was willing to experiment with temple entry because he thought it would be the first step in the solution to the untouchability problem. Most important, there were differences among Untouchables themselves. The Hindu Mahasbhaite Mang leader, K. K. Sakat, united with brahman leader Shripad Mahadev Mate (1886–1957), who was against the direct action at the temple entry satyagraha of Parvati in Pune in 1929. He did join later but left before the satyagraha began.

In this farce, the supposedly silly Maushi initiates a dialogue between the Sudharak (a Dalit radical seeking improvement and progress) Kardak and a Virodhak (a touchable reformer and opponent of Untouchables) by asking, "Is this satyagraha long or short, round or square? Is it something to eat? I still don't know. What is this satyagraha thing about? Not only me, but many women and men do not understand anything about it." In this manner, Maushi, representing ordinary people's misunderstanding of political concepts and strategies, raised thought-provoking questions. To illuminate satyagraha to the ignorant, the Sudharak responds to Maushi,

> I am tired of old traditions. I will join satyagraha.
> I do not want this life of untouchability, stigma, and slavery.
> To destroy untouchability, I will join satyagraha.
> This caste system exploited our fathers, and the same has descend-
>   ed on us.
> Hence, we need to destroy it. I will join satyagraha.
> I am abandoning old traditions, and uprooting untouchability.
> Kardak is requesting you [community], let's join the satyagraha.[57]

Like Ambedkar, Jalsakars attacked the hierarchical structures of caste slavery that exploited them. At the end of the song, Kardak and his associates also explain the meaning of the Nashik Satyagraha farce. He continues, "As

Untouchables started uniting and fighting through satyagraha, touchables brutally battered and boycotted Untouchables. As a result, Untouchables could not have access to even common commodities like salt and oil."[58] When Untouchables tried to seek access to public spaces, including temples and water tanks, there were several repercussions. Touchables attacked them and boycotted them, cutting off Untouchables' access to food and water. After explaining the significance of satyagraha, the Virodhak and the Sudharak present their perspectives.

The Virodhak responds by challenging Untouchables' idea of satyagraha:

Has not your aim of going to the satyagraha changed?
At least now, you should open your eyes.
These leaders [Ambedkar, Dadasaheb Gaikwad] have started satya-
   graha in Nashik
However, you, poor people have to face the actual consequences on
   the ground!
Do you have any idea how Untouchables, especially Mahars are op-
   pressed in the villages?
Drop this *nada* [devoted pursuit] of satyagraha [under the leader-
   ship of Ambedkar] and do not succumb to lies. . . .
At least, become wise now.

To the Virodhak, Untouchables leaders were dangerously provoking adani and poor Untouchables to assert their rights. Moreover, to him, Ambedkar's staunch and aggressive stance of satyagraha with majority Untouchables following him was nothing short of trouble to touchable caste Hindus.

The song below follows the Virodhak's argument and exhortation to Mahars to abandon the Satyagraha and to stop Untouchables' pursuit of rights and freedom.

Why are you doing satyagraha? It is an unnecessary trouble to the
   adnyan [non-intelligent].
Because you did satyagraha, you have been immensely oppressed.
You have been beaten up, unnecessary trouble to the adnyan.
They say Mahars are having an upper hand, and hence they have

excluded you from markets. You cannot find [basic cooking in-
gredients like] oil and salt, your homes have been burned out,
and [due to the boycott by savarnas] people in many villages do
not get water to drink or food to eat.
They call Mahar a *chor* [thief], and all this loss is due to satyagraha!
At least now leave this *chhanda* [impatient desire].
Stop the Nashik satyagraha! Unnecessary trouble to the adnyan
people.[59]

The Virodhak wanted Untouchables, especially Mahars, following Ambedkar to
think about the negative impact of their anticaste radicalism, which included
not just boycotts but vengeance and violence. Hence, the Virodhak implored
Untouchables to end their satyagraha.

The Sudharak refutes the Virodhak's argument,

Educated Sir! Whatever you say is correct.
Our majority brothers have faced immense oppression due to this
satyagraha.
We, too, understand. Nevertheless, some svabhimani [self-respect-
ful] people have joined the satyagraha on their own accord.
The social revolution requires the sacrifices of many patriots and
social workers.
To regain our manuski, we are ready to face the oppression of savarna Hindus who have robbed us of it.[60]

The Sudharak emphasized that Untouchables were not blindly following their
leader; instead, they were exercising their critical faculties and agency. They
were aware of their exploitation at the hands of touchables and were ready
to face enormous hardships to become free manus. The Sudharak's riposte is
followed by a song:

Do not show us the fear of prisons.
We do not care for our lives. We will go to jails to claim our rights.
Why are you unnecessarily blabbering and misguiding and making
us lose our right path!
You do not care about our manuski and obstruct our struggle for

[our] rights [and freedom].

We will give up our lives [for manuski]. . . . Let's participate in satyagraha. We do not care for our lives.[61]

The Sudharak clearly illuminated that Dalits were ready to regain manuski
and even put their lives on the line and risk everything for manuski and the
revolution it would bring about. By the mid-1930s, as I discussed in the last
chapter, Ambedkar adopted an aggressive stand vis-à-vis touchables. Kardak
effectively pointed out these problems between touchables and Untouchables,
promoted the Dalit movement, and prepared Dalits to gain confidence and
power through events like the Kalaram Temple Satyagraha.

However, after struggling for five long years, Dalits did not achieve temple
entry. This failure deeply disappointed Ambedkar, and he announced dharmantar in 1935 in Yeola, in Nashik District: "I will not die a Hindu." Inadver-
tently, he seems to have agreed with the Hindu majoritarian and Gandhian
construction of Hinduism that Untouchables and caste Hindus belonged to
the same religion. As the discussions around the 1931–32 Round Table Conferences clarified, Gandhi argued that Harijans were an indivisible part of the
monolithic Hindu community. Vinayak Damodar Savarkar (1884–1960) of the
Hindu Mahasabha also encouraged the building of special temples exclusively
for Untouchables, so that it would delay finding a solution to the problem.[62]
As a result, Ambedkar rejected Gandhi, Congress, and Hindu reformers and
turned to economic and political radicalism.

Thana Boarding Farce

Kardak takes up Ambedkar's radicalism and his frustration with Gandhi's
politics in his Thana (Mumbai) Boarding Farce, a dialogue between Congress and Ambedkar bhaktas (devotees) set during the infamous 1932 Poona
Pact clash over separate Dalit legislative representation between Ambedkar, who supported the pact, and Gandhi, who opposed it. For a decade,
the two had clashed over who was the true representative of Untouchables
and what role Untouchables should play in addressing their own condition.
Gandhi homogenized all Untouchable castes in the image of a Bhangi (sanitation labor caste)—romanticizing sanitation, hygiene, and cleanliness as

"noble"—and attempted to identify with them by calling himself a scavenger and collectively labeled them Harijan (People of God).[63] Though many Untouchables embraced the term, many opposed it as paternalistic and patronizing. Ambedkar argued that the term not only did nothing to alleviate the conditions of Untouchability and caste slavery but, in fact, naturalized those conditions, deepened casteism, and exculpated touchables from their role in perpetuating them and it. Regarding the term "Untouchable," Ambedkar argued that "'Untouchable' is a bad name that repels and stinks, but it is better for the wrongdoer that the wrong is there still to be redressed."[64] Not only did Ambedkar retain the term *Untouchable*, but he insisted on its assertive capitalization (a practice I follow in this book and throughout all my publications).

Gandhi, however, persisted in assuming an authority to speak on Untouchables' behalf, founding new weeklies—the English-language *Harijan*, *Harijan Sevak* in Hindi, and *Harijan bandhu* in Gujarati—and the League Against Untouchability, which became the Harijan Sevak Sangh (HSS). Despite its objective of social advancement for Untouchables, the HSS had no Dalits in decision-making positions; Gandhi did not believe they possessed the agential capacity to work on their own emancipation and instead appointed savarna Congressmen to those positions. Gandhi considered Untouchables objects of reform for caste Hindus and insisted the former devote their energies to promoting cleanliness and hygiene by continuing with their unclean occupations.[65] This was the cruel paradox: to promote cleanliness, Harijans could not abandon their unclean occupations. The HSS was especially active in promoting education,[66] establishing schools and residential hostels; providing training in the trades of tannery, shoemaking, tailoring, and weaving; and offering scholarships to help Depressed Class students. But when the HSS faced financial problems, it reduced the scholarship by half at the Thana Boarding House. This sudden cut in their scholarships led to hardships for poor Untouchable students, who complained that they could not survive on the reduced scholarship. As a result, the Thana Boarding House closed, putting students in further peril.

When news of the Thana Boarding House closure reached Kardak's troupe, they "resolved to collect funds or even beg their own poor Untouchable brethren to somehow support the students."[67] Kardak's attempts to revive and fund the school also afforded him an opportunity to use Jalsa to illuminate the complex educational, social, ideological, and political struggles that were the context for the Poona Pact clash between Ambedkar and Gandhi. The farce opens:

> Congress *bhakta* (devotee): Namaskar [Greetings], people!

> Ambedkar bhakta: Yes, Namaskar! How come you have entered [our polluted space] here, *deshbhakta* [patriot]?

> Congress bhakta: What are you asking about? This has become a regular business of us patriots. As a part of our program for the welfare of Harijans, we visit them in their neighborhoods. We aim to serve the Harijans and do away with their untouchability.

The opening of the farce establishes a clear equation between Congress, Gandhi, and India, having the Congress bhakta deploy the term *Harijan* and assume the label *deshbhakta* (patriot.) This equation was crucial to Gandhi's mass politics, and marginalized communities, including Dalits, would have to consistently prove their honesty and loyalty to each. Following this logic, because Ambedkar and his followers opposed Congress and Gandhi, they were potentially *deshdrohi* (enemies of the nation, anti-nationalists) in the eyes of many touchables. The farce also alludes to Gandhi's symbolic practice of visiting Untouchable neighborhoods, which Congress volunteers began to imitate from the 1930s.

On seeing the unfamiliar face of the Congress bhakta in her neighborhood, Maushi mockingly asks, "Who is this gentleman?" The Ambedkar bhakta responds, "Maushi, as I explained earlier, these Congressmen dressed in white clothes are trying to trick the followers of Dr. Babasaheb Ambedkar and pull them into the HSS. They want to entice them and kill their svabhiman." The Ambedkar bhakta is mocking the Congressmen dressed in their clean white clothes, which were in stark contrast with the Untouchables' supposedly dirty, dark world of caste slavery. The Congress and Ambedkar bhaktas lived in the same city, yet their perspectives, worlds, and methods of fighting caste discrimination and prejudice were different. While Congress bhaktas following Gandhi wanted Untouchables to depend on them, Ambedkar bhaktas, following Ambedkar, asserted their agency.

The Ambedkar bhakta also notes that the Congress bhakta has donned the

Gandhi *topi* (cap) as evidence of his patriotism.[68] The Congress bhakta explains the significance of his Gandhian topi: "[Yes,] we are donning the Gandhi topi as a marker of Gandhi's divine exhortations and ideology. It encompasses the nation's *hita-ahita* [good-bad], *niti-aniti* [moral-immoral], *hinsa-ahinsa* [violence-nonviolence], *satya-asatya* [truth-falseness], and so on." In this way, the Congress bhakta reinforced the equation between Gandhi and India. Most importantly, he also transformed Gandhi into a saintly figure providing divine moral guidance to Congress and larger Indian society.[69] Maushi immediately interrupts to mock the Gandhian discourse, moving her hand in a circle to signify a wheel: "And just sit on the charkha [spinning wheel that signified Gandhian spirituality] spinning, isn't it?" To Gandhi, the spinning wheel would help Indians materially in weaving their own cloth, becoming self-reliant nationalists, and especially help women spiritually in building their moral strength. While many followed Gandhi, even his friends and critics like Rabindranath Tagore ridiculed him.

Nevertheless, continuing the dialogue, the Ambedkar bhakta requests that the Congress bhakta "not address us as 'Harijan,'" explaining that while Gandhi and Congress may love their new name, "self-respectful Untouchables hate the word." The Ambedkar bhakta also issues a warning, charging the Congress bhakta with assuming "every little power to bind Untouchables to the villages, and by labeling us as Harijan, you are reviving peshvai" (brahman hegemony and rule in precolonial Western India, which upheld caste distinctions and legitimized casteism). "Beware if you address me or those sitting here with the *halkat* [inferior] term Harijan!" The Ambedkar bhakta equates Congress and Gandhi with revitalizing the exploitation of Untouchables, and then uses the proverb "Nav Sonubai ani hatat kathaleche vale" (Her name is Woman of Gold and she has bangles of lead) to highlight the contrast between the name and the adornment and illuminate the limits of, even the deception entailed by, referring to Untouchables as "Harijans":

"Nav Sonubai ani hatat kathaleche vale."
Only because you call us Harijan, has our untouchability gone?
Some *samaj-drohi* [anti-community] Harijans for money may be tricked; however, those Untouchables proud of their caste, truly respectful, with high morals will never be deceived by you.

The Congress bhakta, however, disregards the Ambedkar bhakta's argument and request to not addressing him as Harijan. This was typical of Congress and Gandhi. The Congress bhakta continues to teach the Ambedkar bhakta: "We are under the colonial domination of the English. We are not free. We are bound by the British. We feel bad that we are *gulam* [slaves]. For complete independence we suffer." In denying the relevance of peshva for touchables, the Congress bhakta wants Untouchables to forget the precolonial and focus on the present colonial situation. Congress and Gandhi wanted to homogenize marginalized communities, such as Dalits, Muslims, Christians, and women, to forget their social problems and unite under Congress leadership to create a united front and fight British colonialism.

Gandhi and Ambedkar shared many ideas and yet there were differences. They competed over the meaning of, origins of, and remedies for the removal of untouchability as well as over imagining Dalits as *subjects of history*. They proposed two different paths to achieve an Untouchable revolution—the social/religious and the political. Historically, there is a circulatory logic between the theologico-political practices adopted by Gandhi and Ambedkar: Gandhi begins with religion and deploys it for political aims, and Ambedkar works from within state-centered politics, moving toward faith, belief, and reason of Buddhism. Scholars have yet to study this. To Gandhi, like many touchables, political and economic transformation was a priority, and it would be followed by social reform. As such, before the Poona Pact, his social reform agenda, like that of many savarna reformers, focused exclusively on touchables, thereby excluding Untouchables. They paid lip service to social reform among Untouchables. Yet, during the debates and deliberations of the Poona Pact, Gandhi argued that Untouchables were an inseparable part of Hindu society. He also emphasized that he represented the Untouchables. By contrast, Ambedkar was not disgruntled about the sequence of the transition—whether social reform should precede political. He argued that social and political transformation could be in tandem.

Ambedkar was reluctant for a patient penitent and declared that the "Untouchable question is not *Hindunchya gharcha prashna* [a private one to be resolved inside Hindu family], but it is a national and to go further, it is an international problem."[70] He thus challenged Gandhi, who thought that the question of Untouchables, like those of women and the working class, should be resolved within the Hindu home. Underscoring Dalits' nationalism, he affirmed that just as "brahmans [like the extremist B. G. Tilak] thought that Swaraj [self-rule, political independence] was their birthright, so do the Mahars think."[71] While Gandhi argued that he was fighting for the whole country, of which Untouchables were a part, Ambedkar retaliated that "he was a part apart," that he was separate from the rest and did not belong to the Indian community, affirming that the Indian National Congress's fight would not bring real *svarajya* (self-rule), but in fact would precipitate *amchyavar rajya* (internal colonialism, a rule over Dalits), in which there would be scarce chances of *surajya* (good rule).[72] Although decolonization would free India from British rule, at the same time it would also replace the British with dominant castes, thereby reinforcing internal brahmani colonialism and accelerating caste. Yet, Ambedkar faced a deeper dilemma about the status of Untouchables: could they be integrated into Hindu society and the Indian nation?

Congress's preoccupation with British colonialism attenuated any focus on internal brahmani colonialism. In the farce, the Ambedkar bhakta draws attention to the inadequacy of the Congress bhakta's arguments for Untouchables:

> You are *besharm* [shameless]! You are crying because the English
> have enslaved you and you are not free.
> Our forefathers died in your slavery for thousands of years.
> Still, you never think that [Untouchables should have] ordinary human rights and rights to public spaces.

The Ambedkar bhakta reminds the Congress bhakta that "this sabha is assembled to raise funds for the Thana Boarding Hostel." Pouncing on this line of thought, the Congress bhakta counters, "Instead of struggling so much and squeezing poor people, why don't you hand over the boarding [back] to us, the HSS? Gandhi and the Congress have established the HSS for Harijan uplift." In this manner Congress and Gandhi wanted the marginalized to fall in line and support the larger independence movement, instead of fighting for their rights and manuski.

The Congress bhakta's argument is followed by his song praising Gandhi's efforts for Harijans: "Established HSS for service, to uplift the Harijan, the leader Gandhi is commendable that he strives for the vulnerable." The Congress bhakta wants to reenter the debate and assume control of the Thana Boarding, especially after Kardak starts collecting funds to revive it. He continues to praise Gandhi and HSS:

Thakkar Bappa is striving for us, recommending education, cleanliness.

However, instead of being grateful to him, *your* Ambedkar has decided to hate him and envy him.

We provide free textbooks, scholarships, clothes, and so on; yet Ambedkar's *shepoot vakade tey vadakech* [tail is always already twisted].

And after all our efforts, you are still blaming us and depicting us Congress [as] evil enemy! Is this manuski? Is this justice?

The Congress bhakta creates a distinction: us and them, our touchable Gandhi and your Untouchable Ambedkar. Dalits, Muslims, women—the marginalized—were to be thankful to the Congress and its devotees for the crumbs showered upon them.

Following his party's agenda, he vilifies Ambedkar and praises HSS efforts. Moreover, he insults Ambedkar, dehumanizing him by depicting him as a dog with a crooked tail. The full proverb in Marathi is *kutryache shepoot vakade tey vakadech* (a dog's tail is always crooked). It means that whatever one does for a dog, it will never be satisfied with its gains and ask for more. The Congress bhakta cunningly uses this proverb, omitting the word *dog*, but retaining its crooked tail to refer to Ambedkar. He wants to impress on Untouchables that whatever Congress provided, or did for them, Ambedkar was never happy or satisfied with it. Instead, he continued to fight them aggressively, asking for more, ignoring and confronting them, and following his own different and radical path toward freedom of Untouchables. It was to challenge such animalistic, ashlil treatment that manuski was important to Dalits. Congress never listened to Ambedkar or tried to understand what he wanted; it was merely engrossed in his agenda of reforming from the outside.

By now, the Ambedkar bhakta is frustrated, and he explains the importance of manuski and internal regeneration:

Why don't you just give us what we really want

We are hungry for manuski, then education.

Because without manuski, education is useless!

Why are savarnas discarding our demands for equality and throw-
ing tidbits of cleanliness, education, and the name "Harijan" at
us?

The Ambedkar bhakta continues to illuminate the problem of touchables ignoring Untouchables' demands. Pointing out their double standards to Untouchables, he sings:

The cunning Congress is showing love, which is a pretense.

Your Congress is like the demoness Putana [disguised as a young
beautiful woman], feeding the free milk of education [to Un-
touchables].

It aims to deprive [you] of svabhiman, so that you don't think of
manuski.

The Sangh has its several branches and has created divisions.

It rears the selfish enormous *bhujang* [poisonous snake] Harijan,
which is out to bite Untouchables.

[However,] we will digest the milk, enliven ourselves, pull out the
poisonous fangs of the Harijan snake, and bring those deflected
[to the HSS and Congress] back into the community.

This is our decision of sanghatana [organized community]![73]

Time and again, Kardak reveals the significance of manuski for Untouchables and the samaj as a whole. Through his Jalsa, he illuminates the politics of Gandhi, HSS, and the Congress that deprived Dalits of manuski. Ambedkar emphasized the same in his writings and speeches. Kardak uses Congress bhakta's animal-istic metaphors and calls Congress a demoness and Harijan a poisonous snake. Putana, a demoness disguised as a beautiful woman, is well known for her at-tempt to kill the infant Hindu deity Krishna by offering him milk from her poi-soned breast; she was, however, sucked to death by the god.[74] Kardak transforms Congress into an evil woman and Dalits into a revered male god. Like Krishna, Untouchables would counterattack by defanging Congress and HSS and deplet-ing them of their strength. This subversion was important for organizing Dalits.

Consequently, Kardak concludes:

Gandhi has crushed us, as he is driving the cart of the nation.

He is regularly meeting the British Viceroy and asking for power.

He excludes the minorities and is killing the Untouchables.

He accepts differences in caste communities.

He is not giving political rights to Untouchables, but grants them to Musalmans [Muslims].

He propounds his philosophy of truth and nonviolence, but he practices truth through *dambhikpana* [hypocrisy] and nonviolence is a farce.

This is the homogenizing deceptive politics of Congress. How much do I tell you about this?[75]

Kardak reveals the politics of corruption, *kutil niti* (bad morals), *dhongi and dhambhik* (hypocritical politics), prestige of capitalism, and breach of trust of Untouchables, especially in the context of the Pune Pact. He illuminates how Congress and Gandhi negotiated differently with different marginalized groups—Muslims and Untouchables. In so doing, the former would try to divide and rule, just as the British colonial government had with Indians as a whole. Gandhi would, however, defend his stance, arguing that, unlike Muslims, Untouchables were always a part of the Hindu community. As such, he would try to resolve the Untouchable question inside the Hindu home. However, Ambedkar disagreed with Gandhi. When they met for the first time in 1931, Gandhi questioned him about his sharp criticism of Congress, which corresponded to criticizing the struggle for the Homeland, Ambedkar's famous reply was, "Gandhiji, I have no homeland. No Untouchable worth the name would be proud of this land." He did not have a home inside the Hindu community, in Congress, or in India.

Kardak and many Dalit youth, intoxicated by freedom, aggressively used their art to engage in different political and historical moments of the Dalit movement and most importantly, connected intimately with the most untouched Untouchable. He reversed the strategy of Congress bhakta and now reviled Gandhi and revealed his double standards. Following Ambedkar, he illuminated the problems of Gandhi's politics of not granting agency and freedom to Untouchables.

Challenges and Futures

The success of the NJYSSJ was complicated by contradictions and contestations within the Dalit community, as Dadasaheb Pagare, president of the NJYSSJ, underlined:

> Dalit youth are working hard. [However], they face much opposition from Dalits and non-Dalits. The youth are totally impressed with Dr. Babasaheb's new ideas and guidance. They started with their own villages and rebelled against the *budrukh mandali* [the venerable elite, high castes].

Pagare recognized the differences and tensions inside the Mahar community, as well as between Mahars and savarnas. Unlike people in cities, villagers posed a serious challenge to modernizing young Dalits. They argued:

> You people have jobs, earn well, dress up in good clothes, get your clothes washed. You visit saloons to get a shave. What do we have in the villages? Do we have the facilities that you enjoy in the city? You visit the village for 8–10 days, and then flee to the city. You do not have to face the touchable Hindus here and you need not think about them. Because you are self-dependent and we are depending on touchables. Hence, we have to lead our lives while accommodating the whims and fancies of touchable Hindus.[76]

Villagers were well aware that if Mahars rebelled, they would be further oppressed or boycotted by dominant castes. Their accommodation to the social order was a survial strategy. They felt that educated, urban Dalits who visited them temporarily for a week were in no position to understand the real hardships of village folk. Due to these barriers, Untouchables in the villages continued their age-old practices and posed a challenge to the dissemination of manuski and politico-ethics of anticaste liberation.

Many Mahars in the villages were not ready to abandon their traditional fetters and markers of Mahar caste, such as the vatan or sanitation labor. As I mentioned in the last chapter, Ambedkar and some non-brahman leaders such as Shahu Maharaj led a movement against khoti and vatan, duties that upper castes forced upon Untouchables in perpetuity over generations through caste slavery. Paradoxically, although extremely exploitative and stigmatizing, the vatan work at the same time provided limited means of livelihood to Untouchables. Some also looked upon them as their "customary rights." Hence, many Mahars challenged Ambedkar's agenda to abolish vatan and argued, "We will participate in Dr. Babasaheb Ambedkar's satyagrahas for tanks, temple, well, bore[wells], and ponds; however, do not express your discontent with our traditional Maharki [duties of Mahar]."[77] As a result, Pagare and his associates decided to spread Ambedkar's movement throughout the entire district. Pagare and his associates in Mumbai first focused their efforts on Nashik district. They started their prachar karya for social regeneration in areas dominated by Untouchables from Nashik in Mumbai: Shivadi, Vadala, Matunga, Sion Kolivada, Kurla, Ghatkopar, and so on. They continued their Jalsa activities while attending to their jobs (in textile mills, dockyards, and railways) and families for twenty years and became immensely popular.

Ambedkar immensely valued the poetics-politics of Jalsa. Ambedkar also enjoyed different popular arts: Tamasha, Lavani, and Shahiri. He noted:

> Many lament that Lavani is inferior; yet, taking into consideration *lalitya* [prose] and *navinya* [novelty], such forms cannot be considered inferior. I feel very sad that such forms are on the decline. I did want to preserve this literature once upon a time; however, I have had no such time due to working on many fronts.[78]

Cultural regeneration was significant to Ambedkar's multipronged approach that encompassed social, political, and ideological transformation. Throughout his career, along with educational institutions, political parties, and constitutional legislation, Ambedkar spent much of his time building the Samata Sainik Dal (Army for Equality), reviving literary and artistic works, and constructing a social center for Untouchables. The social center could potentially house Jalsa gatherings and would be most important to building solidarity in the community.

As a law minister in Delhi in the 1950s, Ambedkar also sought funds from the "Princes and People of India" to support a social and cultural center, youth clubs, and Jalsa Mandals. He appealed for a donation of Rs. 325,000 to build a social center for the Untouchables,[79] which he believed would "serve not only as a model for social, economic, and educational activities for the uplift of the Untouchables, but also as a center radiating new ideas and coordinating the different activities into a harmonious whole," including Jalsa.[80] He repeated his truism: "Without raising the Untouchables, the country cannot rise, and in their salvation lies the salvation of the country."[81] The social revolution from below, centering on the most exploited Dalits, would be deeply transformative.

The "Social Center for the Untouchables in Bombay" focused on different purposes, including the promotion of well-being among Untouchables and providing a permanent source of income to maintain and sustain its activities. However, to Ambedkar, the most important aim was to create a place that would function as a center for disseminating knowledge and providing cohesion and inspiration for Untouchables. Moreover, such a place would, he continued, "provide a meeting ground for the Untouchables for exchanging ideas, or performing social and religious functions, and as a center of culture in which they can take pride."[82] The center would be important for Jalsa events. Ambedkar emphasized the role of Jalsa Mandals:

> Untouchable youth in the Bombay Presidency have formed clubs and staged dramatic performances at marriage celebrations and other religious and social functions. These are amateur dramatic clubs giving performances of self-composed plays depicting the evils of baneful social customs on improvised stage before illiterate villagers. It is intended to organize on a sound basis this very useful activity for dissolving old and disseminating new ideas among the masses and to guide it and make it more effective.[83]

To fund the Social Center, the NJYSSJ performed in 1956 at Damodar Hall, Parel (Mumbai), earning Rs. 101.

Postcolonial and Post-Ambedkar Shahiri

Following Ambedkar's death and the disbanding of the NJYSSJ in 1956, other troupes and shahirs filled the void. Many shahirs experimented with musical forms, drawing on, for instance, music from Bollywood films. Shahir Bhimsen Gaikwad, who performed roughly from 1958 until 2015, was at the forefront of this experimentation. I interviewed Gaikwad in Dombivili-Mumbai in June 2017 (figure 4.4). Kardak and Gaikwad mainly focused on Ambedkarite shahiri; however, unlike Kardak, whose poetics-politics foregrounded social and political themes in his Jalse, Gaikwad conducted more aesthetic experiments (just like sangeet-natak and kirtan also drew upon existing popular forms to create new arts), developing a poetics-politics that crossed boundaries to connect low and high cultures, especially before his conversion to Buddhism in the 1970s. Gaikwad used his shahiri to bring together different art forms, content, singing traditions, tunes, languages, and social and political movements in the context of postcolonial and neoliberal Mumbai. He bridged Ambedkarite and non-Ambedkarite shahiri, romance-laden gaulan focusing on the play between Krishna and his maidens and devotional *kavvali*, and Marathi and Hindi songs. As such, he interacted with Tamasha performers, such as Patthe Bapurao (see chapter. 2), as well as with radical Ambedkarite Jalsakars, and closely connected the sringarik Tamasha of Mahars with radical Ambedkarite Jalsa.

Gaikwad used his shahiri skills to not only sing songs motivated by the Ambedkar movement at important events such as Ambedkar and Buddha Jayanti, but also sang a variety of Marathi and Hindi songs during Hindu public programs like Ganesh chaturthi. As I discussed in chapter 3, Dalits had been banned from Hindu public festivals in the late colonial period, and many Dalits, following Ambedkar, had abandoned the Ganesh festival. Post-Ambedkar and post-independence, some Shahirs, like Gaikwad, reentered these spaces and reengaged with these traditions. Gaikwad's embrace of non-Ambedkarite singing and his inclusion and recognition as a Dalit shahir by non-Dalits exposes the changing politics of caste and the emergence of new social and economic mobility as well as the management of caste difference and marginality in postcolonial Mumbai.

Gaikwad underlined propriety, especially with regard to women, because, like Kardak, he was troubled by the likelihood of future promiscuity through song, fearing that Tamasha would plant the seeds of temptation and frivolity. As a result, Gaikwad emphasized *dharma* (morality) and, like Kardak, declared, "Nothing *phajil* [useless, vulgar], no phajil songs," supporting Kardak's and Ambedkar's politics and ethics of respectable women and men, abiding by the values of the patriarchal home. Nevertheless, close attention to the contradictions and tensions reveals how Dalits were forced to oscillate between hope and despair during Kardak's as well as Gaikwad's times. They tried to find a way out of the problem of how to respond to persistent and violent

FIGURE 4.4. Shailaja Paik (front left) with Gaikwad (center), his wife (right), and nephew and grandson (rear) in Gaikwad's home in a chawl in Dombivili-Mumbai. Source: Photo courtesy of author.

hierarchies of caste, sexuality, and gender in contemporary Mumbai (and in India more generally). Shahirs, like Ambedkar and other Dalit leaders, faced contradictions and tensions, but the moral fault lines between the ashlil and manuski that they were navigating ran directly through the bodies of women.

Gaikwad's father, a man named Barku, hailed from a family of farmers whose menfolk worked during the non-farming season as traveling Tamasha artists. Barku Gaikwad had originally migrated from Shel-Pimpalgao (Pune District) to Pune City to join Tamasha, but he left for Mumbai around 1951 or 1952 after the troupe broke up. In Mumbai, he met famous theatre owners like Dadu Indurikar and Madhukar Nerale of New Hanuman Theatre, Lower

Parel, where he soon found work. Bhimsen Gaikwad thus grew up in Mumbai surrounded by poetry, music, and dance. He recalled how almost every night there was some kind of performance:

> I was more interested in singing and writing songs than attending night school. I was not formally trained in singing. I simply watched, heard, and absorbed everything—*tal* [a musical measure], *sur* [tune], *antara* [interval], *kalpana* [idea], if the song was difficult or easy, and how the audience and actors interacted.

Gaikwad developed a passion for singing, training, and rehearsing on his own and learning *khatyal* (sensual and playful) Lavanya and film songs, as well as devotional Hindi bhajans.

Gaikwad embraced Mumbai; "Pune was like a village," he recalled, "but Mumbai was a city with so many [electric] lights." Since the late nineteenth century, Dalits' flight to the city was a great human experiment. They thought the modern, cosmopolitan city of Mumbai would embrace all castes. They refused the backward, caste-ridden village and struggled desperately to make a different kind of life. By offering a new social mobility away from the shackles of caste slavery and untouchability in the village, the city signaled accomplishment and triumph to Gaikwad. Yet, the theoretical modernity was complicated by real lived experiences of caste on the ground. Gaikwad remembers,

> People of different caste and religious communities: Christians, *Apale* [our people; here, Dalits], *Halbe* [Scheduled Tribe], *maratha* [peasant-cultivators, Other Backward Classes], *Phulvale* [flower sellers], and so on. Even police lived in the six chawls. Everyone worked in their [caste] community circles. There was no intermingling as such. Of course, they attended our weddings and other ceremonies; however, they did not participate in Ambedkar or Buddha *Jayanti* [birth anniversary festivities].

Thus, Gaikwad emphasized the cruel paradoxes of spatial proximity and social distancing among people of different religions and castes in Mumbai; people came together for certain activities like birthdays or weddings, yet distinctions and differences were apparent, particularly during caste-specific events like Ambedkar or Buddha Jayanti.

Gaikwad worked at odd and sundry jobs during the day, but his nights were devoted to music and singing, especially "using *sope, sadhe shabda*" (easy-to-pronounce, simple words). Activists associated with the Dalit movement—Shantabai Dani, Ghanshyamrao Talvatkar, Sumantrao Gaikwad—attended these events and praised Gaikwad. To Gaikwad, like Kardak and Pagare, simple words were significant to reach the adani Untouchable. He participated in Jayanti celebrations of community heroes like Jotirao Phule, Ambedkar, and the Buddha, as well as in pan-Maharashtrian festivals celebrating Shivaji, the non-brahman king and icon of Maharashtra, protector of Maharashtra dharma. Eventually, financial exigences forced Gaikwad to establish his own Sanghmitra Gayan (Singing) Party at Chandanvadi-Girgao. He performed for people of all religions, castes, and classes, "Muslims, marathas, Kolis, and Agris, whoever provided us some advance to cover our travel and also gave us food, tea, betel leaves and betel nuts, and water. We also used to sing at public events." Gaikwad set his shahiri and Jalsa to popular Hindi film songs, melodies that would be easily recognizable to audiences of all castes.

However, his lyrics addressed issues of caste discrimination, untouchability, and social injustice. For example, in one song, Gaikwad instructs dominant castes to keep quiet and bow their heads, and to give their daughters in marriage to the Dalit sons—a reference to Ambedkar's famous political strategy from the mid-1930s of advocating for intercaste marriage, thus directly attacking the caste mechanism of endogamy (see chapter 3) to abolish caste hierarchy and distinctions. Ambedkar was convinced "that the real remedy is intermarriage. Fusion of blood can alone create the feeling of being kith and kin, and unless this feeling of kinship, of being kindred, becomes paramount, the separatist feeling—the feeling of being aliens—created by caste will not vanish."[84] Working on these lines, Gaikwad sang, "mukatyane jhukava maan, dyavi mulgi amchya mulala" (lower your neck without a word, and give your daughter to our son) to the famous tune of the song "Pyar kiya to darna kya" (Why fear when you love someone, from the classic Hindi film *Mughal-e-Azam*). This was a seductive and covert method to promote Ambedkar's political strategy: luring in the audience with familiar tunes, surprising them with unexpected, radical lyrics, spreading social revolution, and bringing about change.

Yet, the significance of these Ambedkarite agendas and lyrics did not go over well with an audience from mixed castes, who identified and marked Gaikwad and his troupe as "Jaibhimvale" or "Ambedkarvali [Ambedkarite] Party." While Gaikwad recalls encountering little caste or religious discrimination, he emphasized that non-Dalits invariably identified him and his party as an "Ambedkar" or "Untouchable" group. Gaikwad and his nephew who introduced me to him did not use the word *Dalit*, which has currency especially in academic and activist circles. Sometimes they used the term "backward classes"; sometimes they used the salutation *Jaibhim*, which non-Dalits had combined with *Ambedkar* to signify a caste: Jaibhim-Untouchable-Mahar-Ambedkar. Gaikwad, however, was not bothered by the caste-based recognition; perhaps, this was his strategy of transcending caste and yet proudly underlining his connection with Babasaheb's (a term of respect and endearment for Ambedkar) legacy. And it is worth noting that they respectfully addressed me as "our madam," signifying my belonging to our community.

Gaikwad spoke of tensions inside the Dalit artist community, as well as between Dalit Ambedkarite shahirs and Dalit and non-Dalit Tamasha performers. "We learned new songs and tunes from Tamasha," Gaikwad explained, "but they did not like us very much because we described their performances as ashlil. And for their part, they made fun of us if we did not sing well." Tamasha artists and many ordinary Untouchables made fun of Jalsa, Jalsakars, and Ambedkari shahirs. These were challenges Kardak and Pagare alluded to in the colonial period as well.

Although there were certain differences between the form of Jalsa and Tamasha and between Dalit Ambedkari shahirs and Dalit and non-Dalit Tamasha artists, Gaikwad affirmed Ambedkar's recognition of the cultural and social significance of Tamasha and Jalsa in the Dalit samaj: "Babasaheb saw Tamasha sometimes. He was proud of our artists. There were many *apale lok* [of our people] in Tamasha. Tamasha artists were respected then." However, things changed over time: "There is no respect for Tamasha art today. It has become a business—people have become more and more *lalchi* [greedy]. Earlier, they roamed in bullock-carts and today they have trucks, they ask for more money. It has become cheap, with [more sexual] songs in there." To Gaikwad, Tamasha lost respect because of the loose morality and luxury enjoyed by some Tamasha artists. The fall of Tamasha touched him too because he was one such artist.

As times changed, artists like Gaikwad negotiated with song and music. He responded to political and social agendas, became more flexible, and cooperated with different singers to learn and bend certain rules to support each other. Gaikwad recalled that after his Ambedkarite group and another Tamasha troupe performed together in a village, "Our people asked [the Tamasha troupe] to organize another event in the Buddhavada/Bauddhavada [Mahar-Buddhist quarters].[85] They agreed and then the Tamasha artists requested that we [teach them] Babasaheb's songs because they felt they would otherwise lose popularity in the village." Tamasha was certainly popular, but so was Ambedkarite shahiri, and the latter would gain momentum in particular political and social moments. As a result, Tamasha artists did not want to be left out of their larger social and political movement, and they learned Ambedkar-inspired songs from Gaikwad. Gaikwad recalls how they mixed different tunes and easily navigated between different forms of folk singing, like *kavvali* (Sufi devotional music), *gaulan* (love songs of Hindu deities Radha-Krishna), and *pavada* (panegyrics), and changed their content.

This relatively easy arrangement of intermingling different art forms changed following Ambedkar's *dharmantar* (religious conversion) to Buddhism in 1956. Gaikwad, reporting the tensions of dharmantar, recalled, "Non-Dalits mocked Dalits regarding dharmantar. They mocked us when we changed the name from Maharvada to Baudhhavada." There were internal challenges too, as I mentioned in chapters 2 and 3. Some Mahars did not undergo *diksha* (conversion to Buddhism) and clung to baluta (traditional portions of grain they received in exchange for their service to the village) and wanted to keep Mahar vatan (hereditary claims in a village, including claims to perform local services). However, Ambedkarite Dalits rejected them. When those Mahars who wanted to retain vatandari faced atrocities and caste discrimination and boycott in the villages, they too wanted diksha. Responding to this social and political moment, Gaikwad constructed a new song: "Why are you so stubborn about not leaving the past caste obligations? You will gain wisdom and understanding, respect and dignity, and so you will become a new manus in Buddhism."

Gaikwad's life changed after his conversion to Ambedkarism and Ambedkarite Buddhism sometime in the 1970s. He explained that although he did not formally convert to Buddhism, the new mentality and modern morality of diksha transformed him completely into a new manus and gave him a new manuski and Dalit consciousness. He affirmed, "Earlier, I did not feel a sense of pride or self. Today I have a sense of respect of myself and of Babasaheb." His conversion to Ambedkarite Buddhism and coming into consciousness compelled Gaikwad to transform his shahiri for social and political propagation. Through his songs, he challenged caste hierarchy, caste labor, violence perpetrated by touchables and reminded them of the change, especially after dharmantar:

> We labored for you like slaves
> we ate the bread you gave us
> while keeping our pockets empty
> Gone are those days, *patil* (dominant caste headman of the village) brother.

When I met Gaikwad in July 2017, he continued to pay tribute to his icon, Babasaheb, by singing for me one of his famous poems:

> Awake, awake, working, working
> Bhimrao [Ambedkar] worked for the people
> He at times stumbled, but still he was tireless
> He broke the chains of caste slavery
> Remember how he fought relentlessly against caste discrimination
>   and untouchability, so we have dignity, rights, and we are not
>   segregated due to caste
> Many mighty had to bow to Bhimrao!

Most of Gaikwad's songs praised the efforts and life of Ambedkar to fight caste discrimination and violence and to work for social justice in modern India.

The humiliation of caste had created a collective state of shame, and hence comportment was important to self-respectful Dalits. As a result, Gaikwad emphasized, "People honor me. I dress up appropriately—jacket, *kurta* [long shirt], *topi* [cap]. *Rahanimana* [status] is important." The full shirt, the singer's shiny embroidered jacket, cap, umbrella, footwear, bicycle, and full sari signified a higher social status, and status decided the virtue of a person. It was especially important to Dalits who sought to improve their self-dignity as well as status, honor, and rise in the eyes of the dominant castes. Drinking and gambling were also ashlil vices ineradicably tethered to Dalitness and hence had to be abandoned, especially after dharmantar.

Before dharmantar, Gaikwad broke boundaries and built bridges, thus improving the intermingling and dialogue between various forms. After dharmantar and the gaining of manuski, it would be difficult for him to mix different arts because now, following Dalit radicals, especially Ambedkar, there was no place for the ashlil in constructing the new Dalit manus. Gaikwad would approve of Tamasha "only if the latter does not engage in phajil [improper and overly sexual], ashlil." To him, "[Tamasha people] should retain respectability, morality, modesty." This was the only moral path towards manuski, in Gaikwad's eyes. As a result, he asserted conclusively, "I now sing dharmic *bhajans* [devotional songs]." This was a major transformation in the twenty-first century. The practices of singing bhajan and kirtan are integral to Hindu collective devotional pratices throughout India. Singing Ambedkarite and Buddhist bhajans provided a means for participants to express their commitment and devotion to Ambedkar and Buddha and model manuski and anticaste democratic political structures.

Nothing Ashlil and Nothing Phajil

To shahirs like Ambedkar, the annihilation of caste and immorality would render untouchability nonexistent. The impossible challenge for Dalits was to carry the conditions of the present forward to bring about a future in which those conditions no longer existed. Dalits recognized well the ways caste and the mechanism of endogamy unleashed sexual violence on stigmatized Dalit women (see chapter 3). As a result, they sought to protect women as actors, characters, and even those in the audience. Regarding the presence of women as actors and characters, Gaikwad underscored, "There was no woman on stage in Ambedkari Jalsa or shahiri. There may have been a few, three or four [performers], but I did not come across them." However, Gaikwad reported the change in contemporary times. He argued, "However, everything is business today and women are on stage, earning very well. Earlier, we were happy with food and coconut. Today people have two or three trucks, and take twelve lakhs for one performance." Gaikwad was angry that Tamasha people were commodifying women's bodies and commercializing everything. Perhaps he was unhappy that this enormous enterprise had neglected him completely. Most importantly, he also forgot that his body was also commodified and commercialized.

Like Kardak, Gaikwad was committed to his political radicalism and devoted to a gendered notion of "proper" morality that revolved around a modest and moral, conservative notion of Dalit womanhood. He differentiated himself from Tamasha: "Tamasha artists' and our paths are different." Gaikwad explained, "Jalsa had *dholki, tuntune* [drum, one-stringed sitar-like instrument—just as in Tamasha], but we did not have *nachya* [male dancers] or *nachi* [female dancers]." Gaikwad thus accused Tamasha nachya and nachi of undermining the community's morality through their gestures, songs, dances, and jokes. "I could slap Pralhad Shinde [a famous shahir]" for what he has done with his singing, Gaikwad raged. "It was shameful!" he continued. "When he performed, he sang one or two songs on Ambedkar and continued with all *altu phaltu* [useless, wasteful] songs for the entire three or four hours." By contrast, he emphasized that his "singing justice" had a high moral character:

> When I present, women sit in the front row. *Dharmala dharun gani* [I sing songs that underscore morality, moral virtues]. [I write these songs in such a manner that] they are *dharmaupadesh* [instructions in morality] and *shikvan* [teachings] for women so that they are also able to sing these songs. For example, one song is about when they are working at the *jata* [grinding stone] in the morning—"*aata kashala ga lajayacha, Jaibhim bolayacha*" [why should we be ashamed now? Say Jaibhim and rise]. Today things have changed because everything is becoming business oriented. It is merely *karamnuk* [entertainment]!

Gaikwad affirmed a specific gendered morality for women. Even their seating arrangement was in the first rows of the audience, marking their distance from the vulgar and rowdy men in the middle or the back of the gathering. Women were like attentive students sitting closer to the poet-activist teacher absorbing his political pedagogical agendas. He sharply critiqued the popular entertainment trend devoid of agendas of social justice in the musical arts. He insisted,

"Ambedkari shahirs should not give in to the entertainment business. They should continue to focus on and dedicate themselves to their leader's agenda of *samaj karya* [social justice and social reconstruction]." Poets like him have a moral task to fulfil, Gaikwad maintains—and not only artists but audience members as well, especially women, whose role in the struggle involves strict adherence to circumscribed codes of modesty and morality. In this song, as in the case of Kardak, Babasaheb possesses a supernatural power, becoming a manly protector, mother, husband, and god for women.

Gaikwad expressed the poignancy he experienced as an expert singer who had to dissociate himself from an art form that he loved but that was rooted in sexual-caste slavery and in which he excelled: "Lavani is not bad. It has story." Yet, due to the liberatory anticaste politics and historical conundrums I analyzed above, Gaikwad abandoned Tamasha and Lavani and focused on propriety and the critical political pedagogy of his song: "It is *bara nahi* [not proper] for me to *prachar* [promote Ambedkar and Buddha's social justice message] through Lavani." He reasoned:

> Lavani has her own *rang* [quality to entice in pleasure, sensuality], *dhang* [disdainful airs and arts of love], *havbhav* [gestures and tendency to excite amorous sensations and coquetry]. We do not want those *saunskar* [culture; here, lascivious, wanton effects] on young girls [present and future]. For example, in the Lavani "soda soda raya, tanu shinali, ghamani sari choli bhijali" [Leave me, o kingly man. My body is worn out due to sexual play. Sex has made me sweat and wetted my blouse]. [It] means raya has held you so tight physically and with all the love acts. So, it is *vait* [bad]. Lavani has to have ashlil words. Its admiring [audience] likes it. There is another one, "You had sex with me for four nights. I am now tired." I did not write or sing such songs. *Nafrat aahe* [I hate them].[86]

Thus, once again, Gaikwad emphasized respectability and morality for future Dalit generations. He differentiated between shil-ashil and different high and low cultures. The likelihood of future promiscuity was troubling. He agreed with the lead woman performer, Mangalatai Bansode, whose performative life I re-create in chapter 6, about the sexual excess of Lavani and Tamasha that has tainted her and other performers.

Conclusion

Shahirs consistently deployed the poetics-politics of Ambedkarite Jalsa to artic-ulate anticaste liberation, commit to manuski, and reflect collectively on their conditions of possibility and social and political transformation. In the process, however, they profiled Tamasha and women as threats to the Dalit commu-nity and manuski. Shahirs challenged Congress, tackled the Hindu-right Shiv Sena, and enabled connections to build solidarities between different castes, subcastes and classes, political factions, and religious communities, thus trans-forming the discourse of political activism. Dalits from different castes and reli-gions engaged in the poetics-politics of Ambedkarite Jalse as they experienced larger structural changes—social, political, economic, and ideological. An an-ticaste liberatory discourse shaped shahiri, and shahirs in turn engaged with the sexual-caste economy, public space, Dalit capitalism, the state's anti-Dalit pogrom, increasing violence, and victimization of Dalits and lower castes to suggest new possibilities—political and beyond the state.

For example, the Dalit (Mang caste) Communist poet-intellectual and nov-elist Annabhau Sathe performed in Tamasha and was very active in politics during the 1940s–60s. He cofounded the Communist Lalbavta Kala Pathak (Red Art Troupe), wrote on themes of class and caste struggles,[87] engaged with the Samyukta (United) Maharashtra Movement (SMM; see chapter 5), and paid tributes to Ambedkar in his famous song:

> Take a hammer to change the world,
> Bhimrao went saying!
> Why is the elephant sitting in the mud of slavery?
> Shake your body and come out, take a leap.
> The rich have exploited us and the priests have tortured us.
> They decided we were low and impure and kept us slaves, for thou-
>   sands of years.
> They heaped insults on us, they created these walls.
> Sitting on the chariot of unity let us go forward
> To win a united Maharashtra and hold on to the name of Bhim!

The SMM, led by savarna—brahman and chandraseniya kayasta prabhu—elites, used Sathe's energy and power, yet left out his hero Bhimrao Ambedkar!

Nevertheless, shahiri flourished, and in 1999, a group of Ambedkarite and left activists formed the anticaste Revolutionary Cultural Movement (Vidrohi Sanskrutik Chalval) to critique the facile distinctions of culture and caste order. It was a major regional movement that discussed the need to rethink, restructure, and mobilize anticaste politics, particularly in the context of new economic reforms and neo-liberalization and rising Hindutva (right-wing, aggressive Hindu) politics through the present-day. Kabir Kala Manch, a Pune-based cultural troupe was founded in 2002 to propagate the revolutionary ideas of Kabir, Marx, and Ambedkar. Many members of the group, including Sheetal Sathe, a woman lead singer, have completely revolutionized the shahiri tradition.[88]

There were contradictions and tensions inside Dalit community and in Dalit politics between the pragmatic and liberatory aspects regarding gender and sexuality. Jalsa destigmatized its reliance on the energy and attractions of Tamasha by leaving the women out of the orbit of performance and reinventing it as a critical and pedagogic form. Yet, these political practices were necessary for liberatory anticasteism while resisting ashlil stigmatization and the making of manuski, a certain morality for the emerging Dalit modern citizen in twentieth-century Maharashtra, and went beyond merely constituting masculinity. We need to pay attention to Dalits' commitment, intentions, and contingent agendas of liberatory anticaste resistance in particular historical conjunctures. For them, ashlil undermined Dalit manus—the two could not coexist—and yet, understanding the marginalization of women in Jalsa through the grounded human reality of shahirs like Gaikwad makes it difficult to sustain our usual academic critiques of Ambedkar and Ambedkari politics as reconstituting masculinity or "Dalit patriarchy."

There were different contradictions for different Dalits—while Ambedkar rescued Dalits' manus from the ashlil and did not challenge the genre of Tamasha, Gaikwad and Kardak wanted to get rid of Tamasha. Ambedkar was more interested in the manus than in the genre. Ambedkar challenged the exploitation and commodification of women, while Gaikwad attacked consumerism. However, for Jalsakars and Tamasha people like Mangalatai (chapter 6), the genre was important for different reasons.

Gaikwad, Ambedkar, and Kardak focused on generating manus and manuski. Indeed, while some contradictions may have set Gaikwad at odds with other articulations of radical Dalit politics, the lifelong work of Vilas Ghogre reminds us that Dalit poetry and song has sought also to *bridge* such rifts—by singing to life shared intentions. To fixate on the contradictions would be to miss the complex context within which Gaikwad formulates these particular ideas and to overlook the intentions and tenuous process of manuski towards which they are directed.

The art and activism of Vilas Ghogre is the subject of Mumbai documentarian Anand Patwardhan's rather hopeful 1985 film *Bombay: Our City*, which follows the tireless work of Mumbai's Ambedkarite Dalit singer-activists to forge alliances with India's socialist movements, labor organizations, and leftist political parties—class-based movements that had often been silent about the violence of caste oppression. Ghogre had made it his life's work to build a left-wing alliance between Bombay's Dalits and Communists, and it was the failure of this caste-class political project—embodied in the poet's suicide in the wake of the Ramabai killings—with which Patwardhan opens his much darker 2012 sequel *Jai Bhim Comrade*.

The next chapter focuses on the imposition of decency by the postcolonial state since the 1940s and especially after the creation of new Maharashtra nation-state. Challenging elites' and the state's discourse of ashlil, Dalit-Bahujans continued to perform and watch Tamasha, turning it into caste-based right and assli practice. While the Jalsa flourished, Tamasha did not completely die. Women like Pavalabai and many others were further degraded and excluded but continued to perform in Tamasha, embracing their denigrated status. Women found new avenues to exercise their art and earn their living.

Part III

Chapter 5

CLAIMING AUTHENTICITY AND
BECOMING MARATHI, POST-1960

Tamasha is the *assli* [legitimate] art-form of Marathi culture; yet it is marginalized and excluded. It has not gained the *pratishtha* [respectability] [from the *pandharpesha* elites] that it deserves.
—Kalu-Balu Khade-Kavlapurkar[1]

The above quote from the famous duo Kalu-Balu Khade-Kavlapurkar, third-generation Dalit (Mang caste) Tamasha artists and brothers whose careers in Marathi popular theatre spanned over fifty years, is a succinct assessment of the tension at the core of this chapter: Tamasha is a quintessential artistic expression of Marathi culture and has been mobilized as such by *pandharpesha* (white-collar, urban, privileged) people, who had assumed positions of power and privilege, in the state of Maharashtra since its creation in the 1960s, and yet it remains a marginal and much maligned art based on persistent characterizations of it and its performers as *ashlil* (vulgar).

The anxious new Maharashtra state played a significant role in sanitizing Tamasha and reconstituting the Marathi social imaginary. On January 29, 1961, Morarji Desai, chief minister of Bombay (1952–57) and finance minister (1958–63) and home minister of India (1978–79), declared, "It is extremely essential to create a strong public opinion against ashlilta [in all forms]."[2] The ashlil practices of the lower classes and castes haunted the new state of Maharashtra and its agents. To rein in Maharashtra's ashlil elements, civil society colluded with the state to ban kissing (*chumban bandi*) on screen, Tamasha, alcohol (*daru bandi*), and prostitution (*veshya bandi*).[3] These bans, however, resulted in increased public discussion; censorship incited people to speak about sexuality in order to better regulate it. Public discourse on Tamasha, Lavani, and *chumban* (kissing) both highlighted the socially threatening potential and normalized narratives of Indian sexuality. Especially after the 1960s, sex was not only subject to judgment but was also administered for utility and the greater good of all Marathi citizens. State governance colluded with brahmani morality, enabling censored objects to circulate even more as they staged an opposition between corrupting and purifying forces. I ask why did the new state want to suddenly protect and patronize Tamasha and turn it into a Marathi icon? What procedures and paradigms did Maharashtrians adopt to become good Marathi citizens when Maharashtra was carved out of the larger Indian state?

The Marathi-speaking state was produced simultaneously and in similar ways to the larger Indian nation. This chapter focuses on how the new Marathi social imaginary was produced and experienced by different people and how it changed the meaning of Tamasha. Although for Kalu-Balu and many Tamasha people (along with some sympathetic touchables and state officials), Tamasha was an *assli* (authentic) Marathi tradition, a *jativant* (caste-based) art, many upwardly mobile Dalits, touchables, and powerful state agents denigrated Tamasha as ashlil. Despite some ambivalence, respectable Marathi citizens seeking social order found Tamasha and its artists to be inherently lewd and indecent. State officials, elite public figures, filmmakers and others in the film industry, and those in the Tamasha community, however, also deployed sanitized versions of Tamasha, harnessing its sociosexual energy and recognizing it as a traditional Marathi art, to politically reinforce a regional-linguistic Marathi identity after the creation of the state of Maharashtra in 1960, compromising their objections to Tamasha to create a regional consciousness and identity and accommodate the new capitalism unleashed by Tamasha film. Tamasha was key to Maharashtra's social imaginary, and Tamasha women, implicitly and explicitly, remained a cipher—for the Marathi nation, for virtue, for culture, for an aesthetic ideal, and for sexual energy.

The iterant performativity, energy, and attractiveness of live Tamasha theatre, Tamasha films, and advertisements for Tamasha films produced certain presumed truths about Tamasha performances as raunchy, feudal-patriarchal, and risqué; about Tamasha women as salacious vamps; and about Marathi identity and people as essentially virile, proud, and nationalistic.[4] The various attempts to sanitize Tamasha when placed along with the Dalit project of manuski produce crucial insights into the historical significance and specificity of the latter. The state and elites appropriated Tamasha and used the social and sexual labor of Tamasha women without paying any heed to Dalits or Tamasha women and their manuski.

Marathikaran (literally, becoming Marathi; here, making Marathi regional identity) occurred through various symbols, identities, and political demands, and Marathi identity was constructed, contested, and deployed for various purposes by different Marathi people. Many ideologues, propagandists, activists, and members of civil society attempted to create an image of Marathi people as a unified political community by discursively eliding ideological, regional, and caste, class, and religious differences in the political moment of the formation of state of Maharashtra. In keeping with their pursuit of a modern, independent Maharashtra, however, pandharpesha Marathis were invested in sustaining the perception of castelessness in the urban context. Although caste became insidious in the city, as Gaikwad reminded us in chapter 4, elites interested in the long march of the modern sought to shield the problem under the garb of modernity. In the process, however, the entanglements of caste with class resulted not in the eradication of caste or the inequities that sustained it but in the shrouding of caste in the cloak of class. Elites obscured caste in the discourse on cultural and the Marathi social imaginary.

These elisions helped Marathi elites to push back against the Hindi film industry in Mumbai, the capital of Maharashtra, and the domineering Hindivalas from the north who threatened their sense of Marathiness. As a result, they emphasized a marathamola identity: masculine, muscular, free, virile, proud, rebellious, and adventurous. However, an assli marathamola identity could only be rooted in the energy of the feudal-patriarchal art of raucous Tamasha, not in genteel pandharpesha progressive politics or arts. Despite pandharpesha ambivalence regarding Tamasha, its carnivalesque, rowdy *masti* (carefreeness, passion, a gamut of affects unleashing unruly masculine sexual energy) was required to carve out a robust, masculine, muscular Marathi state that could oppose the dominance of non-Marathi people from North and South India.

Elites defined Tamasha and Lavani—along with genteel *natak* (drama), *sangeet-natak* (song-drama), and classical singing—as traditional Marathi arts at the core of the process and politics of Marathikaran.[5] Tamasha, however, ranked lower in the hierarchy of arts due to its supposedly polluted language and the alleged ignorance of the nonliterate Dalits who performed it. Elites in general considered Tamasha and its performers to be inferior, thereby denigrating Tamasha and elevating and honoring higher sanskritic arts. It was thus marked by a tension, as elites engaged in the dual processes of sanitizing and asserting the assli status of Tamasha. Michel Foucault's work on the nexus of "power-knowledge-pleasure" helps decipher how live Tamasha theatre, Tamasha films, and Tamasha film advertisements created "truth-effects" and knowledge about Tamasha, enabling its power and pleasure and sustaining an ambivalent discourse about Tamasha sexuality that simultaneously legitimated and prohibited Tamasha. The explicit repression of the sexual energy of Tamasha worked in tandem with its implicit harnessing, the simultaneous approval and disavowal of the ashlil by different social actors from a range of castes wherein men imagined and practiced their vision of Marathiness by writing and engaging in a conversation on sex, sexuality, and social mores in the 1960s. Elite Maharashtrians and their new state agents defined their progressive, modernizing mission in fundamentally gendered terms and especially focused on women's morality marked by caste, class, and religion.

Marathikaran was a hierarchical process where Marathi elites positioned themselves as primary actors and the marginalized Tamasha people responded to changing political situations and reconfigured themselves and their marginality in relation to pandharpesha Marathis. Marathi people resorted to multiple identities, drawing upon, for instance, traditions of sants (saints) and kirtankars (singers of devotional songs). Tamasha and Lavani were, in this regard, significant popular, emotive, and performative cultural symbols recuperated through regional and national identity projects aimed at claiming an authentic identity, central to the common trope of a proud, virile, and patriotic Marathi manus (person; but here, people and identity) and Marathi past. The performance of "essential" and "inherent" Marathi traits of valor, virility, strength, and pride were important tropes to mobilize people on emotional grounds, create a common cultural memory, and produce an illusion of unity in time (from precolonial and colonial to the postcolony) and place. Yet there were complexities; elites shaped, produced, and executed state policy in a way that parsed popular arts like Tamasha from classical arts such as bharatnatyam and kathak. The pandharpesha audiences for natak found Tamasha disgusting and sought to sanitize Tamasha theatre and especially, post-1960, Tamasha films for consumption by elite families by regulating the performance and perceptions of Lavani and Tamasha, whose robust popularity evoked their persistent anxieties of caste, class, and sexuality. Elitist discourse and practices clearly followed the caste logic—they rewarded Dalit Tamasha people who fell in line, consented to their will and whims, and supported them and their agendas of Marathikaran.

Vulnerable Tamasha people responded to the new cultural experiments and the construction of a new Maharashtra by claiming their own authenticity and reworking their positions within the newly formed state and the larger Indian nation. Marathiness, a regional consciousness and linguistic identity underlining Maharashtra's uniqueness, and the contingency of the formation of the new nationalist state of Maharashtra alongside and in negotiation with pan-Indian politics were important processes and politicizations that trained Tamasha people in subordinated behavior as well as in strategizing required to survive in the caste system; they worked in harmony with the state and Marathi elites, foregrounding caste and cultural differences among Marathi people and generating assli status for themselves.

There were deep contradictions, even antagonisms, between Marathiness and Dalitness and Marathi and Dalit identity. The particular constitution of a regional, robust, and rebellious Marathi manus, much like the universal liberal manus, did not extend to include Dalit manus and manuski (see chapters 3 and 4). Dalits were even more victimized by the process of Marathikaran and the elitist legitimization of Marathi identity. Dalits were also ambivalent about Tamasha and Tamasha women. Moreover, the ambivalent aesthetics of a robust Tamasha was a key condition in the affective and effective appeal to assli identity and authority of constructed and contingent nature of the imagination of Marathi manus and community as a whole after 1960.

Tamasha and its practitioners emerged as mere pawns in the process of Marathikaran, and Tamasha women—reformed, sanitized, and assli—were conveniently put in the service of Marathikaran. A sanitized Marathi culture was central to Marathikaran, Marathi identity and authority. Scholars have yet to recognize how culture, especially Tamasha, emerged as a major battleground in defining a Marathi identity within the new state of Maharashtra. Tamasha artists repurposed the dual processes of sanitizing Tamasha and asserting their and their Tamasha's assli status to reinforce their traditional roots, striving to keep their arts alive and new. To them, such caste difference was significant to provide evidence of their legitimacy, their assli status. Dalit struggles in transforming Tamasha from ashlil to assli were thus part of a broader project of post-1960 defining a national identity, rooted in linguistic regionalism, in the context of the creation of the new state of Maharashtra. Marathi film-makers discovered the robust masculine masti of Tamasha and Lavani and devoted themselves to sanitizing Tamasha, making it assli for the consumption by pandharpesha, urban, urbane, educated, dominant-caste, male and female audiences. They made many appeals grounded in already prevalent Dalit-Bahujan discourse regarding the true, assli tradition of Tamasha to improve its status in the eyes of the elite and seek their approval. Although a cross-section of Marathis—both elites and Dalits—participated in sanitizing and reclaiming Tamasha (albeit for different purposes), Dalits in particular consistently struggled to underline their legitimacy and, for the purposes of this chapter, transform Tamasha and themselves from ashlil to assli.

While filmmakers and Tamasha artists protested charges of obscenity and indecency, ironically, the Samyukta (United) Maharashtra Movement (SMM), founded in 1946, intensively used Pavada and Lavani as icons of Marathi unity. Bourgeois politics, responding to Indian mass culture in the latter half of the twentieth century, rendered Tamasha and Lavani as respectable objects worthy not only of acceptance but also consumption by pandharpesha. The state sought to ground them morally and culturally as an alternative to Western and mainstream media. Tamasha and Lavani, with the help of the state and political parties like the Shiv Sena, could claim a particular cultural authority as assli Marathi. To make them respectable and consumable, the state censored Tamasha and other ashlil acts. The state "adopted an indigenized version of the white man's burden: a kind of permanently institutionalized discourse of historical crisis according to which censorship becomes necessary because India is always in a time of transition."[6]

There were underlying anxieties, ambiguities, and uncertainties as progressive and conservative elites sparred regarding ashlil-assli that thrived in the context of the creation of the new state of Maharashtra. The new Marathi manus was created by caste and cultural vigilantes who enforced distinctions of taste and culture and in the process attacked the ashlil. Many petitioned for a ban on vulgar writings, vulgar art and aesthetics, and vulgarity in films. There was a visceral dislike for kissing on screen. They engaged in the protection of culture from the onslaught of Western influence as well as from internal ashlil practices. The fault lines converged on women. People were anxious about changing attitudes and behaviors of women.

Becoming Assli Marathi, Inscribing Marathiness, and Making Maharashtra

The project to sanitize Tamasha as part of a modern Marathi identity was the last major brahmani intervention in pursuit of an assli culture, the agenda for which would be set in later decades by the brahman chandraseniya kayastha prabhu (CKP) and maratha-dominated political groups. Although many brahmans denigrated Tamasha as ashlil, individuals like Ram Joshi in the nineteenth century and Patthe Bapurao in the twentieth appropriated it and excelled in it. The biographies of Bapurao published in the 1940s established his canonical status. At the end of the 1940s, however, the colonial state officially banned Tamasha, though it continued to be practiced in rural Maharashtra as well as covertly in cities, as Gaikwad mentioned in chapter 4. Veena Naregal notes that efforts to canonize Patthe Bapurao's work in the "1940s coincided with the regulation and disciplining of Tamasha and Lavani forms. They culminated in the appointment of the Tamasha Sudhar Samiti (Reform Committee), presided over by Datto Vaman Potdar, who also contributed a preface to Jintikar's Bapurao volumes, to send in recommendations to tackle the obscene elements and humor of the form."[7] To Naregal, such attempts suggest why Marathi elites remained unenthusiastic in seizing opportunities to raise Tamasha and Lavani within the national canon of "classical" performance forms, arguing that while "kathak and bharatnatyam were sanitized, purified of their erotic excess, so as to be fit for middle-class respectability and classical status. Tamasha and Lavani's popularity outside educated and respectable middle-class enclaves limits such a possibility."[8]

It was under such circumstances that Tamasha resurfaced in postcolonial India. In the 1950s, the SMM, as part of the language and culture movement, also appropriated Tamasha, creating new Marathi social imaginaries and also challenging Hindivalas and the Hindi film world, while the Marathi film industry celebrated Tamasha and produced new Tamashe Lavanya for the pandharpesha in the 1950s and 1960s. Popular shahirs of the SMM like shahir Sabale worked with brahman writer Sai Paranjape to sing new vag to sanitize Tamasha in their "ek Tamasha sundarsa" (one beautiful Tamasha).[9]

The elites shaped, produced, and executed state policy to differentiate between the popular and the classical arts. Naregal rightly argues that kathak and bharatnatyam traditions were pliant; thus "accommodating themselves to regional upper-caste/middle-class reformist initiatives enabled their incorporation into post-independence canon of Indian classical dances that would be recognized as part of national heritage and deemed worthy of national-level patronage."[10] In the 1950s and especially after 1960, elites sought to extend reform to Tamasha, sanitizing it to make it worthy of middle-class family consumption by regulating the performance and perceptions of lower-caste Lavani and Tamasha, whose robust popularity evoked their persistent anxieties. The paradoxical appropriation of low-caste art forms for political and commercial success and the continued marginalization of low-caste performers and performances demonstrate how political leaders and their parties have exploited the discourse of caste inequality. They have, along with liberals, continued to relegate these forms as "backward" in the larger story of nationalism, modernization, development, and citizenship. Also, they simultaneously and ironically discard and embrace, condemn and engage in the power and pleasure of the ashlil. Throughout this period, Tamasha was seen as dangerous and desirable at the same time.

SMM and Marathikaran

Since the mid-1930s, Marathi speakers had demanded a sovereign, monolingual political region. As during the colonial period, elite Maharashtrians were committed to governing themselves by creating a virtuous and virile nation within

FIGURE 5.1. Advertisement for *Ek Tamasha Sundarsa* (One beautiful Tamasha). Source: *Rasrang*, September 11, 1971. National Film Archive of India.

postcolonial India. However, political tensions between the central and state governments, resulted in Marathis feeling dominated, even marginalized, by Northern Indian leadership, especially the Congress Party. These political tensions resulted in an increasingly sharper focus on the process of Marathikaran and what constituted ashlil and assli Marathi manus by the SMM in the postcolonial period, especially in the realm of public culture. Many elite reformers, revolutionaries, communists, ordinary Marathi people, politicians, and the state engaged in the ongoing and fraught process of Marathikaran.[11] They disciplined the ashlil in every form, to re-create moral and social imaginaries to become "assli" (legitimate, properly) Marathi manus, by creating an "authentic" identity, legitimacy, and order in the newly created Mahan rashtra (great nation) in 1961. As in the colony, there was renewed interest in discussing the intimate in public spaces, especially in the new state of Maharashtra.

After independence, when the Bombay Presidency became the state of Bombay, comprised primarily of Marathi- and Gujarati-speaking regions, the idea of a separate Marathi-speaking state, with Mumbai as its capital, gained some traction and led to the formation of the SMM in February 1946. The state played a significant role in rethinking and regenerating the new Marathi social. Following the States Reorganization Act of November 1956, which reorganized India's states along linguistic lines and incorporated into the state of Bombay Marathi- and Gujarati-speaking areas previously outside it, the SMM, feeling the act had not gone far enough, continued to agitate for the formation of a Marathi-speaking state. This was realized on May 1, 1960, when Bombay State was partitioned into the Gujarati-speaking Gujarat and the Marathi-speaking Maharashtra. In the new state's early years, arts and public culture were central to the process of Marathi identity creation (Marathikaran), and talented writers and powerful public speakers and polemicist-orators like the deshastha brahman Pralhad Keshav Atre (1898–1969), who had been a central figure in the SMM, played a major role in this larger project.

In his writings of the early 1960s on the creation of the state of Maharashtra, Atre argued vehemently that "Marathi manus [literally, person; here, man] are literally *kondmara* [imprisoned]."[12] Frustrated by the number of non-Marathi speakers working in Maharashtra's service, financial, and film sectors, he added that "*Bigar* [non]-Marathi capitalists and businessmen, such as Gujaratis, Marwaris, Sikhs, Madrasis, and Parsis have attacked Maharashtra from North and South. [As a result], Marathi manus is being systematically excluded from various service sectors. The government needs to stop this in time, or else it will erase Marathi manus from Mumbapuri [Mumbai]."[13] He exhorted Marathi people to revive their "original" past Marathiness by asserting their "Marathi *bana* [pride, valor, and refusal to accept insult and injustice] and Marathi *jidd* [determination to fight] that shone like electricity and fire. His very existence is for independence and his country."[14] To Atre, such a rebellious maratha and Marathiness were critical because in every aspect Marathi manus has been restricted [socially, financially, politically]. In Maharashtra State, Marathi manus should be able to live with pride, honor, respect, and prestige [*abru, sanman, pratishtha*]. . . . Maharashtra State belongs to marathas, meaning those speaking the Marathi language. All power and property should therefore belong to Marathi manus. I openly proclaim that Maharashtra government should stop the attack launched by non-Marathi people.[15]

To Atre, Marathi became a linguistic nationalism, a collective identity and ideology for the newly carved out, linguistically rooted regional nation-state. To him, regional rhetoric merged with national identity; linguistic states were not antithetical to creating an Indian nation—both were integral to achieving complete independence. The making of Marathi identity was significant as Maharashtra consolidated its political boundaries; because non-Marathis dominated certain sectors within the new state of Maharashtra, Marathi identity was formed as a besieged one. As a result, Atre spearheaded the transition from "maratha," a demarcator of a Kshatriya (warrior) caste group, to "Marathi," encouraging rebelliousness among Marathi-speaking people as a whole. The new Marathi man embodied distinct values of fearlessness, leadership, and readiness to sacrifice.

This "whole," however, despite some mention of caste discrimination, Dalit suffering, and assisting Ambedkar, did not easily incorporate Dalits and their manuski as articulated by Dalits themselves, and Atre and other elite SMM leaders certainly did not encourage the same sort of rebelliousness among Dalit women and the Dalit samaj, revealing a deep tension between Marathiness and Dalitness. The SMM was mainly an effort to consolidate an alliance between brahmans and non-brahman elites (such as the CKP) across caste groups and a consensus among the middle classes over a shared Marathi identity.

The SMM was the last political movement in Maharashtra led by brahmans. It drew strongly on the historical memory of the marathas. Once the state of Maharashtra was created, it was dominated by elite marathas, and although the SMM tried to eliminate internal divisions along lines of caste, religion, and class, it failed miserably, and earlier tensions between different castes resurfaced. Atre, a deshastha brahman man, was keenly aware of the history of maratha-brahman power plays in the region as well as the numerical strength and dominance of marathas in politics. He argued against those who wanted to convert Maharashtra into a maratha *rashtra* (nation) by cleverly extending maratha identity beyond the *shahannyav kuli* (high lineage clans) and *kunbi* (lower peasant-caste community) to encompass all Marathi speakers, a strategy in use since the end of the nineteenth century.

Yet the dominance of marathas in the SMM and in Maharashtra politics more broadly meant that Dalits and their political parties, such as the Scheduled Caste Federation (founded in 1942; SCF), the Republican Party of India (founded in 1958; RPI), and the Dalit Panthers (1972), were marginalized. SCF and RPI were wary of brahman leftists who focused on class consciousness and ignored caste divisions. marathas and Dalits were most proximate in the caste hierarchy in villages and as a result, maratha-Dalit relations in Maharashtra were highly tenuous. Marathas represented rural exploitation and discriminated against Dalits, and also paid lip-service to anticaste protests led by Dalits. Ambedkar certainly understood such regional caste politics, and he feared a united Maharashtra wherein rural maratha elites, as one bloc, would be more dominant in regional politics and society would increasingly exploit rural Dalits. As a result, he rejected both brahman and maratha elites and worked on an independent Dalit movement. Yet, even SCF and RPI were factionalized, ambivalent about strategies, and had few alternatives besides joining the Congress Party.

Atre, like his contemporary Balasaheb (Bal) Thackeray, was troubled that North and South Indians infiltrated Maharashtra and dominated the service sector. Thackeray, of the CKP caste and a founder of the new regional, nationalist, Hindu, right-wing and ethnocentric organization Shiv Sena, usurped and gave new shape to the regional rhetoric of the SMM era.[16] He was troubled that non-Marathi—primarily Gujarati and Sikh—capitalists dominated the economic realm. Politically, to him the central Indian government had always already abandoned the Marathi people. Congress offices in Mumbai did not employ Marathis, so the latter were frustrated and angry.

Atre and Thackeray—both through the power of writing and oratory, and Thackeray through formal politics—and their followers attacked Hindi-language speakers and Hindi films, frustrated that Hindivalas from north India

were ruling the film industry in Mumbai. As a result, they focused on sanitizing, strengthening, and improving Marathi public culture—Marathi language,
Marathi drama, Marathi film, and the rearing of Marathi children and youth,
especially women—in ways that often marked Dalit difference. For example,
Marathi elites emphasized the significance of a proper Marathi language as the
central node for a robust collective identity in the new regional and linguistic
state, emphasizing its masculine qualities and promoting its sanskritization.
Both the Congress before independence and the independent Indian government privileged language to determine the viability of regional states. Marathi
language aimed to unite all Marathi speakers and has remained the strongest
ingredient in the political rhetoric of Marathiness to the present day.

Brahmani cultured and sanitized changes in writing and pronunciation
were important in this context because they were the basis on which reformers
could make claim to the authenticity and legitimacy of Marathi. The state and
civil society would lead this revolution in language by standardizing a pure,
nasal-toned, sanskritized Marathi language associated with brahmans. In the
process, however, writers formalized and normalized distinctions between
elites and non-elites, high and low castes, classes, languages, dialects, and
tones, even between the Marathi spoken in private and that spoken in public.

While touchable elites tried to develop a model that stressed respectability
and sanitized Marathi, Dalit writers of 1960s and 1970s created a new Dalit
literature celebrating the ashlil, the transgressive, and shocking stories and
poems that centered around the prostitute, the down and out, and the new
Dalit Buddhist, but they did not spend much time on the sensual. Ironically,
this shocking Dalit literature was celebrated outside Maharashtra and even
internationally, but not inside Maharashtra. Marathi Dalit writers consistently
struggled against brahmani elite hegemony and cunning of depleting the skills
of writing, imagination, and literary creativity from Dalit literature.[17]

Marathi Cinema

Marathi cinema had a particular pride of place in the forging of a Marathi
collective identity in the new state of Maharashtra, both illustrating the bravery of Marathis and highlighting the art of Marathi filmmakers vis-à-vis the
business of Hindi films produced in Bombay. Hindi cinema was more popular

than Marathi, and Marathi film critics lamented the declining popularity of Marathi films: "These days films have lost their Marathiness."[18] After a growing sense of decline and years of public debate, a new movement emerged to reinvigorate Marathi cinema in 1960s. As a result, some demanded, "First, Marathikaran of the Marathi film industry: No [Bengali director] Satyajit Roy [*sic*], [we want elite Marathi directors] Shantaram, Paranjape, Atre."[19] One special reporter to the *Chhaya* argued,

> Maharashtra was excluded in the Golden Jubilee celebrations of the film industry in Mumbai. Even senior Marathi artists were not invited. Hindi has made a business out of art. Marathi people do not have money, are in debt, do not parade in luxuries and don't give big feasts. Are they therefore excluded? The marginalization and exclusion of Maharashtriya in the capital of Maharashtra is not proper, it is disappointing and aggravating.[20]

The writer was utterly frustrated: "*Amarathi* [non-Marathi] capitalists control the industry." Writers like him sang the praises of Marathi artists preserving Marathi bana and their regime before the rise of Hindi film producers and artists. But Marathi bana was the exclusive domain of touchable Marathis—exhibitions of rebelliousness, aggressive masculinity, and sturdy character by Dalits were not tolerated, and thus evocations of bana in the Marathi film industry served to differentiate touchable Marathis from Dalit Marathis. While champions of Marathi films were angry about northern Hindivalas ruling Mumbai and dominating Maharashtra and thus endangering Marathi identity, their invocations of Marathi bana operated according to a logic of internal colonialism and caste politics to marginalize Dalits. In these complex processes, touchable writers rooted the Marathi duality of the besieged and the oppressor: while they were besieged by Hindivalas, they also oppressed Dalits. Such a figure as Shivaji both embodied Marathi bana as a muscular, masculine superman and represented the sort of masculinity Dalits were denied.

Bhalji Pendharkar (1898–1994), aka Bhalba, made Shivaji movies to recuperate Marathi bana and the great maratha (peasant cultivator caste) hero Shivaji. Underlining his legacy in Shivaji movies, one writer called Pendharkar "Shivaji Superman." One writer praised his "brilliant story 'Mohityanchi Manjula' [Manjula of Mohite family] of a young *mard* [muscular, chivalrous, manly] maratha

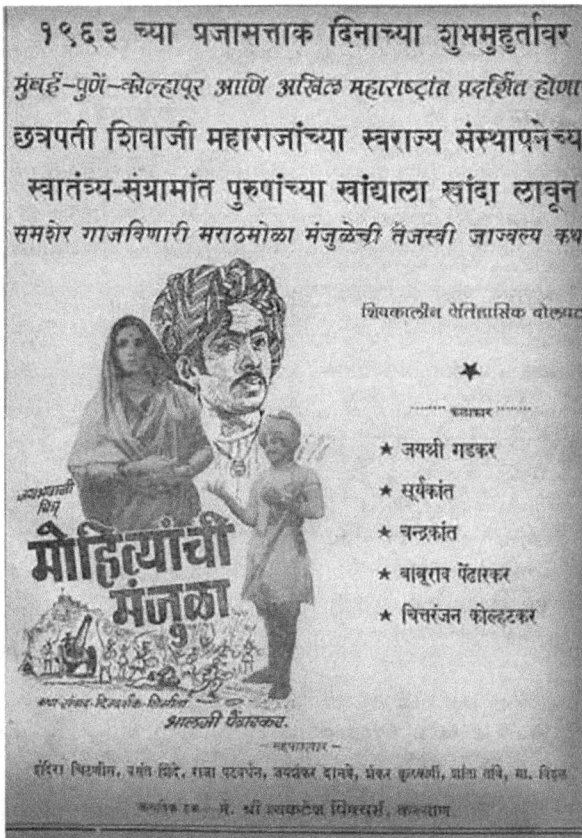

FIGURE 5.2. Advertisement for *Mohityanchi Manjula* (Manjula of the Mohite family). Marathamola Manjula fought along with men in the freedom struggle. Source: *Chhaya*, 1963. National Film Archive of India.

woman. Bhalba has shown how maratha young women moved without fear at night, roamed at village fairs, and could tackle brave men in fights."[21]

The movie *Mohityanchi Manjula* (Manjula of the Mohite family), released on Maharashtra Independence Day, May 1, 1963, portrayed Marathi women in their traditional dress riding horses and wielding swords to protect their freedom from the Mughal army. The film focused on the life of brave Manjula from the Mohite family. An advertisement for the film claimed, "This is the brilliant, energizing story of Manjula of the Mohite family who used her sword, fought along with men in the freedom struggle led by Shivaji" (figure 5.2).

Filmmakers and SMM ideologues presented emotive images based on maratha history in aesthetic ways to create narratives of pride about the Marathi past. In this particular political moment, economic and social reasons led to the rise of the Shiv Sena in 1966. Shiv Sena leaders appealed to Shiv Sainiks (soldiers; here, party-workers of Sena) through a masculinist, muscular, regionalist, rhetorical style, which connected directly with the SMM.[22] Despite their ideological differences, both SMM and Shiv Sena used the regional-linguistic rhetoric and trope of Marathi manus; however, Sena went further in proclaiming itself as the savior of Marathi manus, deploying it as a classless category. This move of the Sena enabled it to have a wider appeal by embracing unemployed, working-class, elite, and white-collar Marathis, who were worried their jobs were taken and that they were exploited by "outsiders" and "antinational" non-Marathis such as South and North Indians, and Communists.

Like Atre, Thackeray too railed against the rise of Hindi films at the expense of Marathi cinema, demanding that "after every three Hindi movies, they [Hindi film makers] should make one Marathi. Producers in Mumbai in five years should be compelled to make a Marathi film."[23] Balkrishna Dandekar, however, challenged the mentality of Marathi "us" versus Hindi "them" in Thackeray's regional nationalism: "His calling on Hindivalas is not due to his boundless love for Marathi, but *phajil premamula* [surplus or spare love]. He has become emotional but without thinking deeply, he made a childish demand."[24] Dandekar disagreed with Thackeray's rhetoric and the immature politics of pitting Hindi against Marathi to strengthen Marathi identity. To him, Thackeray's attack on the national language, Hindi, and denigration of Hindivalas was unhelpful in recuperating regional Marathi language and honoring Marathi identity: "We do not see [his and Marathi manus's hero] Shiv Chhtrapati's self-respect in this demand. Rather there is a *vasa* [odor] of helplessness in this demand. Because his demand is obstructive and stagnating." Dandekar was unsure how scared Hindivale would help Marathi films if they were threatened by Thackeray and his Sena. He attacked Thackeray's constricted ideology of Marathi manus emphasizing, "No Marathi manus [man] has such cheap expectations of Thackeray. Marathi manus expects a lot from him."[25]

Like SMM, Dandekar thus argued for a broader definition of Marathi identity, one that, contra Thackeray, existed in concert with Indian identity and did not consider Hindivalas enemies of Marathis. Attacking Hindi was not the solution to the decline of Marathi cinema. Yet, ignoring such critiques and their expansive vision, in 1996, the cultural minister, Pramod Navalkar, following Thackeray's argument of the 1970s, made it compulsory to show Marathi films in Maharashtra. Speaking at an event that celebrated a hundred years of film, he said,

> The state has made it compulsory for theatre owners to show Marathi films for at least 15 days. This decision was made in a meeting with film producers, distributors, and theater owners. The government reflected on all the obstacles of the film industry, and realized that non-availability of theatres was the biggest hurdle and hence took this step. So, now the producers have to shoulder the responsibility of making *darjedar* [first-rate] movies. Along with Marathi, Hindi film industry should also work responsibly so that Marathi films see good times and take along its younger brother.[26]

With this cunning move, Navalkar kept together the two languages: Marathi and Hindi. Moreover, Hindi as the big brother was made responsible for the protection and prosperity of his younger Marathi sibling. He also masculinized hitherto feminized mother tongues. He affirmed Atre's agenda of "Jai Hind [Victory, India]! Jai [Victory,] Maharashtra!" Although the Thackerays attacked Atre, they and their Sena appropriated his reverberating phrase that summed up his idea of the region and the nation. State agents like Navalkar used state power to force producers to make and theatre owners to support Marathi films to anchor Marathi identity.

SMM, Marathikaran, and the Disciplining of Ashlil Elements

Between 1956 and 1960, the SMM and then after the state of Maharashtra was established on May 1, 1960, Marathi elite ideologues like Atre (and others like Joshi, Bapat, Deo, Dange, and Jedhe) sought to create a politically viable category of "Marathi people." They sharpened their focus on the moral, modest, and modern constitution of Marathiness, on a certain assli regional-linguistic Marathi identity and society. However, there was hardly any mention or allowance for Dalits within this robust marathamola politics. To become fully Marathi and prove that they were now fit to govern themselves, Marathi elites articulated the *shuddha* (sanitized), *naitik* (moral), *samajik* (social), *laingik* (sexual), and *sanskrutik* (cultural) contours of what it meant to be a *new* brand of *shilvan* (genuine, of good disposition) Marathi. In so doing, they intensively debated the boundaries between shil and ashlil and attacked ashlilta as evidence of their assli Marathi identity. This was important to critically carve out their modernity in order to be assli Marathi. Film, literature, and affect that rooted the most ordinary Marathi manus played a major role in reinforcing *gharandaj* (belonging to a family, a lineage and hence of good descent, *kulin*) Marathi status. Emotion, rhetoric, and sensuality were significant to these processes of becoming Marathi and asserting an independent identity. The social imaginary became a powerful weapon to constitute a certain "cultured" Marathi identity, Marathiness, and the larger Marathi society. These were interconnected processes and politics of becoming Marathi, as all actors agreed to create a new Maharashtra.

At the heart of the construction of the new (postcolonial) Marathi identity and nation was the figure of the chaste, virtuous, modest, and modern woman. While men granted some equality to women, they also both bent the rules and imposed certain standards of traditional patriarchy in constituting a new, modern womanhood, revealing their anxiety about displays of women's bodies in public spaces and in the media, women's sexuality, their *purushipana* (becoming manly), and the negative effects of ashlilta on the *kovale* (tender) adolescent minds of those who would become future citizens of the nation. They honored chaste Maharashtrian women and burdened them with the honor of their parents, families, husbands, communities, and the new nation. The burden placed on women in Marathikaran fell especially on those Untouchable women who operated in public spaces, especially women seen as sexually available—prostitutes, Muralis, and Tamasha women. And Dalits' "I too" claims to manus, to be accepted as they are as humans, and now as Marathis, were hardly considered in the constitution of an assli and assli Marathiness; Dalits were rarely mentioned in the articulation of this robust marathamola politics and were frequently the object of reform.

While Marathi elites drew on certain colonial tropes of "civilizing" and "modernizing," they also clearly departed in constructing their own regional identity and legitimacy. Elite Marathis expressed a wide range of attitudes, practices, and anxieties regarding the appropriate boundaries of shil-ashlil, sexuality, language, arts, conjugality, *kulin* (good, decent) women's access to the public realm, and relationships between women and men. While some conversations repeated earlier contestations on similar topics, others took into consideration newer challenges of the changing modern technologies, such as cinema and their connections with actual people. Most of these were prescriptive in character and offered moral lessons for people to follow for the maintenance of healthy bodies and minds. Many elite men and a few women voiced their concerns by writing in magazines and newspapers, as they constituted a new ideal of conjugality. They asserted sexual constraints for both men and women, but the consequences were more serious for women who violated norms of conjugal fidelity.

Becoming Shil-Assli: Decency and Authenticity

Many citizens petitioned the government to prohibit the publication of ashlil literature, songs, novels, or dramas. Censorship of cultural products deemed ashlil did not only or primarily involve repression and denial but led to proliferating discourses on different modes of desire and of being in the world. Prohibition also had the effect of routinizing and inciting desire and transgression. This dynamic is significant to marketing and show business, which thrives on the "strategic deployment of the tease, of provocation as a means of focusing attention, realizing profits, and attracting audiences."[27] Battles over shil-ashlil-assli in the 1960s played out in the pages of newspapers like *Navakal* and magazines like *Rasrang*, *Chhaya*, and *Painjan* (literally, ankle bells, but also a reference to Tamasha through Tamasha women's accessories), and the lack of legal clarity regarding what constituted the ashlil led to many debates.

Speaking at a debate organized by the Mumbai Sahitya Sangha (Literature Committee), the renowned brahman male scholar Gangadhar Gadgil distinguished between romance and pornography. He declared, "There is nothing ashlil in literature."[28] He continued,

> In many people's life there are two motives: you follow one and restrict the other. Similarly, the samaj also draws these lines. There are instructions

that beyond a certain limit there should be no public exposure of sexual emotions. In certain societies the limit is decided at kissing or adjusting the padar [loose end of the sari]. *Kamuktela vikrut valan lavane yala ashlilta mhanta yeil* [When eros is set on disgraceful lines it become ashlil].[29]

Gadgil thus argued that the ashlil emerges basically when sexuality goes awry and, as a result, constraints were important to creating and enforcing a sexual order. He pointed out that the law as well as the Ashlilta Committee formed by the new state were confused about the appropriate boundaries between romance and pornography. To him, there was a need for appropriate boundaries:[30]

> If you want to protect *pativratya* [women's purity and devotion to their husbands], then you have to keep women in *burkha* [veil]. Today, don't [we] send women outside [in the public] for education, jobs? In so doing, don't we accept the danger to pativratya? So, it is not proper to suppress art because it will have negative effects on young people. In India, *dharma-grantha* [books on morality], [naked] sculpture, images of deities are not covered by ashlilta. However, translations in regional languages regarding intensive sexual games from old Sanskrit granth become ashlil.[31]

Gadgil illuminated the sensuality in Hinduism as well as the problem of depicting texts as ashlil. It is no surprise that women became a central cipher in this chaos—woman as nation, woman as virtue, woman as culture, woman as aesthetic ideal, and woman as a locus of dangerous sexual energy. Moreover, Gadgil created hierarchies between Sanskrit and regional languages; he elevated the former and denigrated non-Sanskritic. Sanskrit is also associated with brahmanism and depicted as a divine language. In this context, once again, Dalit women moving and working in public spaces at once emerged as a problem for cultured Marathiness. Any woman in the public realm was presumably licentious or prone to pose a threat. The struggle over relative acceptability of popular Tamasha versus high forms of cultural productions was intensive, as Dalits were burdened with the stickiness of the ashlil.

Taking advantage of the formation of the Ashlilta Committee[32] to discipline the boundaries of shil and ashlil, elite men such as Shirsagar, Gadgil, and Godbole filed a lawsuit against the magazine *Painjan* and wanted the law court to stop the "ashlil" production immediately. *Painjan* had been founded in 1958 and was unabashedly devoted to discussions of sringar (erotic or romantic love). The magazine countered Godbole's attack by filing a defamation suit. The battle raged in Mumbai. In these tenuous moments, *Painjan* boldly declared its unique and main founding objective of "sringar": "*Painjan* is the pioneer in sringar based magazines." This was a bold stance because very few magazines openly declared their devotion to the sensual. In the *Painjan* issue of June 1961, the editor, G. V. Behere argued, "We are not ashamed that people say we focus on sringar." He continued,

> *Painjan* is unique. It departs from other magazines that disseminate *bhi-batsa-vasana* [disgusting-vulgar seduction] in the name of *sringar*. If restricted then she [sringar] becomes *pochat* [hollow, without substance]. If unrestricted she becomes *panchat* [naughty, ribald], and beyond certain measures she is *vikruti* [sickness or disorder]. And if below certain measures, she becomes *bharud* [noisy song-music]. . . . Taking into consideration the love readers have showered upon us, it is appropriate to say that readers have trusted our discretion.

Although Behere robustly defended sringar, he troublingly feminized it, thus endangering it even further. He made a case for the pairing of the concepts shil-ashlil, arguing,

> It is a hope that Marathi magazine remains *sovale, sojval* [pure, decent]. . . . Sringar should be healthy, neutral, innocent, and bringing joy. It should not have *vikruti, halkepana, hinata* [disorder, shallowness, inferiority]. This is [my] earnest request and it has become important to remind the samaj of this. It is difficult to decide the limits of shil-ashlil.[33]

Thus, Behere rightly underscored the difficulties of properly identifying the borders of shil-ashlil and good and bad sringar. Yet, ironically, at the same time, he drew distinctions between higher and lower sringar. Moreover, he asserted, "Yet, I can ascertain that we will never breach the borders,"[34] thereby fortifying the borders of propriety. *Painjan* was unique in portraying the sensual. Even in the headers of some pages, some anonymous writers for *Painjan* report the sexual and sensual: "There is no *rangat* [excitement] unless you kiss in solitude and make love in the night" or "*Varu* [horses] and women can be controlled only with a *lagam* [whip]" or "Tujhi uba, eka disachi, lage hurhur nau masachi" (A day in your warmth leaves me longing for you for nine long months) or "Bharala kanisa dudhana" (The corn cob is full of milk), suggesting the woman is ripe for sex. Despite the bawdiness, the writer unfortunately created similarities between a horse, a nonhuman, and a woman because to him, women did not qualify as humans.

Consequently, contestations and controversies about what constituted the ashlil persisted. In his editorial "The Story of the *Painjan* Trial,"[35] Behere commented, "There is a problem once ashlilta is connected with *nitimatta* [morality, propriety]. Ashlilta means *vishobhit* [without decorum], and hence for the standards of literature anything that is not *sushobhit* [decent] is ashlil." Moreover, to make his point, Behere argued that even Atre's Marathi writings were certainly "not only a torrent of abuse and execrations, but also *bibhatsa* [disgusting] and should be considered ashlil." In the process, he attacked the famous author and pointed out the double standards of the Ashlilta Committee. The committee was partial to the famous Atre and, as a result, did not include the latter's writings in its list of banned literature. This was clear evidence of the committee's prejudice toward non-elite writers and even its timidity about raising any concerns or questions regarding writings of certain stars like Atre. Atre never faced a ban on his writings that bordered on the ashlil.[36] Clearly there were discrepancies on the appropriate borders of shil-ashlil as well as elite-and-non-elite representing the ashlil. Behere concluded his exposé by making an argument about "the difference between using a woman's body and worshipping the beauty of women." He hoped that "it will be helpful if the Ashlilta Committee understands this eventually."[37] Sex-and-love-friendly discourses produced by magazines such as *Painjan* to an extent pushed the boundaries of the acceptable normative Marathi social imaginary. Modern Marathi literature and its creators, who were mostly male brahman and CKP authors, embraced the ashlil in their poetry, prose, and plays, appropriating Tamasha and Lavani and giving it a "high-caste" male voice that appeared "progressive" for its embrace of the ashlil.

Assli Tamasha: Icon, Media, Market, and Identity

The elite politics of decency, civilization, tradition, and modernity penetrated the so-called ashlil realm of Tamasha. Elites had mined the field of high classical arts and rarely commented on lowly Tamasha. Yet, when they did, they depicted Tamasha as *gramya*—rustic, ignorant, an unruly, disorderly art form that either had to be put in order, cleansed, or completely eradicated. However, Tamasha artists and troupe owners actively challenged such elite characterizations. They intensively vocalized their concerns and problems, sought the interventions of the state as well as certain elites in order to raise the status of Tamasha as a respectable art form for the pandharpesha. Tamasha people, presumed to be ashlil, wanted to belong where they did not—among assli Marathis and Indians.

Historically, brahman elites preserved the supposedly inherent respectability of Marathi natak as distinct from disrespectable Tamasha. From the mid-nineteenth century to the mid-twentieth century, elite brahmans strengthened the Marathi natak tradition. Between 1856 and 1862, many brahman men like Parshurampant, Tatya Godbole, Krushnashastri Rajvade, and Ganeshshastri Lele presented natak dramas based on Sanskrit literature. Later, Janardan Kirtane and others produced many translated natak dramas based on historical, mythical, Shakespearean stories.[38] Between 1880 and 1920, Kirloskar, Deval, Kolhatkar, Khadilkar, and Gadkari—took Marathi Rangbhumi to its pinnacle, creating a wave of enthusiasm with their different arts. Tamasha art forms remained mostly ignored and unexplored. Despite being denigrated by elites and banned by the state, Tamasha thrived in the public realm, which is most clearly evident in the rise of Tamasha films in the 1940s. The popularity of Tamasha films and the ashlil elements they promoted threatened elites and their construction of an assli Marathi identity.

As a result, while fighting their political battle for independence from British rule, elites were keen on reinvigorating Marathi language, culture, and theatre. The eminent actor Ganpatrao Bodas, in his April 20, 1947, presidential address in Mumbai at the Annual Drama Festival of the Marathi Culture Committee noted the need to attract Marathi citizens to *rangbhumi* (theatre). He added, "We have to work towards taking rangbhumi to its peak. There should also be new institutions for new dramas. We have to establish a central organization for this purpose, in a city like Mumbai." Most important, Bodas warned, "We [also] have to stop the deterioration of Marathi rangbhumi and show it its earlier days of glory."[39] Following previous efforts in the early twentieth century, Bodas renewed attempts to standardize and institutionalize elite theatre. He created a chasm between us/elites and them/non-elites. He also did not provide details of the perceived deterioration of elite theatre, but was clearly threatened by the rise of Tamasha films.

Significantly, even the renowned scholar of Lavani and Tamasha studies, Madhukar Dhond distinguished between different poets and poetry along caste and class lines—high kavita (poetry) and low Lavani, high *kaviraj/kaviraya* (king of poetry) and lowly shahir. Speaking in Mumbai on January 7, 1961, the anniversary of the death of the famous brahman Lavani singer Ram Joshi, Dhond argued that Ram Joshi was not "an ordinary shahir but Kaviraya [king of poetry]. He possessed rare abilities to make kavita instead of Lavanis, and infused devotional song [*kirtan*] in [sensuous] Lavani. [As a result], he sang cultured Marathi poetry."[40] Brahmani elites like Dhond thus constantly pointed out that intelligent and exceptionally talented brahman men Ram Joshi and Patthe Bapurao sanitized and civilized the "uncultured," "disorderly," "unruly" Dalit Lavanya. Touchable men adopted similar strategies to elevate Patthe Bapurao on a pedestal during colonial times. They easily forgot how brahman Lavanikars appropriated Tamasha and Lavani of Dalits for their own purposes—moreover, they could denigrate them or elevate them as they pleased. Unlike Dalits, they continued to remain decent and legitimate without endangering their caste and class status.

Especially in the context of generating Marathi identity in 1960s, Dhond was invested in elevating the brahman Joshi:

> Ram Joshi lived about 200 years after Eknath and his period was characterized by *vaibhav ani vilas* [prosperity and pleasure]. In such times, Tamasha and Lavani flourished, and hence Joshi was attracted towards Lavanya and Tamashe. He was a brahman. Lavanya unsettled him and [as a result], he later he became *vilasi ani vyasani* [enjoying passions of love, luxury and alcohol]. He indulged in alcohol drinking, women, and other *rangdhang* [dalliances]. He himself became *patit* [polluted], however, he improved the poetry. In this lies his *greatness*.[41]

Thus, to Dhond, like Jintikar and Kelkar, innately intelligent, superior, and exceptional brahman men rescued ashlil Tamasha from its supposedly inferior, ignorant, crude Dalit quarters, sanitized it, and transformed it into decent high poetry. To them, Tamasha and Lavani were inherently polluting, yet this pollution, this ashlil quality, did not stick to brahmans the way it did to Dalits. As a result, brahman men could conveniently purify themselves and become virtuous again. Dalits did not enjoy such a luxury. Dhond could not hide his built-in prejudices against Tamasha, Lavani, and Tamasha women on whom he built his intellectual career. Moreover, Dhond stereotyped them all—Lavani, Tamasha, and women—as polluting, addictive, and full of excess frivolous leisure, which was detrimental to the social order. Most significantly, he also declared, "The Lavanya [Ram Joshi] authored are *not ashlil.*" He continued,

> Joshi's Lavanya lack *pachkal* [silly] sringar. In some of his Lavanya we come across ashlil descriptions; however, he wrote them for Dhondi Mahar [a Tamasha troupe owner] and gave them to him. He retained *nitichi baju* [decent, moral position].[42]

Thus, brahmani elites like Dhond were at pains to sanitize Tamasha and Lavani for their own purposes. They engaged in caste games by creating rankings of human beings, constructing caste hierarchies of shahirs, and elevating brahmans like Joshi and Bapurao and denigrating Dalits. Although both Dalits and brahmans practiced Tamasha, the ashlil stuck only to Dalits. Brahmans were always already decent. Continuing his sanitizing efforts, Dhond added, "[Ram Joshi], in fact, brought Lavani into kirtan and purified [the former]." He continued, "Lavani is a *goda chhand* [sweet hobby]. It is *natyageet* [drama-song] full of *bhava* [emotion], *natya* [drama], *nrutya* [dance], *geet* [song], and so on, and hence it is more effective." Thus, to reiterate, for elites, Lavani performed by Dalits was ashlil; however, the same when performed by brahmans was intensively artistic, full of affect and effect. Brahmani elites ranked knowledge systems and did not grant Dalit arts the same value as that of brahmans.

This high-caste sentiment of "intellect" and "technique" as the appropriate forms of knowledge and practice was echoed time and again in Dhond's writing. He argued, "Joshi thought that if Lavani was brought into kirtan it would be more entertaining. Lavani was more effective than *abhang* [devotional songs]."[43] Thus, to Dhond, Joshi, through his brahman touch, purified and revolutionized Lavani, transforming them into a powerful medium of entertainment. Implicitly in this argument, to Dhond, as to Jintikar (in chapter 2), Dalits were untouched by such power of Lavani, and hence they needed the exceptional intelligence of brahman masters to show them how to perform and practice their arts. Touchable elites like Dhond and Jintikar consigned Dalits with a history of Lavani and Tamasha art to the margins of the growing field of popular culture. Caste defined the past and future of Tamasha and Dalits.

Most importantly, Dhond connected sensual Lavani with devotional abhang. He emphasized that Joshi borrowed from earlier work and hence there was a lot of similarity between Tukaram's abangas and Joshi's Lavanis. The development of Tamasha and Lavani along two tracks reinforced caste differences—Dalit and brahman. With the foundation of the state of Maharashtra and its defining of a linguistic and regional nation for Marathis, elites recuperated brahman and other high-caste heroes in their nation-building; thus Lavanya produced by Dalits were demoted as a form of unskilled labor seen as far less important to state development. In this manner, brahman men used their power of brahmanya, consolidated brahmanism, and conveniently traversed shil-ashlil-assli; they cultivated hobbies, appropriated ashlil, easily converted it into shil and assli.

Jintikar also argued that Lavanis were "lewd and obscene and [that in fact] Tamasha was veiled prostitution."[44] Yet, he canonized Bapurao's Lavanya and elevated them. Elites were a perpetually threatened-feeling lot; they intensively policed the boundaries of proper language, poetry, folk, rural and urban, and so on. They debated whether Tamasha was vulgar or not, while some elevated Tamasha, others denigrated it as rural and vulgar. They also, like Dhond, consistently put brahmans on a pedestal. To Dhond, Joshi even sang Lavanis like "devotional and spiritual [kirtan] inside and the outer expression was [ashlil] Tamasha."[45] To Dhond, Joshi "was not interested in merely the play of poetics. His poetry is full of eros—Radha-Krishna love-play. His Krishna says, 'mukhashi mukha lavuni' [touching mouth to mouth], and entertains and the woman is engrossed in the past memories of sringar." Further, Ram Joshi called himself "Kaviraj and not Shahir. He also called his Lavani a poetry. His greatest contribution is that he provided poetic stature to titillating Lavani fondness." In this manner, Dhond turned his earlier argument on its head. He now cleared the space for devotional eros and Lavani poetry.

The famous nationalist litterateur Mama Varerkar also supported and joined Tamasha troupes to bring about social awakening:

> Tamasha is the most effective literature. Satyashodhaks [Truth-seekers] proved this already.... If the government had used Tamasha to recruit people it would have been beneficial. But our sympathetic government has not realized this. [Further] we should do away with pandharpesha's pesha [occupation]."[46]

Varerkar was aware of the popularity and creative deployment of Tamasha by Satyashodhaks, Dalits, and Communists.

Patriarchal State Patronizing and Policing Tamasha

Despite shortages as well as restrictions on certain materials after the Second World War, Hindi cinema, emerging as a national culture, was given preferential treatment in terms of licensing and acquisition of raw materials.[47] Due to the domination of nationalist politics by North Indians and the Congress Party, Marathi people felt threatened, and their Marathiness emerged from a feeling of besiegement. Marathi people felt the need to push back against the federal dominance of northerners, and in this process, they sought to harness the rowdy energy of Tamasha. Although the colonial state had banned ashlil Tamasha in late 1940s, in the postcolonial period, Marathis converted it into an icon of Marathi identity. The state bans also led to an increased popularity of Tamasha, even as many Tamasha performers lost their means of survival due to the bans. There was also some doubt about the ban; Bhimsen Gaikwad, who was a performer during this period, did not remember any ban on Tamasha. He participated in and watched Tamashe all the time.

Some elites, artists, and lovers of Tamasha pleaded with the government to think creatively about Tamasha. Tamasha was effective for social propagation, and gradually the state and its agents understood this truth. However, rowdy and ashlil Tamasha was unpalatable to the state and civil society. As a result, in 1948, the Bombay state established the Tamasha Sudhar Samiti (Improvement Committee) to sanitize and civilize Tamasha and regulate its dissemination. Headed by Datto Vaman Potdar, a brahman liberal writer, historian, and vice chancellor of Pune University, and counting touchable elites such as Mama Varerkar, N. R. Phatak, and G. L. Thokal among its members, the committee had the charge of approving all Tamasha scripts and lyrics. Under this charge, the committee resolved that "1) Tamasha women should not sit outside Tamasha theatres to advertise Tamasha [by seducing men], 2) ashlil poems, Lavanya, and skits should be eliminated, and 3) Tamasha women should not touch audience members' hands during daulatjada."[48] In 1953, the Drama Censor Committee further regulated *vag* (skits in Tamasha), declaring that Tamasha troupes had to seek approval from the committee. This led to a new practice of writing vag, and writers became important. To avoid banishment and accusations of being ashlil, Tamasha and sangeet baris sanskritized themselves as *Loknatya* (popular drama) or *soubhagyavati* (married women and thus sexually confined to the marriage plot).

After 1960, the new state of Maharashtra launched a broad agenda of institutionalizing and reinvigorating the arts and identity of the Marathi people and the state. The first chief minister of Maharashtra, Yashvantrao Chavan (1913–1984), speaking at the Maharashtra State Drama Festival's prize distribution ceremony, argued that it was essential "to build good theatres for nataks in Mahrashtra."[49] He insisted that there should be "an increase [in] the tradition of old nataks. People should increase their fierce liking of natak. New actors should be produced. Cinemas have attacked Marathi theatre, but still the latter has survived. It should continue its bright and prosperous tradition."[50] To reinforce deep Marathi culture and identity, the government also established a Consulting Committee for Propagating Art and Cultural Education under the Ministry of Education in 1961.

Chavan also made art education a significant part of school curriculum. The government organized festivals of drama, music, dance, popular songs, and popular theatre like Tamasha in cities and small villages. The state also resolved that to support poor people, the entry fee for these entertainment events was to be nominal and local artists were to be encouraged. It granted about Rs. 6,250 in awards to writers, Rs. 3,500 for Shilpa (art) exhibitions, and Rs. 13,000 to Marathi Natya Parishad and resolved to provide financial help to artists with few economic resources.[51] Along with the state, emerging capitalists of the sugar lobby financed Tamasha and the increasingly bourgeois audience also supported it.

The new Maharashtra state also institutionalized Tamasha and other popular arts by involving litterateurs like Sarojini Babar to collate folk traditions, songs, and so on. The Tamasha Sudhar Samiti regulated ashlilta in songs and dance. It also organized regular training camps for artists as well as annual events to promote culture. These actors transformed Tamasha into a form of Loknatya (people's theatre) and facilitated the transition of Tamasha from being performed in open public spaces to enclosed elite theatres in cities and semi-rural areas. Moreover, the Congress Party and other political parties disseminated their political agendas through the frivolous entertainment of Tamasha. Their strategy, to a certain extent, was similar to the manner in which Dalits appropriated Tamasha and converted it into Jalsa. Both appropriated Tamasha art and wanted to capture its energy, attractiveness, and popularity, yet for different purposes. Cleansing Tamasha and Tamasha-based film was important to making them palatable to ruling elites. The first generation of Tamasha films were salacious and unpalatable to urban and urbane elites. Marathi film directors who comprehended these connections and contestations and found good business in Tamasha also joined in the process of appropriating, sanitizing, and commodifying Tamasha.

Clean Tamasha Films Reinforcing Assli
During this period of anxiety and uncertainty about Marathikaran, Marathi films emerged as preeminent sites of public memory and public making. The modern media of film was extremely responsive to public culture and the political context of the 1960s. Walter Benjamin has described cinema as an art form that records the dramatic changes in the very way we see the world. Film influences our perception (*Wahrnehmung*) of the intersection between the aesthetics of art and society. Academic discussions around cinema as a commodity have squarely placed the debate within spheres of consumption and modernity. Especially after 1960, Tamasha became central to the revival of Marathi cinema in opposition to Hindi films in the decades following the Second World War as well as a device of social critique. Significantly, filmmakers replaced social/religious films with feudal-patriarchal Tamasha films. In his interview to *Rasrang*, the successful producer of Tamasha films V. G. Namade argued that despite elite criticism, Tamasha films were "a gold

mine." He continued, "A Tamasha film is like a hen laying golden eggs. Between 1960 and 1970 alone, 15 Tamasha films were made. When Marathi films were declining, it was Tamasha that provided work for artists, technicians, and so on." Rural audiences were central to Tamasha, with or without film. Namade continued,

> The rural audience is the main patron of Tamasha films. They can relate the story to their [lived] experiences. Their numbers are also more than the urban audience. Due to the constant attacks of [large numbers of] Tamasha film, urban audience is disappointed. Newspapers and critics also constantly criticize us; yet we make Tamasha films. From the point of business, Tamasha films set in rural contexts are most successful compared to films based on social and historical themes.[52]

Namade illuminated the urban-rural divide as well as the predominance of rural masses and their love for Tamasha. As people migrated from the rural areas to urban centers, they carried their Tamasha culture to the cities and made the latter assli in both landscapes. Clearly, the rural moral economy and feudal caste-inflected patriarchy, as well as money and markets, drove media and nation-making. This was most significant in 1960s Maharashtra. The urban pandharpesha audience watched Hindi films, while rural Dalit-Bahujan audiences, who were excluded from elite theatres, supported and thrived on Tamasha.

Yet Tamasha as portrayed in film was not authentic. As Namade argued, "What we show is [not true Tamasha]. It is a *nakkal* [copy] of Tamasha. We hire women artists who have an attractive and cute face, they have no idea of Tamasha. Anyway, they later become famous as Tamasha artists." Although Namade argued that films do not portray real Tamasha, there is a reciprocal relationship between the sociality portrayed in film and real life, people's ideas and attitudes. Tamasha troupes increasingly used film songs, and vice versa. There were no clear boundaries. Namade also rightly pointed out the centrality of Tamasha women to the feudal art. It did not matter if these women were hereditary artists or not. The main project was to portray stereotypical feudal-patriarchal Tamasha—that is, a Dalit-Bahujan Tamasha woman enticing dominant-caste men who, following her, would abandon their homes and wives, become alcoholics, and ruin themselves. There could be many versions of this story, but the central plot remained constant. Tamasha women, depicted as prostitutes, were at the core of the feudal, misogynist, patriarchal Marathi plot.

To shine a light on his good film business, Namade also affirmed changes in the attitudes of the larger society towards Tamasha. Yet there were differences among elites that Namade easily erased. Nevertheless, he added,

> In our Pune, the troupe performing in Aryabhushan [a theatre] is now doing the same under the different name of Loknatya and performing in [elite spaces of] Bharat Natyamandir or Bal Gandharva Rangmandir. The [elite] audience of natak who called Tamasha disgusting and bawdy is enjoying it and even appreciating its minutiae. The urban audience who see film mainly for plot and story may find it repetitious; however, they will relish Lavanya, will be enthralled in *saval-javab* [the question-and-answer songs], and immensely appreciate women's energizing dance. . . . We have done good business and opened the region for Marathi and especially Tamasha films.[53]

Despite business-minded directors like Namade, Anant Mane, and V. Shantaram inaugurating a golden age of Tamasha films, few invested in the art form. The success of Tamasha film directors did not go over well with many elites, who insulted Anant Mane, accusing him of being a *"tamashapatache thekedar* [contractor, pimp of Tamasha films]."[54] And though some elites may have criticized Shantaram, the "godfather" of Tamasha films, these criticisms seldom appear in the public record, and perhaps those praises that do survive served to silence his critics.

Nevertheless, like Namade, Mane defended his production of Tamasha films for majority-rural masses as well as for business. He was disappointed that to "elites, Tamasha-centered gramin [rural] films means ashlil films. [As a result], they express their disapproval and disgust by twisting their noses at Tamasha films."[55] Film directors would have to wage a fierce battle to sanitize Tamasha for pandharpesha who fed on Tamasha stereotypes. The supposedly modern liberal, pandharpesha minds could hardly pay attention to rural, ignorant, nonliterate, bawdy, feudal, and caste patriarchy. Caste itself was a subject of presumably traditional society and to those who wanted to roar castelessness, caste did not exist in modern India. Mane continued to illuminate the problem:

> Despite the robust challenge from Hindi films, my gramin films have done well. While I am happy on one level, on the other, I am disappointed that these days an educated audience is not enthusiastic about Marathi films. They think it is lowly to watch Tamasha films. I have in my films held onto [feudal] Tamasha story lines. But while doing so I have not converted the film into Tamasha. I have tried to present some difficulties through Tamasha films. [Elites] should change their perspective about gramin films.[56]

Mane wanted educated elites to change their idea of and attitude toward Tamasha. He wanted more business and high status for Tamasha in the eyes of the elites. Yet, at the same time he was cautious of the reasons why Tamasha became ashlil. He defended his investment in Tamasha:

> I use Lavani in my films because even in literature Lavani has a respectable status. I make it a point to make movies for people in all ladders of the society. I try to keep the songs, dialogues such that an ordinary audience is able to understand it and I keep them simple. 'Simple' doesn't mean '*halke*' [light or hollow]. I make it a point that I show good culture, even through Tamasha film. Tamasha is not ashlil. What is ashlil in Lavani?[57]

Mane, like the Jalsakars, underlined the importance of simplicity and good culture for larger masses. Tamasha was central in communicating with ordinary people. At the same time, everyone, Jalsakars, Dhond, and now Mane here agreed on the problems created by ashlil. As a result, although for different aims, all gentlemen agreed to eliminate the ashlil and retain the shil and assli in Tamasha and Lavani. None of them explicitly mentioned the role of women. Women were implicit in, central to, and yet ruining Tamasha and Lavani.

Mane, in arguing for clean Tamasha and in drawing elites toward Tamasha, unintentionally created distinctions of shil and ashlil, decent and vulgar. His Tamasha was decent and palatable because it focused on good, cultured, social, and moral values. Consequently, he exhorted the elites, "Instead of being frustrated with Marathi [Tamasha] films, the enlightened audience should watch, discuss with us, point out the problems in our films so we can work on them. I want the educated to pay attention to this."[58] He believed in a dialogue between the filmmaker and audience. One elite writer, Vasant Sathe, was sympathetic to Mane's plea. He argued, "It is not a sin to create Tamasha films. It is not wrong to present the art that actually finds roots in marathamola bahujan samaj. While doing this, he did not just force Tamasha for Tamasha's sake."[59] It would take an immense amount of social, economic, and intellectual labor to change the elite's stereotypical opinions and attitudes toward what they saw as boisterous, sexual Tamasha.

Film directors, the main agents of creating and selling the ideology of Marathi manus and sanitizing Tamasha, popularized Tamasha through media—films, advertisements, newspapers, magazines, newsletters, and songs. The prosperity that followed from this newfound popularity helped Tamasha, and Tamasha artists sang the praises of V. Shantaram, Mane, and others. Actors of non-Tamasha backgrounds like Jayashree Gadkar, Sulochana, Usha Chavan, the Chandrakant and Suryakant brothers, Nilu Phule, Arun Sarnaik, and others flourished and carved out their careers with Tamasha films. A few Tamasha women, such as Leela Gandhi, Maya Jadhav, and Madhu Kambikar, also entered films.

However, some Tamasha women pointed out the problems of Tamasha films and their makers. They were angry about the ways renowned directors profited from Tamasha films, especially by casting Tamasha women as ashlil, lewd, and breaking morality, thus reproducing the misogyny of Tamasha art in Tamasha film. The caste and gender performativity of Tamasha films actually reinforced misogyny and stereotypes of Tamasha women as common prostitutes, enhancing the stickiness of the ashlil for Dalit women. Sharing their Tamasha lives with me, the Jagtap sisters in Wakad-Pune on a hot afternoon of July 7, 2017, were furious with V. Shantaram and his ilk:

> Shantaram bapu earned fame in Tamasha. But look what he has done to us! Look what he has done to our image! In his immensely popular Tamasha film *Pinjra* [literally, cage, but also a metaphor for life; 1972], Sandhya [the lead actor], a Tamasha woman, entices the honorable, morally righteous, ideal Guruji [teacher] of the village. It is she who ensnares Guruji in her *mohjaal* [net of love and desire]. She makes him fall in love with her. [She

changes him from Guruji into a Tamasha artist], thereby blotting his character and causing his downfall. Is he a *kukula baal* [small baby] who has no brains of his own to think? How can she alone do things to him and he is all passive, accepting his ruination? Can he not think about what he is getting into?

The sisters vocalized their radical feminism; they were rightly frustrated with filmmakers who made money by characterizing Tamasha women as morality breakers, enticing moral men of high values, bringing out the beast in them by turning them into murderers (as in *Pinjra*), and leading them toward death and downfall. To them, Tamasha filmmakers thus blotted all Tamasha women as corrupt and corrupting, seducing and leading astray prominent men in the village, such as the headman or his son. These processes would further victimize Dalit Tamasha women.

The dangerous desirability of the Dalit Tamasha woman as depicted in films like *Pinjra* is predicated on the interdicts against cross-caste contact, which, of course, were constantly breached. The tension between her as both taboo and attainable was necessary to the perpetuation of the sex-gender-caste complex, and thus caste itself. She was thus subjected to brahmani control, whether on stage or within the film industry—she needed to be tamed to conform on terms that deny her what is hers: autonomy over her art. Moreover, though still dangerous, as a sanitized and respectable production, she was only vaguely recognizable—a specter or, in Jean Baudrillard's terms, a simulacra: an image rather than a reality.[60] Her material reality is elided, and her sexually objectified and socially degraded dancer caste-body is retained to signify desire but immediately resignified as assli. In this perversion of her being is the constitutive perversity of desire, as it emerges in the caste context. This raises questions about how the sexual expressions of Tamasha women become mere convention and belie the complex emotions that are no doubt at work before, during, and after the performance.

Films were cashing in on Tamasha; yet, at the same time, they were reinforcing the stereotype of the predatory nature of ashlil Tamasha and Lavani women. Although it was a copy, as Namade argued above, films learned from Tamasha artists, the overall performative and performance, and reproduced it, in turn making Tamasha assli. Historically, the larger society stereotyped Tamasha women as wayward. Their outcaste status made them more inferior. As a result, films, which joined in on the sanitizing process in 1960s, made it a point to underscore that both Tamasha women and non-Tamasha women were to be disciplined. Deviance from normative womanhood and sexuality had to be severely punished. Caste and cultural vigilantes have continued to entrench their supposedly protective patriarchal politics in twenty-first century Maharashtra. Hindu right activists were invested in maintaining and further consolidating hierarchies of caste and sexuality—elevating respectable womanhood and denigrating dishonorable womanhood in the name of Indian family and culture.

Advertising Assli Clean Tamasha
In order to tackle the anxieties of the educated urban elites, Tamasha filmmakers sought to manipulate them and win them over through Tamasha films and Tamasha film advertisements. Tamasha film advertisements in Marathi newspapers and magazines played an important role in creating and selling the ideology of Marathi manus, disseminating the newly cultivated and cultured Tamasha films, and staging anew Tamasha art for Marathi society. Tamasha film participated in sanitizing and legitimizing Tamasha, using a new genre of Tamasha advertisements to enhance profits and disseminate Tamasha films, especially for consumption by respectable dominant-caste women. Because Tamasha women were stereotypically represented as possessing an untethered sexuality and enticing dominant-caste men and corrupting them, dominant-caste women did not approve of Tamasha and Tamasha women. As a result, men engaged in a regime of covert sexuality, secretly visiting prostitutes or seeing Tamashe and Tamasha films. Tamasha films and film ads elevated their game by seeking to persuade respectable elite women (and men) to see Tamasha. As such, the world of Tamasha had a profound effect on the visual shape of advertisements as well as the actors in them. The process continues vigorously in twenty-first century Maharashtra. Marathi newspapers like *Sakal, Navakal,* and *Loksatta,* are full of Tamasha and Lavani show advertisements..

The success of Tamasha film advertisements relied upon Marathi identity and the new state of Maharashtra to refashion specific "prior meanings" in an effort to create new forms of demand. As Judith Williamson argues, "Advertisers clearly produce knowledge ... but this knowledge is always produced from something already known, that acts as a guarantee, in its anteriority, for the 'truth' in the ad itself."[61] "Effective advertisements do not manufacture meanings out of thin air and impose them on an easily manipulable consumer base," writes Douglas Haynes. "But neither do they simply reflect a fixed set of cultural understandings already present in society in some static shape."[62] In the particular context of Tamasha film advertisements, both Tamasha filmmakers and advertisers actively participated in ongoing processes of Marathikaran, creating Marathi manus, and the cultural construction of Tamasha for a new Maharashtra. They innovatively designed their messages to transform powerful and familiar social and cultural concepts into new forms that they hoped would motivate customers to buy their product: sanitized Tamasha films.

The film *Vaijayanta*, starring Jayashree Gadkar and Suryakant, renowned actors who led Tamasha films, embodied Marathi bana and marathamola culture. In the advertisement for the film in figure 5.3, Gadkar is dressed in a traditional Maharashtrian nine-yard sari, covering her body tightly and fully. Her sari is tightly draped around her so that it would not come loose when she danced. Although she was fully covered and thus displaying modesty, the tight sari also highlighted her figure, calling attention to her chest, midriff, thighs, and hips. This style of Tamasha sari draping is different from both a household sari draping and a brahman style of sari draping. By contrast, Gadkar's traditional Maharashtrian jewelry, replete with necklace, bangles, chokers, arm bands, and waist band, and her hair style of *ambada* (bun) or *veni* (hair plait) adorned with flowers reinforced the sartorial norms of dominant-caste and dominant-class women. Similarly, Suryakant is dressed in a traditional *pheta* (turban headgear), vest, and *kurta-pyjama* (long tunic and tight trousers) or *dhotar* (dhoti), and both Gadkar and Suryakant reinforced Marathi style and identity for new Maharashtra. Moving away from Tamasha characteristics of romance and desire, the advertisement in figure 5.3 highlights decency and devotion.

The advertisement in figure 5.4 for the film *Ram Ram Pavhana* (Greetings, guest) reads, "Sensuality and the erotic can be sold, but not *iman* [honor].

FIGURE 5.3. Advertisement/poster for *Vaijayanta*, "The song-movie popular due to *saval-javab* and more songs. Due to these, people in the theatre applaud it immensely. The movie that Punekars like and is the true representation of life without a smack of vulgarity." Source: *Chhaya*, 1961. National Film Archive of India.

Despite being a Tamasgir, Tulsa behaved with *neki* [morality]." In this manner, Tamasha filmmakers and film advertisers sanitized Tamasha and Tamasha women as morality bearers to better market their films, which also served to reinforce the process of Marathikaran and assli Tamasha.

The advertisement for the film *Bel bhandar* (figure 5.5) popularizes the film as "high-descent based, family oriented, pure and auspicious drama." Further, it emphasizes, "This is an outstanding drama racing towards its 300th show.

FIGURE 5.4. Advertisement for *Ram Ram Pavhana* (Greetings, guest). Source: *Chhaya*, 1951. National Film Archive of India.

You can watch it with the family."[63] Filmmakers and their films transformed the historical stereotype of the Tamasha woman as homewrecker into a family maker—a cinematic figure that brought the family together in their enjoyment of film and Tamasha, underlining auspiciousness that was counter to the image of Tamasha, and without any concern about becoming ashlil.

Even an advertisement for Nerolac Paints (figure 5.6) emphasized Marathi tradition and reinforced colorism (see chapter 2) in its depiction of a Marathi bride. There was no place for a dark bride in Marathi society; she could be slightly

FIGURE 5.5. Advertisement for *Bel bhandar* (fruit and turmeric powder used as offering to Kanderao). Source: *Chhaya*, 1952. National Film Archive of India.

tanned but had to be fair. The paint advertisement is not for a Tamasha film, but it reinforces the stereotype, thus creating the truth effect of the assli Marathi woman.

Some Tamasha film advertisements appealed to respectable women directly. The advertisements for the most successful films, such as *Sangtye Aika* produced in 1959, for instance, reads, "Women have started liking Lavani, just like they did *abhang* [devotional songs]" (figure 5.7). In the eyes of the larger society, while abhang was decent, Lavani was vulgar. Some elites like Dhond, as discussed above, clearly explained these distinctions and even wanted to

FIGURE 5.6. Advertisement for Nerolac Paints. "Wheatish fair
bride, special wedding sari, silky dark peacock blue dots, dark
black bun, bun decorated with yellow shevanti and orange
aboli flowers, crescent red mark on forehead, hands yellow
after the turmeric ceremony and hands full of bangles, and red
henna—full of colors." Source: *Chhaya*, no date. National Film
Archive of India.

convert Lavani into devotional abhang. Similarly, Tamasha film ads, such as
the one in figure 5.7, elevated Lavani to the higher status of devotion so that
it could be consumed by respectable women who had hitherto refrained from
watching Tamasha and Lavani. The ashlil language in Tamasha skits and Lavani
songs were anathema to elites. As a result, the transformation of Lavani into

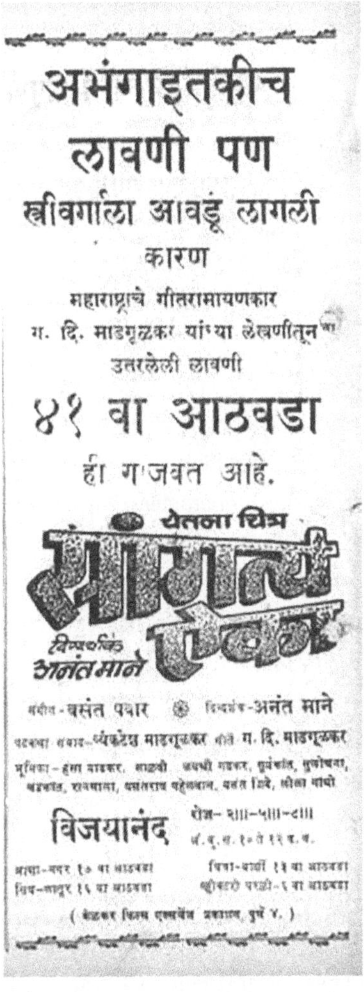

FIGURE 5.7. Advertisement for *Sang-tye Aika* (Listen to what I have to say). Source: *Chhaya*, 1961. National Film Archive of India.

abhang was an important strategy. Moreover, in the case of *Sangtye Aika*, because the Lavani was written by the renowned and always already meritocratic, intelligent, superior brahman poet, writer, and lyricist G. D. Madgulkar, who was hailed as the modern Valmiki (author of the epic Ramayana), it would have been even more easily palatable to elite women.

There is a lack of detailed evidence on attendance numbers, but the caption in figure 5.8 reads, "Even women in Pune unanimously declare that 'Sangtye Aika' is better in comparison with other socially based films and can be seen with family." To target and moreover capture women and larger family audiences, the advertiser conveniently summed up women's voices to make the Tamasha film an important social intervention that held family together (figures 5.10, 5.11, 5.12). Marathi elites put Marathi films on a pedestal to create a magical effect of transforming ashlil Tamasha into palatable Marathi culture.

Adding to its devotional flavor, but now highlighting its assli character, the editor of *Chhaya* wrote about the success of *Sangtye Aika* when the film entered its 100th week (figure 5.8): "Nobody can definitely speak to the reasons for its success, but its assli Marathi bana, the lively characters that are identifiable in everyday life in Maharashtrian villages. It is the sweet fruit of assli Lavanya and songs of Marathi characters, artists, performers, script writers, and so on."[64] This was historic victory for the film. The advertisements for the film (figures 5.7, 5.8, and 5.9) illuminate its dissemination and sanitizing for urban and semi-urban middle classes, especially for women and *their* families.

Again appealing to women and family audiences, the ad in figure 5.13 reads, "Lokshahir Anant Phandi with his melodious voice makes even Lavani famous. Anant Phandi [1744–1819] sang Lavanis [among other songs at the peshve court]. Yet, on [the royal] Ahilyabai Holkar's request he [left Lavanis and] turned to singing devotional kirtan." The ad clearly emphasizes that with his melodious voice, the famous shahir elevated the always already degraded Lavani. Here, the ad suggests that Lavani lacks melody because it is ashlil, but the poet critically transforms Lavani through his beautiful voice. Moreover, he followed the advice of the royal and left Lavani singing to sing devotional kirtan, thereby purifying himself.

The ad for the film *Kalgi Tura* (figure 5.14) strengthens the connection between Marathi valor, masculinity, and virility and Lavani. It reads, "The actress Usha Kiran hoisting masculine Maharashtra's flavorful Lavani's flag in the Marathi film [*Kalgi Tura*]."

The eros of Tamasha and Lavani and its practitioners was fundamental to building Marathi identity, Marathi masculinity, and the Marathi nation.

FIGURE 5.8. Advertisement for *Sangtye Aika*. Source: *Chhaya*, 1961. National Film Archive of India.

FIGURE 5.9. Advertisement for *Sangtye Aika*. This film is the renowned poet and lyricist G. D. Madgulkar's "challenge to those who assert that Lavani and Loknatya cannot be watched with family. Come, see, and let's see if you can detect any vulgarity. Families have watched and praised this film now running into its fifth week." Source: *Chhaya*, 1961. National Film Archive of India.

FIGURE 5.10. Advertisement for *Sangtye Aika*. "Avoiding the enticement of transforming films into vulgar Tamasha, only Marathi films can transform Tamasha into cultural films [or culturize Tamasha]." Source: *Chhaya*, 1961. National Film Archive of India.

FIGURE 5.11. Advertisement for *Sangtye Aika*. "You can watch Loknatya [Tamasha] with family. Eros can be exhibited in good [sanitized] language and this is evident through [this] movie celebrated by Pune's critical audience." Source: *Chhaya*, 1961. National Film Archive of India.

FIGURE 5.12. Advertisement for *Lokshahir* (balladeer) *Anant Phandi.* "'Troublesome path should not be your highway, don't leave the moral, straight path.' [He] popularized Lavani too with his melodious voice, he announced to the peshva in full court, he was honored by Ahilyabai [Holkar] to sing *katha-kirtan* [devotional stories and songs], instead of [the ashlil] Lavani, an effective story of such an immortal shahir." Source: *Chhaya*, 1960. National Film Archive of India.

FIGURE 5.13. Advertisement for *Kalgi Tura* (Feminine and masculine traditions of shahiri). Source: *Chhaya*, 1956. National Film Archive of India.

अंधाराकडून प्रकाशझोतात आलेली

संजीवनी मुळे-नगरकर

० 'सोळा हजारात देखणी' मध्ये माया जाधव आणि संजीवनी मुळे - नगरकर

FIGURE 5.14. Advertisement for *Sola hajarat dekhni* (The beautiful one among sixteen thousand women). "The invention of assli marathamola Lavani: Sanjeevani Mule-Nagarkar who traveled from darkness into limelight." Maya Jadhav and Sanjeevani Mule-Nagarkar in *Sola hajarat dekhni*. Source: *Rasrang*, no date. National Film Archive of India.

Tamasha conflated concerns about sex and sexuality and debates about Marathi society. Away from danger, desire, and delight, these ads highlighted honor and the morality of women and men. Ads also insisted that respectable dominant-caste families as a whole—men, women, children—could watch Tamasha films because there was nothing ashlil in them. Both Tamasha films and ads were sanitizing Tamasha and Lavani. While cinema could offer some respite and freedom from joint families, Tamasha ads reintroduced the *bharkatlela* (waylaid) man into the boundaries of his family. It is intriguing that the stereotype of Tamasha woman as wayward was now used to contain men.

Instead of watching Tamasha and Lavani secretly on his own or with other male-female friends, the dominant-caste elite man could now enjoy it with his family. This was a huge change propelled by Tamasha films and ads. They led to a veritable discursive explosion by inciting dominant castes to speak and do more about sex and sexuality expressed through Tamasha women. Earlier, the dominant-caste elite man had avoided his family members and snuck out of his home to watch Tamasha and participate in the regime of covert sexuality. He somehow had managed to secretly watch and enjoy the devious Tamasha woman to satisfy his sexual and sensual urges. With new Tamasha films, the man and his family, including his wife and children, could sit comfortably in enclosed theatres, watch the sexy Tamasha woman, and consume her even if she was on the screen. They together visualized conjugality, enjoyed the entertainment, pleasure, and violence embodied by Tamasha women. They did not pay attention to her exploitation in the feudal-patriarchal caste-ridden village. Moreover, Tamasha films and ads disrupted the wife-prostitute binary. Both dominant-caste respectable women and men could enjoy the distinctions they were creating along the lines of shil-ashlil as well as respectability and non-respectability. And most important, the man got to enjoy both women—wife and prostitute—at the same time, in the theatre and in real life. As a result, respectable elites won on all counts and inevitably the burden of assli Marathi morality and identity fell on Tamasha women.

Tamasha films addressed both the fantasies and anxieties evoked by the figure of the Tamasha woman. The feudal Tamasha nachi now emerged as a modern girl who embodied the attractions of romantic love and represented a renewed spirit of rebelliousness and unbridled sexuality. Stereotypically, Tamasha was characterized as a family breaker because of the sexually stigmatized erotic nachi and her love affairs with many men. Tamasha films and ads, however, did away with open sensuality so that Tamasha could no longer threaten the destruction of conjugal relationships, love, happy families, and the larger social order. Such a strategy addressed the unease about spousal fidelity, which was a concern among elite women. Tamasha film would now enhance the happiness and comingling of different members of the family. In the process, first, Tamasha film engaged in disciplining so-called hot and highly sexualized Tamasha women in the service of elites and the state. Second, Tamasha filmmakers and ads drew upon the feudal salacious woman stereotype to produce another salacious, but slightly decent woman for the dominant castes. They were steeped in the deep ambivalence of sanitizing, on the one hand, and producing a salacious stereotype of women, on the other. Sex, sexuality, and Tamasha were openly discussed in bazaars, corporate ads, and families. Advertisers reproduced prevailing ideas of reformed assli Tamasha to fashion appeals they hoped would compel readers to see Tamasha films. They participated with Tamasha filmmakers to make Tamasha a powerful new art form.

Tamasha Conferences: Sanitizing, Regulating, and Making Order
State officials organized Tamasha Parishads (conferences) and other events to canonize, enforce standards in, and centralize an otherwise disperse and rebellious art form. They also publicized their organizing efforts, linking the state to Tamasha's newfound popularity. Speaking at the three-day Tamasha conference, the minister of state, Balasaheb Desai, reported, "The government will make every effort for the economic uplift of Tamasha artists. These artists who serve ordinary people deserve all sorts of help. If Tamasha art improves, then it will become the best tool for literacy and entertainment."[65] Desai expressed the state's desire to serve Tamasha artists; yet, he failed to mention the "appropriate improvement" he was looking for. In a similar vein, the president of the Parishad, G. L. Thokal, wanted the Mumbai municipal government to pay attention to Tamasha: "In recent times there has been a lot of damage to the art, and I am sad about it. It's in the city and not the village that the attitudes towards making [a particular kind of] Tamasha have marred Tamasha and art." Thokal took pandharpesha to task for denigrating Tamasha. He also wanted to develop Tamasha and artists to procure an income. Importantly, at this time "about 40,000 people are working in Tamasha and it is their means of livelihood."[66]

The state encouraged Tamasha conferences to refine Tamasha and make it assli. Tamasha people also showed an interest in the conferences. On October 10–11, 1960, the Tamasha Parishad organized its second conference.[67] It had about 300–400 representatives, and every day about 500 people attended the shows of famous artists. In the conference's inaugural address, the minister of education Bharade said, "We need to keep alive the *Lokakala* [people's art] of Tamasha." Similarly, the deputy chief minister of Maharashtra, Madhusudan Vairale, in his presidential address, argued, "The [Tamasha] people should come forward and make some new experiments." Artists and filmmakers were already conducting experiments, as I revealed above. To anchor a robust nationalist identity, Tamasha also needed to be shaped anew.

Like Tamasha films, conferences also sought to make Tamasha respectable through the inclusion of women in Tamasha spaces. Like Tamasha performances, Tamasha conferences attracted mainly men. Very few women were involved. However, after the second Parishad, some educated women litterateurs from respectable families participated. Their presence helped in the renewal of Tamasha. Elites also expressed their staunch opinions. For example, the renowned dominant-caste poet Shanta Shelke, while addressing Tamasha women at the above Tamasha conference, argued, "Tamasha women should sing assli Marathi songs, and they should preserve their culture. They should stop singing cinema songs." Thus, in her view, legitimate Marathi songs and not hybrid cinema songs constituted assli Marathi culture. Like many scholars and laypeople, Shelke reinforced Tamasha as an essential element of Dalit culture and outside Marathi culture—this was the "caste-ing" and culturalizing of Tamasha as Dalit.

These conferences and similar events were also an opportunity for the state to recognize, reorganize, and celebrate Tamasha. During these meetings, the state awarded artists by gifting them turbans, scarves, or money. Even though these events were often poorly organized and only paid mere lip service to Tamasha and its artists (they certainly were not supporting Tamasha to the same extent as they were the classical arts), the state and some rich men emerged as new patrons of Tamasha. Chief Minister Yashwantrao Chavan inaugurated the first Maharashtra state Tamasha Mahotsav (Festival), to be celebrated March 18–20, 1961, at Rangbhavan, Dhobi Talao-Mumbai. About fourteen sangeet baris participated.[68] Education Minister Balasaheb Desai awarded the winner of the competition. This was the first time a Tamasha festival, a public Tamasha competition, an award ceremony, and discussion were held together. Unfortunately, despite these firsts and unlike their elaborate coverage of classical arts, newspapers, including *Navakal,* published no news about the debates and discussions.

The state also used these events to declare its support for new social and cultural practices by building theatres for Tamasha in Mumbai. Speaking at a felicitation event for the legendary Tamasha artist Bhau Bapu Narayangaokar (the grandfather of Mangalatai Bansode), Minister of Social Welfare Trimbak R. Naravane mentioned,

> Tamasha artists have preserved the art of Tamasha even in adverse cir-
> cumstances. . . . But only this is not enough. Tamasha is a unique art of
> Maharashtra. Tamasha has engaged in mass education through entertain-
> ment. Tamasha should not imitate Natak or Bolpat [drama or talkies]. Art-
> ists should pay attention to and strive to preserve *marathamoli bhasha,*
> *thasakebaja Lavanya—the shuddha svarup* [legitimate Marathi language,
> energetic Lavanya in pure form]. They should provide a model for other
> regions to follow.[69]

Thus, to state officials, Tamasha was a unique art to be preserved in its assli rural form by artists. As such, and most important, it was required for marathamola Marathi identity, especially in the 1960s. In the process, the state sanitized and harnessed Dalit Tamasha for its purposes. Tamasha artists like Bhau Narayan-gaokar agreed with the state official, "Yes, we will strive to retain the *shuddha svarup* [pure, assli form] of Tamasha." He had to concede to the terms of state support in order to survive.

To elevate Tamasha and Marathi films as a whole, Marathi elites also at-tacked and denigrated Hindi films as well as the North Indian artists who dominated the Hindi film industry in Mumbai. Speaking about Marathi and Hindi cinemas at Kolhapur's reading hall, the famous writer G. D. Madgulkar emphasized, "Marathi cinema industry has not converted films into Tamashe, [rather, they have made] Tamasha-based films."[70] Madgulkar's statement was counterintuitive—exposing the ambivalent aesthetic of Tamasha. On the one hand, he wanted to underline decency; yet, on the other he was not disturbed by the salacious discourse of Tamasha. However, he attacked Hindi cinema: "Hindi film industry stands first when it comes to making *chitrapatanche* Tamashe [entire films like Tamasha]. There is some *vulgarity* and lack of sringar in Marathi cinemas. However, writers should *not despise this speck of inferiority*. Instead writers should cooperate with cinema producers [to make good movies]."[71] Thus, ambivalent and ambiguous elites adopted double standards of shil-ashlil; they possessed the power to create artificial differences and artificial boundaries between different identities—Marathi/Hindi and savarna/Dalit—paying less attention to the relationality between them.

Such efforts by Marathi elites to differentiate an authentic Marathi culture continued. Yet, there were a few challenges from within elite brahman circles. Speaking on Tamasha and Tamasha people at a meeting of Youth Association, Colaba-Mumbai, on May 28, 1961, the chairperson of the meeting, the renowned socialist writer and brahman woman Durga Narayan Bhagwat (1910–2002) challenged elite brahman men's derision of gramya as "uncultured" Tamasha and rightly argued, "[brahman men] Deshpande-Bapat *Tamasha kala bighadvili* [have damaged Tamasha art]."[72] To her, elite discourse, literature, and drama actually killed traditional Tamasha. She continued, "P. L. Deshpande and Vasant Bapat drew upon and imitated the real Tamasha in their writings. In the process, they ruined Tamasha kala. The way ordinary people saw Tamasha in the past has changed in the present."[73] Bhagavat criticized renowned elite brahman litterateur men who conveniently appropriated and in turn corrupted Tamasha through their writings. They, like the filmmakers discussed above, reinforced stereotypes of Tamasha.

Most importantly, Bhagwat compared the *"vinod"* (joke, humor, fun) in assli Tamasha and P. L. Deshpande's writings:

The true preserver of vinod in Marathi literature is the *songadya* [buffoon character] in Tamasha! We can clearly find the sense of humor the wise class has lost in songadya. P. L. Deshpande's vinod has the capacity to merely make the clerical class laugh and entertain. However, a songadya's vinod has the power to engage everybody, including children, the old, the harassed, and ignorant people. This is absent in P. L.'s writings. The rural folks have lived on vinod. There can be no vinod without a philosophy. Hence there is a unique philosophy behind a songadya's vinod. Indians have *vinodala parkhe* [lost the sense of sport, jesting].[74]

Bhagvat pointed out the limitations of the renowned writer Deshpande's humor that was severely restricted to the urban petit bourgeois, lower-middle-class, and elites alone. She exposed the chasm between two classes—urban and rural, supposedly wise and ignorant. She also illuminated the shallow humor of the educated, which the latter used to poke fun at Tamasha. Urbane Marathi citizens could not grasp the potentials and firmly grounded philosophies of rural masses.

Bhagavat also criticized the government for not heeding her advice and for its half-hearted support of Tamasha. An anonymous writer in *Chhaya* agreed: "The Mumbai State Tamasha Parishad is a bizarre collective." This writer was also uncomfortable with a separate Tamasha conference, because to him state officials created many associations to exhibit their work, yet they were hardly effective. Even political parties had their own fish to fry, as the writer notes:

> Some parasitic people from Congress Party are involved with Mumbai Tamasha people. Balasaheb Patil, Jadhav, Namdeo Vhatkar, and Vishvasrao Vabale, supported by Construction Department person, Balasaheb Desai. They want to use Tamasha troupes in the coming elections. Mama Varerkar has arrived from Delhi to work on using Tamasha in Congress for propagation. The Communists like Amar Sheikh are excluded. Tamasgirs resolved that instead of independent parishad in Mumbai there should be a comingling [*snehsammelan*] of Tamasha people. This was, however, declined by Vhatkar and Patil! There were many contestations. . . . There is a danger of artist's oppression.[75]

The Congress Party, like the Communists, Satyashodhaks, and Jalsakars, also appropriated Tamasha and sought to regulate it for political propagation. The government initiated Tamasha Parishads, and Tamasha people used this opportunity to organize themselves. At this time, they also replaced the traditional cooperative principles on which Tamasha troupes were organized with capitalist, servant-owner culture. There was now a contractor with money who recruited troupes for fixed periods and amounts.[76] State and capital shaped a new Tamasha.

Tamasha Artists Reinforcing Assli Status

Efforts to reform Tamasha, to eliminate its reputation as ashlil and mark it as both shil and assli, and thus have it included in broader Marathi identity, came from within the Tamasha community of artists as well. Two parallel histories of Tamasha were operating at the same time: one rural and the other urban. While urban Tamasha was subject to the sanitizing, standardizing, and institutionalizing forces of the Marathi film industry and state organizations, making it palatable for pandharpesha audiences, in rural areas and especially villages, Tamasha artists continued to face caste discrimination, including harassment from audiences, the police, political parties, and rowdy patrons. Speaking to an audience in the 1979 in Mumbai, Dadu Indurikar, a famous Tamasha artist, remembered, "In 1940, I started my own troupe. However, during this time, there was a lot of touchable-Untouchable *jatiyavada* [caste distinction and discrimination problem]. I was totally burned in this caste struggle. People asked, 'Why see a Mhardyacha [Mahar caste, derogatory Mhardya] Tamasha. They came up with many such insults."[77] Dalits were aware of the ideological work that Marathi Tamasha movies, Tamasha advertisements, and the itinerant performativity of Dalit Tamasha women therein were doing to support their ongoing stigmatization as ashlil and deepen the divide between urban and rural.

Marathi elites, for their part, continued to compare Hindi and Marathi films: they delighted in reporting that "Hindi is experimenting while Marathi movies are focused on [denigrating feudal] Tamasha." They looked down upon rural Tamasha and even derisively characterized some actors, such as the "*ardhi-chhadi*" (short pants) hero Dada Kondke, as feudal, rural, and infantile and hence as uncultured, unruly, uncivilized, and ashlil—that is, lacking shil (good disposition; noble, genuine qualities). In response to the marginalizing effects of these associations of Tamasha, Tamasha artists, and Dalits more broadly in the process of Marathikaran in the new state of Maharashtra, Tamasha artists and troupe managers sought to sanitize Tamasha and Tamasha artists.

Tamasha people spent tremendous energy learning the epithets of assli to survive the violence at the roots of the caste system. Historically, even though Dalits opposed and resisted certain dominant-caste norms, in order to assimilate themselves with the Marathi nation, many Tamasha artists accepted the dominant-caste values of shil-ashlil and agreed with elite and statist sanitizing and organizing efforts in order to improve their own assli status and livelihood. Tired and disgusted by their abjection as animals and stereotypical ashlil status, they wanted to be assli Marathi citizens and seek protection and prosperity in the new Maharashtra. To these ends, they worked on various fronts, including special programs. During the Tamasha conference at Kolhapur on September 7, 1959, for instance, artists arranged a special program for women, which the Mahila Mandal (women's organization) welcomed.[78]

Some in the Tamasha community made public statements about the need to render Tamasha shil to reach pandharpesha audiences through special programs. In 1961, Balkrishna Pant Nerale, the owner of the famous Hanuman Theatre, a Tamasha and Sangeet Bari Theatre, near Lower Parel, Mumbai, declared: "Tamashala pandharpesha samajat karyarat karnyachi sandhi havi" (We need an opportunity to actively engage the respectable, urban, urbane, elite audiences, draw their attention to and root Tamasha in their community).[79] As a result, many people wanted to rescue Tamasha for popular consumption. Nerale continued his "important *svabhimani*" (self-respectful) exhortations: "To permanently uproot ashlilta from Tamasha, it is necessary to change the *abhiruchi* [interests] of the audience. In a similar way, Tamasha programs should gain respectable status in pandharpesha samaj."[80] Speaking at Chhotu Juvekar's Satyanarayan Mahapuja program, Valkeshvar-Mumbai, one Junnarkar was happy to report that "Sangeet Bari (Tamasha) found the hitherto denied space in this *satyanarayan puja* [auspicious event]."[81] As ashlil people, Tamasha artists were excluded from auspiciousness. As a result, inclusion in big, grand, auspicious programs was important for them to gain an honorable, legitimate, and equal status in society. It would provide them a taste of being assli. The newspaper *Navakal* affirmed the effect of a shil Tamasha at such an event as the Satyanarayan Mahapuja program: "It is through many such events that Tamasha artists will be able to improve their status." Many artists, including Master Bhagavan, Shantaram Bhate of the Tamasha Board, and cinema director

Salgavkar attended the program, which ran until 3:00 a.m. According to Bhate, "This event was a new project in the history of Tamasha."[82]

In addition to performing Tamasha as special programs or as part of larger cultural events, the Tamasha community worked in harmony with the state and elites to legitimize its art and preserve its legacy as a traditional art of Maharashtra by recording histories during Tamasha conferences. The preservation of memory, history, and citations was important in legitimizing and authenticating the assli, rural, oral art. An introductory book providing information about Tamasha artists was to be published. And Dagdu Sali and Haribhau's Tamasha literature were sent for publication. To refine the art and deepen appreciation for it among different publics, the state and artists, in addition to publishing books about Tamasha, also started organizing Tamasha training camps, competitions to produce Tamasha literature, and academies for artists, thus institutionalizing Tamasha. Focusing on traditional Tamasha, the Tamasha Kala Kalavant Vikas Mandir (Art and Artists Progress Committee) with its headquarters at New Hanuman Theatre organized competitions for new writers and Tamasha artists to write gangavlans, Lavanya, farces, and vag.[83]

However, many Tamasha artists were not particularly enthusiastic about such regimentation, especially if it happened without their consultation. Bhau Manjrekar, for instance, was upset that only fourteen troupes participated in the Nanded Tamasha Mahotsav organized by the Maharashtra government. He was also angry that artists were not using funds spent by the Maharashtra government on Tamasha, as assistance from the state was rare.[84] It seems, however, that in many cases the government's funding did not reach the artists. As a result, Manjrekar called upon the government to investigate whether its funding had resulting in developing Tamasha. Manjrekar argued, "Tamasha art is Maharashtra's *jativant* [caste-descent-based and hence authentic] art, *bahusankhya vargachi kala* [art of many people]. And hence, to keep it alive the government should consult appropriate people [who work in Tamasha]."[85] Tamasha people began to create a lineage and line of caste-descent to protect their art and profession, which was their key means of survival. As a result, they transformed Tamasha into their cultural capital and caste capital and even termed it *khandani* (of ancestral lineage). They depicted Tamasha as their caste-based right. They wanted Tamasha people to lead the conferences and meetings, instead of elite brahmans, such as Madgulkar, Bhagwat, Vijay Tendulkar, and Vikram Gokhale. Madhusudan Nerale affirmed that Tamasha people did not find affection and affinity with such elites.[86]

Speaking at an event in Jalgao's Haidari Theatre on December 24, 1961, Chhotu Juvekar of Navshakti Tamasha registered his skepticism and frustration with lackadaisical state-led efforts to promote Tamasha: "Government support and competition has become a farce and Tamasha is in a disgraced, dishonored state. Nobody is paying attention to artist's comfort." Shantaram Kate, the accountant of Natya Parikshan Mandal (Drama Censorship Association) and officer appointed for Tamasha countered Juvekar, arguing that he should not blame the government as it was only following the demands of representatives of Tamasha.[87] Kate aptly represented the pretentious, apathetic, and impassive government intervention in Tamasha. He easily dismissed Juvekar's concerns, turning the blame on Tamasha people and artists.

Some Tamasha artists, including the famous twin brothers Kalu-Balu, spoke more directly to the problems Tamasha artists continued to face, especially in rural areas: "People drink alcohol and attend Tamasha. There are more of this variety these days. When they create chaos, it is difficult to calm them down. There is *gundgiri* [rowdyism]."[88] In articulating these issues, Kalu-Balu pointed to the rural-urban divide as a major factor: "There is difference between the city and the village. In the village police, patil rules. There is less of such fear in city." Moreover, to them,

> audiences in the city are scared that their reputation, their social status, might fall into disrepute if they see Tamasha. And they are also used to seeing natak and films, sitting in [modern, Western] chairs [unlike sitting cross-legged or squatting in open air on open maidans for Tamasha]. Some people think seeing Tamasha is [not acceptable because it is inferior, ashlil]. Very few people are sympathetic toward Tamasha. [In general] the elite avoid Tamasha, [and as a result] we are sad [that we are excluded by them]. People think Tamasha is only for

people in rural areas. This misunderstanding is still prevalent. Some elites are [now] curious to see Tamasha.[89]

Kalu-Balu illuminated the differences between urban/urbane and rural/ uncouth audiences. Because elites were used to sitting in Western chairs in theatres, they looked down upon squatting or sitting cross-legged in open spaces. Elites also argued, *"Ashuddha ani aspastha* [impure and incoherent] pronunciations make Tamasha boring."[90] As a result, they stereotyped Tamasha as ashlil and characterized Tamasha artists as uncivilized and lowly and excluded them.

In the 1970s, Kalu-Balu also asserted the importance of training new hereditary and non-hereditary artists entering Tamasha, but state-sponsored and state-organized Tamasha training camps often revealed tensions between the interests of the state and those of the artists.[91] Appasaheb Inamdar and Madhukar Nerale organized some camps. Inamdar noted,

> Tamasha art was dying. Today it has become difficult for boys to stand upright with adorned turbans. The practice of singing film songs in Tamasha is increasing. Film Lavanya are entering Tamasha, and to stop this intrusion we need *shibir* [training camps devoted to Tamasha Lavani]. But many a time we had to cancel the camps because of different priorities of politicians. Some state officials show no affection for shibir. About 22 girls and boys participated in this shibir and immensely benefitted from it.[92]

There was a discrepancy between the rhetoric of reform and the limited opportunities provided by the state and the organization and execution of those opportunities on the ground. Although artists responded favorably to statist institutionalization, sanitization, and regimentation, they faced difficulties in praxis due to the vacillating and at times apathetic state and Marathi elites.

Despite training and standardization, as well as ongoing attempts by the state and Tamasha artists to reform Tamasha, artists continued to face elites who were disgusted with their art. One anonymous Tamasha devotee pointed out the reasons:

> The *daulatjada* [throwing of money, jewelry at women artists] in san-
> geet bari theatres is extremely disgusting. Barring a few exceptions, the
> pandharpesha cannot relish Tamasha with family. And hence Tamasha
> is on its death bed. It is disgusting *dhanda* [profession/business]. One
> good reason is the shameful practice of *baithak* [private entertain-
> ments]. If some social reformers do not pay attention to rid it of its
> immoralities, the future of Tamasha will be very difficult.[93]

Like this writer, many writers sought anonymity while writing about the
ashlil. They did not want to reveal their identity while commenting on
anything ashlil. Moreover, the author was angry that "Tamasha has entered
luxurious theatres in 1965 . . . [as well as elite] natak now. Tamasha is vulgar
and disgusting dhanda and whatever *ghanerde* [dirty] jokes we found in
there, we find more in natak now. If you see nataks in Chhatrapati Shivaji
Mandir, you will be completely convinced that Tamasha from [public]
tents has entered [private] theatre, and drama from theatre has moved to
tents."[94] Elites wanting to maintain and reinforce boundaries between the
classical natak and unruly Tamasha did not approve mixing the two arts.

Nevertheless, some artists were able to find new avenues. They entered
films and carved out a niche. Yet, they were not as prosperous as non-
Tamasha actors who performed copies of Tamasha. Some artists also tried
to abandon Tamasha in order to be included and assimilated into elite
natak. The famous artist Sanjeevani Bidkar detailed the discrimination she
faced at the hands of urban theatre people: "The world of natak is never
ready to forget that I have come from Tamasha."[95] She wanted to be an actor
in elite theatre, which "resented the *bhadak* [ostentatious] environment
of Tamasha." As a result, she left her *painjan* (ankle bells typically worn in
Tamasha) in order to be included in pandharpesha theatre. But she failed,
her dream was not fulfilled, and she continued to struggle:

> I performed stale roles, so that the natya world understands my acting
> skills. Both audience and producers appreciated them. Yet, the produc-
> ers with whom I was already working did not give me a chance for new
> nataks. They reasoned that 'I can't talk [pure, sanitized, sanskriti lan-
> guage], may not be able to act.' I came with a dream, but it has become

my fate to live with the broken pieces of my dream. Marathi theatre does not allow me to forget the work I have been trying to abandon. Because I came from Tamasha, I was denied main roles. Later, I denied the role of Tamasgir in Natak. . . . I am very disturbed when I think about Marathi theatre. I have now turned to Gujarati.[96]

Although Bidkar wanted to change from ashlil to assli, she could not do so easily on her own due to prevalent caste and class discrimination. She would need the support of a variety of elite people in the profession and to change her language, lifestyle, and herself. Yet, there was no guarantee that she would be included in the exclusive club of Marathi theatre. The forms of discrimination and distinction became sophisticated and changed with time and place.

The journey from ashlil to assli also forced theatre owners to change the names of their theatres and even the vocabulary used to describe performances. For example, sangeet bari and Tamasha came to be known in a broad sense as Loknatya (people's theatre). Madhusudan Nerale changed the name of Hanuman Theatre to New Hanuman Mangal Karyalay (Wedding Hall) in 1994. Pandurang Ganpat Nerale had established Hanuman Theatre in 1949 in Lower Parel-Mumbai. Initially a set of plywood walls and a tarp roof, until Pandurang Ganpat Nerale constructed the theatre in 1955–56, Hanuman Theatre had been famous for Tamasha and sangeet bari shows. And although it was one of many Tamasha theatres in the working-class neighborhoods of Mumbai—Vadacha naka, Naigao, Ambevadi, Delisle Road, Bhayakhala, and Pilahouse—it was unique in that it was the only one to have an academy for training in Tamasha.[97] And though the Hanuman Theatre (along with Pilahouse) survived the state ban on Tamasha in late 1940s,[98] it couldn't survive the name change nor the larger process of Marathikaran and the sanitization and standardization of Tamasha that accompanied it, and it closed in 1962–63.

However, after deciding to participate in the making of assli Tamasha, Madhusudan Nerale reopened the theatre as New Hanuman Theatre in 1965 with the help of Chhotu Juvekar and others "to save and serve Maharashtra's traditional popular art."[99] Yet, in 1994, he found that circumstances had changed: "Underworld gangs increased, termites consumed the wood in the building, and [we] had to close down the theatre." As a result, he was "forced to convert it to New Hanuman Mangal Karyalaya in Lower Parel."[100] The journey of Hanuman Theatre from a Tamasha and sangeet bari theatre to a wedding hall emphasizes the disciplining and even erasure of unbridled sexuality and lower caste, lower class to emphasize tight strictures of auspiscious marriage ceremonies. This would enhance the reputation of the theatre and mark sanitizing and assimilating processes.

The struggle from ashlil to assli was reinvigorated in the 1980s and 1990s as India advanced into the neoliberal era. In 2001, commenting on his innovative Lavani program *Sola hajarat dekhni* (The one woman attractive among 16,000 women; figure 5.15), featuring lead artists Maya Jadhav and Sanjeevani-Mule-Nagarkar, producer Mahonar Nare emphasized his innovative Lavani program "*is assli, not ashlil.*"[101] He was proud of his "assli marathamola discovery of Lavani" and asserted, "I want to produce a Lavani program that will be popular in the city."[102] In this, he joined a long line of film directors, producers, writers, contractors, and artists who took up the task of making Tamasha assli for Marathi identity and legitimacy. Artists took every rare opportunity to present their excellent art and thrive. Avinash Chitnis covering the above event for *Rasrang*, reported Nare's "invention" as "assli marathamola." He further argued that it was very rare for men and their families to listen to Lavani or see Lavani dance, especially because the elites were anxious about and feared Lavani. For Chitnis, like Kalu-Balu, "the main hindrance to [the elites] was the unique audience that gathered for such programs and their *vahiyat* [frivolous, lecherous] behavior." Yet, Chitnis reinforced Nare's *Sola hajarat dekhni* as "invention of assli marathamola Lavani" and the performers, who were confident about bridging the rural and urban divide. They asserted that their shows would be appreciated by both urban and rural audiences. Everyone—Chitnis, Nare, Jadhav, and Nagarkar—affirmed the effect of the dual processes of sanitizing and asserting the already assli status of Lavani on their shows.

Chitnis was at pains to show that the *Sola hajarat dekhni* program was *svaccha* (literally, clean; here, devoid of ashlil):

> The participants have taken utmost care to make it *dekhani* [attractive] and svaccha entertainment. *Nakhra, sringar, ada* [gestures and eros]

'माझ्या लावनीवर प्याचडी करायचीय? पन त्यासाठी तुमाला हॉंगकॉंग, पॅरिस, लंडन, न्यूयॉर्क, अटलांटा असं
कुठंतरी यावं लागल बगा. मी फकस्त निथल्या थिएट्ररस्त्या जत्रेतच नाचते.

FIGURE 5.15. Advertisement for Tamasha Mahotsav. Source: *Rasrang*, 2005. National Film Archive of India.

are at the core of Lavani. The audience will be attracted to them, but not take them to be *onghal, ashlil* [overtly obscene, vulgar]. Maya Jadhav has paid minute attention to this while setting the dance moves, even her "Padala pikalaya amba" [famous Lavani song literally titled "Ripe Mango," suggesting full, ripe breasts] is done with *kamalichi safai* [wonderful cleanliness without vulgar gestures] and is very attractive.

Safai—social, sexual, linguistic, verbal—was important for assli Marathi identity. Chitnis illuminated elitist ambivalence, the consistent efforts to erase the ashlil but still engage in the covert regime of sexuality. Tamasha and Lavani were to be clean and devoid of ashlil. Yet the clean deliberately contained hints of the unclean and vulgar to make it attractive. Elites clearly gained from Tamasha energy, yet they repressed and sanitized it further for popular consumption. Most important, Chitnis started and ended his essay by emphasizing decency that was most important for an assli Marathi identity.

The liberalization and globalization of the 1990s created new competitions within media and, to an extent, changed lives of Tamasha and Lavani women. Women enhanced their skills and learned different dancing and singing skills. They moved from performances in the open maidan to luxurious air-conditioned theatres and auditoriums. They started recording their songs, advertised on television and in newspapers and magazines. Most important, they produced CDs and videos of their performances and even had shows in different countries. For example, the Maharashtra Mandal of Boston and New York invited the lead artist Surekha Punekar for a Lavani performance.

Even the cultural minister of Maharashtra, Pramod Navalkar, boasted that he was the first person to organize Tamasha and the boisterous Lavani Mahotsav over two days in Yashwantrao Chavan air-conditioned theatre. He argued:

> Lavani would charge you to any extent. . . . The artist girls, who were totally neglected and ignored by the society, they were in that dirty area. Two days' performance was held. And those girls gave performances, dressed up to respectable people like Naushad [Ali, legendary Hindi film music and composer]. Now there are shows going all over Maharashtra. [Lavani singer] Surekha Punekar is on the top of the world now. She said, "On that day, I was introduced to a real audience, and now my life has changed."[103]

The potency of sexually charged Lavani was at the core of asserting assli Marathi culture in the elite realm.

Government and corporate support for sexually charged Tamashe/Lavanya programs and training and the institutionalization and regularization of these arts reached new heights in the twenty-first century. To exploit the new popularity of and demand for Tamashe/Lavanya, in 2004, the state of Maharashtra through the University of Mumbai established the Lokkala Academy—that is, a department of Popular Culture and Performing Folk Arts (PFA)—to train students in the "scientific knowledge of folklore and performing folk arts."[104] The Lokkala Academy involved leading Tamasha and Lavani women as instructors, especially to train non-hereditary artists from a variety of caste backgrounds in the assli popular arts of Maharashtra. It focused on "regimented and rational aims and objectives" to implement a master's and certificate course in supposedly folk arts, in order to encourage professionalism, academic ambience, research, and documentation, to connect traditional and innovative approaches, and to help non-hereditary students "*exploit* opportunities in the field of PFA and seek self-employment.[105] The academy wanted its students to "*exploit* the possibilities in Performing Folk Arts, Folk Performances Administration, Folk Research and mass education and communication through Folk Performances which will help students to work with print media and electronic media through Folk-Culture background."[106] The academy thus *exploited* ashlil Tamasha art and "train[ed] all round [non-Dalit] folk-theatre professionals, who will provide leadership to the folk-theatre culture of the country and work as facilitators for National and International folk-theatre."

Lokkala Academy, under the aegis of Shahir Amarsheikh Adhyasan, also started documenting shahirs and shahiri "who [contributed] to the freedom movement of nation and Maharashtra."[107] It organized workshops and folk festivals, sometimes with assistance from the government. Lokkala Academy organized a Parampara (tradition/culture) festival in 2007 and 2008 and wanted to continue the tradition. The festival was organized with the help of West Zone Cultural Center and the Cultural Affairs Department of the Government of Maharashtra. The academy conducted workshops on folk songs, folk dances and folk plays during Parampara Festival in which supposedly expert exponents of folk music and folk drama imparted knowledge to students.[108]

Building on this new interest in popular culture, activists and intellectuals have only recently turned their attention to Tamasha and Lavani. The *Rasrang* magazine advertisement in figure 5.15 from 2005 amply illustrates the renewed scholarly interest in Lavani. This caption reads, "You want to do a Ph.D. on my Lavani? For that you have to visit Hongkong, Paris, London, Atlanta, and so on. I only dance in fairs in theatres there."[109] The ad highlights the popularity and transnational travel of Tamasha-Lavani artists, arts, and students pursuing these popular theatrical forms for different purposes, most importantly financial. Significantly, the caption uses a typical rural pronunciation of Ph.D., as "patch D" and "*phakast*" (only) instead of the elite "*phakt*."

FIGURE 5.16. Vithabai's phad dance at the 18th Maharashtra State Tamasha Mahot-sav. Jayant Vaishampayan, "18th Tamasha Mahotsav: Kalavantanche haal [troubles of Tamasha artists]." Source: *Rasrang*, April 12, 1980, 28–29. National Film Archive of India.

Yet, hereditary Tamasha artists continued to be marginalized, excluded, and exploited. They faced enormous difficulties as Vithabai Narayangaokar (1935–2002), daughter of Bhau-Bapu Mang poignantly emphasized in 1980, "Saheb, lokanchi ji hagindari ti amchi vatandari" (Sir, *the land where people defecate and is used as venue for our Tamasha performances, we turn it into our inheritance rights and lineage of Tamasha*).[110] Like her co-artists, she reinforced Tamasha as her caste-based-culture-and-right as well as her right to livelihood. Referring to the 18th Maharashtra Tamasha Mahotsav, held in Nashik, she continued:

> The venue hosting Tamasha artists did not have basic water facilities. So, we have set up our *birhad* [ourselves with our equipment, clothing and accessories, and families] behind this theatre. The place where all people urinate, defecate—that is where we cook, eat, and along with our young children, sleep in the bitter cold. Under such circumstances, how will artists participate in Tamasha Mahotsav and then how will the state be successful in supporting Tamasha artists?[111]

Despite Vithabai's and Vaishampayan's (the reporter covering the event) complaints, the state social officer Garbe shrugged off his responsibilities and also took credit for the meagre facilities that were provided to Tamasha artists. He noted, "We were not provided any instructions from higher authorities. Whatever organization you see is our work."[112] The government spent little money on Tamasha, starving Tamasha artists of resources. State representative Garbe, like others before him, immediately protected wavering statist intervention and also pointed out that Tamasha artists should be grateful to him for the scarce facilities he provided. Whenever Dalits asked questions or challenged the status quo, dominant castes and the state shut them down, and only rewarded them for falling in line. Caste stole the material and psychic resources of Dalits. Destitute Dalit Tamasha artists make do with the tidbits thrown to them surviving the quiet mundanity of caste. But then there are women like Mangalatai Bansode, Vithabai's daughter who worked through subjection, poverty, and vulnerability, actualizing this vatandari-right-and-caste-based lineage, and turning it into a thriving business enterprise. Her life illuminates her negotiating ashlil-manus-assli status, as she continues to be degraded as a Tamasha woman falling in iterant performative cycles of ashlil business.

Conclusion

Tamasha and Lavani were paradoxically attractive, threatening, and desirable at the same time. The sexual-caste economy rendered the Tamasha woman as a specter, even if the state and elites reframed her and her art as respectable. Elites retained her caste-body as a sexually objectified and socially degraded dancer to signify desire, but immediately resignified to answer the notions of assli. I illuminated the discourse and processes of claiming legitimate Marathi identity for different actors—elites and Tamasha people—in the new state of Maharashtra. The category of "Marathi" embodied certain perceived features of Marathiness drawing on "commonsense" notions of Marathi people through a gamut of myths, stories, common past, virility, valor, cultural past, pride, regionalism—rhetoric drawing on images in popular history and stereotypes about Marathi people. The Maharashtra state deployed Marathi manus as a political weapon against non-Marathi people. Regenerating Maharashtra was a process to create a new Marathi culture and a new identity after the violence of independence. The moralizing Maharashtra state sought to repress pleasures, unruly sexuality, and childish behavior to create a proper Marathi manus.

The constitution of Marathi identity was a hierarchical process between elites and Tamasha people. Although the pandharpesha invested in modernity and its resulting castelessness denied caste-, class-, religion-, and region-based differences to create a united Maharashtra and Marathi identity since SMM, their efforts were limited and vacillating.Throughout the twentieth century, in the social and political realm, elites adopted inclusion/exclusion and worked on reforming Dalits from the outside. They did not engage with Dalits as subjects or address Dalit manuski. Even though Marathi elites and the State of Maharashtra made intense efforts to redefine and renew Tamasha, to take pride in it as an iconic form of Maharashtrian identity and art, the ashlil did not stick to them the way it did to Dalit performers. These efforts at creating assli Marathi cultural authenticity reproduced in the realm of popular culture and cinema, as anxious, hesitant, and fearful elites inaugurated the standardization, canonization, and regulation of ashlil Tamasha. Tamasha filmmakers and advertisers of Tamasha film struck a gold mine in Tamasha and pounced on the supposedly traditional art to revive Marathi film and Marathi identity. The multiple efforts by different elite actors to generate assli stripped Dalitness from Tamasha and were striking for the absence of manuski for Dalit. They along with the state spoke of assli Marathi manus without Dalitness. To tackle the dominant-caste hegemony, subordinated Tamasha people engaged in varied maneuvers to rework their caste difference and repurpose Tamashe as caste and cultural capital and their traditional roots and to establish their status as assli. They reinforced their right to perform in Tamasha. They made difficult choices under constraints, though at times they challenged and twisted hegemonic norms to create a new Tamasha. But they also accommodated, to make peace with and internalize some elitist discourse of sanitization, and shared their program of regimentation and standardization to prove their worthiness and traditional belongingness to an assli Marathiness and Indianness.

Chapter 6

FORGING *NEW* FUTURES AND MEASURES OF HUMANITY

When I met with Mangalatai Bansode,[1] the daughter of the legendary Vithabai Narayangaokar, on October 9, 2004, she sang a famous Lavani attributed to her mother:

> laaj dhara pavana janachi manachi
> potasathi nachatey mee parva kunachi
> dava dola jhakun khunavu naka, ho asa tumhi hinavu naka
> aathavan dete mee tarnya panachi
> potasathi nachatey mee parva kunachi

> (O guest, maintain your shame for others as well as for yourself. I
>   am dancing to
> earn my livelihood; I do not care for anybody else. Do not make
>   sexual gestures
> by winking your left eye at me. You are actually mocking me. I am
>   helping you
> remember your youth. I am dancing for my everyday living. I do not
>   care for anybody else.)

Through this Lavani, Vithabai asserted her humanity, and yet troubled Tamasha women's precarious relationship to *manus* (the human). Through such pointed and piercing songs, Vithabai interpreted her Tamasha life as a ritual of "rough music"[2] and cruelty, sharply ridiculing her male audience. She transformed her performance art and the expected performativity of Dalit women's sexual availability into a site of Dalit women's resistance, into a performativity of Dalit femininity and sexuality rooted in an improper caste politics.

How might we consider Vithabai's and Mangalatai's iterative use of

Tamasha, of performance art to illuminate the political economy of caste slavery, daily practices in the production of and resistance to Dalitness, the reproduction of brahmani patriarchy, and strategies for resistance and redress? In deploying her Lavani as a political double entendre to exhibit the tension between the performativity of seduction and the lyrical refusal of her sexual availability, Vithabai coded it as a text of protest. She foregrounded Tamasha women's exploitation, used her body to evoke pleasure, and engaged in covert acts of resistance to record the persistent production of her Dalitness as abject, threatening, dependent, irrational, entangled in violence and humiliation and, at the same time, dissenting and resilient against caste discrimination and patriarchy. Pleasure was fraught with violence, exploitation, and desire as well as challenges to domination.

Even in the postcolonial state of Maharashtra, Mangalatai, like her colonial counterpart Pavalabai, did not measure up to brahmani standards of manus or womanhood. Fifty years after Pavalabai, Mangalatai combined old and new Tamasha cultures, performing both her social struggle and the ambivalent legacy of the ashlil, manuski, assli, and freedom on stage. She expressed desires, exorbitant and excessive, that were consistent with neither radical Dalit politics nor the brahmani norms and ideals of womanhood.

The precarity of Mangalatai worlding ashlil and assli Dalitness simultaneously challenges and consents to the authority of touchables' framing of Tamasha as Dalit cultural identity, hierarchizing the ashlil and the assli and distinguishing between fallen (Dalit) and respectable (touchable) womanhood, on the one hand, and navigating the radical Dalit politics of manuski, self-determination, and anticaste liberation, on the other. She was both an ashlil and an assli Tamasha woman. To her, unlike Ambedkar and Ambedkarite Jalsakars, there was no dichotomy between the ashlil and the assli, between private and public, as she negotiated the entangled politics of caste, sexuality, and state-making. This chapter shows how, despite all the effort that had gone into the revision, regulation, and rehabilitation of Tamasha, and despite the attempts of radical Dalits like Ambedkar and Ambedkarite Jalsakars to remake Dalit women and sanitize Tamasha of its *sringarik* (erotic) elements, there still exist a significant number of Dalit women performers struggling to navigate the sticky stigmatization of being ashlil. From Pavalabai to Mangalatai,

Tamasha women have had to negotiate the conditions of the sex-gender-caste complex, the stickiness of the ashlil, and the possibilities for forging an assli human future through the precarious performance and performativity of their labor, sexual and otherwise.

Working in the *Hagandari* (Defecation Field) of Tamasha

On October 9, 2004, Mangalatai performed on a stage built quickly overnight in the defecation field in Kada village, Ahmednagar district. I had met Mangalatai, a nonliterate Tamasha dancer, a month earlier, during her performance at the famous Bal Gandharva Rangmandir auditorium in Pune (see figure 6.1). In the many hours we spent together in Pune and more so in Kada, Mangalatai remembered her past and narrated her present while also speculating about her actions in the future. Epistemologically and politically, our listening presence helped Mangalatai evoke forgotten moments, name her anger and discontent with her life situation, and record her resilience and frustrations, both to herself and me. We chatted away that hot afternoon as the other artists continued with their card games, relaxed or slept before the evening performance, checked their equipment, and ate their meals in the shade of the tents. This was their everyday way of life for eight to nine months every year. In Mangalatai's words, *our* common caste background— she a Mang and me a Mahar-Dalit-Buddhist—facilitated my entering into sequestered spaces that were often out of bounds to elite scholars,

> I do not take riks [risks], I am a little concerned about who is interviewing, what will they do with my information, and where it will end up? However, I am very happy to talk with you because you belong to *aapla samaj* [our community]. It is because of that that I am sitting with you, or else, we live or die, who cares for us?

Mangalatai did not want to invite trouble from non-Dalits. The deeper caste-community cord was very significant to Mangalatai. She was more comfortable talking with me as a person who belonged to "our" samaj. Moreover, by deploying her own low-class and low-caste vocabulary of "riks, Mhar, nhai," Mangalatai challenged elite, cultured, sanitized, and sanskritized language practices of "risk, Mahar, nahi." After some persuasion, she talked unhindered,

FIGURE 6.1. Mangalatai leading the Lavani performers in September 2004 at Bal Gandharva auditorium, Pune. Source: Photo courtesy of author.

and we built on our common connection. Thinking about Tamasha in this manner, distinguishing the dilemmas that Dalit Tamasha women endured from those of Dalits in search of manuski, was not a possibility until and unless the social and political conditions for such thought had emerged. My presence as a Dalit researcher sensitive to Dalit manuski for Tamasha women, in a reflexive and generous mode, created the conditions for that possibility.

Mangalatai was a generous host, offering me the best *methichi bhaaji* (vegetable dish made from fenugreek leaves) and *bhakri* (bread) cooked on a *chul* (open hearth) (see figure 6.2), and I am grateful to her for spending time with me and sharing her life experiences. While we chatted away for hours, I noticed some women and men in the troupe viewing me with skepticism. "What is she, a middle-class-looking [fair-complexioned, neatly dressed] lady, doing here?" they may have thought. I noticed that during our conversation, Mangalatai was very alert and kept a close watch on eavesdroppers who could overhear her story. To be more cautious, we constantly shifted from one location to another: inside the tent that was a temporary home for artists, outside to the fields, and at times to the area around the tent, where we walked. In this manner, she

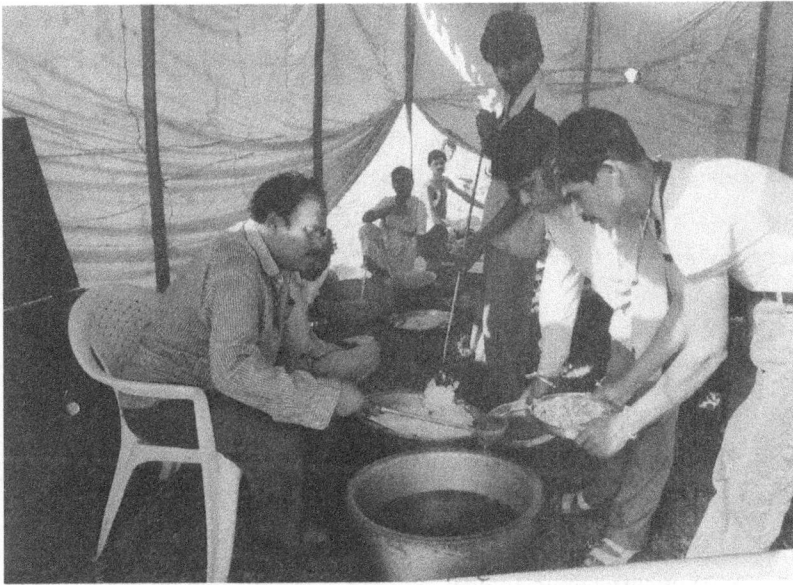

FIGURE 6.2. Meals cooked on the *hagandari* (fallow land used for defecation).
Source: Photo courtesy of author.

could also keep a watch on workers attending to their duties as she continued to share her experiences of poverty, politics, and the titillating performances of sringarik Tamasha and Lavani.

Policing Women and Producing Tamasha

Tamasha women, though at times in control, were also at the mercy of men and women in their family and the audience as well as the contractors and managers who policed them in the interest of producing Tamasha. Mangalatai and other Tamasha women deployed their body politics, their itinerant performativity of their sensual and sexual selves and informal sexual relationships, as an economic resource. As a result, women's bodies and especially women's sexuality became property, a form of wealth for the family—as such, women were at the mercy of their patrons. At the same time, many women negotiated patriarchal power and bent it to suit their own purposes, engaging the sexual economy of erotic excess and normative societal structures of caste, gender, sexual, and familial labor by manipulating their bodies.

Women were (and are) sometimes able to appropriate their own sexuality, selling it, abandoning marriage, and keeping the benefits that they accrue for themselves. In these processes, gender and sexuality emerge as generative activities in a particular way: as source and effect of exchange. However, Mangalatai's modes of life "exceed the logic of capital itself"[3] because families increase the value of women by keeping them inside the family and community and not selling them off as objects of barter and exchange or gifts in the marriage economy.

Poverty and Hunger

We need to challenge critiques located in an West/East, willfull/willless, consent/coercion, or resistance/domination binary that often buries the complexity of Dalit Tamasha women's experiences. Most Tamasha women and Tamasgirs as a whole concurred that they were pushed to perform because of poverty. Mangalatai recounted her days of poverty and hunger: "When I was with my mother, it was hard to procure food. We had name and fame, but no money to even buy food. My father, uncles (both maternal and paternal), looted my mother." Women were the breadwinners of the entire family, and it is poverty as well as their generational ties to Tamasha that enabled them to draw upon their bodies as an economic resource by performing in Tamasha. Mangalatai underscored that although her mother was a very famous artist, as a child Mangalatai often starved. Moreover, men who depended on women's familial, social, and sexual labor and at times supported them also often further oppressed those women.

Seconding Mangalatai, the highly reputed Lavani *samaradni* (Lavani empress) Surekhatai Punekar, a Dalit (Mahar-Buddhist) Tamasha woman, recounted her overlapping and complicated struggles:

My maternal grandparents were in Tamasha. My father was a *hamal* [head loader] at Pune Railway Station. He continued with his *hamali* during the daytime and engaged in *bailgadicha* [bullock cart] Tamasha in the nights. Once the bullock cart met with an accident, and I got a deep cut on my leg. During those times there was only *jhada khalcha* [under the tree] Tamasha. There was no proper stage. Tamasha women also did not earn the kind of income they do these days. I was introduced to the stage when I was only eight years old. I liked to dance and sing. My father also instructed me to sing well. He did not allow me to sleep and *phatke dyayache avaj chadhavanya sathi* [punished me so I would sing higher]. I stood on a chair and sang.[4]

Thus, Surekhatai endured physical beatings because she knew without her wages there would be no food at home. Hunger was common, she reported:

We went from village to village to perform. When we got to the village, we first begged for bread and curry, and then after collecting everything, ate together at a village common hall and performed in the nights. After three, four months we went home until Divali and worked as maids for 10–12 families. We never had food to eat in our home. I remember my days of my poverty, sometimes we got only black tea [because there was no money to buy milk] and hard baked bread.

Surekhatai, like Mangalatai was constantly afflicted by hunger and poverty during her childhood.

Over the years, however, the larger poverty narrative proved to be complicated and sat uneasily with some non-hereditary young artists who entered Tamasha and Lavani willingly to make money and learn the art from lead-artists. Mangalatai mentioned, "These days girls, college students from even higher castes [brahman], at times due to poverty but also to earn easy pocket money, participate in my troupe. They want to work with me." Although touchable women have performed in Tamasha and Lavani shows or in films since the 1940s, these were typically temporary monetary arrangements for them. They were not stigmatized like hereditary Dalit Tamasha women; the ashlil did not stick to them. Even though they also performed in Tamashe, they were always already assli. They rode their scooters to the theatres, danced and sang, and after the show returned to their respectable homes as normal, modern, and modest women. They also danced in films and television shows and became attractive star artists. However, abject Dalit Tamasha women were excluded from such fame and they did not enjoy this privilege and luxury—they were afflicted by poverty, the stickiness of the ashlil, and the stigma of caste. For hereditary artists, their poverty was further compounded by ignorance and illiteracy.

Pedagogy of Tamasha

Tamasha women's education was the dance and song training they received from their parents or family members. The Tamasha stage was transformed into a classroom where parents, like schoolteachers, inflicted *phatke* (beatings) to discipline children and instill the pedagogy and body politics of song and dance ritual. Surekhatai was not sent to school because her migratory lifestyle could not allow for this luxury. She reasoned:

> My parents were alcoholic. Because my father was *kalechya nadat* [engrossed in the art], he did not send me to school. We were six siblings. I must say that while my parents sent my sisters to school to be educated until the third grade, I was never given such an opportunity. I do not know the reason. My mother said she did not know either.

In a similar vein, Mangalatai recalled that her mother, Vithabai initiated her into Tamasha:

> When my mother performed in her Tamasha, there were fewer women performers. She needed more women in her troupe and hence, she discontinued my schooling when I was in class two and pushed me on to the Tamasha stage when I was merely nine years old. Today, I am fifty-five and I am still dancing. My mother is my *guru* [teacher]. I am famous because of her. My mother also danced from when she was seven years old. Initially, I was scared of men in the audience, but gradually I became bold and I could tackle them as I turned fifteen or sixteen. My son Nitin was also introduced to the Tamasha stage when he was only seven years old. We tried our best, but he did not study at all.

Education for Mangalatai was the actual pedagogical training and practice of Tamasha on and off stage. Mangalatai transformed her mother into a guru and herself into a *shishya* (disciple), thus reinforcing her khandani of Tamasha and the guru-shishya practice of higher classical arts to establish new traditions in Tamasha. To accentuate their khandani caste-based arts, at times, artists hired dance and music experts to train them, but not all women prefer to dance, as Mangalatai's sister Kranti reported:

> I do not like to dance. I always wanted to sing, but my mother only brought me out to dance. I have studied until the fifth class, but I was not interested in school. My mother used to dance and move around, and we were left with some caretaker who fed us, clothed us, and sent us to school. It was like we were just dancing as a hobby, or since it was in the family, our condition was quite good. After my mother's death, I am now with my elder sister.

Many women were busy earning for their families, and consequently, they could not pay attention to their children. They could barely spend time with them or think about their rearing.

After the Tamasha parishads and reforms of 1970 and 1980s, like elite classical artists, Tamasha artists spent long hours learning dance moves, singing, and rehearsing. They wanted to exhibit their assli status to savarna pandharpesha both through ancestry as well as additional training. As a result, some like Surekhatai also enrolled for classical *kathak* dance lessons. Mangalatai also learned to dance, sing, perform a variety of skits, and engage in a confident and bold manner with the mixed-caste, mostly dominant-caste male audience.

The pedagogical goals of Tamasha people for everyday survival thus contrasted with those of respectable, middle-class Dalits who aggressively sought manuski, education, and employment to cultivate decency and proper conduct and focus on self-and-community building, as I illuminated in chapters 3 and 4. To upwardly mobile Dalits, self-esteem, self-reliance, dignity, self-assertion, assertive manuski, and community power were significant to adjust to their new status as free *manus* (human beings) in independent India. Feminine virtue, domesticity, and privatization of family and marital relations were central to these processes of self-in-community-making.[5] To achieve modernity, morality, and manuski, respectable Dalits did not approve of the unbecoming conduct in terms of ashlil dress, tone of voice, pronunciations, demeanor, multiple companions, and free movement of Tamasha people. To them, Tamasha, Murali, and the slum were metaphors for Dalit lives and they sought to escape from them. The Tamasha woman, in their eyes was a commodity—used, abused, ravaged, discarded, raped and as such Tamasha women rendered the Dalit samaj weak, disrespectful, and ashlil. Tamasha women's good conduct could not mitigate the rule of coercion, violence, and resentment against them. In pursuing their agendas, upwardly mobile and middle-class Dalits at times decontextualized and paid less attention to unequal conditions of different Dalits. They followed Ambedkar's dictum, "Self-respect is more important than bread." By contrast, Tamasha women made different choices under constraints because, as they argued, "self-respect does not guarantee bread."

As I have revealed throughout the book, Tamasha people sought different ways of governing and managing their lives. Tamasha parents, kin, and associates engaged in pedagogical injunctions to paradoxically embrace their status as both ashlil and assli. This meant abstaining from overt assertions of equality, liberty, and oppositional consciousness and continuing old forms of caste servility and obsequiousness. At the same time, they encouraged, educated, and trained women to be alert, bold, and smart, to manipulate male managers and otherwise be attractive, to engage the audience, and to cater to men's sensual and sex(ual) demands. Both paths of formal and informal politics taken by different Dalits were tortuous and did not guarantee them full equality, liberty, and manuski. Dalits had to keep on struggling to become assli manus!

Work/Play, Body Politics, and Erotic Excess

The "fun and play" Tamasha was *kala* (art), hard *kama* (work), and performance of sensual play for Tamasha women, and it was relaxation, amusement, entertainment, and an opportunity to feel like a "real" man for touchable men in the audience. I reiterate, Tamasha was a fraught performativity, accommodating, negotiating, and switching the meaning of work and play. Tamasha women's work enabled men to laugh, joke, make lewd comments and gestures, pat each other on the back, flirt, dance, drink and make merry, and strengthen male bonding and masculinity at the expense of Tamasha women. Tamasha women performed to amuse men, and they were playful in the service of the oppressor. Men structured manliness and masculine behaviors mainly with Tamasha women who excited and stimulated them. And the everyday work and sustenance of Tamasha women depended on their complying, challenging, negotiating, bending, and transgressing brahmani patriarchy through an excessive performance of the sringarik and exotic. Although agents of the colonial and postcolonial Maharashtra state, women and men from a variety of castes and classes sought to sanitize Maharashtrian society. Mangalatai underlined the necessity of ashlil and sringarik excess:

> Some old, traditional Lavanya have ashlil words. We have to dance and make ashlil gestures in tune with these words because people in the audience like them. For example, the words "choli majhi taatali, kaya majhi bhijali" [my blouse is tight because of full breasts and my body is wet]. How do you show this? How do you show you have full breasts and hence the choli is tight and the body is covered with water [clearly revealing the private body parts]? There's another Lavani: "kiti mi halavu, kiti mi halavu, thand garava?" [how much do I shake, how much do I shake in this cool breeze?] One has to show everything, enact, and bring to life these ashlil words.

Mangalatai indicated that to earn their living, Tamasha women engaged in the play of deploying ashlil words and a body politics of erotic excess to entice and fulfill men's desires.

It was thus a titillating vicious circle of the Tamasha performativity: men in the audience wanted more sensual and sexual titillation, and women provided it because they thought that was exactly what audiences wanted. As a result, women on stage and men in the audience participated in a mutuality of desire through a sexual and erotic body politics of gestures, including winking the left eye, biting lips, continually shaking hips and breasts, and accentuating particular body parts.

Although Mangalatai felt the injury, pain, and predicaments produced by the circular logic of Tamasha, she also underscored that artists depended on the audience: "Public demands ashlil Lavanya. We have to satisfy them, and everybody does it. So, we cannot really help it, or we will lose." Much as in scholarly econometrics, everybody in the Tamasha occupation and business understood the operations of the law of *magani tasa puravatha* (demand and supply). There was a double system of work and play in Tamasha—work was concealed behind play and most important, the meaning of play was fashioned to accommodate that of work.[6] Yet, the work of Tamasha women was depicted as nonwork in the culture of India that values hard work and as a result, "time off" or "time pass" has a negative connotation.

Tamasha women deployed and exaggerated their femininity as a device to enhance men's self-image and the imagination of marathamola Woman and Man, constructed manliness and femininity, and male and female sexuality. As a result, Tamasha not only reflected social relations but also constructed, reproduced, and sharpened them. Constructed as a sexually dirty, disrespectable, and dangerous Tamasha woman, Mangalatai was important to men for the latter's enjoyment, relaxation, and having a good time. This was the double-sidedness of being a Tamasha woman: she was enjoyed and degraded at the same time. Mangalatai was willing to indulge men in the audience in the expression of their desires, flattering their egos, enticing them sexually by becoming an image of an ideal desirable woman men would want to have sex with. In this manner, women created an imaginary sexual world and sold it to men.

Different motivations propelled women into Tamasha and Lavani: young college students wanted pocket money to buy new clothes and accessories, and wives needed to supplement their husbands' income; some young women wanted to dance in the hitherto forbidden performance art. But financial motivation was most significant for Tamasha women.

Deviant Sexuality and Patriarchy

Tamasha women and men fought with and supported each other. Women, the main breadwinners, easily incorporated family members into the practice of Tamasha. Tamasha women and men bent patriarchal rules, partnered with each other, and together shared the tasks of singing, dancing, helping with chores, and taking care of the younger children. Yet men also exploited Dalit women's social and sexual labor in various ways. Tamasha enhanced the gender imbalance and raised the potential for sexual abuse by men. Men secured their ties of manliness, marathamola masculinity, by playing with Tamasha women. In other words, "Marathi men" were constructed out of the abuse of Tamasha women, and this potent danger continued for Mangalatai, as she was fashioned as a desirable and necessary commodity. She noted:

In the beginning I was scared to face the public. However, gradually I learned to handle the public. *Hey lok cheshta kartyat, maskari kartyat, pan kunibi haat nhai laval ajoon . . . mee kadak bai haye* [These people make fun of me, ridicule me, but nobody has so far touched me physically . . . because I am a very strict woman]. *Me ek lakh deto, don lakh deto, jhopaya ye . . . ashe mhas prasang hote* [I will give one or two lakh rupees, sleep with me . . . there were many such incidents], but I never gave in and just continued with my Tamasha. My family has been attacked; I have faced caste discrimination in my village, but this is life!

This is the peripatetic life of a Tamasha woman: insecure and unstable, oppressed by the conjugated technologies of caste, gender, and sexuality and contesting patriarchies; however, the caravan is always on the move. Due to her engagement with the public and lowly Tamasha, Mangalatai was always already discriminated against as a promiscuous Dalit woman by men of all castes. Nevertheless, over the years, she learned to work with men, and found ways to protect herself through an assli performativity.

The brahmani patriarchal ruling classes of colonial and postcolonial Maharashtra created (and create) a normative hierarchy of caste, gender, and sexuality. As a result, they graded femininity focusing on caste lines and tightly tied (and tie) mobile Tamasha women to the lowest ladder of sex and sexuality and even depicted (and depict) their sexuality as deviant because, to them, unlike elite women, low-status Tamasha women were not sexually monogamous. Tamasha women engaged in flexible relationships, though some were legally married and stayed in monogamous relations. Especially during the colonial period, driven by social, sexual, and (national) cultural anxiety, ruling elites engaged with the "woman question" that was rooted in caste. To construct a "moral," "respectable" Indian woman they created the binary of "good wife" and "bad prostitute," thus strengthening the connection between chastity and higher caste and excluding Dalit Tamasha performers. Touchable women and men reinforced the "loose" morality of Dalit women to amplify their own upper-caste morality and caste power. Tamasha women were thus in constant and potential danger of being violated physically and faced many other *vyap* (difficulties), as Surekhatai and Mangalatai recounted.

Performing Tamasha, and the Dalit women's performativity entailed by it, also meant learning new and sometimes frightening local traditions. While mentioning some unusual practices in a village, Mangalatai reported:

> One evening I was made to sit in a vehicle and told that the show was in some other village, and I got scared. I took my cousin along and visited that village. There was a typical tradition of dance in that village. The dancers were to dance in a mobile bullock cart. We got into the carts, trying to balance ourselves, and started dancing. The crowd shouted and whistled at us; they also threw things at us. It was a dreadful experience. I will never forget it.

Mangalatai and other Tamasha women understood and gradually learned to negotiate with men, to entertain their ego and maleness, and to bend and transgress public patriarchy. Once in 1980, Mangalatai was dancing to the song "Bango bango" from the movie *Kaidi* (Prisoner). She continued:

> My troupe was competing with Tukaram Khedkar's in Shivdi, Mumbai. Just for my dance, the public [audience] went wild. They started screaming, whistling, dancing, and were rowdy. After my co-associates informed me of this behavior as I was finishing my makeup, I immediately took charge. I slowly walked through the aisles, talked to them, then ascended the stage, and requested them to stop the nuisance. You will not believe it, but 10,000 people calmed down in merely one minute. It was a big reward for me! I was very happy. There were and are better-looking and younger girls than me but the public demanded me—a Tamasha dancer-mother of four children.

Her son Nitinkumar affirmed that Mangalatai was the main attraction of their troupe and the main earner: "The audience knows her, watches Tamasha for her, so she has to be there. I do not allow her to exert a lot, so we give her a few Lavanya [dancing] and some singing. Although she is in her fifties, she still dances energetically and looks like a sixteen-year-old on stage and so she should continue as long as she can."

Mangalatai remains the lead artist and nucleus of her troupe, yet significant hazards in the life of Tamasha haunt her:

> I remember I was made to dance in what is called a *jhadakhalcha* Tamasha—that is, Tamasha under a tree. There was no stage and we were danc-

ing with all the people around us. I had to walk to the men to take the money from them and at that instance they used to pull my sari or even try to paw me, wanting to touch or hug me. We were helpless. Sometimes we tried to smile and get away and at times some men from the troupe intervened. What to do . . . *publicach mai baap* [the public is our mother and father, a protector and provider]. I will continue to dance for at least ten years, as long as the public wants me.

Thus, Mangalatai reiterated how the performativity as a Tamasha woman exposes the caste and patriarchal order: touchable men looked at her as a sexually dirty and expendable Dalit woman who could be trifled with and who would approve of their socially illegitimate desires. Degraded Dalit women reinforced touchable men's masculinity, made them confident, bolstered their ego, and yet men devalued, insulted, and ogled them, considered them deviant, and denigrated them.

Men forgot that Mangalatai was taking money from them and in turn offering a dream of sex, her sexuality, but not sexual intercourse. Men wanted to be flattered, not rejected by her or any woman for that matter. To men, Mangalatai's sexually charged body was only to serve the men and their masculinity. She was a commodity, a thing, an item, and her sex(uality) in public was important to the construction of their manliness, and to them, her value was merely sexual. Men ogled and pawed at Tamasha woman's body as if she were an animal, and she was in turn confirming their masculinity, reinforcing their domination, and constructing her Dalit femaleness. It was men who exhibited rowdy behavior and their animalistic tendencies by screaming, joking, jumping frantically, drinking, acting in a frenzy, and also treated Tamasha women as animals, not humans. Her thingification stripped her of her individuality and identity, denying Mangalatai her manus and manuski and confirming the ashlil that stuck to her as a Dalit Tamasha woman. After playing dirty with her, men went home to be with their modest and respectable wife and family; they remained decent while Mangalatai was stigmatized forever, and her sexuality rendered deviant.

At times, although she was in control, she could also not openly challenge men or co-opt their authority. She also was troubled by the fear of rape. Once while she was dancing in a village in a half-sari draped to her knees, her dance was so seductive that after she performed, some ruffians entered her chamber with knives demanding she accompany them to their village. Mangalatai pleaded and begged the men, "I am in the middle of a show. People will get mad if I leave now. I am also a mother of three children, so please try to understand." After some more pleading, the men calmed down and agreed that she would accompany them after the second dance. However, by the time they returned for her, Mangalatai's co-workers hid her in the Tamasha equipment truck. The men searched every nook and corner in the tent, but they could not find her. Fortunately, the police arrived by this time and the ruffians' plan was frustrated. Meena Javale reported lack of resources and more dangers for Tamasha women,

> I was performing in a village and there was no bathroom. I was trying to take a bath in a small corner shielded with flimsy bed sheets. Some man found this out, and he walked close to me and kissed me from outside the sheet. I yelled, and the man ran away. Though my people will do the best and protect me, but there is fear of sexual violence.

Sometimes family members faced limitations too. Nitin was frustrated about sexual overtures towards his mother, Mangalatai:

> I get very angry when people make comments or wink at her. But, I cannot help it when it happens when I am performing on the stage. This is art, and I cannot answer sback [or respond aggressively] when I am on the stage. However, if this happens off stage, I will not tolerate it. This is our tradition, our business, our life, and is everything to us. We have to bend before all [political] parties, audience, and powerful people.

Nitin emphasized the precarity and predicament of the ashlil and assli in Tamasha. They were assli Tamasha artists always subjected to brutal exploitation of the ashlil. In their khandani art they had to tolerate touchable men mocking their timidity and inability to protect Dalit women on stage. Most important, Nitin summarized the power of the routine violence Tamasha women's performativity invited: "Sagalyana sambhalun karava lagata" (We have to continue it, accommodating, bending, challenging, consenting, and compromising with everyone). Tamasha people had to avoid inciting social turbulence and remain in their place. These were the tragic limits they lived under.

Nevertheless, after struggling over long years, Mangalatai also improved her economic status and propelled upward mobility for her family and troupe. At the time we met in 2004, Mangalatai owned eight trucks to accommodate her traveling troupe, plus two cars and a jeep for her own family's transportation. One truck also had a power generator and needed a regular supply of diesel. It produced enough electricity for two villages. This was significant when she performed at night, especially in rural areas. She argued that the government should provide some concession in diesel rates to Tamasha artists who were always on the move.

Yet life for Tamasha women was unstable. Surekhatai recounted her misfortune in finding a trustworthy life partner:

> During my Tamasha life, I fell in love with [a Muslim man] Baba Pathan, a contractor. Of course, he never took me to his house because I was a Tamasha dancer [a loathed object nobody wants to associate with]. He used to lock me in a room at a lodge and visit his family, whenever he wanted to. After a few years, I was pregnant and Pathan abandoned me. My family was furious with me over this relationship. I still continued to dance.

Surekhatai's silence and discomfort while reflecting on her relationship with her partner suggest the flexibility and illegitimacy of such "affairs." Unlike Surekhatai, Mangalatai, a Mang woman, had a fairly stable marriage with a Mahar-Buddhist man. She reported:

> My husband worked in my mother's Tamasha. He wrote skits and poetry. My father was a maratha and did not approve of my Mhar [Mahar] husband. In Tamasha line, first of all Tamasha women have no husbands, or if they do, they keep changing. [Due to flexible arrangements,] a Tamasha woman has no one husband and the children do not know their father. I did not want such precarity for my children, and as a result, I managed the relationship [despite violence]. He also is aware who the main earner is.

Both Surekhatai and Mangalatai faced violence from their lovers and husbands, with whom they had stable relationships. They were brave women who managed men in the audience, but they could not escape domestic violence. Mangalatai's life also illuminates the fluidity of transgressing caste boundaries in Tamasha—her mother was Mang, her father a touchable and dominant-caste maratha, and her husband a Mahar-Buddhist. Yet, she struggled against the stickiness of the ashlil.

Both Mangalatai and Surekhatai entrenched a new patriarchy and enacted a different modernity and robust body politics by donning a thick and long gold *mangalsutra* (a necklace that a Hindu groom ties around his bride's neck) and creatively refashioned their emotional and corporeal selves. Intimate bodily experiences of intentionally donning mangalsutra and full, clean dress emerged as powerful practices of presenting Dalit women's transformed personhood and social and moral status. Yet their body politics of erotic excess were not robust: both women acceded to the modest and moral traditional brahmani patriarchy by donning its marker, the mangalsutra. It is through such practices as the politics of mangalsutra that Dalits, in their march to modernity from the early decades of the twentieth century, continually appropriated and disrupted caste norms and deprived dominant castes of their powers.

Mangalatai and Surekhatai twisted tradition and modernity, and they innovatively redeployed marriage, chastity, and motherhood to forge new moral meanings as wives. Modern mangalsutra and marriage offered Mangalatai a hitherto denied morality and modesty. It was a survival strategy to avoid flirtations and sexual advances from men. Following Ambedkar and Navayana Buddhism, many Dalit women abandoned the black-beaded mangalsutra to don a necklace of yellow beads. Many elite feminists also abandoned the brahmani sign of mangalsutra. However, such elite feminist liberatory politics rarely engages with despised Dalit women's practices. By showing off her thick mangalsutra, Mangalatai displayed her womanly virtue as well as her moral and modern self. She was not merely imitating married women or seeking complicity with patriarchy as in the case of savarna women. She instead negotiated and renegotiated, selectively appropriating certain traditional brahmani practices, mimicking them, and generating broad possibilities and power for herself.

The tripartite masculine patriarchies—the colonial and postcolonial Indian state and dominant and lower castes—looked down upon marriages of Tamasha women and their alternative practices because they are often open contractual relationships that can be made and broken by free will. Hence, to them, Tamasha women were not bound to the monogamous strictures of marriage and were therefore believed to be lower in the social and sexual ladder. However, many Tamasha women continued to live with single partners throughout their lives. There were no clean lines. Although mangalsutra provided some respectability for monogamy, bodily autonomy, and power for married Tamasha women, at the same time, women also internalized rigorous disciplining of their subjectivity and performed as second wives with lower status and without honor.

Tamasha in the Patriarchal State of Maharashtra
The state and the national government committed violence in adopting a double standard: at times they sought to protect, include, and extend patronage to some artists, and at the same time they neglected them and further exacerbated their vulnerability. After 1960, the newly independent state of Maharashtra sought to carve out its own robust Marathi identity. To accomplish this task, along with elitist emphasis on brahman-activated, high-culture sangeet natak, the state also incorporated the supposedly degenerate and rural Tamasha art. Both art forms were popular and thrived, however differently. State agents sought to protect and preserve the so-called adulterated art of Tamasha by setting up committees and boards to collate literature, publish volumes of popular arts, fund events, and even to give awards to artists. Although respectable Dalits and touchables looked upon Tamasha as a degraded practice, to mobilize support for linguistic formations and regional nationalism, many touchables along with the state deployed it as a tool and appropriated its rebellious, carnivalesque energy; underscored its essentially legitimate Marathi manus identity; and re-appropriated the social and sexual labor of Tamasha artists in the service of the state and stigmatized it further. The exploitation, discrimination, and stigmatizing of Tamasha women ensured the production and reproduction of Dalit labor for a sexual-caste and political economy. Ambedkar and his followers consistently fought against such caste practices. Nevertheless, the state and touchables cunningly worked within the caste logic, which dictated and hierarchized cultures, further reified caste cultures, and culturalized Dalit identity.

As a result, some artists sought to work from inside the state machinery and entered the overt political realm. Political parties hired them to perform and disseminate their political agenda. Mangalatai, however, was not keen on entering politics:

> Some people say they are entering politics to serve the needy. However, that is not the case. My mother was also invited to do so. But nothing concrete takes places. The picture is very rosy though. *Mothe lok jagu denaar nhai* [big people will not allow us to survive there]. If we enter politics, they will harass us, *chhedtaat amhala* [tease us] as they do here in Tamasha. It is the same when a girl tries to enter the field of modeling or cinema; she has to satisfy everybody [sexually] on her way to success. This has been my mother's experience and our experience too, so I just do not want it.

Mangalatai was celebrated by politicians; however, that did not stop her from openly criticizing them or taking them to task for troubling artists. She wanted the government to help artists. She continued:

> I have won the Maharashtra Gaurav Puraskar [Honor Award]. I would like a national award just like my mother received. Then I will feel that my art has acquired its true value. On other fronts, I am very contented. I have no regrets. I am happy. All Tamasha artists are in debt today, so the government should help us a little. It is all the [debt to contractors] so the government should help us a little to repay or do away with that.

Mangalatai wanted the state government to help non-elite, hereditary artists. As a result, she negotiated and selectively aligned with some political parties at particular moments. She complained that the state's stricter rules were ruining the art of Tamasha; however, she was a thorough businesswoman who controlled her Tamasha empire astutely and wisely. Though Tamasha was an exploitative art form, ironically, it was also financially empowering for the Bansode family—including its male members and other employees.

The colonial and postcolonial state of Maharashtra and its agents, as well as dominant-caste women and men constructed Tamasha women through an erotic gaze and denied them moral gains. Yet Tamasha women have repeatedly performed both their art and their Dalit womanhood on the Tamasha stage, deployed the obscene and the sringarik, and negotiated with patriarchy to their economic benefit. Unfortunately, they have been too easily associated with sex

FIGURE 6.3. Mangalatai putting on makeup in her makeshift tent, getting ready for her performance. In April 2017, thirteen years after I first met her in 2004, Mangalatai continued to perform her *khandani* (cultural and caste capital) Tamasha at the Tamasha capital, Narayangao, as she had promised. Source: Photo courtesy of author.

work. I am not vilifying sex workers, but I want to emphasize that Mangalatai categorically asserted, "We do not dance in bars or engage in sex work. We also do not work in Lavanis and sit in one place. We are on the move earning our livelihood." Although in general, the larger society conflated them with prostitutes, Mangalatai created hierarchies and marked distinctions between Tamasha women, Lavani women, and bar-dancer women. By holding onto a sense of herself as an assli Tamasha woman, she resisted depictions of her as a prostitute selling sex through liminal, contingent, provisional, and submerged forms of contestation (see figure 6.3).

Tamasha also emerged as a privileged practice because its mobility allowed artists to escape sexual labor under specific patrons as in the case of Lavani or sangeet bari forms. Lavani artists from banner shows lacked such agency. Mangalatai commented, "We can also do that [kind of Lavani singing and dancing] by sitting in one place; however, we do not. We move around villages with a troupe of one hundred fifty and perform." Tamasha theatre constantly traveled among villages and cities. By contrast, Lavani artists carved out stability by sticking to the city and performing only a few famous songs. Moreover, Lavani troupes were also not as big as those of Tamasha, and hence the financial risks were lower. Mangalatai further complained that unlike Tamasha, which was in the open and a public performance, some Lavani artists performed in the secluded, private *baithaks* (sittings) for political leaders, *amdars*, *mantris*, and *khasdars*, which further reinforced both the art form as sexual and the loose sexuality of Tamasha women.

Tamasha as *Khandani* Capital

Five generations of Mangalatai's family were in Tamasha: her grandparents, parents, five sisters and three brothers, children, and grandchildren. Kailas, Mangalatai's brother (figure 6.14), continues to organize a troupe in his mother's (Vithabai Narayangaokar) name. Malati Inamdar, Mangalatai's sister also has her own Tamasha troupe (figure 6.4). Like Surekhatai, her sister Lata Punekar was also famous (figure 6.23). Surekhatai and Mangalatai's family members drew upon and built on *khandani* (family occupation, hereditary lineage, and caste and cultural capital.) Tamasha for their livelihood. Kailas asserted, "We [my mother and I] had no other option. There are other businesses too, but Tamasha is our Lakshmi [goddess of wealth]. This is not a business. It is our service to the public. We entertain people, forgetting our own sorrows." In this manner, Tamasha people exploited the cracks in the institution of caste that reduced them to work as laborers and entertainers. Tamasha people worked at serving dominant-caste men and were implicated in the very regimes of power and sexual-caste violence that oppressed them.

Tamasha provided many generations of women and men artists with economic capital, as well as khandani, which was and is the social and cultural capital they have acquired, accumulated, and skillfully cultivated over long years.[7] In depicting Tamasha as khandani, Mangalatai and Nitin also transformed it into their *jativant* (caste-based) cultural capital and caste capital, thus reifying it as a Dalit identity, culture, and art form. In doing so, they essentialized Tamasha as Dalit culture, tradition, art, and reinforced their right to perform it.

Moreover, families gendered khandani capital by easily associating women with dance and associating men with managerial work or playing musical instruments. Hereditary Tamasha families deployed the cheap and readily available labor inside the family. As parents and kin, women were always already recruited to serve in roles critical to the integrity of familial labor and household as well as to the sexual economy of Tamasha. Caste and cultural ideology disciplined the division of not only labor and laborers, as Ambedkar argued, but also of sexual labor. Family members also competed with each other to prove their assli khandani status and created new practices like guru-shishya parampara. Mangalatai competed with her sisters' and brother's Tamasha troupes, and rivalries ran deep as each tried to outwit the other. (See photos of their troupe tents in figures 6.4, 6.5, and 6.6).

In addition to Mangalatai and her family, other families, which included one hundred fifty to two hundred women and men, depended on Mangalatai for their livelihood. Mangalatai also emphasized that Tamasha was not for minting money, but to serve the various (especially sensual) needs of the larger public: "To serve the audience and to earn their living, the artists often had to give up their own needs." While other artists depended on her labor, Mangalatai in turn depended on the dictates of politicians and the state:

> The political parties dominant in the village, *sarpanch, patil* [headman], the landlord who gives us this place to put up our stage, and the police all torture us. Anybody can come and bully us, kick us. We are so helpless . . . *hittha log hagatyat titha amhi khato, nachato* [people defecate here and we eat our food in this very place and dance here]. Despite all this, I have to continue with this [complicated life], for I have one hundred fifty people to feed. We have to keep everybody happy in this line [of Tamasha], and I have been tolerating these people since I was nine. I just smile at them and get away. Sometimes the public gets mad and political party people are a great nuisance They start shouting from the gates, "Ours is the ruling party now, give us free entry. Let our twenty men enter for free." How do we live in such circumstances?

Thus, like her mother, Mangalatai argued that she transformed others' fallow lands and hagandari (used for defecation) into her khandani of making

FIGURE 6.4. Mangalatai's sister Malati Inamdar's troupe *rahuti* (the tent where managers enter contracts for the year) in Narayangao, 2016–17. Source: Photo courtesy of author.

FIGURE 6.5. Mangalatai's brother Kailas Narayangaokar's *rahuti*, Narayangao. 2017. Source: Photo courtesy of author.

FIGURE 6.6. Many *rahutis* of Tamasha troupes in Narayangao, 2017. Source: Photo courtesy of author.

money in Tamasha. Similar to her son, she underlined the precarity of Tamasha women, at the mercy of everybody—ordinary men as well as politicians.

Many Tamasha women, both hereditary and non-hereditary, who hailed from Pune continued to live in the city. Surekhatai owned an apartment in Kasba Peth, Pune, and lived among respectable neighbors. Her name was on the list of residents usually exhibited at the entrance of her apartment complex. She thus found some acceptance, at least in residential terms, among honorable members of the society. She did not live in segregated or separate neighborhoods like the common prostitutes of the red-light district in Budhvar/Ravivar Peth.

Mangalatai was an entrepreneur, a businesswoman. She maintained a thick *hajeri ani pagar pustak* (register) for daily accounting. While we were talking, her son Nitinkumar demanded three hundred rupees. She immediately raised her eyebrows and questioned him, "Why do you need the money?" Nitinkumar responded that it was for diesel for the vehicles. Mangalatai reminded him

FIGURE 6.7. Artists wearing makeup and getting ready for the show in Narayangao, 2017. Source: Photo courtesy of author.

FIGURE 6.8. Tamasha woman wearing makeup as her daughter watches and plays with her powder and lipstick. Source: Photo courtesy of author.

FIGURE 6.9. Artists getting ready for the performance. Source: Photo courtesy of author.

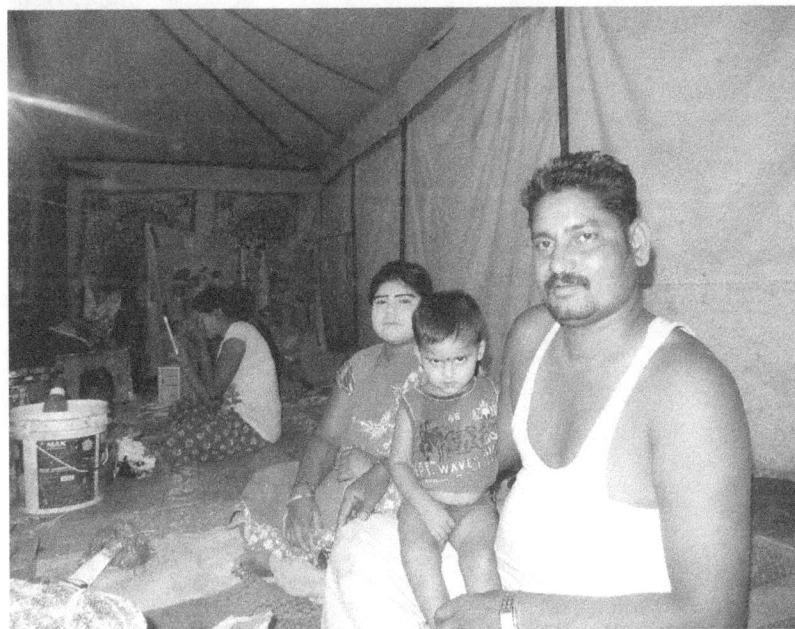

FIGURE 6.10. Tamasha family: wife, husband, and child in Tamasha. Source: Photo courtesy of author.

FIGURE 6.11. Sakutai getting ready for her dance. Her makeup box, clothes bag, and basket with milk, water, and bread. Source: Photo courtesy of author.

FIGURE 6.12. Artists carry their belongings in trunks, and they also carry utensils in case they have to cook. Source: Photo courtesy of author.

FIGURE 6.13. Tamasha people sleep in bunks built in trucks. The trucks are transformed into temporary homes, replete with a cooking stove, buckets, and so on. Source: Photo courtesy of author.

FIGURE 6.14. Author with Vithabai's son and Mangalatai's brother and rival Kailas Narayangaokar and his son Mohit. Source: Photo courtesy of author.

that she had bought diesel just the day before. However, instead of haggling in my presence, she preferred to give him the money from her *tijori* (locked case to store valuables), which she kept a close eye on. She also insisted that Nitinkumar bring her the receipt.

Mangalatai controlled her troupe's finances. When I first met Mangalatai at Bal Gandharva and asked about who kept track of her income and expenses, Mangalatai mentioned that her sons and husband took care of everything. However, during deeper conversations in Kada, I noted discrepancies between this account and her activities. Revenue and this income from Tamasha can be inconsistent, and Mangalatai was critically involved in making ends meet day-to-day. In the middle of a performance, for instance, she was cramming all the cash collected that evening inside her tijori. She sat in her special chamber in the tent, wearing only a bra and petticoat, counting all the cash, and put the money in the tijori (locker). Unlike elite modest women, she did not seem inhibited by her minimal dress among her people. She also asked a male worker how much food grain and vegetables would be required for the entire troupe. She calculated the money to feed everyone and admonished the worker to remember that she was also paying for the grinding of wheat.

Nonetheless, despite her thorough accounting skills, Mangalatai reported that she had incurred a debt of Rs. 500,000 and that Tamasha was not as lucrative as it once was. Many Tamasha artists were in debt from taking loans for weddings, schooling, clothing, and family support. Surekhatai seconded this hardship: "I used to fall sick, but I worked undeterred. I got my brother and sisters married. I got my cousins married. Everything is settled now. I have earned up to Rs. 80,000 for a show when things were fine. However, I am in debt today and I have to start afresh." She started performing again and still was when I caught up with her again in 2016—selective Lavani shows focusing mainly on the sensual play of *adakari* (gestures).

Most Tamasha and Lavani women, including Mangalatai and her immediate and extended family, were able to capitalize on the opening of markets in a liberalizing and globalizing world since the 1990s. Although there were certainly challenges, they were able to explore the limits of their social, economic, and political potential as a result of a Lavani revival through "banner shows." Banner-show Lavanya featured professional and lead dancers performing for two to three hours. Women successfully exploited the opportunities and changes in ideological, social, and political milieus by experimenting with new and different technologies and forms, appropriating them, and bending them to suit their own purposes.

As a result, they adopted different strategies in various markets: they entered films; collaborated with local television networks to produce and appear as special guest judges in Tamasha and Lavani competitions; released CDs of their songs; made YouTube videos of their Tamashe and Lavanya; hired choreographers and rehearsed their dances; deployed new technologies of music, dance, and remix songs; and collaborated with political parties and their leaders, including cultural ministers, to seek pensions and awards and to institute changes in Tamasha and Lavani. Local Marathi newspapers exploded with the exuberance of Tamasha and Lavani shows from the end of the twentieth century. Benefitting from these opportunities, Surekhatai also traveled to Boston and New York to present her renowned Lavanya—"Ya ravji, basa bhavji, kashi rakhu me tumchi marji" (Come o guest, do sit, how do I maintain your desire) and "Pikalya panacha deth kiti hirva" [literally, the stalk of a ripe leaf is so green; here, suggesting that a woman's private parts are strong and ready for penetration] for the largely touchable-caste Marathi diaspora in the United States. Many Marathi people showcasing their modern casteless selves were and are globalizing Tamasha and Lavani and reinforcing the assli identity of Marathi manus outside India. Some male choreographers like Ravi Sangamnerkar (figure 6.15) and Ashish Desai (figure 6.16) trained and worked on Tamasha and Lavani women's gestures and dances, turning them into successful dancers.

Mangalatai also lamented that Tamasha was losing in the entertainment race because of decreasing audience numbers: "Now is the world of remix, and orchestra, vulgar mixes and so there is less public [audience] for Tamasha." Other forms of performance and musical medleys competed with Tamasha. While commenting on the change over time and the difference between other popular forms of entertainment and Tamasha, Mangalatai reported, "Earlier the public used to announce prizes, jalsa was popular, and men touched women artists' hands, or pressed them as they do at [sangeet bari] of Chauphula and at Aryabhushan Theatre. But we do not have that kind of physical proximity in Tamasha."

FIGURE 6.15. Renowned choreographer Ravi Sangamnerkar. Source: Photo courtesy of author.

FIGURE 6.16. Choreographer Ashish Desai. Source: Photo courtesy of author.

राष्ट्रपती आर.वेंकट राघवन , सुनितादेवी व गिरिष कर्नाड
यांच्या समवेत विठाबाई नारायणगांवकर

FIGURE 6.17. Vithabai Narayangaokar presented with an award by the president of India Ramaswamy Venkataraman (president, 1987–1992). The president is mistakenly named Venkat Raghavan in the photograph. Source: Photo courtesy of author.

FIGURE 6.18. The procession celebrating Vithabai, her father, and grandfather. Source: Photo courtesy of author.

Tamasha women agreed that, unlike in forms such as Gondhal or sangeet baris, where the audience sits closer to the performers, Tamasha was "safer" because women performed on a platform above at a distinct distance from the male audience. It provided some power to women to look down on men. Surekhatai underscored Mangalatai's views:

> Tamasha has changed its form over the recent years and has become lewder and raunchy, because the public is not the same as earlier. Today, there is a lot of money and less of the art form; clothes and adakari are changing immensely and if this is the state of the art today, what will happen to future dancers?

Tamasha women like Surekhatai, Mangalatai, Seematai, and Meena and Veena Javale were concerned about the change in comportment and dance styles of younger women. As a result, Tamasha women took up this issue with their union. Veena reported, "We actively participate in our union. We have decided on an acceptable code of dress that women will adhere to. It is important to regulate as women are performing sexy dances in skimpy and sexy clothes." Women also mentioned the changes in saris: "Earlier, the sari was thick, but today women wear only net-saris," with fabric as thin as net, thus revealing the body. Although Surekhatai complained about the change in dress when I met her in 2004, she also assimilated with new Tamasha and wore a net-sari in 2017 (figure 6.19). This was important for her business.

Mangalatai and Surekhatai continued to use their talents and art to accumulate respect as assli Tamasha artists but also worked for the betterment of the community at large. Surekhatai mentioned:

> I perform Lavanya. Some of them are very famous. I visited villages and performed anti-liquor, anti-dowry, anti-AIDS government programs, and fetched an honorarium. I traveled to many villages for this social propagation. I performed not only for men but also women because women never attended and I wanted them to do so. I also won a prize of two lakhs at the 1998 Lavani Mahotsava [festival].

Surekhatai was thus involved in social activism as well. She was also sensitive to gender discrimination rampant in the society: men enjoyed watching

FIGURE 6.19. Surekhatai (right) in her makeup room with author. Source: Photo courtesy of author.

dishonorable, low-status, degraded Dalit women dance on the Tamasha stage and provide entertainment to men; however, they would not allow their own respectable genteel women to watch these shows.

Consequently, Surekhatai questioned hypocritical dominant caste men who constructed hierarchies of caste, class, gender, and sexuality. She performed "special" Tamasha shows only for women (figure 6.20). During such events, she herself stood at the door of the public hall to welcome women who came to watch her dance with a *mogryacha gajara* (string of jasmine flowers used to decorate women's hairstyle; in performances, men wrapped it around their wrist and inhaled the fragrance as they watched women dance or sometimes showered the flowers on women, as if they were showering love) and *panacha vida* (a mouth-freshening roll of betel leaves, areca nut, cloves, and rose petals, chewed on during performances). Significantly, the Bal Gandharva Theatre has retained the annual Ladies-Special Lavani Event as part of the Pune festival that celebrates Marathi art and culture through the present day.

Such ladies-only events lasted two to three hours and were free of charge, unlike usual Tamasha and Lavani shows. As a result, many women attended the show. These ladies-only shows and the mobilization of the labor of Tamasha and Lavani women therein were empowering moments for all—mixed-caste, mixed-class, elite, and ordinary—women, for they afforded them opportunities to enjoy themselves immensely and transgress patriarchal and gendered boundaries. For example, they whistled loudly, thrusting their thumb and index finger in their mouths, waved their hands rapidly in the air, danced, and made merry in the theatre just like men did. In case they could not whistle, many women brought plastic whistles to the auditorium to thoroughly enjoy themselves and participate in the caste, gendered, and sexual performative. In this instance, for once, the Tamasha theatre, typically a masculine space constructed for a male gaze, engendered proximity between Tamasha and non-Tamasha women and a liberatory possibility and power for many women from a variety of castes.

Theirs, however, was a tentative pleasure. All women—performers and audience—enjoyed song and dance, easily forgetting the sexual-caste labor of Dalit Tamasha women. For these temporary and transient moments, sisterhood beyond caste seemed triumphant. However, dominant-caste women were not bothered by the stigmatized, corrupt, dirty enticer, the Tamasha woman on stage, and momentarily enjoyed dancing with and like Tamasha women. Like men, touchable women unmarked by caste easily occluded the ways the performative and their supposedly innocent amusement exploited Tamasha women, its deep roots in sexual-caste labor that entrenched Tamasha women's degraded status rendering them as free women, eliding the difference between violation and volition.

Most importantly, in this moment of empowerment, respectable women transgressed the boundaries of the performativity of proper womanhood to supposedly act like Tamasha women. They abandoned their modesty and moderation for three hours in order to engage, breathe, perform, and live the ashlil. For example, in response to the infamous song "Dhagala lagali kala, pani themb themb gala, java tujha ni majha jula, angala bhidude anga" (When clouds burst, water drips; , and let our bodies come together. when you and I come together, water drips; when we kiss, water drips; when we have sex, water drips), one woman, in her fifties, raised her two hands and danced frantically, closing the fingers of each hand and energetically colliding them against each other, as if they were a couple kissing and making love. The original song was performed by Dada Kondke, who in the eyes of the elites, always already represented the paradigmatic ashlil and his songs always had a double meaning. Elites dismissed Kondke as ashlil, infantile, and wayward, as I discussed in chapter 5.

By her particular gesticulation, the woman at the ladies-only show challenged the boundaries of modest womanhood by embodying Kondke's ashlil song to present the sexual play with her hands. This woman could make this gesture only in the confined premises of the theatre during the ladies-special Lavani program. Yet, outside the theatre she enjoyed the privilege of dismissing the song, Kondke, and Tamasha women as ashlil. No Tamasha and Lavani woman made the gestures as depicted by the respectable woman, and yet there was never any threat of the ashlil sticking to the latter.

It is the constant repetition of the performativity of the ashlil, assli, and the decent in the most mundane of daily activities that creates and reinforces the hegemonic and normative social conventions and ideologies of sex-gender-caste complex. To maintain their respectability, elite women were complicit in maintaining the dichotomy of the wife and prostitute, thereby reinforcing their normative ideal womanhood located inside the logic of caste. They could be sexy, frivolous, show off their curvy bodies, and perform like a Tamasha woman but only inside their private bedroom. Even if they did so in dances in the public, in films, or other events, the ashlil did not stick to them. Tamasha women did not enjoy such luxury of privilege, protection, and privacy. Even if Tamasha women enacted alternative performativities of womanhood, entrenched caste hierarchies and the ashlil dented their subversive dreams. Their life was a constant struggle against the ashlil and hegemonic caste and contested patriarchies.

Mangalatai remembered how Tamasha life tortured her mother and family, robbed, and terrorized them:

My mother used to dance a lot and she even delivered a baby on the stage. Our contractor said that the Tamasha had to close down as Vithu [Vithabai] could not dance. So, we were put again in a temporary rest home. We had thought that the contractor would at least give us something to survive on for some time, but he never returned to inquire about us. When we visited our mother at the hospital, she had no food or clothes for the newborn. There was no money. So, someone suggested that we could keep the harmonium as collateral and get some money on that. But I refused because the harmonium and *chaal* [ankle bells] are Lakshmi [our wealth]. How can we take a loan on that? I went out and requested the contractor to give us some money and told him that we needed help. But he said that nothing could be done unless the Tamasha started again. There was another sangeet party in Jalgaon, and I asked them for some money, saying that I was Vithabai's daughter and that she was in the hospital. That lady agreed to give me 1,000 rupees, but I had to dance every evening. I was very happy. I bought food for everybody and mutton biryani [a delicacy they could rarely afford] for my mother and clothes for the newborn.

Poverty and hunger haunted Tamasha women, who lacked economic and social resources.

Artists also affirmed the hierarchy of wages: main artists like Surekhatai were paid the highest, and the payment decreased as one descended the ladder. There was and is much borrowing of music, dance, and styles between Tamasha and Marathi and Hindi films. Films provided artists another opportunity to present their art and, moreover, earn more money and fame. Mangalatai also acted in Marathi movies. However, she could not pursue movies because, as she reinforced, "I have to feed these families." There was another compelling cause. Although Mangalatai entered the film industry, she seemed perpetually troubled by dishonor and the blot of her stigmatized life as a nachi (inferior dancer):

> People come and go, but the *batta* [blot] of a *nachanarin* [or nachi, dancing woman] stays forever. Nobody respects us [in or outside films]. Men have their affairs. Their keeps do not move around with their children, but we are not like that.

As a Tamasha woman, Mangalatai was aware of the potentials and difficulties of Tamasha: she was successful financially; however, she believed she could not challenge her stigma as ashlil, an immoral, disrespected public dancer. She was the empress of her empire, married to a man, a "good" wife and mother who bore sons (and daughters) and worked for their success; still, she is successful because she is a nachi, an inferior dancer marginalized by casteism. Her Tamasha life provided many possibilities, and at the same time, it was dangerous and a potential threat because it was constructed by the logic of caste.

Unlike Mangalatai whose children were in Tamasha, Surekhatai did not want her children to be associated with her world of Tamasha. Uneducated but lucratively employed, she sent her children away to fancy boarding schools at Panchgani, near Pune. Due to the itinerant nature of her work, she felt that she could not otherwise give them a stable education. She wanted to educate her children and keep them away from the world of Tamasha—of dance and of her life. Yet, ironically, her sons and her family severed ties with her. Nevertheless, when I met her again in 2016, her two sons and her former partner Baba Pathan were the managers of Lavani programs featuring Surekhatai and new dancers. Thus, although initially she had tried to sever her children's ties with Tamasha, on gaining adulthood, they entered their khandani profession. However, instead of ordinary musicians or technicians, they were a level up the ladder, managing the entire troupe and show and making important decisions.

Mangalatai's sisters and brother residing in Narayangaon also created new traditions to assert and celebrate their khandani. For example, in the month of August, villagers in Narayangao celebrate the local goddess Muktai on the day of a fair in Narayangao. Women carry ablutions to worship the goddess. Vithabai's family picked this same day to celebrate Vithabai and their ancestors Bhau-Bapu Khude Narayangaokar with a loud, musical, and brightly lit procession along the village main roads. In this manner, Vithabai's family created a new tradition by celebrating their khandani ancestry in Tamasha and in Narayangao at the same time as the celebration for the local goddess and her touchable devotees, even if for a few hours every year (figures 6.27 and 6.28).

Mangalatai also kept her children with her throughout her life. She celebrated Tamasha and wanted her children to follow their ancestral khandani of Tamasha. Yet not all her descendants are in the practice. Her granddaughter is a medical doctor—the first doctor in her Tamasha family. Mangalatai believed that Tamasha was an art gifted to them by their khandan, and they are following this hereditary art form like other classical arts. Tamasha people often inscribed their investment in the art, especially to challenge the poverty

FIGURE 6.20. Happy, smiling, mostly touchable-caste-Hindu, middle-class, respectable women enjoying a special ladies' Lavani show. Source: Photo courtesy of author.

FIGURE 6.21. A Tamasha family: the woman/wife/mother dances, the man/husband/father sings and acts in skits. They are trying to earn wages to educate their son, seen in the middle. Source: Photo courtesy of author.

FIGURE 6.22. Lata Punekar, Surekhatai's sister and rival. She wants to travel to Boston like her sister did. Source: Photo courtesy of author.

FIGURE 6.23. Vithabai honored by state agents, film actors, and civilians. Source: Photo courtesy of author.

भारताचे पहीले राष्ट्रपती डॉ. राजेंद्र प्रसाद यांच्या हस्ते
सत्कार स्विकारताना बापुराव खुडे नारायणगांवकर

FIGURE 6.24. Mangalatai's grandfather Bapurao Khude Narayangaokar honored by the first president of India, Rajendra Prasad. Source: Photo courtesy of author.

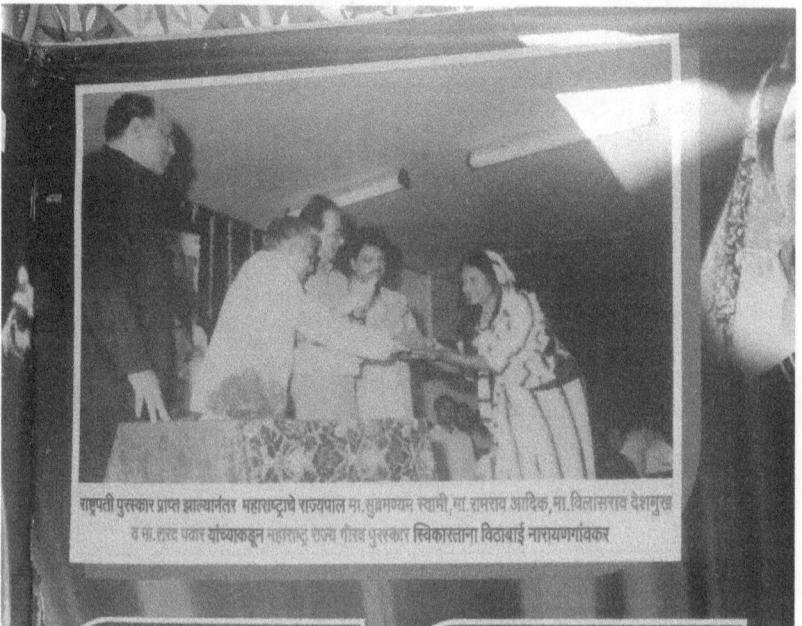

राष्ट्रपती पुरस्कार प्राप्त झाल्यानंतर महाराष्ट्राचे राज्यपाल मा. सुब्रमण्यम स्वामी, मा. रामराव आदिक, मा. विलासराव देशमुख
व मा. शरद पवार यांच्याकडून महाराष्ट्र राज्य गौरव पुरस्कार स्विकारताना विठाबाई नारायणगांवकर

FIGURE 6.25. Vithabai awarded a Maharashtra state honor by state governor Subramaniam Swamy, Ramrao Adik, Vilasrao Deshmukh, and Sharad Pawar. Mangalatai wishes to gain the same popularity and felicitations. Source: Photo courtesy of author.

FIGURE 6.26. Narayangao also boasts of Vithabai's statue, which is abandoned and insulted. A cobbler set up his business in front of Vithabai's statue in Narayangao. Source: Photo courtesy of author.

FIGURE 6.27. Villagers in Narayangao celebrate the local goddess on the day of a fair. Women carry ablutions to worship the goddess. Source: Photo courtesy of author.

FIGURE 6.28. Vithabai and her parents and grandparents are celebrated once a year in a procession in Narayangao, 2017. Source: Photo courtesy of author.

paradigm that engulfed Tamasha. But this khandani performative was conflicted: it burdened as well as offered Mangalatai financial security. Many elite Dalits considered Tamasha as a lower form of art, especially because it stigmatized Dalit women. To move away from such denigration, they trained their children in classical dance forms of kathak or bharatnatyam.

Although Mangalatai gradually asserted her power, paradoxically, she was also powerless. Her complex life represents her ideas, intentions, and actions, continually entangled in the intersecting webs of her triumphs and tribulations, transformations and tensions, suppression and subversion. I illuminated the deep tensions in her *double living*—the private and public and the personal and professional—as well as the super-exploitation and discrimination she faced due to the conjugated oppressions of caste, gender, and sexuality. There were no clean boundaries: the multiple oppressions constantly crept into, challenged, and complicated each other, puncturing her seemingly triumphalist life narrative.

Conclusion

Caste camouflaged as culture, art, and khandani controlled the alienated sexual labor of the most unfree Dalit Tamasha woman. Mangalatai's stigmatization ensures the consistent reproduction of Dalit labor for a sexual-caste economy. Her degraded and stigmatized body and being as a Dalit Tamasha woman is intimately tied to the valorizing of respectable Marathi (and Indian) womanhood. To negotiate this sexual-caste politics, Mangalatai, her children, and other family members asserted and culturized their Dalit identity by capitalizing on their particular caste culture and the sociosexual labor of women, consolidated their hereditary assli khandani, and right to Tamasha performance. In the process, they provided livelihood and social and economic mobility for their future generations. Yet, khandani Tamasha rooted in the sexual-caste economy reproduced lowness, the ashlil, and offered a few positives beyond economic rewards.

I reiterate that we need to pay attention to the violence of sexual-caste slavery and the ambivalences of Mangalatai's so-called consenting agency to govern her life. The liberal and paternal gifts of free will, an autonomous self, and humanity disguise the domination, power, and brutality of caste slavery. Although she, as a Dalit Tamasha woman, inhabited the sumptuary excess of profligacy, dirtiness, and idleness; exhibited the failures of character and improper womanhood; and embodied the fear, uncertainty, and anxiety of the larger society, she simultaneously exercised her constrained agency to reify her Mang caste culture, which the larger society rendered low and degraded. She reinforced her right to her khandani cultural capital of Tamasha to challenge her powerlessness, build her business, and provide the livelihoods of two hundred troupe members. In so doing, she transformed Tamasha into her cultural-and-caste-capital. Yet, her critical labor of redress did not fully change her condition. She was implicated in the caste logic that dictated her life; she was a burdened, dirty, dangerous, and threatening Dalit Tamasha woman, for hers was not a robust sexuality or ideal womanhood, and she remained a wayward woman acquiring fame and wealth for herself and her troupe. Thus, the performativity of her Tamasha as a practice of consent, resistance, and redress is quite tentative. The significance of her performative was less about overcoming the ambiguous and precarious status of Dalit or providing remedy to her injury and pain than it was about creating the conditions for a different politics of resistance and transformation, at times on a constrained individual level and sometimes on a collective level for Tamasha people. Yet, these moments of assertion on individual levels did not extend to the Dalit community.

The ongoing precarity of Tamasha women's lives is stark, and the persistence of what Ambedkar termed a negative form of the law of contract—that is, social boycott—continues to shape their lives. Even though artists risk not being able to survive by the means afforded by Tamasha, they persist with the form and find it hard to sustain themselves through other means. The complicity demanded of them is a form of social boycott.[8]

Acting like a hero-heroine duo on the Tamasha state, Mangalatai and Nitin's sex play in Tamasha was fraught: Mangalatai exaggerated her femininity, accentuated her sexuality, flirted and erotically played with her son, Nitin. Their performance of play, of sensual song and dance—the hugging, caressing, and Nitin hitting Mangalatai's bottom, as if engaging in sexual intercourse—disguises the Dalit labor for a casteist economy that performatively enacts Dalits as ashlil, working to sell the dream of sex to the men in the audience. Nitin's second wife, a supposedly inferior nachi in the hierarchy danced beside her mother-in-law and her husband, who were performing the sensual work to excite and arouse the audience of mostly touchable men. She continued to perform her dance work with an emotionless face, seemingly unbothered by the play between her mother-in-law and her husband. The performativity of play by both Mangalatai and her daughter-in-law, rooted in the exploitation of Tamasha women's caste and sexual labor, demanded that nonliterate Dalit Tamasha women consent to the sex-gender-caste complex, the social-sexual, cultural, and patriarchal norms that stigmatized them as low and degraded and ensured the that caste economy thrived. Modern, educated, respectable Dalits certainly disapproved (and disapprove) of such sociosexual work for genteel and respectable women.

The audience's awareness that this was sex play between mother and son, with the son's wife looking on, mark this as a truly very complex moment in the dynamics of performative power around the sex-gender-caste complex. It raises questions about the excess of play and cultural traits, forms of sexual expression, of sex play, that Tamasha performance and performativity authorizes, how certain gendered, caste, and class performativities become Tamasha conventions, and how those performative conventions belie the complex emotional labor that is no doubt at work before, during, and after the performance. From Pavalabai to Mangalatai, we see a continuing thread of precarity, and a continuum of both sexualized and other forms of labor that Tamasha women perform. The perversion of desire assumed different forms, from Pavalabai to Mangalatai, and is most evident in the attempts to tame the Tamasha woman, appropriate her art, and limit her aesthetic autonomy and one expression of her sexuality to ensure the perpetuation of the sex-gender-caste complex.

QUEERING THE "VULGAR"
Tamasha without Women

In the evening of April 14, 2017, the Dalit Panchsheel Social Foundation and Machhindra Eknath Gaikwad Foundation celebrated the renowned Dalit La-vani dancer and film actor Megha Ghadge as a star attraction and special guest-of-honor at their annual Ambedkar Jayanti Celebrations at Tadivala Road/Dhole Patil Road, Pune (figure 7.1). During the event, she was on stage flanked by respectable women and men of prominence, including local Dalit and touchable corporators. Her neat image, including the full white dress, as ex-pected for a community public event, struck a stark contrast with her skimpily draped sensual body projected on the screen, accompanied by a song from her movie *Kata Kirr*. The entire spectacle—life-size portrait of Ambedkar, movie screen surrounded by big banners with Ambedkar's image and announcements of his birth anniversary celebrations, blasting music, ostentatious lighting, and crowds of men joyfully dancing to sensual lyrics and intoxicated with masti—represented everything Ambedkar and Jalsakars opposed, but times had moved on.

No one—neither Ambedkar, nor the Dalit community, and nor touch-ables—ever anticipated that these new transformations and disparate notions of freedom, self-making, provisional resistance, and reconstructive practices would be deployed by Tamasha women at the end of the twentieth and into the twenty-first century. These formed an acquisitive, responsible, and self-interested ethic through which Tamasha women could remake themselves and their families. A new generation of artists transformed the meaning and prac-tice of Tamasha in the context of new political and sexual-caste economy. They were agents in creating and preserving masti historically produced in Tamasha. They displayed wealth and preserved their honor, identity, personhood, and

FIGURE 7.1. Megha Ghadge at Ambedkar Jayanti celebrations, Pune. "Panchasheel Social Foundation, Machhindra (dada) Eknath Gaikwad Foundation's best wishes on Bhim Jayanti, Dr. Babasaheb Ambedkar's 126th birth anniversary celebrations. Many, many salutes." Megha Ghadge dressed in full white in center looking at her phone. Source: Photo courtesy of author.

name before others. Some leading Tamasha women also enjoyed the pleasure of power and continued to negotiate precarious public political realms. Tamasha women rearranged complex ideological relations of assimilation or challenge for different purposes.

This book has centered Dalit Tamasha women at the heart of modern Indian society *in both their oppressed subjectivities and their resistant practices*. The Marathi idiom of shil/ashlil, manus/Untouchable, assli/non-authentic that marked the Tamasha woman's condition and that were used to differentiate the desirable from the undesirable was constitutive of modernity in a caste society and points to its provisional, fragmentary and ongoing constitution. A Tamasha woman's life rooted in what I have called the sex-gender-caste complex and the tripartite politics of ashlil-manuski-assli that rendered her a vamp brings into stark relief the centrality of caste, gender, and sexuality in the formation of political constituency and political rights in India—two central building blocks of modernity since they underlie the ideas of the political citizen (of a nation) and the human subject (with rights) respectively. Although Tamasha was considered ashlil, touchables and Dalits energetically appropriated it at different moments throughout the twentieth century and attempted to control it for different purposes. Deploying the vernacular as a method and working with diverse Marathi archives, the book records the politics of Tamasha in three phases: pre-Ambedkar, Ambedkar, and post-Ambedkar.

The book tracks how the precarious performativity of Tamasha violently guarded the moral economy of shil-ashlil (decent-vulgar). At the turn of the twentieth century, the ashlil deployed through Tamasha sharpened caste distinctions and reinforced Dalit oppression, underlined both Dalits' untouchable status and caste divisions, and was connected with discourses about honor, respectability, racial identities, and the governance of presumably indecent Dalit communities. Perversion and sexuality were major concerns for the state and brahmani elites. Victorian and brahmani ideologies thus pitched modernity against backwardness and enabled only certain brahman-Hindu traditions to form the bedrock of modern India and liberal democracy. As a result, the ashlil underscored Dalitness and became the key modality or form of caste by excluding Dalits from the realm of manus.

Focusing on Maharashtra, the book illuminates how concerns over the ashlil reveal a multitude of sensoriums and visceral feelings that strategically encode caste structures. I demonstrate that vulgarity through Tamasha was sometimes mobilized to obscure social change, while at other times, it was explicitly politicized at certain moments of conflict and transition to foreground particular interests, to define identities, build civility and politeness, and inscribe decency in order to marginalize and malign social and economic competitors. Touchables, Dalits, and the state negotiated and reimagined the political concept of the ashlil. The ashlil-manus-assli of Tamasha was challenged by three different movements: first, Ambedkar's movement for Dalit manuski, which sought to eliminate the exploitation of Tamasha women and his followers, which sought to erase Tamasha itself; second, the postcolonial Maharashtrian nationalist movement, which sought to create an assli Marathi identity not by erasing but by sanitizing and repurposing Tamasha; and third, Tamasha women, who inhabited, disputed, denied, manipulated and ambiguously reclaimed the ashlil, manus, and assli in and beyond Tamasha.

Although on the exterior some passed as touchables, Dalits could not easily escape the *stickiness of the ashlil* or separate their caste from their lower

Conclusion

status to become casteless and always already assli like modern touchables. All touchable actors—Bapurao, male audiences, the state, and middle-class women—mobilized the ashlil, reshaped it, and associated with Tamasha to varying degrees without the ashlil sticking to them. In the process, the ashlil was linked to the masses, had proximity to sexuality, and commonality with caste. It also had the power to regulate the social order, organize castes, and exclude certain members of society. Although the ashlil was regulatory in one form, it fluidly moved through binaries of coercion and consent, through different castes, with multiple affective dimensions in practices of caste—touch, body, shame. In this sense, the ashlil may not necessarily be depicted as vulgate, but it could allow connections with manuski.

Rather than the art per se of Tamasha, its performance, the repertoire of gestures, the music, the musical instruments, lyrics, song, and dance, my objective has been the analysis of its historical, institutional, material, and ideological politics of cultural realities rooted in systemic sexual-caste violence. As a first step in unravelling key secrets of Indian society and Marathi caste politics, Tamasha women help us understand the nature of an ever-contested, vibrant political sphere in modernity. In this process, the book also tracked the extraordinary reach of vernacular Marathi concepts, concepts that are rooted in particular social, historical, political, ideological contexts and cultural realities and that contribute to a global history of social inequality, sexuality, gender, and humanity. Normative politics and generative processes of gender, caste, and sexuality continue to shape Dalit identity, agency, and citizenship in present-day India as Tamasha women negotiate their status as ashlil and manus.

Especially after the 1920s, under the leadership of Ambedkar, Dalits challenged brahmanism, which dehumanized them as ashlil. They appropriated, debated, and challenged Marathi elites' discourse of liberalism, rights, progress, new public morality, and modernization to selectively appropriate certain high traditions and to solidify a respectable, licit, national culture and ideology in colonial India and especially in the new state of Maharashtra. I analyzed the dialectic, the two discourses of Dalit efforts of manuski and brahmani dehumanizing of Dalits, which were complementary processes operating in conjunction. Dalits consistently fought to be recognized as equal manus, human beings, and to establish an equal and just society. They struggled to recuperate their manuski and lift themselves up, raising their moral status in the eyes of the dominant castes and the colonial and postcolonial government to assert their assli status under sheer contingencies. Ambedkar's and Ambedkarite Jalsakars' liberatory anticaste project of manuski aimed to rescue manus from the ashlil to carve the Dalit political subject, rights, and constituency.

The Ambedkarite call to manuski reinforced a more just, equal, and fulsome humanity and the revolutionary potential of the modern moment as well as the anxieties and contradictions that attend the making of revolutionary subjectivity. Ambedkar's project of manuski was to recuperate personhood and humanity of Dalits and end the exploitation of Tamasha women, and his position on Tamasha women and prostitutes illustrates the complexity of totally escaping patriarchy. His commitment to manuski and the consistency of his thought was remarkable, given the complexity of his ideas. His own anxieties about ashlil Tamasha and the contingency of constituting the Dalit as manus left the social force of the ashlil intact. Manuski could be recuperated only by unsticking the ashlil from Dalits, especially from Dalit women in relation to, for example, vatandari or prostitution. In the process, however, Ambedkar and his followers identified certain women's aberrant sexuality as threatening to their radical politics and divided Dalit women along an axis of sexual propriety and social respectability, creating a dichotomy between the dangerous and endangered. Yet Ambedkar's ideological constructs and commitment went far beyond any of these processes, creating immense possibility and new meanings for the Dalit samaj.

For Jalsakars, Tamasha had an instrumental value for public outreach, and due to the politics of the ashlil, they sought to peel away the ashlil that had stuck to their caste status. Unlike Ambedkar, for Gaikwad, the entire genre and commodification of Tamasha and culture of consumption was a severe problem. Both Ambedkar and Gaikwad derided consumerism. But importantly, for Tamasha women, the genre was their livelihood. They could not give up the genre and performance because it was also a form of survival. Dalits' liberatory anticaste theory of manuski thus got engulfed in the sheer historical limits of conceptualizing humanness, humanity, and masculinity, which constituted each other.

Pavalabai and Mangalatai's strategies, agency, and subjectivity were removed from Ambedkar's formal politics of oppositional consciousness, heroic action, and direct confrontation, or the poetics-politics of Jalsakars' promotional work for social regeneration. Like Pavalabai, Mangalatai invested in her body as a sensual and desire-producing machine, amplified her femininity and sexual availability, and summoned manliness and male sexuality. She engaged in difficult practices, in the work and play of Tamasha, to both consent to and disrupt the caste mechanism to create possibilities for herself, her family, and her troupe. Her lack of education and resources, the threat of starvation, and her want of property and protection defined her precarious social position. However, gradually, as she achieved success and recognition in Tamasha and became the lead performer, Mangalatai applied the principles of good management to all aspects of her life—personal hygiene, finances, sexuality, child rearing, self-in-community, renunciation of intemperate habits, and moral restraint.

The postcolonial Maharashtra state's goal is striking in its absence of manuski for Tamasha performers and Dalits as a whole. The state sanitized, policed, and patronized Tamasha and appropriated the social and sexual labor of Tamasha people, without dealing with the Dalit body or with manuski as generated by Dalits. Maharashtra repurposed Tamasha and even made it iconic, and yet acted hypocritically toward Tamasha people. Moreover, the state stripped Dalitness from Tamasha, making it consumable for touchables and especially the elite. The government shaped the ashlil anew in the present day. The postcolonial state was involved in producing a sanitized Tamasha for general consumption and creating an assli Maharashtrian identity and nationalist culture away from the bawdy; yet this construction did not affect Tamasha performers who remained ashlil. The sexual-caste politics of Tamasha proves an allure, and it is this which is renewed, remade, and repurposed. The illicit desire that Tamasha encodes is constantly drawn into a licit sphere, but ironically, for that to happen, the illicit must be kept alive.

Media and the Marathi film industry also joined elites and the state in legitimizing the assli identity of Tamasha for the new Marathi citizen within the newly independent state of Maharashtra, by selling the ideology of marathamola Marathi manus, once again without paying attention to Dalits. Benefiting from this new awkward and contingent assli status, Tamasha women asserted their constrained humanity, enhanced their social and financial capital, and improved their lives. They rode the wave of market neoliberalization and the attendant moral changes, and gained national and international visibility, which Ambedkar and his followers would have never anticipated or approved of. Yet only a select few lead artists were successful, while the majority Tamasha people struggled to survive.

While these are homological developments, the Ambedkarite agenda is yet singular: here, the Tamasha woman is an incitement to humanity but cannot desire to be human on her own terms. And given that the ashlil of what she does sticks to her, she has to unpeel herself from her performance, her Tamasha self, so to speak, to access manuski. Yet the Ambedkarite agenda is anything but simplistic: its prophetic and historical strengths go beyond what it sets out to do with regard to Tamasha, and this is borne out by the ironic presence of a Tamasha artist as a chief guest at an Ambedkarite event. The Dalit subject of history is inexorably and inevitably the universal human subject, however this universality is acknowledged. The study has pointed to the power of this liberatory politics, as well as noted the tragic ironies that attended its heralding. No calm is possible with these wounds.

Tamasha remained a fraught performativity—it was work, violence, play, and amusement. While Tamasha was exploitation rooted in caste violence and hard work and was the only means of earning livelihood for Tamasha people, especially Tamasha women, it was play, nonwork, individual and social relaxation, pleasure, fun, and sexuality for men in the audience and respectable society as a whole. Men's personal relaxation, expression, and pleasure were commodities available to purchase with their labor as a worker and a male. Tamasha women made men feel good, and to this end, they sold their sexuality, but not sexual intercourse. If they developed extended relationships with men outside the Tamasha theatre, that was a different matter.

Tamasha and Tamasha women were central to male bonding and to constructing manliness and male sexuality. Women cultivated this *dhanda* (business) of Tamasha and provided the service of sexual pleasure to men. Beyond the sexual and the voyeuristic, this service generated the pleasure of belonging, bonding, and male homosociality. Men laughed, joked, patted each other on the back, and sat with their arms around each, having a good time watching

Tamasha. They enacted their manliness and male bonding in the enjoyment of degrading Tamasha women. In other words, Tamasha women were central to the construction of the male ego, virile manliness, muscular masculinity, and male bonding. Tamasha women were successful if they made men feel appreciated, approved, loved, and recognized, and this success perpetuated economies of caste, class, gender, and sexuality.

Success in the drama between Tamasha women and their male audiences was measured not in coercive acts of sex but around the routine rituals of sexual interest, accentuated sexuality, flirtatious plays alluding to sex, romance, sexual intimacy, and fantasy of sex. Tamasha reproduced differences of caste, gender, and sexuality, while it simultaneously constructed marathamola Woman and Man, produced male and female sexuality, and exaggerated the inequality of caste, gender, and sexuality and made it pleasurable. Women build muscular men by flattering them.

And yet, as this book shows, Tamasha degraded and stigmatized the woman but not the man—denigrating Dalit women was merely a means to sharpen the sexual--caste economy. Tamasha women were stigmatized permanently, and their bodies were appropriated to serve men of all castes. Tamasha certainly brought out the animalistic side in male audiences composed of mostly touchable men—they exchanged lewd jokes, laughed, made lewd gestures to women, drank, danced, and screamed. And yet, animality and the ashlil did not stick to them. It was Dalit women whose abject and dirty status was intensified in Tamasha, the sexual-caste mechanism consistently mutated and updated to differentiate and discriminate human beings.

If this book is an account of the caste logic that holds contempt for the ashlil and bibhatsa and its main practitioner, the Tamasha woman, a logic that continues to hold sway, I want to end by illuminating a very different project that sought to appropriate, assimilate, and twist the old, and create new definitions of the ashlil, assli, and manus as artists pushed the boundaries of respectability, vulgarity, and honor in present-day India.

In the mid-1990s, a group of men—straight and gay—started experimenting even more with Tamasha by introducing troupes called Bin Bayakancha Tamasha (Tamasha without Women) in Mumbai. Madhusudan (Madhu) Shinde, a Dalit-Chambhar (leatherworker caste), transgender, plump, jovial artist in his early fifties, reported, "Some [dominant-caste] artists like Anil Vasudevan and Pramod Kandalkar—both of whom were trained as Bharatnatyam [classical] dancers—experimented with Bin Bayakancha Tamasha."[1] Vasudevan and Kandalkar made innovations to their own dance programs by appropriating Dalit arts and eventually organized an all-male dance troupe. As a result, some leading straight but mostly gay male artists worked with other men, trained them through repeated rehearsals, and reintroduced them to perform as women. Many gay and straight men attended these shows.

Madhusudan preferred to be called "Madhu" (honey)—the ambiguous twist being in the name, which could be a woman's or a man's name and it means sweet as honey. Madhu wanted themselves and their co-workers to portray the "perfect" and "real" woman: "My dancer friends think by increasing the size and lifting up their padded chests, they look sexier [like women]. However, this picture of breasts—big, tight, with upward push—is artificial. Had you seen them earlier, you would have laughed your head off. One of the fundamentals of portraying a woman is to have 'downward-slanting small breasts.'" Along with dancing, Madhu is also a choreographer, arranges for dance costumes, and manages dance performances for the government, schools, private housing societies, and so on.

Bin Bayakancha Tamasha queered Tamasha and Lavani and mocked the ashlil of Tamasha through an exaggeration of heteropatriarchal assumptions in neoliberal India. The dancers experimented with new ideas, new sites of contestation and variability, new performativities, to once again both transgress and reinforce gender boundaries and hyperpatriarchy, thus signaling a need to inquire into the formation of homosexualities in Tamasha and in India. Bin Bayakancha Tamasha exposed the failure of heterosexual regimes and brought into relief the supposed quality of heterosexual performativity. Anand Satam, a Vani (grocer, high caste) transgender (or "TG" as they called themselves) artist who worked with Bin Bayakancha Tamasha for seven years, emphasized that Vasudevan and Kandalkar said, "This idea is going to fly, just [wait and] watch! And it did, eventually. You attended the performance and you found it fantastic and successful!"[2] Similarly, Ravi Sangamnerkar, a male choreographer training Tamasha and Lavani women, was ecstatic about Bin Bayakancha Tamasha: "Look how [these men are] outperforming women,"[3] he

FIGURE 7.2. Mostly gay male troupe Lavanya Shiromani (Epitome of Graceful Beauty) starting their performance with a worship seeking blessings from gods for a successful show. Source: Photo by author.

FIGURE 7.3. Lavanya Shiromani TG leaders Anand Satam (second from left) and Akshay(a) Malvankar (first from right) and their co-artists. Anand Satam's mother in the center attended the show. Akshay's co-artists referred to them as Akshaya. While Akshay is a man's name, Akshaya is a woman's name. Source: Photo by author

FIGURE 7.4. Author with TG artists. Source: Photo by author.

stated, and yet he forgot how gay men were excluding women but also preserving the figure of the Tamasha woman through their exaggerated feminine
identity, thereby contesting and reproducing norms (see figures 7.2, 7.3, 7.4).

Bin Bayakancha Tamasha people appropriated Dalit Tamasha legacies and
reconstructed the hypersexualized femininity as a fundamental function of
dominant-caste patriarchies and re-idealized bourgeois forms of heterosexual
exchange by inhabiting idealized notions of sexuality. However, at the same
time, some like Madhu repeatedly mocked, inverted, and invaded patriarchal
power with their swelling feminine presence and breached it with the plump
belly that could not be controlled by the waistband. In the new millennium,
touchable transgender communities have increasingly turned to Tamasha and
Lavani as modes of sexual expression, art, and livelihood. In doing so, they
exceeded the limitations of dominant culture, broadened the coordinates
of the Dalit struggle, and opened a space for new alliances, solidarities, and
politics. And yet, none of TG artists I interacted with said anything about
their reinventing and mobilizing of Bin Bayakancha Tamasha being rooted

in the sex-gender-caste complex that led to differentiation, exploitation, and stigmatization. At least, they did not mention it. I reiterate, sexuality is not free floating, and as this book has done, we need to analyze it in the contexts of caste violence and caste patriarchy. The all-male sociability that Bin Bay-akancha Tamasha invites and constitutes persists, eliding the Dalit woman performer's labor and the sexual-caste logic that dictates it. Like Dalit Tamasha women, transgender men rearranged complex ideological relationships of as-similation, appropriation, and challenge for a different purpose and political possibility; however, they did not adopt an anticaste perspective or worldview or pay attention to the logic of the caste order and brahmanism that transcends individuals. Nevertheless, no one vision, one anticaste thought, or one resolu-tion is possible for this history.

This book examined the ambivalence of Tamasha prohibition, production, and proliferation—subjugated, subaltern Tamashe and Lavanya and their prac-titioners negotiated characterizations as ashlil to carve out their own manuski and assli status. Tamasha and Lavani programs are raging in present-day Ma-harashtra. Historically, intelligent Dalit singers and dancers deployed their weapons of the weak to exploit cracks in the institution of caste in order to transform their violated, abject, subjugated bodies into the play, entertainment, and pleasure of Tamasha. Elites and state agents depicted them and their arts as ashlil, impure, lowly, and corrupt and blamed them for modern India's ills. As a result, Dalits sought to be everything opposite the ashlil and insisted on manuski and modernity unblemished by backwardness and denigration. Although Dalit radicals consistently struggled to discard everything ashlil and become shil manus, it was not to be. In the postcolonial period, elites and the state of Maharashtra claimed Tamasha and Lavani as authentically Marathi, systematically appropriating and mobilizing ashlil Dalit arts and their Dalit practitioners in the service of state- and nation-building projects.

The government and civil society strengthened their own exclusivity and legitimacy, policing morality and boundaries of the "good" and "bad," simulta-neously deepening or temporarily suspending differentiations between castes and classes, and making themselves and Dalits more visible in postcolonial India. In so doing, they manipulated the violence of the vulgar and made the assli identity possible. A Dalit Tamasha woman being a figure charged with sexual surplus produced by the endogamous as well as moral economy of the caste order is strictly not required for the making of this economy, but is necessary in order to affirm and naturalize its logic. These contests illuminate the persistence of the violence of caste into the making of the modern Indian republic—the figure of the Tamasha woman bears the burden of this public and rather embarrassing secret.

These supposedly rational, scientific, and academic approaches to Tamasha artistry represent new wounds in the battles between the proponents and opponents of shil-ashlil-manus-assli and continue to hurt hereditary Dalit artists whose lives were easily indexed as backwards, disgusting, dirty, vulgar, and corrupt. Dalits cited, twisted, queered, and deeply engaged with the assli discourse of the Marathi state and painfully reiterated elite norms. The success of their politics lay not in producing a pure, political opposition but in forging possibilities for their futures from presumably impure resources and precarious positions and expanding categories of manus and assli. Dalit artists' virtuous selves entangled with their community continue to puncture the neat, educated, and smart Dalit modernity of their caste fellows to exercise their few modes of agency surviving the structural violence of ashlil caste and untouchability. Their politics, different voices and dialogues deserve attention as it continues with recent insurgencies, transplanted to an even more diverse global theatre.

Introduction

1. *Tamasha* literally means "spectacle." I have conducted ethnographic fieldwork with Dalit and touchable Tamasha, Lavani, and Sangeet Bari performers in Maharashtra since 2003. I also spent summers and extended time in 2016–2017 interviewing artists in cities and rural areas. I am using pseudonyms for artists, unless otherwise noted. Also see Shailaja Paik, "Mangalatai Bansode and the Social Life of Tamasha," *Biography* 40, no. 1 (Winter 2017): 170–98.

2. The terms in quote marks appear in the historical record and I use quote marks here, on their first appearance, to call into question their usage and construction in historical time and space. Hereafter, I use them without quote marks.

3. I am grateful to Projit Mukharji for his insight on stickiness. For details, see Sara Ahmed, *The Cultural Politics of Emotion* (New York: Routledge, 2015) on "sticky signs." Stickiness, as conceived by Ahmed, is *"an effect of the histories of contact between bodies, objects, and signs"* (90, emphasis in original); it is the outcome of repeated impressions, an effect that emerges from "histories of contact." The meaning of that emotion emerges from cultural and personal exchanges; as those exchanges repeat, meaning and resonance collect, and what results is an "accumulation of affective value" (92): this is "stickiness."

4. Bhimrao Ramji Ambedkar, "Away from the Hindus," in *Babasaheb Ambedkar Writings and Speeches* [hereafter *BAWS*] vol. 5, ed. Vasant Moon (Bombay: Maharashtra Government, 1989), 419. I thank V. Geetha for this insight.

5. Interview with author, Pune, July 7, 2016.

6. Sianne Ngai, *Theory of the Gimmick: Aesthetic Judgment and Capitalist Form* (Cambridge, MA: Harvard University Press, 2020).

7. I thank Christian Lee Novetzke for these discussions.

8. Feminist scholars only recently have dealt with Ambedkar's exposé of surplus woman and endogamy. See Durba Mitra, "'Surplus Woman': Female Sexuality and the Concept of Endogamy," *Journal of Asian Studies* 80, no. 1 (February 2021): 3–26; V. Geetha, *Bhimrao Ramji Ambedkar and the Question of Socialism in India* (Palgrave Macmilan: 2021), 171.

9. Brahmaprakash Singh's recent work has also borne this out. Singh, *Cultural*

Labour: Conceptualizing the 'Folk Performance' in India (New Delhi: Oxford University Press, 2019).

10. For "sexual economy" see Nair and John, *The Question of Silence: The Sexual Economies of Modern India* (New Delhi, Kali for Women, 2000). I build on and deepen their work by centering the violence of caste.

11. I am building on Ambedkar's theorization of caste. See Ambedkar, "Castes in India," *BAWS*, vol. 1 (Bombay: Maharashtra Government, 1979), 5–22; "Untouchables or the Children of India's Ghetto," *BAWS*, vol. 5; "What Path to Freedom?," speech, May 31, 1936, in *BAWS*, vol. 17, 113–47, and so on in Ambedkar, *BAWS*, vols. 1–5, 17. Also, for details on the sexual-caste economy, see Paik, "Ambedkar and the 'Prostitute': Caste, Sexuality, and Humanity in Modern India," *Gender & History*, August 16, 2021, https://doi.org/10.1111/1468-0424.12557.

12. Ambedkar, "Away from the Hindus," in *BAWS*, vol. 5, 18.

13. See Balmurli Natrajan "Cultural Identity and Beef Festivals: Toward a 'Multiculturalism *against* Caste,'" *Contemporary South Asia* 26, no. 3 (2018): 287–304, doi:10.1080/09584935.2018.1504000, for a review of scholarly discussions about the politics of reclaiming Dalit arts and culture.

14. See Judith Butler, *Gender Trouble: Feminism and the Subversion of Identity* (London: Routledge, 1990); and Judith Butler, *Bodies That Matter: On the Discursive Limits of "Sex"* (London: Routledge, 1993). I am deploying Butler's analysis of performativity to analyze both the performance and performativity of Tamasha. Butler is influenced by Lacanian psychoanalysis, phenomenology, structural anthropology, and speech-act theory in her understanding of the "performativity" of identity. To her, gender is a "stylized repetition of acts." Butler argues that social reality is not a given but is continually created "through language, gesture, and all manner of symbolic social sign." In the act of performing the conventions of reality, by embodying those fictions in our actions, we make those artificial conventions appear to be natural and necessary. In *Undoing Gender* (New York: Routledge, 2004), Butler revises her earlier argument: "Performativity is not just about speech acts, but also about bodily acts. . . . Significations of the body exceed the intention of the subject" (198–99).

15. I am building on Pierre Bourdieu's concept of game. He explains his idea of "homo ludens": that "human beings are constituted by the games they play giving rise to a notion of social structures as rules that guide individual strategy." For details, see Michael Buroway, "The Roots of Domination: Beyond Bourdieu and Gramsci," *Sociology* 46, no.2 (2012): 187–206.

16. On social death, see Orlando Patterson, *Slavery and Social Death: A Comparative Study* (Cambridge, M.A.: Harvard University Press, 1982).

17. Homi Bhabha, *The Location of Culture* (New York: Routledge, 2004).

18. On affect and untouchability see numerous works in Dalit literature as well as theoretical discussions in G. Guru, ed., *Humiliation: Claims and Context* (Delhi: Oxford University Press, 2009); Joel Lee, "Disgust and Untouchability: Towards an Affective Theory of Caste," *South Asian History and Culture* 12, no. 2–3 (2021): 310-327, doi:10.1080/19472498.2021.1878784.

19. Ambedkar, "The Annihilation of Caste," *BAWS*, vol. 1, 25–80.

20. Ambedkar, "The Annihilation of Caste."

21. For details, see Ambedkar's analysis of caste in "The Annihilation of Caste."

22. For details, see Shailaja Paik, *Dalit Women's Education in Modern India: Double Discrimination* (London: Routledge, 2014).

23. On brahmans, see Shefali Chandra, *The Sexual Life of English: Languages of Caste and Desire in Colonial India* (Durham, NC: Duke University Press, 2012); Anna Schultz, *Singing a Hindu Nation: Marathi Devotional Performance and Nationalism* (New York: Oxford University Press, 2013). On Dalits, see Anupama Rao, *The Caste Question: Dalits and the Politics of Modern India* (California: University of California Press, 2009); Sharmila Rege, *Writing Caste/Writing Gender: Narrating Dalit Women's Testimonials* (New Delhi: Zuban, 2006), Paik, *Dalit Women's Education*; Clarinda Still, *Dalit Women: Honor and Patriarchy in South India* (New Delhi: Social Science Press, 2014); Lucinda Ramberg, *Given to the Goddess: South Indian Devadasis and the Sexuality of Religion* (Durham, NC: Duke University Press, 2014).

24. Madhukar Dhond, *Marathi Lavani* (Pune: Mauj, 1988); V. K. Joshi, *Loknatyachi Parampara* (Pune: Thokal Prakashan, 1961); Gangadhar Moraje, *Marathi Lavani Vangmay* (Pune: Moghe Prakashan, 1974); Namdeo Vhatkar, *Maharashtrache Loknatya Tamasha Kala ani Sahitya* (Kolhapur: Yashashree Prakashan, no date); and Tevia Abrams, "Tamasha: People's Theatre of Maharashtra" (PhD diss., Michigan State University, 1974). Some have even focused on select leading men *lavanikars* (Lavani performers), such as Honaji Bala, Saganbhau, Patthe Bapurao, and Ram Joshi, and Lavanya or Tamasha women, such as Vithabai Narayangaokar, and recorded their lives. Many writers have confined themselves to the detailed literary modes and instruments used in Tamasha and thus objectified Tamasha artists. Some writers have stuck to the textual realm and rarely stepped outside their middle-class apartments to interact or travel with Tamasha artists to examine their ideas, experiences, and lives. A few scholars have worked well, combining history and ethnographic methods. Nevertheless, a significant problem is that most writers do not provide detailed information on or analysis of the Marathi sources they procured. Their failure to examine the social life and the sexual economy of caste has hindered their analysis. Some journalists, like Sandesh Bhandare and Shirish Shetye, have traveled to open and enclosed Tamasha theatres to produce photographic books on the everyday life of Tamasha artists.

Sandesh Bhandare, *Tamasha: Ek Rangadi Gammat* (Mumbai: Lokvangmay gruha, 2006).

25. Sharmila Rege, "The Hegemonic Appropriation of Sexuality: The Case of Lavani Performers in Maharashtra," *Contributions to Indian Sociology* 29, no. 1–2 (1995): 24–38.

26. Susan Seizer, *Stigmas of the Tamil Stage: An Ethnography of Special Drama Artists in South India* (Durham, NC: Duke University Press, 2005); Ramberg, *Given to the Goddess*; Davesh Soneji, *Unfinished Gestures: Devadasi, Memory, and Modernity in South India* (Chicago: University of Chicago Press, 2012); Priyadarshini Vijaisri, *Dangerous Marginality: Rethinking Impurity and Power* (New Delhi: Indian Council of Historical Research, 2016); Kunal Parker, "A Corporation of Superior Prostitutes: Anglo-Indian Legal Conceptions of Temple Dancing Girls," *Modern Asian Studies* 32, no. 3 (1998): 559–633; Janaki Nair, "The Devadasi, Dharma, and the State," *Economic and Political Weekly*, December 10, 1994, 3157–67; Leslie Orr, *Donors, Devotees, and Daughters of God* (New York: Oxford University Press, 2000); Amrit Srinivasan, "Temple 'Prostitution' and Community Reform: An Examination of the Ethnographic, Historical and Textual Context of the Devadasi of Tamil Nadu," PhD diss., Cambridge University, 1984.

27. I thank Prathama Banerjee and V. Geetha for these discussions.

28. V. Geetha, *Ambedkar*, 214.

29. Rao, *The Caste Question*, 67.

30. Rao, *The Caste Question*, 61.

31. See Rao, *The Caste Question*; and following her, Ramberg, *Given to the Goddess*; and Charu Gupta, *The Gender of Caste* (Seattle: University of Washington Press, 2014).

32. Gupta, *The Gender of Caste*, 142.

33. Gupta, *The Gender of Caste*, 163.

34. Gupta, *The Gender of Caste*, 165.

35. For details, see book review, Shailaja Paik, "The Gender of Caste: Representing Dalits in Print, by Charu Gupta," *South Asia: Journal of South Asian Studies*, 2017, doi:10.1080/00856401.2017.1379230.

36. Linda Gordon, "Internal Colonialism and Gender," in *Haunted by Empire: Geographies of Intimacy in North American History*, ed. Ann Laura Stoler (Durham, NC: Duke University Press, 2006), 441.

37. Ramberg, *Given to the Goddess*.

38. Rita Rozario, *Broken Lives: Dalit Women in Prostitution* (Karnataka: Ambedkar Resource Center, 2000); Rege, *Writing Caste/Writing Gender*; and Sharmila Rege, *Against the Madness of Manu: B. R. Ambedkar's Writings on Brahmanical Patriarchy* (New Delhi: Navayana, 2013).

39. Rege, *Against the Madness of Manu*, 148.

40. Rege, *Against the Madness of Manu*, 148–49.

41. J. Lorand Matory, *Stigma and Culture: Last-Place Anxiety in Black America* (Chicago: University of Chicago Press, 2015), 333.

42. On agrarian caste slavery in South India, see Sanal Mohan, *Modernity of Slavery: Struggles against Caste Inequality in Colonial Kerala* (New Delhi: Oxford University Press, 2015); Rupa Viswanath, *The Pariah Problem: Caste, Religion, and the Social in Modern India* (New York: Columbia University Press, 2014).

Chapter 1

1. Sharmila Rege, "The Hegemonic Appropriation of Sexuality: The Case of Lavani Performers in Maharashtra," *Contributions to Indian Sociology* 29, no. 1–2 (1995): 24–38.

2. V. K. Joshi, *Loknatyachi Parampara* (Pune: Thokal Prakashan, 1961), 130.

3. "Maharashtra," *Data Highlights: The Scheduled Castes*, Census of India 2001, https://censusindia.gov.in/Tables_Published/SCST/dh_sc_maha.pdf.

4. Madhukar Dhond, *Marathi Lavani* (Pune: Mauj, 1988), 56; V. K. Joshi, *Loknatyachi Parampara* (Pune: Thokal Prakashan, 1961), 34–51; Tevia Abrams, "Tamasha: People's Theatre of Maharashtra" (PhD diss., Michigan State University, 1974), 12.

5. Balwant Gargi, *Folk Theatre of India* (Calcutta: Rupa, c1991), 74.

6. Rege, "Hegemonic Appropriation," 23.

7. Interview conducted with Madhu Shinde by author, Mumbai, 2016.

8. For details on baluta, see Sumit Guha, *Beyond Caste: Identity and Power in South Asia Past and Present* (Leiden: Brill, 2013), 86–115.

9. For details on Indian caste feudalism, see Bharat Patankar and Gail Omvedt, "The Dalit Liberation Movement in Colonial India," *Economic and Political Weekly* 14, no. 7/8 (annual number, Caste and Class in India; February 1979): 409–24.

10. Hiroyuki Kotani, *Western India in Historical Transition* (New Delhi: Manohar, 2002), 123. Unfortunately, he does not provide evidence or details.

11. As Patankar and Omvedt refer to it, "Dalit Liberation Movement," 413.

12. Phule, "Gulamgiri," *Mahatma Phule Samagray Vangmay*, edited Y.D. Phadke (Mumbai: Maharashtra Government Culture Association, 1991), p.118.

13. Interview with author, Kandivili-Mumbai, August 1, 2016. Emphasis mine.

14. Some dominant-caste critics have argued on these lines. For example, see Pantanwane's introduction to Rustum Achalkhamb, *Tamasha Lokrangbhumi* (Sugava: Pune, 2006). Pantawane does not provide details.

15. Achalkhamb, *Tamasha Lokrangbhumi*, 8.

16. Achalkhamb, *Tamasha Lokrangbhumi*, 77.

17. Ambedkar notes that peshve also did not spare daivadnya sonars and pathare

prabhus who tried to imitate peshve practices. For example, when sonars started wearing dhotis and using salutations of "namaskar" like the brahmans, peshwe got the East India Company to issue a prohibitory order. Ambedkar, "The Annihilation of Caste," *Babasaheb Ambedkar Writings and Speeches* (Mumbai: Government of Maharashtra, 1979), 39.

18. Ambedkar, "The Annihilation of Caste," 39–40.

19. Ambedkar, "The Annihilation of Caste," 39–40.

20. V. S. Naipaul quoted in Gopal Guru, *Humiliation* (Delhi: Oxford University Press, 2009), 14.

21. Rege, "Hegemonic Appropriation," 26–28.

22. Hiroshi Fukazawa, *Medieval Deccan: Peasants, Social Systems, and States* (Delhi: Oxford University Press, 1991).

23. Rege, "Hegemonic Appropriation," 26–28.

24. For more about the Koregaon memorial, see Shraddha Kumbhojkar, "Contesting Power, Contesting Memories: A History of the Koregaon Pillar," *Economic and Political Weekly* 47, no. 42 (October 20, 2012). Violence erupted at the monument in 2018 when brahman fundamentalists attacked Dalits.

25. Shailaja Paik, *Dalit Women's Education in Modern India: Double Discrimination* (London: Routledge, 2014).

26. I have benefitted from Michel Foucault, *The History of Sexuality*, vol. 1 (New York: Pantheon, 1978).

27. I thank V. Geetha and Prathama Banerjee for these discussions.

28. For a similar strategy in Bengal, see Samita Sen, "Offences against Marriage: Negotiating Custom in Colonial Bengal," in *A Question of Silence? The sexual economies of modern India*, ed. Mary E. John and Janaki Nair (New Delhi: Kali for Women, 1998), 77–100.

29. Only one historian, Veena Naregal, analyzed the normative, institutional, and ideological maneuvers of dominant-caste elites for and cultural ascendancy. See Veena Naregal, "Performance, Caste, Aesthetics: The Marathi Sangeet Natak and the Dynamics of Cultural Marginalization," *Contributions to Indian Sociology* 42, no. 1–2 (2010): 79–101.

30. Michael David Rosse, "The Movement for the Revitalization of 'Hindu' Music in Northern India, 1860-1930: The Role of Associations and Institutions" (PhD diss., Univ of Pennsylvania, 1995), 98, cited in Anna Schultz, *Singing a Hindu Nation: Marathi Devotional Performance and Nationalism* (New York: Oxford University Press, 2013). Emphasis mine.

31. Giorgio Agamben, *Homo Sacer: Sovereign Power and Bare Life* (Stanford, CA: Stanford University Press, 1998).

32. Janaki Bakhle, *Two Men and Music* (New York: Oxford University Press,

2005), has analyzed brahman men's shaping of the Hinduized public sphere and Hindu ascendancy by marginalizing and even excluding Muslim musicians. Yet, she fails to pay attention to the privilege of dominant brahman caste status of the actors who appropriated elements from Dalit art forms and Parsi theatre. Their caste status enabled them to conveniently dabble with everything high, low, and in between and yet retain their brahman hegemonic apparatus.

33. "Shimga," *Sudharak*, March 20, 1893. For similar cleansing processes regarding Ramlila and Holi festival in North India, see Nita Kumar, *The Artisans of Benares* (Princeton, NJ: Princeton University, 2017); and Nandini Gooptu, *The Politics of the Urban Poor in Early Twentieth Century India* (Cambridge: Cambridge University Press, 2014), 237–45.

34. *Navakal*, October 21, 1926.

Chapter 2

1. C. B. Khairmode, *Dr. Bhimrao Ramji Ambedkar yanche charitra*, vol. 3 (Pune: Sugava Prakashan, 1964), 141–42; R. M. Bivalkar and Jhumbarlal Kamble, *Mahadcha Muktisangram* (Mahad freedom struggle) (Pune: Rajhans Prakashan, 1977), 12, 47,

2. B. M. Jintikar, *Patthe Bapuraochya Dilkhush Lavanya, Patthe Bapurao yanchya dholki varil bhedik Lavanya* (Pune: Jintikar, 1958). Although Jintikar provides different dates—that is, her birth year as 1881 and death year 1930—he does not have details on her compared to Bhalerao. I am following the dates provided by Pavalabai's nephew, Lahuji Namdeorao Bhalerao. Lahuji Bhalerao, "Namchand Pavalabai Tabaji Bhalerao Hivargaokarin," 1.

3. Balwant Gargi, *Folk Theatre of India* (Calcutta: Rupa, c 1991), 75.

4. See Frantz Fanon, *Black Skin, White Masks* (New York: Grove Press, 2008); Margaret L. Hunter, "If You're Light, You're Alright: Light Skin Color as Social Capital for Women of Color," *Gender and Society* 16, no.2 (2002): 175–93.

5. Chandrakumar Nalge, *Maharashtra's Sculptor: Patthe Bapurao* (Mumbai: Maharashtra State Literary and Cultural Association, 2003).

6. Govind Purushottam Dange, *Dholkivaril Lavanya*, part 3, as in Jintikar, *Bapurao*, 21.

7. Jintikar, *Bapurao*, 19.

8. Dange, *Dholkivaril Bapurao*, 8.

9. Lahuji Bhalerao, "Pavalabai," unpublished memoir, 13.

10. Jintikar, *Bapurao*, 26.

11. Bhalerao, "Pavalabai"; cf. 1881 date in Jintikar, *Bapurao*.

12. Bhalerao, "Pavalabai," 3.

13. Bhalerao, "Pavalabai," 3.

14. Bhalerao, "Pavalabai," 3.

15. While Lahuji Bhalerao refers to him as Nama Dholvadkar, Jintikar, Kasbe, and Achalkhamb call him Namdev Dhulvadkar. I am retaining Lahuji's version.

16. Kanta Achalkhamb also mentions Pavalabai's association with Haribaba Gholap. See Kanta Achalkhamb, "Namchand Pavalabai," *Asmitadarsha, Divali Ank* 1, no. 3 (1982): 156–58.

17. Milind Kasbe, *Tamasha: Kala ani Kalavant* (Pune: Sugava, 2007),17.

18. Bhalerao, "Pavalabai," 4.

19. Dange, *Dholkivaril Bapurao*, 12.

20. Also see Deepti Priya Mehrotra, *Gulab Bai: The Queen of Nautanki Theatre* (Delhi: Penguin, 2006).

21. Bhalerao, "Pavalabai," 5.

22. Bhalerao, "Pavalabai," 5.

23. See Jintikar, *Bapurao*, 10

24. Quoted in Jintikar, *Bapurao*, 10. Emphasis mine.

25. Jintikar, *Bapurao*, 18; Dange, *Dholkivaril Bapurao*, 6.

26. Interview by the author, Mumbai, 2016. Gaikwad spent his childhood in Ravivar Peth-Pune, where his family and Bapurao were neighbors. Gaikwad and Bapurao spent hours together, writing Lavanya and sharing music and lyrics. Gaikwad did not mention Pavalabai during our interview; she was dead by the time he and Bapurao knew one another and Bapurao was then associated with other women.

27. Veena Naregal, "Performance, Caste, Aesthetics: The Marathi Sangeet Natak and the Dynamics of Cultural Marginalization," *Contributions to Indian Sociology* 42, no. 1–2 (2010): 79–101.

28. Dange, *Dholkivaril Bapurao*, 7.

29. Dange, *Dholkivaril Bapurao*, 7.

30. Jintikar, *Bapurao*, 19.

31. Dange, *Dholkivaril Bapurao*, 7.

32. Dange, *Dholkivaril Bapurao*, 8.

33. Dange, *Dholkivaril Bapurao*, 6.

34. Jintikar *Bapurao*, 18 as well as; Dange, *Dholkivaril Bapurao*, 6. Emphasis mine.

35. Dange, *Dholkivaril Bapurao*, 6.

36. Dange, *Dholkivaril Bapurao*, 6.

37. Nalge, *Maharashtra's Sculptor: Patthe Bapurao*, 15, 19.

38. For details see Nalge, *Maharashtra's Sculptor: Patthe Bapurao*, 5, 15, 19, 21.

39. Bhagvan Thakur, *Ambedkari Jalse* (Pune: Sugava Prakashan, 2005), 85.

40. Jintikar, *Bapurao*, 26.

41. Interview with Hasanbhai Pativadekar conducted by author, July 14, 2016.

42. Interview with Madhukar Nerale. Interview conducted by author. August 11, 2016.

43. Jintikar, *Bapurao*, 26.

44. Interview with Gaikwad, Dombivili-Mumbai, August 3, 2017. Emphasis mine.

45. Interview with Gaikwad, Dombivili-Mumbai, August 3, 2017.

46. Bhalerao, "Pavalabai," 5.

47. Kasbe, *Tamasha*, 17.

48. Bhalerao, "Pavalabai," 7.

49. Bhalerao, "Pavalabai," 7.

50. Bhalerao, "Pavalabai," 7.

51. Bhalerao, "Pavalabai," 7.

52. Dange, *Dholkivaril Bapurao*, 11.

53. Dange, *Dholkivaril Bapurao*, 11.

54. Bhalerao, "Pavalabai," 7.

55. Bhalerao, "Pavalabai," 8.

56. Bhalerao, "Pavalabai," 8.

57. Bhalerao, "Pavalabai," 8.

58. Dange, *Dholkivaril Bapurao* 9.

59. For example, my interviews with Somnath Waghmare, June 12, 2015, and July–August 2016.

60. Dange, *Dholkivaril Bapurao*, 10.

61. Bhalerao, "Pavalabai," 8.

62. Bhalerao, "Pavalabai," 8.

63. Kasbe, *Tamasha*, 17; Rustum Achalkhamb, *Tamasha Lokrangbhumi* (Sugava: Pune, 2006), 121. Neither provides any evidence.

64. Bhalerao, "Pavalabai," 9.

65. Bhalerao. "Pavalabai," 9.

66. Bhalerao, "Pavalabai," 9.

67. Bhalerao, "Pavalabai," 9

68. Bhalerao, "Pavalabai," 9.

69. Jintikar, *Bapurao*, 23–24.

70. Achalkhamb, "Namchand Pavalabai," 156.

71. Dange, *Dholkivaril Bapurao*, 10.

72. Achalkhamb, "Namchand Pavalabai," 156.

73. Dange, *Dholkivaril Bapurao*, 10.

74. Vijay Prashad, *Untouchable Freedom: A Social History of a Dalit Community* (Delhi: Oxford University Press, 2001), 139.

75. I thank V. Geetha for these discussions.

76. Dange, *Dholkivaril Bapurao*, 10.

77. Dange, *Dholkivaril Bapurao*, 10, Achalkhamb, "Namchand Pavalabai," 156.

78. Dange, *Dholkivaril Bapurao*, 10.

79. Achalkhamb, "Namchand Pavalabai," 157.

80. Shahir Lahri Haider, Kolhapur, March 15, 1958, quoted in Jintikar, *Bapurao*, vol. 3, 8.

81. Bhalerao, "Pavalabai," 10.

82. Bhalerao, "Pavalabai," 10; and Achalkhamb, "Namchand Pavalabai," 158.

83. Achalkhamb, "Namchand Pavalabai," 158.

84. Dange, *Dholkivaril Bapurao*, 12. Emphasis in original.

85. Dange, *Dholkivaril Bapurao* 12. Emphasis in original.

86. Kailas Jhodge, "Ram Joshi," *Rasrang*, June 9, 1984, 21–22.

87. Dange, *Dholkivaril Bapurao*, 14.

88. Bhalerao, "Pavalabai," 11.

89. Bhalerao, "Pavalabai," 11.

90. Bhalerao, "Pavalabai," 12.

91. Bhalerao, "Pavalabai," 13.

92. Dange, *Dholkivaril Bapurao*, 13. Emphasis mine.

93. Dange, *Dholkivaril Bapurao*, 13.

94. Dange, *Dholkivaril Bapurao*, 15.

95. Dange, *Dholkivaril Bapurao*, 15.

96. Dange, *Dholkivaril Bapurao*, 16.

97. Dange, *Dholkivaril Bapurao*, 16.

98. Achalkhamb, "Namchand Pavalabai," 158.

99. Dange, *Dholkivaril Bapurao*, 17.

100. Janaki Bakhle, *Two Men and Music* (New York: Oxford University Press, 2005), 92.

101. Bakhle, *Two Men*, 89.

102. Achalkhamb, "Namchand Pavalabai."

103. Jintikar, *Bapurao*, 19.

104. Jintikar, *Bapurao*, 3.

105. Jintikar, *Bapurao*, 5.

106. Jintikar, *Bapurao*, 5.

107. Jintikar, *Bapurao*, 10.

108. In Jintikar, *Bapurao*, 8.

109. Nalge, *Maharashtra's Sculptor: Patthe Bapurao*, 89.

110. For details on spatial segregation in Pune, see Shailaja Paik, *Dalit Women's Education in Modern India: Double Discrimination* (London: Routledge, 2014).

111. Thanks to V. Geetha, for her insights.

112. Also see Christian Lee Novetzke, "Brahmin Double: The Brahmani Construction of Anti-Brahmanism and Anti-caste Sentiment in the Religious Cultures

of Premodern Maharashtra," *South Asian History and Culture* 2, no. 2 (April 2011): 232–52.

113. Dange, *Dholkivaril Bapurao*, 17.

114. Interview with Changdeo Bhalerao, Nagar, August 1, 2017.

115. Lahuji Bhalerao, "Pavalabai," 14.

116. I am following Bhalerao, "Pavalabai," 14; and Kasbe, *Tamasha*, 18. Jintikar mentions the year as 1930. Kanta Achalkhamb does not provide dates but mentions that she died at Duncan Road, Nagpada (Mumbai).

117. Kasbe, *Tamasha*, cites the date as December 12, 1945. Jintikar is more reliable than Kasbe.

118. "Patthe Bapuravanche Tyanchya Gavi Smarak Karun Tamasgiranni tyanchey ruun phedun takave," *Navakal*, April 10, 1961.

119. *Rasrang* 35, no. 14 (March 10, 1992): 25.

120. Jintikar, *Bapurao*, 30.

121. *Pudhari*, Ahmednagar, 27 April, 2017.

Chapter 3

1. *Dnyanprakash*, January 1, 1930.

2. *Nirbhid*, December 15, 1935.

3. *Nirbhid*, December 15, 1935.

4. Ambedkar, "Who Were the Shudras," *BAWS*, vol. 7, 182–85.

5. Shailaja Paik, *Dalit Women's Education in Modern India: Double Discrimination* (London: Routledge, 2014), 155.

6. Since the early 1900s, many elite reformers, the colonial British state, and Dalits contested the boundaries of appropriate sexuality for women. They conflated all non-wives, disproportionately Dalit, who were given to local deities as "prostitutes." As Durba Mitra, *Indian Sex Life: Sexuality and the Colonial Origins of Modern Social Thought* (Princeton, NJ: Princeton University Press, 2020) argues, they correlated all forms of sexual deviance with prostitution.

7. "Bhaginnino samajala batta lavanarya dhadya pasun mukta vha" (Sisters, liberate yourself from the profession/business that blots the community), *Janata*, July 4, 1936.

8. Emile Durkheim, *The Elementary Forms of the Religious Life* (London: Allen and Unwin, 1915).

9. Following Louis Althusser, "contradiction" is a conjuncture. See Warren Montag, "Althusser's Lenin," *Diacritics* 43 (2015): 48–66.

10. Mitra, *Indian Sex Life*; Ashwini Tambe, *Codes of Misconduct: Regulating Prostitution in Late Colonial Bombay* (Minneapolis: University of Minnesota Press,

2009); Swati Shah, *Street Corner Secrets: Sex, Work, and Migration in the City of Mumbai* (Durham, NC: Duke University Press, 2014).

11. B. R. Ambedkar, "Castes in India: Their Mechanisms, Genesis, and Development," first printed in *Indian Antiquary* 46 (May 1917); reprinted in *BAWS,* vol. 1, 3-22. Emphasis in original.

12. Giorgio Agamben, *Homo Sacer: Sovereign Power and Bare Life* (Stanford, CA: Stanford University Press, 1998), 27.

13. In a different context of England, Judith Walkowitz examines the isolation of prostitutes from working-class women, *Prostitution and Victorian Society* (Cambridge: Cambridge University Press, 1980).

14. For Gandki's ideas on women, see Ashwini Tambe, *Codes of Misconduct*; Sujata Patel, "Construction and Reconstruction of Woman in Gandhi," *Economic and Political Weekly*, February 20, 1988, 377–87.

15. Ambedkar, "Castes in India."

16. Ambedkar, "Castes in India."

17. Ambedkar, "Castes in India." Emphasis in the original.

18. Only recently, feminists have analyzed Ambedkar's examination of endogamy and surplus woman. See Durba Mitra, "'Surplus Woman': Female Sexuality and the Concept of Endogamy," *Journal of Asian Studies* 80, no. 1 (February 2021): 3–26.. Also see Prathama Bannerjee's forthcoming paper "Gender, Sex, and Caste in Ambedkar's Early Thought."

19. Urmila Pawar and Meenakshi Moon, *We Also Made History* (New Delhi: Zubaan, 2008), 58.

20. *Bahishkrut Bharat*, May 3, 1929.

21. *Bahishkrut Bharat*, May 3, 1929.

22. Gayle Rubin, "Thinking Sex," in *Pleasure and Danger: Exploring Female Sexuality*, ed. Carol Vance (New York: Routledge, 1984), 3–44.

23. B. R. Ambedkar, speech, Khairmode Collection, Mumbai University.

24. *Bahiskrut Bharat*, February 3, 1928.

25. *Bahiskrut Bharat*, June 21, 1929.

26. *Janata*, July 4, 1936.

27. Paik, *Dalit Women's Education.*

28. Shailaja Paik, "Ambedkar and the 'Prostitute': Caste, Sexuality, and Humanity in Modern India, " *Gender & History*, August 16, 2021, https://doi.org/10.1111/1468-0424.12557.

29. Ambedkar, "What Path to Freedom?"

30. Ambedkar, "What Path to Freedom?"

31. Subramanian Shankar, *Flesh and Fish Blood* (Berkeley: University of California Press, 2012), 100.

32. Shankar, *Flesh and Fish Blood*, 99.

33. *Bahishkrut Bharat*, March 29, 1929.

34. *Janata*, March 7, 1936

35. Paik, *Dalit Women's Education*.

36. Paik, *Dalit Women's Education*.

37. Paik, *Dalit Women's Education*.

38. I have benefitted from Black theorists, in particular Fanon, Sylvia Wynter, Saidiya Hartman, and here Achille Mbembe, *The Critique of Black Reason* (Durham, NC: Duke University Press, 2017), 135. Ambedkar was not in conversation with any of these Black theorists; however, it has been generative to put them in conversation to understand Dalit humanity constructed under caste slavery.

39. Mbembe, *Critique of Black Reason*, 31.

40. I am building on Foucault's insights on governmentality.

41. *Bahiskrut Bharat*, December 23, 1927

42. *Bahiskrut Bharat*, December 23, 1927.

43. V. Geetha, *Ambedkar*, 114.

44. *Bahiskrut Bharat*, December 23, 1927.

45. In the context of Uttar Pradesh, Charu Gupta illuminates how sanitation castes claimed their monopoly over "customary rights" to collect and sell nightsoil, sweep homes, and clean private latrines. See Charu Gupta, *Gender of Caste* (Seattle: University of Washington Press, 2014), 148–51.

46. Sylvia Wynter, *On Being Human as Praxis*, ed. Katharine McKrittrick (Durham, NC: Duke University Press 2015), 138.

47. *Janata*, March 7, 1936.

48. *Janata*, March 7, 1936.

49. *Janata*, March 7, 1936.

50. *Dnyanprakash*, January 1, 1930.

51. *Dnyanprakash*, January 1, 1930.

52. *Janata*, November 5, 1932.

53. *Janata*, October 8, 1932.

54. *Bahishkrut Bharat*, December 23, 1927.

55. *Bahishkrut Bharat*, December 23, 1927.

56. *Bahishkrut Bharat*, February 3, 1928.

57. See Jose Munoz, *Disidentifications: Queers of Color and the Performance of Politics* (Minneapolis: University of Minnesota Press, 1999), 31. I thank Shefali Chandra for this insight.

58. *Bahiskrut Bharat*, February 3, 1928.

59. Paik, *Dalit Women's Education*.

60. Paik, *Dalit Women's Education* .

61. *Bahishkrut Bharat*, May 3, 1929.

62. *Bahishkrut Bharat*, May 3, 1929.

63. *Bahiskrut Bharat*, March 29, 1929.

64. Ambedkar, "What Path to Freedom?" in *BAWS*, vol. 17.

65. There are significant parallels here between Ambedkar and Fanon who argues, "a Black is not a man."

66. *Janata*, October 15, 1932.

67. *Janata*, October 15, 1932.

68. *Janata*, February 25, 1933.

69. *Janata*, February 25, 1933.

70. *Janata*, November 19, 1932.

71. Fanon, *The Wretched of the Earth* (New York: Grove Press, 1963), 36–37. I am reading Fanon and Ambedkar together.

72. Ramchandra Hari Bandasode, *Ashprushyanchi Dishabhool*. Unfortunately, the publication information is not available on the tattered pages at the archives. The events suggest that the booklet may have been published in mid-1930s Mumbai.

73. Bandasode, *Ashprushyanchi Dishabhool*, 32.

74. Bandasode, *Ashprushyanchi Dishabhool*," 11.

75. Bandasode, *Ashprushyanchi Dishabhool*," 33.

76. Bandasode, *Ashprushyanchi Dishabhool*," 34.

77. Janata, September 13, 1936.

78. *Bahiskrut Bharat*, 23 December 1927.

79. *Bahiskrut Bharat*, 23 November 1928.

80. *Bahiskrut Bharat*, 23 November 1928.

81. Fanon, *Wretched of the Earth*, and Judith Butler note the hybridity of the human. Butler's gender as praxis and performative is helpful here.

82. *Janata*, July 4, 1936.

83. *Janata*, July 4, 1936.

84. *Janata*, July 4, 1936.

85. *Janata*, July 4, 1936.

86. *Janata*, July 4, 1936. Emphasis mine.

87. *Janata*, July 4, 1936.

88. V. Geetha, *Ambedkar*, 188.

89. *Janata*, July 4, 1936.

90. *Janata*, June 2, 1936.

91. Christophe Jaffrelot, "Sanskritization vs. Ethnicization in India," *Asian Survey* 40 (2000), 756–66; Balmurli Natrajan, *The Culturalization of Caste* (London: Routledge, 2012).

92. *Dnyanprakash*, January 1, 1930.

93. *Janata*, July 4, 1936.

94. *Prabuddha Bharat*, October 26, 1956.

95. *Dnyanprakash*, January 1, 1930.

96. *Janata*, July 4, 1936.

97. *Janata*, July 4, 1936.

98. *Janata*, January 22, 1949.

99. *Janata*, January 22, 1949.

100. Pawar and Moon, *We Also Made History*.

101. Shailaja Paik, "Mangalatai Bansode and the Social Life of Tamasha," *Biography* 40, no. 1 (Winter 2017): 170–98.

102. Paik, "Mangalatai Bansode."

103. *Prabuddha Bharat*, July 21, 1956.

104. *Prabuddha Bharat*, October 26, 1956.

105. *Prabuddha Bharat*, October 26, 1956.

Chapter 4

1. Raymond Williams, *Marxism and Literature* (Oxford: Oxford University Press, 1977), 131.

2. B. D. Kardak, *Ambedkari Jalse: Svaroop va Karya* (Mumbai: Abhinav Prakashan, 1978), 6.

3. Kardak, *Ambedkari Jalse*, 6.

4. My reading of Tamasha challenges the relatively positive view of scholars regarding the cultural politics of anticasteism around, for example, reclaiming the parai.

5. Bhagavan Thakur, *Ambedkari Jalse* (Pune: Sugava Publications, 2005); Krishna Kirvale, *Ambedkari Shahiri: ek shodh* (Pune: Nalanda Publications, 1992).

6. Kardak, *Ambedkari Jalse*, 10, 12.

7. Kardak, *Ambedkari Jalse*, 4–6.

8. *Janata*, March 7, 1936.

9. They shared common ground in this regard with the communists, who also drew on a repertoire of folk forms and sought to refashion them.

10. In colonial Tamil Nadu, former Devadasis joined the anti-nautch campaign groups and spoke, wrote, and sang against the conditions of their existence. Some came to be active as nationalist songsters and performers. "Special drama" artists (mostly Bahujan and at times Dalit men)—the most stigmatized group—also likewise took to featuring popular-critical themes in their performance. In the 1940s, when the Scheduled Caste Federation was active in northern Tamil Nadu, they were active in seeking a civic withdrawal from beating the parai, the drum

that Dalits were enjoined to beat during various rites of passage, especially death. I thank V. Geetha for this information.

11. I am following Dalit feminist Bebitai Kamble, who details these processes in her autobiography, *Jina Amucha* (Our living) (Pune: Sugava, 1980).

12. The Arya Samaj also discussed Dalitoddhar, but it was for a different politics of building majoritarian Hindu power.

13. For details on culture as a power resource, see Pierre Bourdieu and Loic J. D. Wacquant, *An Invitation to Reflexive Sociology* (Chicago: University of Chicago Press, 1992), 19.

14. Kardak, *Ambedkari Jalse*, 3.

15. Kardak, *Ambedkari Jalse*, 10, 12.

16. Bourdieu and Wacquant, *An Invitation to Reflexive Sociology*, 19.

17. Kardak, *Ambedkari Jalse*, 21.

18. Kardak, *Ambedkari Jalse*, 21.

19. Kardak, *Ambedkari Jalse*, 21.

20. Kardak, *Ambedkari Jalse*, 21.

21. Kardak, *Ambedkari Jalse*, 56.

22. Kardak, *Ambedkari Jalse*, 51.

23. Kardak, *Ambedkari Jalse*, 22.

24. Interview, August 1, 2016.

25. See Meera Kosambi, *Gender, Culture, and Performance: Marathi Theatre before Independence* (New Delhi: Routledge, 2015).

26. Kosambi notes that Vishnudas Bhave was supported by Shankarshet and Lad, yet in general was almost ostracized in Sangli in 1840s. Kosambi, *Gender, Culture, and Performance*, 21.

27. R. B. More autobiography, p. 130.

28. Pagare, quoted in Kardak, *Ambedkari Jalse*, 10.

29. Pagare, quoted in Kardak, *Ambedkari Jalse*, 10.

30. Kardak, *Ambedkari Jalse*, 10.

31. Pagare, quoted in Kardak, *Ambedkari Jalse*, 10.

32. N. G. Bhavare, "Dr. Babasaheb Ambedkaranchya Dalitoddhar Chalvalitil Dalit Shahir" (Dalit shahirs in Ambedkar's struggle for uplift of Dalits), *Asmitadarsha, Divali Ank* (1982), 28.

33. Thakur, *Ambedkari Jalse*, 33.

34. Thakur, *Ambedkari Jalse*, 39.

35. Cultural troupes of the Rashtra Seva Dal and Communist Party also deployed Jalsa in the same vein.

36. Kirvale, as in Thakur, *Ambedkari Jalse*, 43.

37. Thakur, *Ambedkari Jalse*, 43.

38. Sharmila Rege, *Against the Madness of Manu: B. R. Ambedkar's Writings on Brahmanical Patriarchy* (New Delhi: Navayana, 2013), 150. I have relied on Rege, especially pages 150–51, for information on Ram, Sita, and Krishna.

39. Thakur, *Ambedkari Jalse*, 85. Thakur is drawing this information from elsewhere; however, he provides no details.

40. Thakur, *Ambedkari Jalse*, 87.

41. Appasaheb Ranpise, "Ambedkar Banyachi Shahiri" (Ambedkarite Shahiri), *Asmitadarsha, Divali Ank* (1982), 23.

42. Bhavare, "Dalit Shahir," 29.

43. Sharmila Rege, *writing caste/writing gender* (New Delhi: Zubaan, 2006), 38.

44. For details on Phule, see Shailaja Paik, *Dalit Women's Education in Modern India: Double Discrimination* (London: Routledge, 2014).

45. Quoted in Rege, *writing caste/writing gender*, 38.

46. Kardak provides details in *Ambedkari Jalse*, 12.

47. Krishna Kirwale, 1992, quoted in Rege, *writing caste/writing gender*, 36.

48. Thakur, *Ambedkari Jalse*, 170–71.

49. Thakur, *Ambedkari Jalse*, 141.

50. Thakur, *Ambedkari Jalse*, 167.

51. Ranpise, "Ambedkar Banyachi Shahiri," 21.

52. Ranpise, "Ambedkar Banyachi Shahiri," 21. Later, Shahir Vamandada Kardak (1921–2004) and his disciple Lakshman Kedar established the Chandrodaya Natya Mandal in Shivadi-Mumbai

53. Paik, *Dalit Women's Education.*

54. Ramchandra Kshirsagar, *Dalit Movement in India and Its Leaders, 1857–1956* (New Delhi: M. D. Publications, 1994), 242.

55. Kardak, *Ambedkari Jalse*, 12.

56. Most touchables, including Gandhi, believed that Untouchables must not agitate for their rights and freedom in the radical Ambedkarite vein but silently cooperate with their touchable Hindu Congress trustees. Gandhi was against Untouchables trying to organize satyagrahas on their own initiative because, in his eyes, they were weak and vulnerable, without a mind of their own. As a result, like women, they had to be herded by touchables toward achieving reform. Ambedkar challenged Gandhi's attempts to cosmetically achieve reform without attacking the caste mechanism of endogamy and the caste slavery that produced untouchability in the first place. Yet, as Jaffrelot notes, Gandhi was the first—and only—Indian politician to make the abolition of Untouchability central to swaraj and to act so single-mindedly in order to challenge it. As a result, he was detested by the orthodox Hindus who figured so largely in the Congress.

57. Kardak, *Ambedkari Jalse*, 20.

58. Kardak, *Ambedkari Jalse*, 22.

59. Kardak, *Ambedkari Jalse*, 22–23.

60. Kardak, *Ambedkari Jalse*, 22–23.

61. Kardak, *Ambedkari Jalse*, 25–26.

62. "Ashprushyakarita khas devalay" (Special temples for Untouchables), *Bahiskrut Bharat*, April 12, 1929.

63. The term *Harijan* is deeply contested. For details, see Paik, *Dalit Women's Education*; and Shailaja Paik, "Mahar-Dalit-Buddhist: The History and Politics of Naming in Maharashtra," *Contributions to Indian Sociology* 45, no. 2 (2011), 217–41.

64. Ambedkar, *BAWS*, vol. 5, 363.

65. M. K. Gandhi, "Statement on Untouchability," November 14, 1932; for details on Gandhi and HSS see Joel Lee, *Deceptive Majority: Dalits, Hinduism, and Underground Religion* (Cambridge: Cambridge University Press, 2021).

66. Eleanor Zelliot, *From Untouchable to Dalit: Essays on the Ambedkar Movement* (Delhi: Manohar, 1992, 169); and Christophe Jaffrelot, *Dr. Ambedkar and Untouchability: Analysing and Fighting Caste* (Delhi: Orient Longman, 2005), 70.

67. Kardak, *Ambedkari Jalse*, 149, 159

68. The Gandhi topi became an important marker, even the famous Martin Luther King Jr. and his followers, who embraced Gandhian principles, especially nonviolence, would don it.

69. In *Event, Metaphor, Memory: Chauri Chaura 1922–92* (Berkeley: University of California Press, 1995), Shahid Amin traces a similar process through which subalterns who may never have seen or heard their leader and yet reinforced a Gandhian discourse, thereby converting Gandhi into "mahatma," the great soul in the 1920s Uttar Pradesh, North India.

70. *Janata*, January 22, 1936.

71. *Times of India*, January 1, 1919.

72. *Times of India*, February 28, 1920.

73. Kardak, *Ambedkari Jalse*, 149–158.

74. "Putana," *Encyclopedia Britannica*, https://www.britannica.com/topic/Putana.

75. Kardak, *Ambedkari Jalse*, 165–66.

76. Pagare, quoted in Kardak, *Ambedkari Jalse*, 10.

77. Kardak, *Ambedkari Jalse*, 10.

78. Thakur, *Ambedkari Jalse*, 93, draws on one author, Ranpise. No details provided.

79. Ambedkar, "An Appeal to the Princes and People of India for Funds for A Social Center for the Untouchables in Bombay," Khairmode and Ambedkar Collection, University of Mumbai. (No date on the original, but I suspect it is in the 1940s.)

80. Ambedkar, "An Appeal," 4.

81. Ambedkar, "An Appeal," 11.

82. Ambedkar, "An Appeal," 3.

83. Ambedkar, "An Appeal," 14.

84. Ambedkar, *The Annihilation of Caste: The Annotated Critical Edition* (New Delhi: Navayana, 2014), 285.

85. About half a million Mahars following Ambedkar converted to Buddhism on October 14, 1956. As a result of this political revolution, they changed the name of their residential quarters from Maharvada to Bauddhavada/Buddhavada. Gaikwad alternated between the words, but the meaning is same.

86. Interview with Gaikwad conducted by author, Dombivili-Mumbai, August 3, 2017. Emphasis mine.

87. For details on Sathe and Dalit literature, See Juned Shaikh, *Outcaste Bombay: City Making and the Politics of the Poor* (Seattle: University of Washington Press), 2021.

88. For details on Sheetal Sathe, see Rasika Ajotikar, "'Our Song Impure, Our Voice Polluted': Conversations with Activist and Musician Shital Sathe," *Feminist Review* 119, no. 1 (July 1, 2018): 154–62.

Chapter 5

1. Quoted in Ulhas Rahane, "Tamasha," *Rasrang*, April 22, 1978.

2. "Ashlilte virodhi janmat tayar karane attyavashyak aahe" (It is extremely essential to create a strong public opinion against ashlilta [in all forms]), *Navakal*, January 29, 1961.

3. These forms of repression and censorship continued from colonial times well into the twenty-first century. The state banned bar-dancer women in 2005, thus forcing many of them to abandon their profession and livelihood, go underground, and practice prostitution. Yet, in 2013 the Supreme Court overruled Maharashtra State's decision about cultural disciplining and reopened dance bars. These debates between the state and its subjects reveal the contests over caste, moral, and cultural policing of dancing women in twenty-first-century India. They illuminate contemporary concerns such as the increase of right-wing fanaticism and revitalize our understanding of ashlil. Yet, caste-inflected patriarchal-feudal efforts were not without challenges.

4. For details, see Shreeyash Palshikar, "Breaking Bombay, Making Maharashra: Media, Identity Politics, and State Formation in Modern India" (PhD diss., University of Chicago, 2007). The Dar Commission, formed after independence to consider linguistic states, generalized, "The marathas are an able and virile people and an invaluable asset to the Hindu race and nation," in Robert King, *Nehru and the*

Language of Politics (New Delhi: Oxford University Press, 1998), 10. On transformations in the term *maratha*, see Rosalind O'Hanlon, *Caste, Conflict, and Ideology: Mahatma Jotirao Phule and Low-Caste Protest in Nineteenth-Century Western India* (Cambridge: Cambridge University Press, 1985)' and Prachi Deshpande, *Creative Pasts: Historical Memory and Identity in Western India, 1700–1960* (New York: Columbia University Press, 2007). Although the term *maratha* had been previously used to depict participation in Marathi military culture, maratha elite and royal families, and Marathi speakers in general, by the end of the nineteenth century, it was available to a wider range of Marathi speakers, excluding brahmans. Shahirs were central to creating a mass movement and active masculine energy around the demand of Maharashtra. Enduring popular songs of the 1950s by shahir Krishnarao Ganpatrao Sable, such as "Jai Jai Maharashtra majha, garja Maharashtra majha" (Victory, victory to my Maharashtra, my Maharashtra is roaring), written in 1952, became a popular masculine anthem frequently used in cultural and political events.

5. For example, see P. K. Atre, *Jai Hind! Jai Maharashtra, Selected Essays* (Mumbai: Manorama Prakashan, c1997), and more details below.

6. William Mazzarella, *Censorium: Cinema and the Open Edge of Mass Publicity* (Durham, NC: Duke University Press, 2013), 72, 75.

7. Veena Naregal, "Performance, Caste, Aesthetics: The Marathi *sangeet natak* and the Dynamics of Marginalization," *Contributions to Indian Sociology* 44, no. 1–2 (2010): 85.

8. Naregal, "Performance, Caste, Aesthetics," 83.

9. *Rasrang*, 11 September 1971.

10. Naregal, "Performance, Caste, Aesthetics," 83..

11. For one example, see P. K. Atre, *Jai Hind! Jai Maharashtra, Selected Essays* (Mumbai: Manorama Prakashan, c1997).

12. "Jai Maharashtra," May 1, 1964, in Atre, *Jai Hind! Jai Maharashtra*, 36.

13. Atre, *Jai Hind! Jai Maharashtra*, 40.

14. Atre, *Jai Hind! Jai Maharashtra*, 12, 14, 36.

15. Atre, *Jai Hind! Jai Maharashtra*, 36.

16. Keshav Sitaram Thackeray (aka Prabodhankar) and his sons Bal and Shrikant Thackeray were propgandists for the SMM. Prabodhankar was a social reformer of the 1920s and 1930s and an anti-brahman polemicist and activist. Bal and Shrikant worked for Atre's newspaper *Navayug*, and later Thackerays started newspapers like *Marmik* in 1960 and *Samna* in 1989, as well as launched the Shiv Sena on October 30, 1966.

17. See Baburao Bagul, Gangadhar Pantawane, Nagnath Kotapalli for debates on Dalit literature.

18. *Rasrang*, May 12, 1967.

19. R. T. Kamble and M.H. Tamboli from Solapur writing for *Chhaya*. June 1. 1962.

20. *Chhaya*, July 15, 1962.

21. *Chhaya*, May 8, 1963.

22. Thomas Blom Hansen, *The Saffron Wave: Democracy and Hindu Nationalism in Modern India* (Princeton, NJ: Princeton University Press, 1999); Mary Fainsod Katzenstein, *Ethnicity and Equality: The Shiv Sena Party and Preferential Policies in Bombay* (Ithaca, NY: Cornell University Press, 1979).

23. *Rasrang*, 28 March, 1970.

24. *Rasrang*, 28 March, 1970.

25. *Rasrang*, 28 March, 1970.

26. "Marathi chitrapat dakhvine saktiche" (Compulsory screening of Marathi films), *Rasrang*, July 27, 1996.

27. Mazzarella, *Censorship*, 11.

28. *Navakal*, March 12, 1961.

29. *Navakal*, March 12, 1961. Emphasis in original.

30. *Navakal*, March 12, 1961.

31. *Navakal*, March 12, 1961.

32. "Painjan khatlyacha kissa" (The story of the *Painjan* law suit), *Painjan*, September 1963.

33. *Painjan*, September 1960.

34. *Painjan*, September 1960.

35. "Painjan khatlyacha kissa," *Painjan*.

36. "Painjan khatlyacha kissa," *Painjan*.

37. "Painjan khatlyacha kissa," *Painjan*.

38. Anubhavi Pradhyapaka, "*Marathi Natake* [Drama]," *Navakal*, January 4, 1956.

39. "Marathi Rangbhumi Bhavishya" (The future of theatre), *Navakal*, April 23, 1947.

40. Dhond, "Ram Joshi hey shahir nasun kaviraya hote" (Not a shahir but king of poets), *Navakal*, January 10, 1961.

41. Dhond, "Ram Joshi." Emphasis mine.

42. Dhond, "Ram Joshi." Emphasis mine.

43. Dhond, "Ram Joshi."

44. For this information, I have relied on Sharmila Rege, "The Hegemonic Appropriation of Sexuality: The Case of Lavani Performers in Maharashtra," *Contributions to Indian Sociology* 29, no. 1–2 (1995): 30–31.

45. Dhond, "Ram Joshi."

46. *Navakal*, 2 March, 1945.

47. Rege, "Hegemonic Appropriation," 30.

48. M. R. Lamkhade, *Tamasha and Lavani* (Pune: Navin Indalkar, 2014), 82.

49. "Maharashtrat natakan karita changali theatare bandhanaar" (Will build good theatres for Marathi drama in Maharashtra), *Navakal*, January 17, 1961.

50. "Changali Theatre," *Navakal*, January 17, 1961.

51. "Natak adi Kalana Uttejan Denyache Sarkarche Dhoran" (Government supports encouraging drama and arts), *Navakal*, January 26, 1961.

52. Sharad Gokhale, *Rasrang, Diwali ank* (1971): 12

53. Sharad Gokhale, *Rasrang, Diwali ank* (1971): 12.

54. Vasant Sathe, "Anant Mane's utkrusta kalakriti [best artistic creation]," *Rasrang*, August 9, 1980.

55. Nandkumar Prabhune, *Rasrang*, October 5, 1966.

56. Nandkumar Prabhune, *Rasrang*, October 5, 1966.

57. Nandkumar Prabhune, *Rasrang*, October 5, 1966.

58. Nandkumar Prabhune, *Rasrang*, October 5, 1966.

59. Sathe, "Anant Mane's utkrusta kalakriti," *Rasrang*, August 9, 1980.

60. I thank V. Geetha for these discussions.

61. Judith Williamson, quoted in Timothy Burke, *Lifebuoy Men, Lux Women: Commodification, Consumption and Cleanliness in Modern Zimbabwe* (Durham, NC: Duke University Press, 1996), 3.

62. Douglas Haynes, "Selling Masculinity: Advertisements for Sex Tonics and Making of Modern Conjugality in Western India, 1900–1945," *South Asia: Journal of South Asian Studies* 35, no. 4: (April 5, 2012): 790.

63. *Rasrang* May 12, 1973.

64. "Historic Victory of 'Sangtye aika' Entering Its 100th Week," *Chayya* (1961).

65. "Marathi Tamasha kshetratil kalavantanna Desainche ashvasan" (Desai's support to artists in Marathi Tamasha art), *Navakal*, September 21, 1959.

66. "Marathi Tamasha," *Navakal*, September 21, 1959.

67. "Marathi Tamasha," *Navakal*.

68. "Rajya Tamasha Mahotsav, spardha, bakshish samarambh, ani parisamvad" (State Tamasha Fair, Competition, Awards, and Debate), *Navakal*, March 18, 1961.

69. "Khas Tamashasathi Mumbai shaharat chalu varshi theatre bandhanyachi mantrayanchi ghoshana" (Minister declares to build theatres especially for Tamasha in Mumbai city), *Navakal*, March 20, 1961.

70. *Navakal*, January 2, 1961.

71. *Navakal*, January 2, 1961. Emphases mine.

72. *Navakal*, May 28, 1961.

73. *Navakal*, May 28, 1961.

74. *Navakal*, May 28, 1961.

75. *Chhaya*, June 13, 1961.

76. Shittivala (Whistle-blower), "Tamashache ekamev vidyapitha: Lalbagche New Hanuman Theatre" (The one university for Tamasha: Lalbaug's New Hanuman Theatre), Dholki Tuntune, *Mumbai Sandhya*, September 25, 1981.

77. "Tamashachi pichehat" (Decline of Tamasha), *Rasrang*, March 24, 1979.

78. "Mahilansathi khas Tamasha" (Special Tamasha for women), *Navakal*, September 9, 1959.

79. "Tamashala Pandharpesha Samajat Karyarat Karnyachi Sandhi Havi" (Need an opportunity to establish Tamasha in elite society), *Navakal*, May 7, 1961.

80. "Tamashala," *Navakal*, May 7, 1961.

81. "Tamashala," *Navakal*, May 7, 1961.

82. "Tamashala," *Navakal*, May 7, 1961.

83. "Tamasha sahitya nirmitisathi lekhanspardha" (Writing competition for Tamasha literature), *Rasrang*, May 10, 1980, 1.

84. "Tamasha spardhevishayi kalavantat nirutsaha" (Some artists unenthusiastic about Tamasha competition), *Navakal*, January 8, 1962.

85. "Tamasha spardhevishayi kalavantat nirutsaha," *Navakal*.

86. Interview, Mumbai, 2016.

87. "Tamasha spardhevishayi kalavantat nirutsaha ," *Navakal*.

88. Rahane, "Tamasha."

89. Rahane, "Tamasha."

90. Rahane, "Tamasha."

91. Shashi Tayshete, "Tamasha training camp in Mumbai" *Rasrang*, November 18, 1978.

92. Tayshete, "Tamasha training camp in Mumbai."

93. *Rasrang*, September 14, 1974, 26–29.

94. *Rasrang*, September 14, 1974, 26–29.

95. *Rasrang*, *Diwali ank*, 1978, 122. No author.

96. *Rasrang*, *Diwali ank*, 1978, p. 122. No author.

97. Shittivala, "Tamashache ekamev vidyapitha."

98. Shittivala, "Tamashache ekamev vidyapitha."

99. Madhukar Nerale, interview with author, June 14, 2016.

100. Nerale, interview with author, June 14, 2016.

101. Avinash Chitnis, "Assli marathamola Lavaninrutyavishkar," (Invention of real Lavani dance), *Rasrang*, April 1, 2001. Emphasis mine.

102. Chitnis, "Assli marathamola."

103. As quoted in Mazzarella, *Censorium*, 72.

104. Lokkala Academy, University of Bombay, https://mu.ac.in/lok-kala-academy.

105. https://mu.ac.in/lok-kala-academy. Emphasis mine.

106. https://mu.ac.in/lok-kala-academy. Emphasis mine.

107. https://mu.ac.in/lok-kala-academy.

108. https://mu.ac.in/lok-kala-academy.

109. *Rasrang*, January 11, 2005, 61.

110. Jayant Vaishampayan, "18th Tamasha Mahotsav: Kalavantanche haal" (Troubles of Tamasha artists in the great event), *Rasrang*, April 12, 1980, 28–29. Emphasis mine.

111. Vaishampayan, "18th Tamasha Mahotsav."

112. Vaishampayan, "18th Tamasha Mahotsav."

Chapter 6

1. The quotes from Mangalatai and her son Nitin in this chapter come from my interviews with them on September 9 and 10, 2004, and September 1, 2016.

2. I am departing from the traditional elite depiction of Tamasha as "rough music" and deploying the term here especially to mark the directed mockery of or hostility against certain individuals who offended Vithabai.

3. Gayatri Chakravorty Spivak, "Criticism, Feminism, and the Institution," *The Post-Colonial Critic: Interviews, Strategies, Dialogues*, ed. S. Harasym (London: Routledge, 1990), 251.

4. The quotes from Surekhatai Punekar in this chapter come from my interviews with her on October 1, 2004, and October 20, 2016, Pune.

5. Shailaja Paik, *Dalit Women's Education in Modern India: Double Discrimination* (London: Routledge, 2014).

6. See Roland Barthes on the concept of "alibi" in *Mythologies*, trans. Annette Lavers (New York: Noonday Press, 1972), 123. To Barthes, the relationship between form and meaning is one between signifier and signified combining into a sign. This form is then borrowed by a "metalanguage," which adds a different meaning.

7. I am deploying and building on the French sociologist Pierre Bourdieu's conceptualization of "capital." Moreover, I am also gendering the concept.

8. I thank V. Geetha for her insights here.

Conclusion

1. Interview with Madhu conducted by author, October 15, 2016.

2. Interview with Anand conducted by author, November 1, 2016.

3. Interview with Ravi conducted by author, September 20, 2016.

BIBLIOGRAPHY

Abrams, Tevia. "Tamasha: People's Theatre of Maharashtra." PhD dissertation, Michigan State University, 1974.

Achalkhamb, Kanta. "Namchand Pavalabai," *Asmitadarsha, Divali Ank* 1, no. 3 (1982): 156–58.

Achalkhamb, Rustum. *Tamasha Lokrangbhumi*. Pune: Sugava, 2006.

Agamben, Giorgio. *Homo Sacer: Sovereign Power and Bare Life*. Translated by Daniel Heller-Roazen. Stanford, CA: Stanford University Press, 2016.

Ahmed, Sara. *The Cultural Politics of Emotion*. 2nd ed. Edinburgh: Routledge, 2014.

Ambedkar, B. R. *Dr. Babasaheb Ambedkar: Writings and Speeches [BAWS]*, vols. 1–5, 17. Mumbai: Government of Maharashtra, 1979–1989.

Amin, Shahid. *Event, Metaphor, Memory: Chauri Chaura 1922–92*. Berkeley: University of California Press, 1995.

Atre, P. K. *Jai Hind! Jai Maharashtra*. Mumbai: Manorama Prakashan, c1997.

Barthes, Roland. *Mythologies*. Translated by Annette Lavers. New York: Noonday Press, 1972.

Bhabha, Homi K. *The Location of Culture*. Routledge Classics. London; New York: Routledge, 2004.

Bhalerao, Lahuji. "Namchand Pavalabai Bhalerao." Unpublished memoir, no date.

Bhavare, N. G. "Dr. Babasaheb Ambedkaranchya Dalitoddhar Chalvalitil Dalit Shahir" (Dalit shahirs in Ambedkar's struggle for uplift of Dalits). *Asmitadarsha, Divali Ank* (1982): 25–34.

Bivalkar, R. M., and Jhumbarlal Kamble, *Mahadcha Muktisangram* (Mahad freedom struggle). Pune: Rajhans Prakashan, 1977.

Bourdieu, Pierre. *Distinction: A Social Critique of the Judgement of Taste*. Translated by Richard Nice. Cambridge, MA: MIT Press, 1984.

Burke, Timothy. *Lifebuoy Men, Lux Women: Commodification, Consumption and Cleanliness in Modern Zimbabwe*. Durham, NC: Duke University Press, 1996.

Buroway, Michael. "The Roots of Domination: Beyond Bourdieu and Gramsci." *Sociology* 46, no. 2 (2012): 187–206.

Butler, Judith. *Bodies That Matter: On the Discursive Limits of "Sex."* New York: Routledge, 1993.

———. *Gender Trouble: Feminism and the Subversion of Identity.* Cambridge, MA: Harvard University Press, 1982.

———. *Undoing Gender.* New York: Routledge, 2004.

Chandra, Shefali. *The Sexual Life of English: Languages of Caste and Desire in Colonial India.* Durham, NC: Duke University Press, 2012.

Deshpande, Prachi. *Creative Pasts: Historical Memory and Identity in Western India, 1700–1960.* New York: Columbia University Press, 2007.

Dhond, Madhukar. *Marathi Lavani.* Pune: Mauj, 1988.

Fanon, Frantz. *The Wretched of the Earth.* Translated by Constance Farrington. New York: Grove Press, 1963.

Foucault, Michel. *The History of Sexuality.* Vol. 1, *An Introduction.* Translated by Robert Hurley. New York: Vintage, 1978.

Fukazawa, Hiroshi. 1991. *The Medieval Deccan: Peasants, Social Systems and States: Sixteenth to Eighteenth Centuries.* Delhi; Oxford: Oxford University Press, 1991.

Gargi, Balwant. *Folk Theater of India.* Calcutta: Rupa, c1991.

Geetha, V. *Bhimrao Ramji Ambedkar and the Question of Socialism in India.* Palgrave Macmillan, 2021.

Gordon, Linda. "Internal Colonialism and Gender." In *Haunted by Empire: Geographies of Intimacy in North American History,* edited by Ann Laura Stoler (Durham, NC: Duke University Press, 2006)

Guha, Sumit. *Beyond Caste: Identity and Power in South Asia Past and Present.* Leiden: Brill, 2013.

Gupta, Charu. *The Gender of Caste: Representing Dalits in Print.* Seattle: University of Washington Press, 2014.

Guru, G., ed. *Humiliation: Claims and Context.* Delhi: Oxford University Press, 2009.

Hansen, Thomas Blom 2001. *The Saffron Wave: Democracy and Hindu Nationalism in Modern India.* Princeton, NJ: Princeton University Press, 1999.

Hartman, Saidiya. *Wayward Lives, Beautiful Experiments: Intimate Histories of Social Upheaval.* New York: W.W. Norton, 2019.

Haynes, Douglas. "Selling Masculinity: Advertisements for Sex Tonics and Making of Modern Conjugality in Western India, 1900–1945." *South Asia: Journal of South Asian Studies* 35, no. 4 (April 5, 2012): 787–831.

Hunter, Margaret L. "'If You Are Light You Are Alright.'" *Gender & Society* 16, no. 2 (2002): 175–93.

Jaffrelot, Christophe. *Dr. Ambedkar and Untouchability: Analysing and Fighting Caste.* Delhi: Orient Longman, 2005.

———. "Sanskritization vs. Ethnicization in India." *Asian Survey* 40 (2000): 756–66.

Lee, Joel. *Deceptive Majority: Dalits, Hinduism, and Underground Religion.* Cambridge: Cambrdige University Press, 2021.

———. "Disgust and Untouchability: Towards an Affective Theory of Caste." *South Asian History and Culture* 12, no. 2-3 (2021): 310–27. doi:10.1080/19472498.2021.18 78784.

Joshi, V. K. *Loknatyachi Parampara.* Pune: Thokal, 1961.

Kardak, B. D. *Ambedkari Jalse: Svaroop va Karya.* Mumbai: Abhinav Prakashan, 1978.

Khairmode, C. B. *Dr. Bhimrao Ramji Ambedkar yanche charitra,* vol. 3. Pune: Sugava Prakashan, 1964.

King, Robert. *Nehru and the Language of Politics.* New Delhi: Oxford University Press, 1998.

Kosambi, Meera. *Gender, Culture, and Performance.* London: Routledge, 2015.

Kotani, Hiroyuki. *Western India in Historical Transition.* Delhi: Manohar Press, 2002.

Kshirsagar, Ramchandra Kamaji. *Dalit Movement in India and Its Leaders, 1857–1956.* New Delhi: M. D. Publications, 1994.

Lamkhade, M. R. *Tamasha and Lavani.* Pune: Navin Indalkar, 2014.

Matory, J. Lorand. *Stigma and Culture: Last-Place Anxiety in Black America.* Chicago: University of Chicago Press, 2015.

Mitra, Durba. *Indian Sex Life: Sexuality and the Colonial Origins of Modern Social Thought* (New Jersey: Princeton University Press), 2020

———. "'Surplus Woman': Female Sexuality and the Concept of Endogamy." *Journal of Asian Studies* 80, no. 1 (February 2021): 3–26.

Mbembe, Achille. *The Critique of Black Reason.* Durham, NC: Duke University Press, 2017.

Moraje, Gangadhar. *Marathi Lavani Vangmay.* Pune: Moghe Prakashan, 1974.

Muñoz, José. *Disidentifications: Queers of Color and the Performance of Politics.* Minneapolis: University of Minnesota Press, 1999.

Nair, Janaki. "The Devadasi, Dharma, and the State." *Economic and Political Weekly,* December 10, 1994, 3157–67.

Nair, Janaki, and Mary E. John, eds. *A Question of Silence: The Sexual Economies of Modern India.* London: Zed Books, 2000.

Naregal, Veena. "Performance, Caste, Aesthetics: The Marathi Sangeet Natak and the Dynamics of Cultural Marginalization." *Contributions to Indian Sociology* 44 (2010): 1–22.

Natrajan, Balmurli. *The Culturalization of Caste.* London and New York: Routledge, 2012.

Ngai, Sianne. *Theory of the Gimmick: Aesthetic Judgment and Capitalist Form.* Cambridge MA: Belknap Press of Harvard University Press, 2020.

Novetzke, Christian Lee. "The Brahmin Double: The Brahminical Construction of

Anti-Brahminism and Anticaste Sentiment in the Religious Cultures of Precolonial Maharashtra." *South Asian History and Culture* 2, no. 2 (2011): 232–52.

O'Hanlon, Rosalind. *Caste, Conflict, and Ideology: Mahatma Jotirao Phule and Low-Caste Protest in Nineteenth-Century Western India.* Cambridge: Cambridge University Press, 1985.

Orr, Leslie. *Donors, Devotees, and Daughters of God.* New York: Oxford University Press, 2000.

Paik, Shailaja. "Ambedkar and the 'Prostitute': Caste, Sexuality, and Humanity in Modern India." *Gender & History*, August 16, 2021. https://doi.org/10.1111/1468-0424.12557.

———. *Dalit Women's Education in Modern India: Double Discrimination.* Routledge Research on Gender in Asia Series. London: Routledge, 2014.

———. "Mahar-Dalit-Buddhist: The History and Politics of Naming in Maharashtra." *Contributions to Indian Sociology* 45, no. 2 (2011): 217–41.

———. "Mangalatai Bansode and the Social Life of Tamasha." *Biography* 40, no. 1 (2017): 170–98.

———. "Review of Charu Gupta, *The Gender of Caste.*" *South Asia: Journal of South Asian Studies*, 2017, 1–3. doi:10.1080/00856401.2017.1379230.

Palshikar, Shreeyash. "Breaking Bombay, Making Maharashtra: Media, Identity Politics, and State Formation in Modern India." PhD dissertation, University of Chicago, 2007.

Parker, Kunal. "A Corporation of Superior Prostitutes: Anglo-Indian Legal Conceptions of Temple Dancing Girls." *Modern Asian Studies* 32, no. 3 (1998): 559–633.

Patankar, Bharat, and Gail Omvedt. "The Dalit Liberation Movement in Colonial India." *Economic and Political Weekly* 14, no. 7/8 (February 1979; annual number, Caste and Class in India): 409–24.

Patel, Sujata. "The Construction and Reconstruction of Woman in Gandhi." *Economic and Political Weekly* 23, no. 8 (February 1988): 377–87.

Patterson, Orlando. *Slavery and Social Death: A Comparative Study.* Cambridge, MA: Harvard University Press, 1982.

Pawar, Urmila, and Meenakshi Moon. *We Also Made History: Women in the Ambedkarite Movement.* Translated by Wandana Sonalkar. New Delhi: Zubaan, 2008.

Phule, Jotirao. *Mahatma Phule Samagray Vangmay.* Edited by Y. D. Phadke. Mumbai: Maharasthra Government Sahitya Culture Mandal, 1991.

Ramberg, Lucinda. *Given to the Goddess: The Sexuality of Religion amongst South Indian Devadasis.* Durham, NC: Duke University Press, 2014.

Ranpise, Appasaheb. "Ambedkar Banyachi Shahiri" (Ambedkarite Shahiri). *Asmitadarsha, Divali Ank* (1982): 21–24.

Rao, Anupama. *The Caste Question: Dalits and the Politics of Modern India.* Berkeley: University of California Press, 2009.

Rege, Sharmila. *Against the Madness of Manu: B. R. Ambedkar's Writings on Brahmanical Patriarchy.* New Delhi: Navayana, 2013.

———. "The Hegemonic Appropriation of Sexuality: The Case of the Lavani Performers of Maharashtra." *Contributions to Indian Sociology* 29 (1995): 23–38.

———. *Writing Caste/Writing Gender: Narrating Dalit Women's Testimonials.* New Delhi: Zuban Publications, 2006.

Rozario, Rita. *Broken Lives: Dalit Women in Prostitution.* Karnataka: Ambedkar Resource Center, 2000.

Sanal, Mohan P. *Modernity of Slavery: Struggles against Caste Inequality in Colonial Kerala.* Delhi: Oxford University Press, 2015.

Schultz, Anna. *Singing a Hindu Nation: Marathi Devotional Performance and Nationalism.* Oxford: Oxford University Press, 2013.

Sen, Samita. "Offences against Marriage: Negotiating Custom in Colonial Bengal." In *A Question of Silence? The Sexual Economies of Modern India,* edited by Mary E. John and Janaki Nair, 77–100. New Delhi: Kali for Women, 1998.

Seizer, Susan. *Stigmas of the Tamil Stage: An Ethnography of Special Drama Artists in South India.* Durham, NC: Duke University Press, 2005.

Shaikh, Juned. *Outcaste Bombay: City Making and the Politics of the Poor.* Seattle: University of Washington Press, 2020.

Shankar, Subramanian. *Flesh and Fish Blood.* Berkeley: University of California Press, 2019.

Singh, Brahma Prakash. *Cultural Labour: Conceptualizing the "Folk Performance" in India.* New Delhi: Oxford University Press, 2019.

Soneji, Davesh. *Unfinished Gestures: Devadasi, Memory, and Modernity in South India.* Chicago: University of Chicago Press, 2012.

Srinivasan, Amrit. "Temple 'Prostitution' and Community Reform: An Examination of the Ethnographic, Historical and Textual Context of the Devadasi of Tamil Nadu." PhD dissertation, Cambridge University, 1984

Still, Clarinda. *Dalit Women: Honor and Patriarchy in South India,* New Delhi: Social Science Press, 2014.

Tambe, Ashwini. *Codes of Misconduct: Regulating Prostitution in Late Colonial Bombay.* Minneapolis: University of Minnesota Press, 2009.

Thakur, Bhagavan. *Ambedkari Jalse.* Pune: Sugava, 2005.

Vhatkar, Namdeo. *Maharashtrache Loknatya Tamasha Kala ani Sahitya.* Kolhapur: Yashashree Prakashan, no date.

Vijaisri, Priyadarshini. "Contending Identities: Sacred Prostitution and Reform in

Colonial South India." *South Asia: Journal of South Asian Studies* 28, no. 3 (2005): 387–411.

———. *Dangerous Marginality: Rethinking Impurity and Power*. New Delhi: Indian Council of Historical Research, 2016.

Viswanath, Rupa. *The Pariah Problem: Caste, Religion, and the Social in Modern India*. New York: Columbia University Press, 2014.

Walkowitz, Judith R. *Prostitution and Victorian Society: Women, Class and the State*. Cambridge: Cambridge University Press, 1980.

Williams, Raymond. *Marxism and Literature*. Oxford: Oxford University Press, 1977.

Wynter, Sylvia. *On Being Human as Praxis*. Edited by Katherine McKittrick. Durham, NC: Duke University Press, 2015.

Zelliot, Eleanor. *From Untouchable to Dalit: Essays on the Ambedkar Movement*. Delhi: Manohar, 1992.

Newspapers
Dnyanprakash
Janata
Prabuddha Bharat
Bahiskrut Bharat
Times of India
Navakal
Mooknayak
Sudharak

Magazines
Chhaya
Rasrang
Painjan

Bourdieu, Pierre, 360n15, 382n7

brahmans: Ambedkar on, 126; and art reform, 186; Bapurao's reputation among, 86–92, 94; and caste slavery, 53–54, 57–59; and Gandharva's caste privilege, 85; and Jalsa, 192–93; and Marathikaran, 235, 238–41; Marathi arts defined as respectable by, 251–55; Pavalabai and Bapurao threaten, 98, 99–101, 102–3; public sphere shaped by, 365n32; in Pune, 93; and reform, 65–70; and the sex-gender-caste complex, 132–37; Tamasha performed by, 37, 52; and the sanitization of Tamasha, 255–57, 280

brahmani society: and Ambedkar, 162, 167; Bapurao's relationship to, 73, 91, 116, 118–20; and clothing, 152; and Dalit radical politics, 154, 158; and endogamy, 9–10; and Jalsa, 192, 196; Pavalabai and Bapurao threaten, 98, 99–101, 102–3; and the mangalsutra, 314–15; and patriarchy, 7, 25, 28–31, 98, 133–34, 135; and purity/pollution, 58; and respectability, 1, 10–11, 37, 59–70, 347; and the sanitization of Tamasha, 235, 241, 252–53; SSD challenge to, 143; and state censorship, 230; and Tamasha women, 298, 307, 309

brahmanya: and appropriation, 254, 365n32; and the arts, 67; and Bapurao, 73–74, 80–81, 86–92, 94–95, 102–3, 113–16; Bapurao's relationship to, 116, 118–20; Bapurao and Pavalabai threaten, 95; and Dalit humanism, 152; and dehumanization, 58; criticized in Kardak's Thana boarding farce, 205–7; and patriarchy in Pavalabai's life, 103–4, 105–7, 110–12; in Pune, 93

British colonialism, 59–65; and the ashlil, 16; and legitimacy, 21; and masculinity, 29, 142; in Thana boarding farce, 206, 207, 210

Butler, Judith, 12, 360n14, 372n81

canonization: of Bapurao, 73, 112–20, 235, 254; of Tamasha, 277–82, 295–96

capital, 382n7; and caste privilege, 68, 75, 121; khandani as, 41, 318–43; Tamasha as, 16, 285, 296. *See also* appropriation; caste privilege; khandani

caste privilege, 54, 68–70: and appropriation, 365n32; and Bapurao, 73–74, 80–81, 86–92, 94–95, 102–3, 121; and the sex-gender-caste complex, 7, 24, 132–37; and sexual violence, 56, 126, 127, 152–53. *See also* appropriation; brahmanya; sexual violence; stickiness

caste slavery: and Ambedkarite Jalsakars, 189; Ambedkar's opposition to, 119–20, 125–32, 375n56; and the ambivalent position of Tamasha women, 64; and Black theory, 371n38; and Dalit body politics, 153, 155; and the Dalit question, 24, 28, 29; and Dalit radical politics, 39, 174–75; and Dalit womanhood, 2–4, 5–6, 37, 171; and Dalit women's bodies, 39; and dharmantar, 156, 157–58, 159, 164–65, 167–68; feminist inattention to, 29; Gaikwad on, 216, 217, 220, 221, 223; Jalsa's challenge to, 183, 184–86, 192–97; in Kardak's farces, 199–202, 205–7; and Mangalatai, 341–43; and manuski, 20, 140–41, 142, 144; and Pavalabai's sexual availability, 98–99, 120–22; and performativity, 12–13; and the peshva regime, 363–64n17; and the sex-gender-caste complex, 7–11, 132–37; Tamasha and the performativity of, 50–59, 298–99; and Tamasha, 14–15, 345; and Tamasha films, 276; and Tamasha as khandani capital, 318–19; and Tamasha shows for ladies, 332–34, 335; and vatandari, 146–51, 211–12

censorship, 229–30, 234, 235, 247–50, 255–56, 377n3

Chakravarti, Uma, 190

chandraseniya kayastha prabhu (CKP), 235, 239, 240, 250

Chavan, Yashvantrao, 246, 279

Kardak's Thana Boarding farce, 208, 209; and manuski, 143–44; of Pavalabai, 79, 104, 105–6, 107–8, 111; and the performativity of Tamasha, 311; of Untouchables, 58; and vatandari, 149–51; of women in *Painjan*, 250

Depressed Classes Conference (1935), 125

Desai, Ashish, 327, *329*

Desai, Morarji, 229

Deshpande, P. L., 280, 281

desire: Pavalabai as object of, 75–78, 97–99; Mangalatai entices men's, 307–8, 311; and sexual violence, 56; and Tamasha, 6, 56, 102; and Tamasha films, 262; Tamasha film advertisements downplay, 262, 264, 273; and the work/play of Tamasha, 48–50, 306–18. *See also* audience; masti; play; pleasure; sex-gender-caste complex

Devadasis, 30-31, 128–29, 373n10

dharmantar: and Ambedkar's radical Dalit politics, 125, 127–28, 132, 174–75, 202; and the ideal Dalit woman, 170–71, 172–73; Gaikwad on, 219–21; by Mahars in 1956, 377n85; as manuski, 150, 155–69; and vatandari, 149–51

Dholvadkar, Namdeo (Nama): 84–85, 85–86, 96, 104, 107

Dhond, Madhukar, 252–55

diksha, 219–20. *See also* dharmantar

dress. *See* clothing

education: and arts in Maharashtra, 122, 256–57, 278, 279; Jalsa as, 40, 183–86; and Kardak's Thana Boarding Farce, 203–4, 208–9; manuski not achieved solely through, 137–38, 212; for Tamasha artists, 284, 286, 291–92; for Tamasha women, 304–6. *See also* prachar karya

endogamy: and the sex-gender-caste complex, 7–8, 9–10, 72, 129, 130, 132–34; Gandhi fails to attack, 375n56. *See also* sex-gender-caste complex

English (language), 4, 24, 32–33, 47, 179

ethnography, 34–36, 359n11; and Dalit identity, 52, 56, 218, 299–301

family: Ambedkar on, 190; and the new Dalit woman, 170–72; and Tamasha film advertisements, 265–66, 270–72, *274*, 274–77; and Tamasha as khandani capital, 318–41

farce, 48, 192, 198–210

feminist scholarship, 25–31, 72, 83, 128–29, 153, 171, 174–75

films: advertisements for, 263–77; on Ambedkarite performance art, 179–80, 226; about Bapurao and Pavalabai, 118, 119, 120; and Gaikwad's music, 217; about Ram Joshi, 117; Mangalatai in, 335; and Marathi identity, 36, 236, 240–45, 280, 350; and Tamasha, 40–41, 67, 230–35, 257–63, 282–83; Tamasha women in, 303, 327

food, 95, 101–2, 173, 302–4, 326

Foucault, Michel, 232. *See also* governmentality

Gadkar, Jayashree, 261, 264

Gaikwad, Bhimsen Barku, 40, 55–56, 179, 186, 213–23, 225–26; on Bapurao, 87–88, 95, 101, 366n26; on Tamasha bans, 255; on commodification of Tamasha, 349

gan, 50, 190–91

Ganapati, 50, 51, 191

Gandharva, Bal, 85. *See also* Bal Gandharva Theatre

Gandhi, 376nn68–69; and Ambedkar, 131, 155, 158, 160, 164, 192375n56; compared to Bapurao, 101–2, 103; and Kardak's farces, 198, 202, 202–10

gaulan, 50, 189, 214, 219

Ghadge, Megha, 42, 345, *346*

Ghogre, Vilas, 226

globalization, 291, 326–27

governmentality, 16, 60–65, 145. *See also* Foucault; respectability

hagandari, 41, 299–301, 320

denied, 104, 105–6, 107–8, 111; Tamasha films and Marathi manus, 263, 264; Tamasha women denied, 56; Tamasha women as threat to Dalit manus, 305–6; and vatandari, 149–51. *See also* dehumanization; manuski

manuski, 15–16, 19–20, 346–51; and Ambedkarite Jalsakars, 189, 195–97; Ambedkar's fight for, 119–20; and the ashlil, 18; Bapurao and Pavalabai threaten, 95; negated by caste and patriarchy, 106; and Dalit body politics, 151–55; and the Dalit question, 25–26, 27, 28, 30, 31; and Dalit radical politics, 7, 11, 39, 125–32, 174–75, 356, 373n10; and the Dalit samaj, 137–46; and the new Dalit woman, 171–74; and dehumanization, 58; dharmantar as, 155–69; Gaikwad's on, 221–23; and Jalsa, 40, 176–79, 182–86; and Kardak's farces, 198–99, 201–2, 207–9; Mangalatai denied, 311; and marathikaran, 231; and respectability, 1–2; and the sex-gender-caste complex, 136–37; and Tamasha women, 3, 121–22, 225–26, 305–6; and vatandari, 146–51

marathamola: and assli identity, 21; and Bapurao's Lavani, 89–90; and Lavani, 289; and Marathi films, 231, 350; and the work/play of Tamasha, 49–50; and SMM, 246; and Tamasha, 261, 279, 352; and the abuse of Tamasha women, 308–15; embodied by actors in *Vaijayanta*, 264. *See also* Marathikaran; masculinity

marathas (caste), 53, 54, 238–40, 242–44, 377–78n4

Marathi (language), 15–22, 347, 348; and assli Lavani, 289, *290*; and Dalit radical politics, 39, 139–40, 141; and films, 40–41, 67, 244–45; and Marathikaran, 238–39, 240, 241, 377–78n4; and the Tamasha archive, 31–33; and Tamasha studies, 24–25, 47, 361n24. *See also* vernacular

Marathi film industry: and advertisements for Tamasha films, 263–77; Mangalatai in, 335; and Marathi identity, 36, 230–35, 236, 240–45, 280, 350; sanitizing Tamasha, 257–63, 282–83; and Tamasha films, 40–41, 67, 230–35. *See also* films; Hindi film industry

Marathi identity, 229–96: as assli, 2–3, 16, 20–22; and bans on ashlil practices, 69; and the Dalit question, 25–31; and the globalization of Tamasha, 327; and masculinity, 378n4; and performativity, 12–14; and respectability, 61–62, 66–70; and the sex-gender-caste complex, 8; and Tamasha, 40–41, 315, 350–51; and Tamasha artists, 41. *See also* marathamola; Marathikaran

Marathikaran: 3, 13, 20–21, 40–41, 229–96. *See also* Marathi identity

marriage: Ambedkar on, 7, 132–36, 153, 154, 167, 190; Bapurao's, 89, 100, 101; and caste, 52, 130; and the new Dalit woman, 169–72; Gaikwad on, 217; Muralis and, 82–83; and Pavalabai, 117, 121; and Tamasha women, 8, 64, 256, 302, 309, 313–15. *See also* endogamy; family; respectability; sex-gender-caste complex; surplus women

masculinity: of Ambedkar in Jalsa, 191; of Ambedkar in Gaikwad's shahiri, 223; and Bapurao's canonization, 113–16; and British governmentality, 63; and the Dalit question, 27–30; and the new Dalit woman, 153–54; ethnographic observation of, 34–36; and Jalsa, 195–96; and Marathi films, 234, 242; and Marathi identity, 231, 378n4; and manuski, 138, 141–46; and Pavalabai's sexual availability, 98–99; and the sex-gender-caste complex, 9; and Shiv Sena, 244; and Tamasha, 6, 10, 351–52; in Tamasha film advertisements, 273 and the work/play of Tamasha, 49–50, 306–18. *See also* marathamola; masti

only Tamasha shows, 333–34; savarnas unaffected by the, 68–69, 295; and Tamasha audiences, 92–93; and Tamasha films, 261; and Tamasha women, 3, 298–99; touchable Tamasha women escape the, 303–4

sudharana, 66, 68, 140, 188. *See also* manuski; respectability

Surekhatai, *332*; on domestic violence, 213–14; on the economics of Tamasha, 326; and khandani, 318, 335; on modern Tamasha, 330–31; on the pedagogy of Tamasha, 304; performances in the US, 291, 327; on poverty and hunger, 302–3; residence, 321

Suryakant, 264

surplus women: and Ambedkar, 151, 153, 163, 171; Meena Javale, 1; Muralis as, 83; Pavalabai, 73, 97–99; prostitutes as, 130; and the sex-gender-caste complex, 7–9, 132–37; Tamasha women as, 13, 64–65, 193. *See also* endogamy; sex-gender-caste complex

svabhiman, 140: and Ambedkarite Jalsakars, 184, 189; of Dalits, 129; and Dalit body politics, 154–55, 306; and ideal Dalit womanhood, 169–74; of immoral women, 127; and manuski, 137–38, 141, 143, 144, 146. *See also* manuski; vernacular

Tamasha conferences, 41, 277–82, 283, 284

Tamasha Kala Kalavant Vikas Mandir (Art and Artists Progress Committee), 284

Tamasha Mahotsav (Maharashtra), 279, 284, 293, *294*

Tamasha Sudhar Samiti (Reform/ Improvement Committee), 235, 255–56, 257

Tamil Nadu, 373n10

temple entry, 128, 155, 160, 198–99, 202

Temple Entry Bill (1933), 128, 160. *See also* temple entry

Thackeray, Balasaheb (Bal), 240–41, 244–45,

378n16. *See also* Samyukta (United) Maharashtra Movement (SMM)

Thackeray, Keshav Sitaram (Prabodhankar), 195, 378n16. *See also* Samyukta (United) Maharashtra Movement (SMM)

Thakur, Bhagvan, 189, 194

Thana Boarding Farce, 202–10

Thana Boarding House, 177, 203–4

theatres: as ambivalent spaces, 102; Aryabhushan Theatre (Pune), 87, 259, 327; and assli performances, 288–89; effect of British rule on, 60; as erotic spaces, 98–99; and ethnographic field work, 34–36; Hanuman Theatre (Mumbai), 283, *284*; and licensing, 64; New Elphinstone Theatre (Mumbai), *61, 62*; in red light districts of Mumbai and Pune, 93–94; state support for, 279; Pavalabai's performances in, 84, 86; and urbanization, 85

urbanization, 85, 170, 186, 216, 258

urban Tamasha, 34–36, 112; compared to rural, 281–83, 285–86, 289. *See also* cities; Mumbai; Poon; rural Tamasha; theatres; urbanization

vag, 50, 104, 236, 256

Vaijayanta, 264, *265*

Varerkar, Mama, 255, 256, 281

vatandari: and Ambedkar, 39, 136–37, 138, 146–51, 156, 165–66; Mahars challenge Ambedkar on, 211–12, 239, 293; and Mangalatai, 41, 294

vernacular, the (language), 4, 15–22, 347, 348; and Dalit radical politics, 39, 139–40, 141, 145, 152; and Jalsa, 177, 182; and the Tamasha archive, 31–33; and Tamasha studies, 24–25, 47, 361n24. *See also* Marathi (language)

Vhatkar, Namdeo, 60, 280–82

Victorian morality, 16, 59–70, 167, 347. *See also* respectability

The authorized representative in the EU for product safety and compliance is:
Mare Nostrum Group
B.V Doelen 72
4831 GR Breda
The Netherlands

www.ingramcontent.com/pod-product-compliance
Lightning Source LLC
Chambersburg PA
CBHW030729280326
41926CB00086B/560